T0248295

This Is Not Who We Are

What kind of country is America? Zachary Shore tackles this polarizing question by spotlighting some of the most morally muddled matters of WWII. Should Japanese Americans be moved from the west coast to prevent sabotage? Should the German people be made to starve as punishment for launching the war? Should America drop atomic bombs to break Japan's will to fight? Surprisingly, despite wartime anger, most Americans and key officials favored mercy over revenge, yet a minority managed to push their punitive policies through. After the war, by feeding the hungry, rebuilding Western Europe and Japan, and airlifting supplies to a blockaded Berlin, America strove to restore the country's humanity, transforming its image in the eyes of the world. A compelling story of the struggle over racism and revenge, *This Is Not Who We Are* asks crucial questions about the nation's most agonizing divides.

Zachary Shore is Professor of History at the Naval Postgraduate School, Senior Fellow at UC Berkeley's Institute of European Studies, and a National Security Visiting Fellow at Stanford's Hoover Institution. He is the author of five previous books, including *Blunder: Why Smart People Make Bad Decisions* and *A Sense of the Enemy: The High-Stakes History of Reading Your Rival's Mind.*

This Is Not Who We Are

America's Struggle Between Vengeance and Virtue

Zachary Shore

CAMBRIDGE
UNIVERSITY PRESS

CAMBRIDGE
UNIVERSITY PRESS

University Printing House, Cambridge CB2 8BS, United Kingdom

One Liberty Plaza, 20th Floor, New York, NY 10006, USA

477 Williamstown Road, Port Melbourne, VIC 3207, Australia

314–321, 3rd Floor, Plot 3, Splendor Forum, Jasola District Centre, New Delhi – 110025, India

103 Penang Road, #05–06/07, Visioncrest Commercial, Singapore 238467

Cambridge University Press is part of the University of Cambridge.

It furthers the University's mission by disseminating knowledge in the pursuit of education, learning, and research at the highest international levels of excellence.

www.cambridge.org
Information on this title: www.cambridge.org/9781009203449
DOI: 10.1017/9781009203418

© Zachary Shore 2023

First published 2023

Printed in the United Kingdom by TJ Books Limited, Padstow Cornwall

A catalogue record for this publication is available from the British Library.

ISBN 978-1-009-20344-9 Hardback

CONTENTS

FIGURES

PROLOGUE
The Friendship Train

Everyone wanted to be there. It was the kind of spectacle that only Hollywood could produce. Scores of searchlights crisscrossed the night sky, illuminating the fancy floats below. Ten live bands filled the grounds with music fit for the extravaganza. And the stars came out in force. John Wayne was there, and so was Mickey Rooney. The "Brazilian Bombshell" Carmen Miranda enchanted the crowd, while others swooned at the French-born actor Charles Boyer, still glowing from his performance in the hit film *Gaslight*. More than one hundred of the most renowned celebrities performed, mingled, and jockeyed to be seen. Half a million spectators braced the cold November chill, since most did not yet own a television.[1] In 1947, TV was just beginning to penetrate American homes as the long postwar economic boom began, and TV crews were there to capture the event. The comedian Danny Thomas got a raucous laugh by shivering on stage, reflecting what the crowds were feeling. He bowed in mock reverence at California's Governor Earl Warren, who was seated with his wife on stage. The mood that night was ebullient, a striking contrast to the abject suffering that had brought them all there.

Across the Atlantic, Europeans were starving. The war had crippled food production. The massive bombing of roads, bridges, canals, and railway lines had shattered transportation routes, making the transit of food to cities that much harder. Drought had withered crops, further depleting what little food remained. More than two years had passed since Germany's surrender, but the lives of average people had only worsened. Tens of millions of children were enduring malnutrition, stunted growth, and disease. Mothers jostled and shoved their way into the scrums surrounding canned food distribution sites. Others picked through garbage dumps, searching for any edible scraps.[2] With winter rapidly approaching, Europeans desperately needed nutrients or millions would soon die. The continent was facing a grim postwar apocalypse, and Americans were being asked to help. The half a million who gathered that night in Hollywood had come to launch a distinctly American solution: the newly minted Friendship Train.

It began as a publicity stunt, the brainchild of Drew Pearson, America's best-known syndicated columnist. Pearson had witnessed Soviet Army forces in France being lauded for supplying food aid while American shipments went unnoticed. Pearson wanted America to get credit for its own humanitarian efforts. Since early 1946, some Americans began eating less to make more food available for shipment to Europe. At President Truman's urging, Americans observed "meatless Tuesdays," cut down on bread consumption, and tried to reduce food waste. Exports rose, but it was not enough. By the fall of 1947, the situation had grown dire. The government intensified its efforts, but the public had to pitch in more. In one of Pearson's columns he proposed a Friendship Train that would race across America collecting food for Europe's hungry masses. He thought that if celebrities could accompany the train, the crowds would gather and donations would rise. Europeans would then see the true heart of the American people. But neither Pearson nor any others could have imagined just how ardently Americans would get on board with the idea of simple giving.

As the train prepared to leave Los Angeles, the nation's most celebrated songwriter, Irving Berlin, led the crowd in a round of "God Bless America," a song he had introduced less than a decade earlier.[3] Hollywood's showstopping sendoff contained eight freight cars full of food, including 160,000 pounds of sugar given by Hawaii, whose governor of course attended the glamorous event.[4] From Hollywood the train sped through California's bread basket. Bakersfield supplied 80,000 pounds of grain. Fresno donated crates of raisins. Merced gave more dried fruit and canned milk. In Stockton, people held up signs reading "Hunger is the enemy of peace," "Food for our Friends," and "Bonjour, vive La France." Oakland, San Francisco, and Bay Area cities provided even more, throwing in a $10,000 cash donation.[5]

The train picked up more food in Reno, where both the mayor and governor came out to greet it.[6] Omaha added 50,000 pounds of flour plus more cash contributions.[7] Stunned by the extent of average Americans' generosity, French Foreign Minister Henri Bonnet flew to meet the train in Omaha and witnessed for himself the spontaneous outpouring of support. He called it "America's far-reaching gesture of amity."[8] And that reach just kept extending.

It was not just white Americans who joined in giving. Black Americans donated across the country. A group of Black Americans in Los Angeles pooled their funds to purchase a truckload of groceries for the train.[9] Native Americans gave as well. Sioux Chief Ed White Buffalo, his wife, and their three children, all in traditional dress, presented the train with seventy-eight ears of corn. Rich as well as poor folks gave. Henry Kaiser, a leading industrialist and future founder of the healthcare company Kaiser Permanente, made sure to be photographed loading boxes onto train cars as part of his contribution. A seventy-three-year-old small-town grocer, Frank Tessier, donated a sack of flour from his store. Even little children joined in the event. One four-year-old boy donated 400 pennies to the cause, providing perfect footage for the newsreels.[10]

Cities vied to give the most of whatever they had. The tiny town of Sidney was not even on the schedule for a visit, but the town's leaders convinced the train to stop and accept their contributions. One boy literally offered the shirt off his back, which was immediately auctioned for the cause. Though the town barely numbered 10,000 residents, it raised $12,000. In Aurora, John Crumm made a special effort to gather food for the train. Crumm had been a prisoner of the Japanese during the war and knew the pain of hunger. He organized a group to pick the corn that still remained in the fields and that would otherwise have gone to waste. It was enough to sell for $825 worth of flour.[11] By the time the train reached Council Bluffs, it stretched to fifty-seven cars. And that town added five more. The train then rumbled on through Iowa, picking up more food and money everywhere it went. But Kansas broke all records, adding eighty-three boxcars of wheat. Governor Frank Carlson addressed an audience of thousands saying, "We have so much, the need is so great, and it takes so little from the individual that we must not fail to do our duty."[12]

Try as they did, no city could top the fanfare that New Yorkers gave: forty cars of food plus a ticker tape parade. More than 100,000 New Yorkers lined the streets to celebrate this extraordinary act of giving. Even Hollywood's audacious send-off could not compare with

Figure 0.1 The Friendship Train Cargo sets sail for Europe on November 17, 1947, in New York. Originally, it hoped to collect eighty train carloads of food, and the train ultimately collected over 700 cars ($40 million value) of food, clothing, and fuel, paid in part by monetary donations. Photo by Irving Haberman/IH Images/Getty Images.

the show that New York put on. Two railway barges laden with food took victory laps around the Statue of Liberty as jets of water one hundred feet high arced across them in majestic streams. Then the Friendship Train's supplies were loaded onto the first of four ships that would cross the Atlantic to deliver its cargo to France. With the smashing of a champagne bottle on its bow, the USS *Leader* was re-christened the "Friend Ship" and sent on its way. Those shipments would go not just to the French but also to Italians, Germans, and Austrians, America's former foes.

Politicians of both parties attached themselves to the popular phenomenon. New York's Republican Governor Thomas E. Dewey, eyeing yet another run at the presidency, called the train "an important contribution to world peace."[13] New York City's Democratic mayor, William O'Dwyer, convened a ceremony at City Hall, where thousands of children, released from school, were invited to participate in the festivities. The mayor proclaimed the episode "a material symbol of the desire of our people to relieve the hunger and suffering of our fellow humans in Italy and France."[14] Warren Austin, America's ambassador to the United Nations, called it simply an act of "peace mongering."[15]

New Yorkers gave an additional $73,000 toward the purchase of food. And throughout the episode, every corporation and labor union – from teamsters to dock workers, from railways to shipping lines – provided its services entirely free of charge. The hope had been to deliver the food to France and Italy by Christmas. At the ceremony, the French consul general referred to the captain of the Friend Ship as "a real Santa Claus."[16]

By the close of its journey, the Friendship Train had swelled to an astonishing 481 cars, with the first shipment of food to France weighing more than eight million pounds.[17] The film producer Harry Warner, chairman of the train committee, declared that "No other humanitarian appeal in history ever had such a quick and tremendous response." The committee had chosen Warner (of Warner Brothers Studio) to oversee the effort precisely because it wanted him to generate footage to play in movie theaters across Europe. The entire project was intended as a propaganda bonanza, a chance to showcase America's goodness on film. It was as if Americans were desperate to show the world who they truly were. But why?

Looking back, this orgy of ostentatious giving, the mugging for the camera, the battles over who could donate more or whose sacrifice could be more noble, seemed to have a performative dimension. Was it all just generosity for show, a public relations ploy, or worse – a neo-imperialist plot to hook the world on US goods? Or did the Friendship Train stem from a deep-rooted sense of kindness, a virtue hardwired into the American psyche. Cynics and true-believers can debate, but most people harbor multiple motives for their acts. Whatever their intentions, the fact is that American giving saved lives. Years later, that was how it would be remembered, as Europeans made their gratitude known. And certainly, at the time, the donations were welcomed as a lifeline. Thank you letters arrived from overseas. From Vienna one man wrote to the Friendship Train Committee chair of Hartford, Connecticut, "We cannot fully measure what this noble help means." He said that people like him could hardly have survived without the help that Americans so freely gave. A German man in Lüneburg described how much Germans looked forward to the many CARE packages Americans sent.[18]

Americans at the time did believe that they were especially good, exceptional in their behavior, a shining city on a hill. But this conviction did not square with their egregious actions of the past few years. During the war, America had engaged in many needlessly cruel acts against the innocent – actions that even the frenzy of wartime hatred could neither excuse nor explain. The triumphal postwar narrative declared that America had helped to rid the world of a vicious evil, and that was certainly true. But soon after victory, a number of influential Americans began reexamining some of the country's less charitable decisions toward its enemies, and they wanted to atone. They wanted to ensure that Americans lived up to the ideals they so often espoused. And above all, they wanted the world to see Americans the way they saw themselves, as a kind and decent people. This handful of leaders recognized that their notions of American goodness had at times been derailed, and even after the war, its occupation policies were exacerbating misery to no good end. But to climb aboard the Friendship Train, to reach a point of virtue, Americans first had to wrestle with their most recent vengeful acts.

INTRODUCTION
From Vengeance to Virtue

In the end, there was chaos in Kabul. Thousands thronged the airport, desperate to escape the return of Taliban control. Convinced he could have no future in his homeland, seventeen-year-old Zaki Anwari frantically clung to the wheel of an American C-17 aircraft as it took off. He and a dozen others either fell to their deaths or were crushed by the airplane's unforgiving landing gear.[19] They were not the only victims of the botched withdrawal. Amidst the panicked crowds, a suicide bomber murdered 170 Afghans, thirteen US troops, and wounded an estimated 150 others.[20] As the mayhem continued, day after excruciating day, Americans looked aghast at their country's quandary. To remain in Afghanistan meant spending billions more on what seemed like a forever war, but exiting meant abandoning millions of Afghan allies to the nightmare of extreme Islamist rule. Most Americans wanted the war to end, but they never wanted it to end this way. They were left appalled at what their government had done. A rare murmur of consensus echoed across the land as Americans lamented: this is not who we are.

It was far from the first time Americans felt this way. Their sentiment resembled how they reacted during an entirely different episode in the summer of 2018, when news media broadcast scenes of migrant children at the southern border locked in cages. The public listened to the wails of toddlers calling for their mothers and were sickened by the sound.[21] Again, Americans insisted that this is not who we are. Most Americans wanted secure borders, but few wanted children to pay the price. As in Afghanistan, the government was grappling with a dilemma, and the public recoiled at the result.

There have been many moments when Americans objected to their government's behavior, but few episodes are as compelling as those suffused with moral ambiguity. As a historian, I decided to look back at an earlier time when Americans also declared, "This is not who we are." I wanted to see how the country grappled with its government's humanity at a pivotal moment in the nation's past. What I found surprised me.

America emerged from World War II as the undisputed superpower. Its defeat of Nazism's radical racial ideology and Japanese militarism was total. Its enemies were vanquished, its allies were hobbled, and its one true rival, the Soviet Union, was reeling from the loss of some twenty million citizens.[22] But during the war, the United States committed numerous inhumane acts against the innocent. It imprisoned thousands of American citizens in concentration camps because of their race. It used nuclear weapons on entire cities, indiscriminately killing some 200,000 civilians. And it imposed a punishing peace on Germany, which for two painful years caused countless children and adults to starve. As I explored the process that produced these decisions, I fully expected that racial animus and wartime hatreds alone would explain them. But it couldn't. To my surprise, the majority of key decision makers, along with much of the American public, opposed these harsh measures. The most remarkable aspect of these policies was precisely how little support and how much ambivalence they actually produced.

In the internment affair, the shock of Pearl Harbor sparked a fear of saboteurs, but many questioned whether security required removing thousands of citizens from their homes. The government's own surveys of public opinion found that, initially, a paltry fourteen percent of west coast residents approved of forced evacuation of Japanese Americans. The percentage was higher among those in southern California, but even there the surveys found only limited support for internment. If you had been alive at the time, you could easily have had the impression from newspapers and politicians that most Americans were demanding the removal of Japanese Americans from the coast and insisting on their confinement to concentration camps, but the polling data suggests the opposite, that in the first few months after Pearl Harbor, there was no groundswell of support for this drastic action. While racism undeniably fueled hatred toward Japanese

Americans, that anger had its limits. The public had to be convinced that forced relocation was a sensible idea. As the internment unfolded, discomfort with the policy and degrees of opposition to it slowly began to mount.[23]

Something similar happened with the atomic bombs. The use of this remarkable new weapon might end the war and ultimately save lives, but it would require the killing of hundreds of thousands of innocent people. An oft-cited Gallup poll taken just days after Hiroshima showed that eighty-five percent of Americans supported the nuclear attack. But most Americans had no idea what an atomic bomb was. The vast majority, including the president, had no college education (fewer than one in twenty did), and most could not begin to grasp the effects of a nuclear strike. An earlier Gallup poll, in 1944, revealed that most Americans opposed the use of poison gas against the Japanese. It is almost inconceivable that Americans would have opposed poison gas yet approved of a nuclear attack, since the latter is many times more horrific and long-lasting. Had Americans understood that the atomic bombs were more than just a very powerful conventional bomb, they likely would have opposed its use as well. In fact, as time passed and Americans learned what the bombs had actually done to innocent civilians, with all their gruesome effects, support for the decision plummeted. It has fallen to roughly fifty-six percent today.[24]

The same was also true regarding the Roosevelt administration's scheme to cripple Germany. If that nation were reduced to an agrarian state, it could hardly make war on the world again. But what if such extreme treatment only inflamed Germans' thirst for revenge, ultimately igniting the very war that the punishing peace was intended to prevent? The government initially considered the harshest measures. When word of the punitive Morgenthau Plan leaked to the press, Americans recoiled. Even FDR himself tried to distance himself from it, and his Republican opponent in the presidential election used it against him in the campaign. Yet it was a modified version of Treasury Secretary Morgenthau's plan that became official US policy for the first two years of occupation. While hatred toward the German people undeniably rippled across America, soon after the war average Americans were confronted with images of starving German children, and their anger quickly ebbed. Remarkably, Americans voluntarily ate less in order to have more food available for Germans and others in desperate straits. Polling data showed a substantial majority, over sixty percent, in favor of feeding the needy, including America's former enemies. With respect to each of these three brutal acts against civilians, average Americans appear to have embraced kindness and mercy over cruelty and revenge.

My primary interest, however, was not with the American public's views. As I dug deeper into these decisions, I found an even greater surprise. The brutal actions that the American government inflicted on the innocent were not only actively opposed or uneasily accepted by the public but were also opposed, or at least not endorsed, by most of the nation's top leaders. In each of the three vengeful decisions, a majority (and sometimes an overwhelming majority) of key officials argued against vengeance and favored mercy. But if most of the government's top leaders supported mercy, how and why were these vengeful policies adopted? That is the crucial question that drives Part I.

Part II tackles the flip side of the puzzle. It asks how American leaders sought, in essence, to atone for some of its own wartime cruelties. After the war, the United States undertook a dramatic series of measures. By leading a massive food campaign that fed millions of people during a global food shortage, by rebuilding western Europe and Japan, and by heroically airlifting supplies to a blockaded Berlin, America did more than just rescue countless civilians from hunger and oppression; it transformed its image in the eyes of the world.

I had expected to find that after years of sacrifices by the American public, from rationing to war bonds, Americans would be tired of giving. The opposite turned out to be true. While a sizeable minority still wanted to punish its wartime enemies, the majority was inclined toward forgiveness. Still, the nation's better angels had to be directed. President Truman cleverly recruited an audacious advertising whiz kid, Charles Luckman, who, with Truman's strong backing, encouraged Americans to eat less in order to save millions overseas. The Friendship Train was only one of many successful drives that Luckman engineered. The astonishing aspect of America's postwar sacrifices was how much of it was directed toward its recent former foes. Anti-communism and the desire to check the spread of Soviet influence can only partly explain these decisions. When we probe deeper into individual motives, we find a complex collection of causes, with the humanitarian impulse being an important factor in the mix.

This is the story of how destructive decisions overlapped and intertwined and how the country then tried to reverse course. It traces the connections between heroes, villains, and victims in each virtuous and vengeful act, weaving a new kind of through line across America's past. But unlike the Hollywood version of history, the real heroes and villains proved far more complex, often assuming both roles. Many of the same people were intimately involved in each of these pivotal decisions, and they sometimes switched sides. For reasons both pragmatic and personal, idiosyncratic and ethical, the proponents of harshness in one case became the defenders of mercy in another, and vice versa. These were ethical dilemmas, complex and confusing. Even the person most known for her support of human rights, Eleanor Roosevelt, sometimes found herself defending decisions that many felt were cruel. Again, I wanted to learn why.

Some leaders, such as War Secretary Henry Stimson, remained remarkably consistent – consistently ineffective. Stimson's Christian values convinced him of the wrongness of many governmental actions during the war, but he could not overcome the forces around him, from his Cabinet rivals to the generals he supposedly oversaw. He harbored deep ambivalence about the internment, objected to the fire bombings of Japan, and agonized over the use of atomic weapons. He worked hardest to prevent the punitive plans for Germany, yet there, too, he faltered.

Herbert Hoover, the nation's first Quaker president, consistently stood for mercy, but his fortunes fell in tragic fashion. Hoover had been an international icon, having organized relief efforts during World War I. A gifted mining engineer with a knack for logistics, Hoover's actions as a private citizen to deliver food and medicine to occupied Belgium earned him the moniker "the Great Humanitarian."[25] For a time, he was arguably the most admired man in America, but as president he failed disastrously to lift his country out of the Great Depression. Shunned by both parties and scorned by the public, Hoover toiled in political purgatory. Even Franklin Roosevelt, when encouraged to invite the former president to the White House for consultations, quipped, "I'm not Jesus Christ. I can't resurrect him." And then, to everyone's amazement, the postwar food crisis brought Hoover back into the limelight. The Great Humanitarian dusted off his rescue playbook, speechified his Christian values, and embarked upon a worldwide mission to once more feed despairing nations. How he came to be in the position of global savior is as compelling as the mission itself, for his resurrection had everything to do with the vicious Washington intrigues being waged behind the scenes.

Hoover and Stimson did not stand alone. Several key officials strove to prevent or undo the vengeful actions of their nation. Some labored from within, such as the millionaire magnate Will Clayton, a Texas cotton king who served his country through the State Department, at first helping shape the bitter peace for Germany, then recoiling after witnessing the cruelty of its effects. Some consider Clayton the true father of the Marshall Plan: the billion-dollar transfer of American wealth that remade Western Europe. Another voice for mercy came from Joseph Grew, the Bostonian aristocrat and longtime ambassador to Tokyo. After six months as a prisoner of the Japanese Empire, he returned to America on a speaking tour aimed at softening hatred toward the people of Japan. Had he succeeded, the atomic bombs might never have been used.

And there were others, lower down, who pressed for mercy, calling on the American sense of fairness. A lieutenant commander of naval intelligence risked his career to combat the Japanese-American relocation. Two young attorneys in the Justice Department heroically attempted to expose a cover-up about internment. And there were those outside of government, from Quaker Friends to Protestant clergy, driven by a Christian conviction that fairness and decency should form the basis of any action. They all believed that harming innocent civilians, especially children, was "not who we are" as a nation, and they said so in strikingly similar words. Each, in his or her own way, sought to ameliorate the worst effects of wartime anger and racial animus. Yet their opponents cannot be seen as sinister, for they, too, believed that their actions were morally justified.

The advocates of mercy wanted to build a better world, and that same desire drove the ones who demanded retribution. The man behind the harsh peace for Germans genuinely believed that his plan to cripple Germany would form the foundation of a lasting peace. The men who devised and enforced the concentration camps for Japanese Americans did so in part because they believed it was essential to secure the nation. And the few who advocated the use of atomic bombs against civilians believed it necessary for the future stability of world order. Or at least that was what they told themselves and others, but the truth was more complex. None of these decisions was straightforward or clear-cut. Each involved degrees of moral ambiguity. And all of the key players grappled with shades of gray. We will meet each of these leaders within these pages. We will learn their stories and the reasons why they thought the way they did. And we will look beneath the surface of their convictions to find sometimes a hopeful faith in humanity, and at other times a misplaced longing for revenge.

These are truly human dramas, full of noble aspirations mixed with baser needs. Efforts at world peace were fueled by individual ambitions. Calls for punishing an enemy in the name of the public good were often driven by hunger for private gain. The quest for global security flowed not in a direct line from A-bombs to occupation zones but in stutter steps from vengeance to virtue. America's emergence as number one came at the needless cost of hundreds of thousands of innocent lives but was then cemented by the saving of millions more.

This Is Not Who We Are spotlights America's struggle to be good at the moment it was becoming great. It asks why the United States treated its enemies cruelly when most American leaders and the public supported mercy. It shows how a handful of officials managed to impose their will upon a flawed policy process, thwarting the kinder intentions of the majority. But the book also shows how the country tried to atone for its inhumane actions by leading the world in humanitarian acts. To suggest that America reclaimed some of its humanity in the years just after the war is not to claim that the country suddenly became morally pristine. The list of injustices committed against others, domestically and abroad, is a catalogue of moral failings.[26] But if we are to be objective, we must also examine the many humane acts that Americans pursued – for those actions alleviated suffering and saved lives. I show how the cruel and the compassionate deeds were intertwined and cannot be understood in isolation.

My previous books have dealt with the problem of enemies: how we assess them, how we try to predict their behavior, why we often fail to read them correctly, and just as important, why we sometimes succeed. In this book, rather than examining enemy assessments, I instead focus on the way that enemies were treated. My larger aim is to offer a historian's take on judgment. I believe that the decisions about how to treat enemies (both actual and perceived) can offer us a unique window on wisdom. But to access those insights, we must explore how people grappled with hard ethical choices when the stakes were the highest they could be.

Background and Approach

It has been more than thirty-five years since John W. Dower published his acclaimed study of racism in the US-Japan conflict, *War Without Mercy*,[27] and since that time, most scholars assume that racism explains the ferocity of that war. Racism was so deep and widespread across the United States in the 1940s that it was not surprising that Dower found ample evidence of racist attitudes on the part of American leaders and the public. But while racism clearly intensified the battle-space, racism alone cannot explain some of the harshest wartime policies. Many high-level American leaders tried hard to prevent not only some of the most vengeful measures against Japanese and Japanese Americans but also those directed against the German populace. This book spotlights the intense struggles within the highest echelons of American government to create what many leaders saw as humane policies. And though they ultimately failed, their efforts demonstrate that at least in the innermost circles of government, rather than being a war without mercy, WWII was in many ways a war over mercy. It was an ongoing series of struggles between those who pushed for vengeance and those who favored moderation.

This book also challenges the recent depiction of the United States offered by Stephen Wertheim in *Tomorrow the World*.[28] Like many works in the vein of William Appleman Williams's *The Tragedy of American Diplomacy*, Wertheim and scores of like-minded scholars have argued that American leaders often single-mindedly sought economic and military imperialism around the globe. This book offers a more complex view. It affirms that certain officials did pursue American expansion, but it emphasizes the considerable efforts to spread American power for what those individuals saw as humane reasons.

The Williams lineage of scholarship has advanced our understanding of America's rise, but it has tended to focus on singular motives for expansion, whether economic, military, ideological, cultural, or other. The problem with that approach is that motives are typically mixed. Individuals and governments act out of multiple motivations. Isolating a single factor can be illuminating, but it tends to skew our perception of the intricate process of decision making. This book does indeed focus on a particular motivation – mercy toward one's enemies (or perceived enemies) – but it tries to present this subject within the context of numerous competing drives: the thirst for vengeance, the craving for power, the demand for security, the hunger for personal gain, the desire to outflank individual rivals, the yearning to repay acts of friendship, and the noble hope to act with honor. Just as Thucydides observed more than two and a half millennia ago, wars bring out the vast range of human motivations, and no single cause can explain it all.

Although most of the historic decisions I cover in this book have been studied in depth, they have typically been studied in isolation. Scholars have given us countless weighty monographs on subjects such as the Marshall Plan, the atom bombs, the internment, and related matters. But the decisions that produced these actions must be seen as an organic process. Only when we view their interconnections can we grasp how and why they came to pass. Because many of the same people took part in each decision, they learned from their interactions. The dynamics of one decision shaped the outcome of the next. Historians have too often overlooked this crucial element in the story of America's rise, and that is unfortunate, because decisions are never made in a vacuum. I hope that this book can heighten the importance of studying decision webs.

Every book is by nature limited in scope. In order to do justice to certain subjects, I had to omit others. There is still more to be said about the fire bombings of Japan, the aerial bombings of Germany, the rebuilding of postwar Japan, the nature of humanitarian aid, and so many other morally complex issues. One reason I chose to focus on the three cases in Part I was because they involved interactions among many of the same individuals, though the cases themselves were each distinct. This made them excellent examples of group decision making over time. But another reason for studying the Japanese-American internment, the initial occupation policy for Germany, and the atomic bombings is that they hold special relevance for a study of moral judgments: each eventually came to be seen by many as immoral. Within two years of Germany's surrender, the punitive occupation policy had to be reversed by the Marshall Plan. Decades later, the internment was declared an injustice, and the government paid restitution to the survivors. And although the wisdom of the atomic bombings of Japan remains debated, shortly after the war a movement arose among some American Christians to atone for these attacks. The penultimate chapter details that drive, and how it transformed into an effort to Christianize the Japanese.

Because I focused on the ethical struggles that American leaders confronted both during and after the war, I necessarily had to examine some of their religious views. It is important that readers distinguish between my own views and the views of the people I present. Readers will find that most of the main characters in this story were Protestants, who spoke unselfconsciously of their Christian values. When I write about their Christian virtues, I am neither endorsing nor deriding those beliefs; I am simply reflecting how those individuals viewed themselves and the world. Their speeches, and also their private writings, frequently employed references to the Christian duty to one's fellow man. Today, much of their language can seem sexist, pious, and out of step with America's secular mainstream. But if we want to comprehend these decision makers' moral judgments, we cannot ignore their religious beliefs, even when their words might make some of us uncomfortable. As a historian, it would be professionally negligent, and an act of cultural erasure, to omit this important aspect of their world view.

The phrase "This is not who we are" is likewise not a reflection of my own view of America. To me, it seems unreasonable to claim that any nation is good or bad. Rather, I see countries as collections of individuals, groups, and institutions that engage in varying degrees of good and ill at various points in time. But the sentiment "This is not who we are" did reflect how many of the people in this book viewed America in the 1940s. They frequently spoke of the goodness of the American people. They commonly referred to its Christian character. And they often did this precisely as their government's actions flagrantly belied those vaunted values. But at other times they conjured notions of American virtue in order to encourage sacrifice and compassion for strangers overseas. When they employed phrases like "This is not who we are," we should interpret those words not as their declarative affirmations of the country's character but rather as their aspirational ideals. The phrase "This is not who we are" should therefore not be taken literally. It is merely, yet profoundly, an expression of a wish. They were really saying, "This is not who we want to be."

It is easy to look back and say what should have been done. That is the luxury of being a historian, spared from the pressures of the moment, freed from the crushing weight of consequence. And that is one more reason why I felt drawn to the three cases of vengeance in Part I. Each involved people struggling with life-altering, world-changing choices. They found themselves tied up in morally ambiguous knots that no one could easily sever. Some of them tried to use their virtues as their guide. I wanted to explore that process in the hope that we might profit from what they learned.

For the past fifteen years I have had the honor of teaching military officers about great power competition. My students come not only from the United States' armed services but also from allied nations around the world. One lesson I hope to convey to them is that power is never just about tanks, planes, and guns. It is more crucially about ideals. If power is the ability to get what you want, then that ability is enhanced when a country acts in accordance with attractive principles. When a country treats others with decency, dignity, and a deep sense of fairness, it not only enhances its own power, it also builds a better world. Sometimes the human emotions of anger, hatred, and thirst for revenge can cause leaders and their publics to forget that simple truth. The struggle between those who understood the roots of lasting power and those who didn't formed an underlying tension throughout the 1940s. It is a struggle that still plagues great power conflicts to this day. As America embarks on a new era of great power competition and cooperation, it should remember that its ideals are among its greatest source of strength. But to fully appreciate this fact, we must first learn the story of America's internal conflicts over vengeance. We must know why Americans were insisting that "This is not who we are," at the very moment they began to lead the world.

Part I
Enemies

1 CONCENTRATE

When Francis Biddle stepped before the assembled crowd, he knew that his words would carry weight. This was the eve of a week commemorating the Bill of Rights, and as Franklin Roosevelt's attorney general, Biddle could be counted on as a fierce defender of civil liberties. Tall and slender, with wide-set eyes and a cleft chin, Francis Beverley Biddle was heir to an American aristocracy. The great-great-grandson of America's first attorney general, Biddle enjoyed the privileges of his class: education at Groton, the elite private boarding school for boys, followed by college at Harvard, and capped by a degree from Harvard Law. But Biddle's breeding did not leave him indifferent to the rights of average citizens. Just the opposite, in fact. He cared deeply about upholding America's most treasured values: treating all equally before the law. And the message he came to deliver on this day would resonate with the crowd. He was addressing the American Slav Congress, a group of citizens who understood the need to protect minorities from discrimination and oppression. But Biddle had come to speak about America's commitment to racial justice. He wanted to ensure that everyone knew where the administration stood. He hoped to count on the crowd's compassion for other minorities, non-Slavic peoples, entitled to the same rights as all Americans. And the timing seemed fortuitous. Some in the audience might be in a compassionate, spiritual frame of mind, having come from church that morning, for this was a Sunday afternoon. It was Sunday, December 7, 1941.

Less than thirty minutes after Biddle began his address in Detroit, thousands of miles and six time zones to the west, Japanese aircraft began bombing ships and sailors at the US naval base at Pearl Harbor.[29] In a time before smartphones and instantaneous communications, neither Biddle nor his audience had any knowledge of the attack. Unburdened by the weight of this shocking news, Biddle was free to deliver his speech exactly as planned, denouncing the denial of freedom on the basis of race. He warned his audience against not just military disarmament but spiritual disarmament as well:

> That disarmament threatens every time an attempt is made to build up hatred against any person or persons on the grounds of race, religion, or national origin. It is of aid and comfort to the enemy outside when a wartime national hero descends to the unheroic level of a public appeal to race prejudice. It is of aid and comfort to the enemy when a boycott is directed against a small shopkeeper whose crime has been that his parents or his ancestors were German or Italian or Japanese.[30]

Biddle's message was simple: racism is treason, religious hatred is un-Christian, and discrimination based on national origin is un-American. And as he spoke, Japanese Zeros rained down a storm of destruction, murdering American sailors as they slept.

Biddle reminded his listeners of the wartime hysteria that gripped America in 1917, when American citizens with an accent or a German-sounding name were persecuted by their neighbors.[31] He implored the audience to care for the constitutional rights of all citizens. The moment when anyone becomes indifferent to those rights, or if they try to override those rights, "they are striking, not at our first, but at our last line of defense."

It was a rousing speech against racism, and distressingly prescient. The Attorney General warned that even in the halls of Congress fears can often be directed against those of certain races, religions, or national origins. He pledged that the Justice Department would prosecute any aliens who posed a danger, and it would protect the vast majority of aliens who are peaceful and law-abiding. But he cautioned that no government alone could guarantee the nation's democratic ideals, just as no government alone could destroy it: "In the final analysis, when this nation's ability to survive as a democracy is put to the test, it is we ourselves who will decide. It is up to us."

Shortly after Biddle finished speaking, radios across the country carried the news. Pearl Harbor had been attacked. Several thousand were dead, and the noble sentiments that Biddle had just proclaimed were suddenly less certain. America's spiritual defenses would now be tested, and Biddle would find his most deeply held American ideals under siege. As attorney general, it was his duty to protect civil liberties, but as he observed, it was not his task alone. To ensure that wartime hysteria would not erode the nation's values, the country's leaders, its institutions, and its sensible citizens needed to be mobilized into action. Unfortunately for the roughly 112,000 Japanese Americans living on the west coast, they were about to become the victims of one of America's worst cases of misplaced revenge. Tragically, this would be only the first of many vengeful acts America inflicted upon the innocent during and shortly after the war. And with each destructive deed, a majority of Americans insisted that this is not who we are. Why, then, did the politics of vengeance prevail?

Soon after Francis Biddle concluded his speech in Detroit, he learned of the Pearl Harbor attacks and quickly returned to Washington. The test of his pledge to defend the rights of racial minorities was about to begin. In the weeks and months that followed Pearl Harbor, some Americans called for banning, arresting, and removing those of Japanese descent from the coast and the country.[32] Even some prominent public figures demanded the removal of this perceived enemy, including the California attorney general, Earl Warren. Warren was running for governor, and he shrewdly recognized that he could ride this issue to higher office. A vocal segment of white Americans now felt completely free to voice their deepest racial views. The newspaper columnist Harry McLemore wrote: "Personally, I hate the Japanese, and that goes for all of them." McLemore demanded immediate evacuation and relocation to the worst part of the American Badlands.[33]

Although the government's actions in the initial weeks after Pearl Harbor were limited to FBI roundups of those deemed suspicious, one segment of the public soon pressed for more robust measures, as fears of a second attack swelled. Rumors and false reports circulated in the press and by word of mouth that Japanese people on the west coast had sent radio signals to Japanese submarines to assist the Pearl Harbor strikes. The fear of sabotage led officials to confiscate the cameras and radios of Japanese Americans and to shutter their businesses. FBI officials arrested Japanese-American community leaders. Innocent Japanese Americans hid, burned, or destroyed any possessions from

Japan, including prized family heirlooms, and especially traditional swords. Fear that a fifth column of saboteurs was living on American shores spread through the population of white citizens in California, Oregon, and Washington State. Their calls for action sprang not solely from fear but also from greed.

Japanese Americans owned land, homes, cars, and possessions, all of which were coveted by some white people, who felt that Asians did not belong in America. White farmers had seen Japanese Americans prosper in the produce trade. White fishermen vied with Japanese Americans for the best catches. There were many white west coast residents who saw Asians as competitors and threats to their livelihoods. If forced to relocate, the Japanese Americans would have no choice but to sell nearly everything they owned at a fraction of its true value. The unanticipated attack at Pearl Harbor presented a golden opportunity not merely to remove these perceived outsiders from their land but also to create a windfall for white people who could profit from the fire sale of Japanese-American property. Pearl Harbor created a perfect mix of incentives to scapegoat Japanese Americans while stoking the flames of white rage.

Clearly, the federal government had to answer the voluble outcry from politicians and media figures. If the administration was going to bow to pressure from a segment of angry voices, it needed to base its response on an actual threat. And to assess the extent of that threat, it needed reliable intelligence – not just on Japanese Americans but also on the actual views of most west coast residents.

The Intel

Franklin Roosevelt faced two existential crises as president. He entered office in the midst of the Great Depression, when the nation hovered on the brink of revolution. His expansive use of government to create jobs rescued the nation from that fate. The second crisis involved the rise of militaristic, authoritarian regimes, which made war a looming danger. Fearing sabotage as early as 1936, Roosevelt began ordering investigations into the safety of American installations. His first instinct was to defend Hawaii. On August 10, 1936, FDR told the Chief of Naval Operations that every Japanese person, citizen or not, who makes contact with Japanese ships in Oahu should be surveilled. They should be the first to be "placed in a concentration camp in the event of trouble."[34] His remark, though chilling, was made in a time before the Nazis' death camps became synonymous with concentration camps. By 1941, as the likelihood of war with Japan intensified, Roosevelt requested official reports on the state of Japanese Americans along the west coast.

FDR asked J. Edgar Hoover, head of the FBI, to assess the threat. The President wanted to know whether the country needed to worry about their loyalty. The FBI chief investigated and returned with a definitive answer. He informed the President that there was no reason for concern. The Japanese Americans appeared eager to prove their loyalty.[35]

Around the same time as Hoover's investigations, the Office of Naval Intelligence launched its own study of the situation, spearheaded by Lieutenant Commander Kenneth Ringle. Ringle had good reason to be alert to the risk of sabotage. In June 1941, he had led a nighttime raid on the Japanese Consulate in Los Angeles, exposing a spy ring. If anyone would have been sensitive to the threat from Japanese Americans, Ringle would have been it. But Ringle was not the average naval intelligence officer. He spoke fluent Japanese, having lived for several years in Tokyo as the naval attaché to the US Embassy. While in Japan, he studied Japanese culture as well as the language. Subsequently assigned to the west coast to keep a close eye on Japanese Americans, Ringle developed extensive ties to the community. After evaluating the community as a whole, Ringle concluded that it represented no threat at all.

But Roosevelt was never content to rely solely on the traditional instruments of government to obtain information. He frequently created back channels, bypassing the officials charged with overseeing an area or issue. FDR preferred his own men to the ones he had not appointed and could not entirely trust.

In order to gather his own information on Japanese Americans, Roosevelt commissioned a friend and journalist, John Franklin Carter, to conduct a secret intelligence mission. Carter in turn tasked Curtis Munson, a businessman who had produced reporting for FDR previously, to travel to the west coast and take the pulse of the Japanese-American community. This time the President would get the truth about the threat. What Munson found was striking. He not only confirmed that the thousands of Japanese Americans were overwhelmingly loyal to the United States but also reported that the Japanese Americans had more to fear from west coast white residents than the other way around.

His follow-up reports only reinforced this view, and Carter forwarded Munson's reports to the President.

These three separate intelligence reports should have sufficed to quash any notion of concentration camps, but just to ensure that the President would not act unwisely, Attorney General Biddle also voiced his opposition to any unconstitutional actions against American citizens. Biddle had read the FBI and Office of Naval Intelligence reports, as well as the Munson reports. He understood that any danger of sabotage was slight and already being monitored appropriately. Biddle, however, had a problem. Some Army commanders, in particular General John DeWitt, the head of the Army's west coast command, were insisting that the Japanese-American community be rounded up and removed from the coast. Immediately after Pearl Harbor, DeWitt began forwarding a series of unfounded rumors that Japanese Americans were signaling to ships off the coast and preparing a large-scale uprising. The Federal Communications Commission and the FBI discredited these reports, but DeWitt remained insistent that the Army take preventive action. It was DeWitt's subordinate, Colonel Karl Bendetsen, who pressed for the total evacuation of all Japanese and Japanese Americans from the coast. Throughout the months leading up to and after the President's executive order, Bendetsen acted as a crucial driving force for internment from within the military.[36] Bendetsen frequently drafted letters and memoranda on DeWitt's and Secretary of War Stimson's behalf, crafting documents that reflected Bendetsen's own views. Bendetsen met with congressmen to influence them in support of internment, and he tried to strangle any opposition to his plans. Because Biddle resisted the Army's demands, the Army implored Assistant War Secretary John McCloy to intervene on their behalf.

From Biddle's perspective, the solution was obvious. On Sunday, February 4, 1942, he met with McCloy to propose a joint statement by the Justice and War Departments. They needed to act collectively to calm the citizens' fears. They should explain to the public that the government had thoroughly investigated the Japanese-American community and determined that it posed no threat. The few individuals who did would be dealt with properly, but evacuation of citizens was neither necessary nor appropriate. This was exactly the approach he had outlined in his speech to the American Slav Congress on December 7, barely two months earlier. Round up the few who genuinely presented a danger and protect the rest from attacks by fearful mobs. A joint War and Justice Department statement could have eased tensions and set policy on a sensible course. But McCloy would not agree to Biddle's plan. He wanted to leave open the option of evacuation. Biddle found himself completely unable to persuade McCloy and quickly realized he was losing control of what should be a Justice Department matter. The War Department was exerting influence beyond its purview, and Biddle lacked the know-how to combat it.

With his top intelligence officials and his own secret investigators agreeing that Japanese Americans posed no threat, how did FDR come to issue the directive to uproot and intern them? It did not stem from a malicious racism. Roosevelt's own racial views of the Japanese were mixed. He did not share the anti-Japanese sentiments of the fearful white Americans who were demanding internment. The Roosevelt family had a long history of engagement with Asia. The President's grandfather had lived in Canton, China, for a decade, where he profited in the budding China trade. Roosevelt's family acquired Japanese porcelains and other artifacts to adorn their estate. And Franklin, himself, had befriended at least one Japanese person, a classmate at Harvard. Despite his openness to friendships with Japanese individuals, Roosevelt nonetheless absorbed the commonly held beliefs of his era regarding racial purity. He did not wish to see any mixing of the races that would produce offspring. He believed that the Japanese shared this view as well, wanting to keep their own race pure. But FDR's racism alone would not have produced the internment. He did not initiate the plan, and he seemed largely indifferent to it. His decision required a strong push in that direction. But who exactly was doing the pushing?

The idea that the general public demanded internment is false, and the government knew it. Ever sensitive to public opinion, Roosevelt grasped that some white Americans felt angry over Pearl Harbor, fearful of further attacks, and hateful toward Japanese Americans living among them. The calls for evacuation, however, did not represent all Americans. They may not even have represented the majority. The government had good reason to think that internment was unpopular, because it was conducting its own surveys on the subject.

By executive order, President Roosevelt had recently created the innocuously named Office of Facts and Figures (OFF) in October 1941, an agency officially charged with coordinating information about America's defense efforts, but which actually functioned partly as a propaganda ministry. FDR chose the noted poet Archibald

MacLeish to head the new organization. From February 7 to 13, 1942, two months after Pearl Harbor, OFF conducted polling of citizens in the three west coast states. In these early months following the Japanese attacks, anti-Japanese sentiments might have been expected to run extremely high. But the survey found that outside of southern California, fewer than half those surveyed supported the internment of Japanese aliens, and only a meager fourteen percent favored interning Japanese Americans.[37] In southern California, where anti-Japanese attitudes were more intense, only a third of respondents supported the removal of Japanese Americans. If even west coast citizens, the people supposedly most fearful of sabotage from an enemy within their midst, opposed internment, then the push for this policy could not have come from the general public. As real as racism was, the idea of forcing Americans from their homes and into camps was a step too far for most people.[38] Their consent would need to be manufactured.[39]

Even if a majority of the public had demanded the internment of Japanese Americans, political pressure alone could not explain the President's actions. FDR was an exceptionally artful politician. He knew how to deflect attention and defeat an argument. He had options available to him for addressing public fears without resorting to the evacuation order. He could have described in a fireside chat to the nation the findings of his intelligence chiefs, unequivocally asserting Japanese-American loyalty and stressed the need to avoid retribution against innocent Americans. He could have defended the civil liberties of all citizens, reminding Americans that if one minority is stripped of its constitutionally guaranteed freedoms, then no other group, such as German Americans, Italian Americans, or Catholic or Jewish Americans, could be safe from a similar fate. This is, of course, what his own Justice Department chief, Biddle, was arguing in his opposition to the proposed internment. But with the outbreak of war and the consuming pressures it exerted, Roosevelt had little time to concentrate on the fate of one relatively small ethnic minority, and even less concern at this moment for their rights. FDR had the fate of the world to consider.

The Stakes

America's victory in the war, and indeed the future of democracy worldwide, hinged, counterintuitively, on Soviet Russia's ability to survive. This was just one insight that made Franklin Roosevelt such an exceptional strategist. He possessed the ability to view foreign and military affairs in a genuinely global context. He did not see the Japanese attack on Pearl Harbor in isolation. He did not mount a military response that was solely directed against Japan or even solely against Japan's aggression in the Pacific. Instead, he had the wisdom to step back from the intensity of the moment and survey the political, not just the military, implications of current events.

Since at least as early as the 1920s while composing *Mein Kampf*, Hitler had dreamed of acquiring living space in Eastern Europe. In 1937, Hitler outlined to his generals and foreign minister his intention to invade Russia and instructed them to prepare. In 1941, he amassed the largest invasion force in history. Some three million troops gathered along Russia's western front and managed to catch only Stalin by surprise. Despite overwhelming intelligence reports that the Germans were poised to invade, Stalin refused to believe his own officials, convinced that these reports were part of a Western plot to embroil him in a war with Germany. The Soviet leader assumed that the massing troops were merely training to the east of Germany as a means of avoiding British bombs as they prepared for an attack on the British Isles.

Once the invasion of Russia began on June 22, 1941, the cost of Stalin's paranoia quickly became apparent. Having spent the preceding years purging his military of suspected enemies, Stalin had succeeded in depleting his officer corps of its most competent commanders. Initially the German advance moved swiftly and steadily eastward as poorly led and ill-equipped Soviet troops fell back. Meanwhile, Japanese forces easily routed inadequately defended targets across the Pacific. As Roosevelt looked on in dismay, he had to fret over a nightmare scenario: that Japan might attack Russia in the east, thrusting the Soviets into a two-front war, one which they were likely to lose. Just two years earlier Japanese troops had attacked Russia in the border region of Mongolia, but Soviet Red Army forces decisively defeated them. Following the Nazi invasion in 1941, the Red Army was desperately combating German troops in the west, and this time the Soviets seemed barely able to prevent a total collapse. If forced to divert some of their troops east to battle the Japanese, Russia and its vast resources, including its crucial oil fields, seemed certain to fall to the Axis. If that occurred, the Allies' odds of winning the war would be slim.

Everything had to be done to prevent a Russian collapse from occurring. Japan had to be drawn away from attacking Russia. Roosevelt's strategy throughout the second half of 1941 appears directed toward that end. By imposing an oil embargo on Japan coupled with impossible demands, FDR probably hoped to draw the Japanese into a conflict with the United States in the Pacific and away from an attack on Russia's rear.[40]

This was one of FDR's greatest gifts – the ability to perceive the interlocking puzzle pieces of world affairs with a clarity that others lacked. He recognized that decisions in Japan could cripple Russia's ability to survive, which would strengthen Germany's hand immensely, which would severely imperil America. Roosevelt likely divined a daring solution to that puzzle, one which gave the United States a fighting chance for victory. Unwilling to withdraw from China as America was demanding, and feeling the tightening noose of the US oil embargo, on December 7, 1941, the Japanese launched their fateful strike. Roosevelt at last found himself enmeshed in the war he had long expected, but for which America nonetheless remained ill prepared. Four days after Pearl Harbor, Hitler gave Roosevelt a surprising gift by declaring war on the United States.[41] Roosevelt wanted to pursue a Europe-first strategy for the war. By declaring war on America, Hitler made Roosevelt's position vastly easier. The President could more readily justify sending troops to fight in Europe as well as the Pacific.

The stakes in this conflict were incalculable. From Roosevelt's perspective, nothing mattered more than defeating the Axis completely. Any other concerns had to be secondary to this one objective. If the civil liberties of Japanese Americans had to be sacrificed in the larger aim of winning the war, then so be it. John McCloy, General DeWitt, and Colonel Bendetsen believed evacuation was necessary to safeguard military installations. A vocal minority of white Americans, particularly west coast politicians, was demanding it be done. Despite these pressures, the internment could still have been prevented. In early February, Secretary of War Henry Stimson tried to meet with FDR to discuss it, but Roosevelt told him that he was too busy, indicating it was far from the President's top priority. The following week, Stimson managed to get the President on the phone. Judging by FDR's response, he apparently had no strong feelings regarding internment. FDR was preoccupied with developing strategies to win the war. He could scarcely concentrate on the Japanese-American matter. The President told his War Secretary to handle the issue however he thought best.[42]

And that should have settled the matter against internment, because Stimson was deeply ambivalent. He had no wish to see more than 100,000 innocent individuals evacuated to the country's interior. As a Harvard-trained former US attorney, he knew that mass internment would probably not be constitutional. As a devout Christian, he felt disturbed by the thought of uprooting people on the basis of race. Although he did perceive some threat from a minority of second-generation Japanese Americans, whom he believed were not all as loyal as their parents, he immediately recognized the ugly underlying motivation behind the calls for removal. "We cannot discriminate among our citizens on the ground of racial origin," Stimson recorded in his diary on February 3, 1942.[43] But Stimson also felt that something had to be done to protect military installations along the west coast, and certain elements within the military were pushing for the evacuation. On February 10, he told his diary that "their racial characteristics are such that we cannot understand or trust even the citizen Japanese." At the same time, he acknowledged that attempting to evacuate all Japanese Americans would "make a tremendous hole in our constitutional system."[44]

These back-and-forth arguments with himself were typical of how Stimson wrestled with difficult matters. In short, on his own, Stimson would probably never have insisted on relocation and internment. His mixed emotions meant that he needed a push. If Stimson had joined with Biddle and taken a strong stand against internment, the evacuation would most likely never have happened, especially given Stimson's imposing stature inside the government.

Gentleman Statesman

Henry Stimson enjoyed one of the most remarkable careers in modern American public service thanks to his intellectual gifts and impeccable pedigree. The son of a noted surgeon, Stimson was educated at Phillips Academy, an elite boarding school comparable to Groton. From Skull and Bones at Yale, followed by a Harvard law degree, he glid effortlessly into one of the most influential law firms on Wall Street. There he was mentored by the firm's prominent partner, a former secretary of state and war. Stimson would follow precisely in his mentor's path.

A chronic insomniac prone to occasional bursts of anger, Stimson nonetheless had a reputation as a man who got things done. Perhaps it was the bags beneath his eyes that gave the impression of a workhorse. His sagging jowls, drooping face, and stooped shoulders contrasted with his belief in hearty outdoorsmanship. His appearance notwithstanding, Stimson was seen as a sober-minded attorney, a man to whom people turned when they needed sound advice or problems solved. He was widely respected as a man of great moral rectitude. Those who had divorced were not welcome in the Stimson home. Hunting, fishing, and vigorous exercise built a man's character. Charity, kindness, and Christian virtues made America great. Above all, deference to authority maintained social order. These were Stimson's values: clear-cut and straightforward. He was a nineteenth-century man caught in a morally muddled modern era.

Beneath his stern demeanor lay a progressive Republican in the Teddy Roosevelt mold. His first public service came in the early 1900s, when then President Theodore Roosevelt appointed him as a United States attorney in New York, where he prosecuted corrupt tycoons and crooked corporations. This was the time of Roosevelt's trust-busting campaign, and Stimson devoted himself to the charge. He belonged to the progressive wing of Republicans, those who believed that government should be harnessed to uplift its citizens and give average white Americans a fair shot at success – what TR dubbed "a square deal." He admired Roosevelt's genuine commitment to the common good, and he never lost his respect for him, even when Roosevelt broke ranks with the Republican Party to challenge his own hand-picked successor, the incumbent President William Howard Taft.

Recognizing Stimson's many gifts, President Taft asked Stimson to lead the War Department. From 1911 to 1913, he reorganized the military to reform and prepare it for modern combat. As testament to his deeply held values of duty, once America entered the war in 1917, the nearly fifty-year-old former war secretary volunteered for the Army. He served as an artillery officer in France and was promoted to colonel. It is difficult to imagine today a middle-aged former secretary of defense enlisting to fight in a war, but Stimson's nineteenth-century values made such a sacrifice seem unremarkable.

In 1927, Stimson was again drawn out of private legal practice to act as governor-general of the Philippines, and two years later President Herbert Hoover named him secretary of state. When Japan invaded Manchuria in 1931, he declared the Stimson Doctrine, which refused recognition of territory annexed by force. It was a purely rhetorical stand to take against Japanese expansion, but there was little more that America could do, given its own economic turmoil. The Stimson Doctrine also conveniently overlooked the fact that America's own acquisition of the Philippines had resulted from its war with Spain. This was, in a nutshell, the Teddy Roosevelt tradition: expansion abroad, compassion at home. And Stimson followed that line, always in moderation, sensitive to the limits of American power, but moving ever closer toward American dominance in world affairs. Unfortunately for Stimson, he could not continue his policies for much longer as Hoover was fated to be a one-term president.

The problem that hung over Hoover's presidency, of course, was the Depression. Hoover was blamed for the massive unemployment and suffering of millions of Americans. The failure of Hoover's predecessors to regulate the financial sector had encouraged wild speculation and a stock market bubble that was destined to burst. And it burst just nine months into Hoover's presidency. As unemployment widened and hunger spread, Hoover endured the brunt of bitter humor. The newspapers that homeless men and women used to cover themselves for warmth were dubbed Hoover blankets. Empty pocket linings turned inside out were Hoover flags. Shantytowns were known as Hoovervilles.[45] The President's name had become synonymous with depression, poverty, and loss.

When the Democratic governor of New York, Franklin Roosevelt, Teddy's younger cousin, trounced Hoover in the presidential election in 1932, both Hoover and Stimson left their respective offices and settled into private life. Had Stimson's long career in public service ended there, his achievements would have been exceptional by any measure. Instead, in 1940, President Roosevelt called on Stimson to once more lead the War Department. It was a selection that would have profound repercussions for decades to come. At nearly seventy-three years of age and in declining health, Stimson began one final stint of high-level service to his country, in a role that would place him at the center of several of America's harshest wartime acts.

On Sunday, December 7, 1941, while his assistant John McCloy was at work in the War Department, Stimson sensed an ominous tension. For months he had been tracking the movement of Japanese vessels in the Pacific and assumed that the Imperial Navy would soon strike somewhere in Asia. Secretary of State Cordell Hull was expecting a reply from Ambassador Nomura on this day, and Stimson felt certain that the message would not bode well for peace. In his diary Stimson wrote: "Hull is very certain that the Japs are planning some deviltry and we are all wondering where the blow will strike."[46] Within hours they would have their answer.

The pressures on Stimson in those first few months were enormous. Of the many immediate matters he confronted on December 7, defending the west coast military installations from sabotage ranked high. General John DeWitt, commander of the Army's western defenses, pushed hard for removal of all Japanese Americans from the coast, but Stimson's misgivings led him to seek the President's clear instructions. When Stimson finally extracted a clear direction from the President regarding internment, he was told to handle the problem however he thought best. A war was on, and there were more pressing matters at hand.

But Stimson, too, was overtaxed by the need to manage the military once fighting had broken out. He was not a man to override his generals, and General DeWitt was insisting on internment. In order to avoid confronting DeWitt directly and free himself to focus on gearing up the military for war, Stimson tasked his able assistant John McCloy with taking the lead on the relocation issue. It was a fateful choice. McCloy, like Stimson, would also be tightly enmeshed in some of America's harshest decisions. The internment order was merely the first.

McCloy, more than any other person in government, enabled the internment order. In doing so, he needlessly sent thousands of innocent people to concentration camps. Through extensive machinations, he personally ensured that they remained there for the duration of the war, even when the Supreme Court might have released them much sooner. Oddly, McCloy never intended to be dealing with questions of Japanese sabotage when Stimson hired him. On the contrary, Stimson only charged McCloy with responsibility for internment because of his knowledge of an entirely different enemy.

2 SABOTAGE

At forty-five, McCloy's balding head belied his vigor. An avid tennis player, he had the energy of a man twenty years younger, which no doubt helped to compensate for some of his unhealthier habits. Early mornings, late nights, and weekends found him at his desk alternately puffing on cigars or sucking on chocolate drops. Round-faced, thin-lipped, and intensely driven, he quickly developed into a forceful shaper of America's foreign policy. McCloy sometimes sported a mischievous grin, as though he knew something you didn't, which was usually true. He referred to Stimson as "the Colonel," and sometimes, behind his back, as "Stimmy." In return, Stimson called McCloy and his two other bright young aides "the imps of Satan." Their banter reflected a camaraderie, which helped to break the tension that infused much of their activities throughout the war. Stimson and McCloy in particular developed a powerful rapport despite their considerable age difference. One time when Stimson erupted in a characteristic outburst, he rang McCloy and shouted into the phone, "Where the hell are my goddam papers!" Unfazed, McCloy coolly replied, "I haven't got your goddam papers," and hung up.[47] The younger man had learned how to handle his boss. McCloy, it turned out, was invaluable. Many believed that McCloy was the one actually running the War Department.

Stimson had brought McCloy into the department precisely because of his unique expertise on sabotage. When Stimson hired him in 1940, the War Secretary had anticipated that America would need to know how to prevent and respond to German infiltration, and McCloy, more than any other person in the nation, possessed a deep knowledge of German operations. On December 7, 1941, when the Japanese struck Pearl Harbor, Stimson immediately set matters "going in all directions to warn against sabotage."[48] The irony, of course, was that McCloy's expertise dealt with German, not Japanese saboteurs. Yet he now turned his attention to the Japanese-American community, about which he knew almost nothing. His unique expertise on German spy rings and intelligence methods had come to him essentially by chance. It stemmed from a deadly incident several decades before when McCloy was still a young man.

Black Tom

It looked exactly like a simple lead pencil. When scattered around an office building or factory, it would not draw the slightest notice. But the pencil was in fact a glass tube containing an explosive concoction of sulfuric acid, chlorate of potash, and, to sweeten the pot, sugar. Devised by German chemists, the volatile mixture encased in what looked like a pencil could be set to act as a tiny time bomb. It was the perfect mini bomb that, when planted in large numbers, could remain hidden in plain view. Seeded in a fertile field, such as a warehouse, the pencil bombs could cause immense destruction.

Prior to WWI, America's military was tiny compared with those of Europe. The American Army was even smaller than Belgium's.[49] But what the United States lacked in military might was offset by its burgeoning industrial strength. Although in 1916 the United States had not yet entered WWI, it was supplying the Allies with massive amounts of munitions, with Britain, France, and Russia being the primary buyers. It was in part through arms sales and the sale of related wartime goods that America emerged from WWI as the largest creditor nation, greatly enhancing its financial influence on top of its impressive productive power. But American neutrality did not protect it from enemy attacks, even on its homeland.

Unknown to American officials at the time, the German government was operating a spy ring out of its Embassy in Washington. The effort was led by the German military attaché, Franz von Papen. The son of a wealthy conservative Catholic family, von Papen had joined the German Army in 1898. As military attaché, he organized a string of covert efforts to blow up bridges and canals in the United States. On the night of July 26, 1916, he managed to pull off his most impressive operation. German saboteurs snuck into America's largest ammunitions depot on Black Tom Island in New Jersey and planted the pencil bombs. The island took its name from its shape, which resembled a tom cat.

The bombs ignited millions of rounds of ammunition, blowing the depot and all its contents to what can only be described as "smithereens." The series of eruptions that continued for hours were heard as far north as Connecticut and as far south as Maryland. The blast shattered windows all across Manhattan. It illuminated the night sky with red and orange flames. It sent bullets showering the area in all directions, killing at least one bystander and injuring others. It felt like an earthquake to many, and it ruptured a water main in Times Square. In a symbolic twist, the explosions damaged the Statue of Liberty, penetrating its chest with shrapnel. It took more than a month to extinguish all of the fires. Miraculously only five people were killed in the attack. Similar strikes had been occurring at other munitions depots on the east coast, and another, less destructive, attack took place that same evening. Thanks in part to information from British intelligence officials who had been tracking his activities, von Papen was declared *persona non grata* at the end of the year and expelled from the United States. He returned to Germany to receive the Iron Cross for his achievements. There was little doubt that the Black Tom explosions had been the work of von Papen and his saboteurs. The challenge, from a legal standpoint, was how to prove it.[50]

During the summer when the attack occurred, John McCloy was just twenty-one years old, but he had devoted his summer to an unusual pursuit: preparing himself for war. Believing that America would soon be impelled to fight alongside its allies, McCloy joined the Preparedness Movement and traveled to Plattsburgh, New York, to ready himself at a military-style training camp. Ex-president Theodore Roosevelt served as the camp's co-founder and spiritual leader, appearing in full soldierly regalia to inspire the young men with invigorating speeches of their national destiny. Teddy Roosevelt had aggressively launched America on its mission to supplant Great Britain as the global leader. The first step in that process began with the defeat of Spain in 1899, and the acquisition of Spanish colonies, particularly the Philippines. Opposed to President Wilson's policy of neutrality in the European war, Roosevelt fully expected America's eventual entry, and he wanted its young men to prepare themselves for combat. John McCloy heard the call, as did many others of his generation. But even older men concurred, including the former secretary of war, Henry Stimson. At age forty-nine, Stimson attended the Plattsburgh camp, and when war came, he volunteered to serve. We do not know if Stimson and McCloy met at the camp that summer, but they did meet much later after the war for a one-on-one discussion of the Black Tom incident.

McCloy served in WWI, and when he returned to the United States, he resumed his studies at Harvard Law School. Harvard Law was the launching point for young men in a hurry. It was an especially useful springboard to the career of any man not part of America's elite. McCloy had come from a working-class Philadelphia background. His father had died when John was a boy, and his mother worked as a hairdresser to support them. She longed for her son to break into the upper class, an unlikely prospect for anyone of her station. She sacrificed to ensure John a place at a private preparatory school, which, though not nearly as prestigious as Groton, Andover, or any of the exclusive training grounds for the children of America's aristocracy, nonetheless provided a considerable leg up in the climb toward high society. Admission to Harvard Law was McCloy's ticket to a bright future, as long as he made the right connections.

McCloy lacked the brilliance of many of his peers, like Dean Acheson and Archibald MacLeish. Those boys were among the darlings of their star professor, Felix Frankfurter. They occupied the front rows in lecture halls, whereas McCloy receded into the back of the room. They were invited to Frankfurter's home for drinks and conversation, while McCloy had to do double time in studying, just to keep up with his better educated peers. And while many of the others shared Frankfurter's political perspectives as Democrats, McCloy identified as a Teddy Roosevelt Republican. Though McCloy lacked sparks of genius, he did possess exceptional tenacity. He would work harder, partly out of necessity to keep up, and partly out of sheer drive to succeed. He could focus single-mindedly for extended stretches on a subject until he had covered it from every angle. It was this quality, cultivated at Harvard and perfected in later legal practice, that brought him to Stimson's attention.

In 1930, McCloy was working at a high-powered New York corporate law firm. One of the firm's clients, Bethlehem Steel, wanted to reopen the Black Tom case, as some new leads had emerged linking Germans to the attack of 1916. McCloy was assigned the case, a case that seemed hopeless to most of his colleagues. There was little to go on after all those years, and even if a connection could be proved, which seemed unlikely, the German government would simply deny responsibility. The connection, if it even existed, would need to be between German governmental officials and the saboteurs, the identities of whom were unknown. McCloy would be chasing a wild goose across international lines. Others had worked the case before him and come up empty. But McCloy set himself to the quest, which took him to Germany, Ireland, and the international court at The Hague.

McCloy spent the next nine years investigating, litigating, and essentially obsessing over the case. Colleagues came to think of him as the Black Tom guy. They were entertained by his talk of exploding pencils, disappearing ink, encrypted messages, and all of the mysterious accoutrements cloaking the darker world into which he had descended. Though conclusive evidence of German culpability always felt just beyond reach, periodic openings arose that fueled his hope of an eventual resolution. At the start of 1933, he paid a visit to Secretary of State Stimson, hoping to convince the elder statesmen to lend the federal government's powers to cracking the case. This is the first recorded meeting of the two men, and it did not go especially well. Stimson gave the earnest thirty-six-year-old attorney a half hour of his time, but McCloy failed to make an impression or even to move Stimson in the slightest. The case was too old and not worth reexamining, especially in light of the international tensions brewing at that moment.

The larger problem was that Germany's turn toward instability made any admission of their guilt implausible. By the close of 1932, amidst growing domestic political turbulence, Germany had appointed a new chancellor, none other than the wily saboteur Franz von Papen. Von Papen had hoped to break some of the Nazi Party's excesses, but his tenure as chancellor barely lasted a few months. In a compromise agreement, von Papen accepted the vice-chancellorship in 1933 in the arrangement that made Adolf Hitler the new chancellor. As Nazi violence increased, however, von Papen took a surprising and courageous stand, speaking out publicly against the Nazis' erosion of individual freedoms. Hitler called von Papen "a little worm," and vowed revenge. In the summer of 1934, in what became known as the "Night of the Long Knives," Hitler conducted a purge of internal opponents, rounding up rivals and having them shot. During this mafia-like outburst, the Nazis murdered one former chancellor, Kurt von Schleicher, in cold blood in his home. Another ex-chancellor, Heinrich Bruening, managed to flee the country, eventually settling at Harvard, where he remained. In order to send a message to other potential rivals, Hitler placed von Papen under house arrest, making it unmistakably clear where true power lay – with the one who controlled the Gestapo and the SS. Von Papen never again challenged the Führer.[51]

Meanwhile, throughout the 1930s, McCloy continued to amass evidence against von Papen and the German spy ring. One big break came when a British intelligence official was persuaded to share intercepted and decrypted messages between Berlin and von Papen, revealing the names of some of the saboteurs. McCloy tracked down one of them, an Irish dockworker named James Larkin, who had lent his aid to the Germans during their war against Britain. Larkin resisted revealing anything to the American visitor, but gradually over several days of conversations, McCloy wore him down until he confessed his whole story. McCloy dragged Larkin to a notary public to have the affidavit certified, and then boarded a ship back home. The experience convinced McCloy of the value of dogged determination and relentless tracing of every detail in a case, wherever it might lead. This was merely one of several remarkable breakthroughs that steadily accrued until the point where the evidence was overwhelming. Owing to some legal technicalities and German maneuverings, the case landed in the US Supreme Court, where McCloy emerged triumphant. For all his trouble, he earned $94,000, an extraordinary sum to him at the time, though his boss, the head of the law firm, pocketed $4.4 million.

The financial remunerations aside, McCloy profited immensely from the notoriety. He was now the leading expert on sabotage and a valuable asset to Stimson at the War Department. He had the added advantage of being a fellow Republican in a Democratic regime. Not long after Stimson took charge of the department, he hired McCloy as his principle aide.

McCloy's experience with the Black Tom case had not only given him some small fame, it had also convinced him of the need to ramp up America's intelligence capabilities. He had seen that Germany and Britain were far ahead of America in intelligence collection and analysis. He had read Herbert Yardley's 1931 book, *The American Black Chamber*, which described America's Cipher Bureau and its efforts to decrypt foreign communications after WWI. Yardley had led that bureau until it was shuttered in 1929, when Stimson became secretary of state. Stimson opposed the unethical and unsavory practice of spying on one's own allies, especially foreign diplomats stationed in the United States. These were, after all, elites of Stimson's ilk. He famously (and perhaps apocryphally) remarked that "Gentlemen do not read other gentlemen's mail," and shut the program down. McCloy had come to think otherwise. If America was to supplant Great Britain as a global leader, it would need a robust intelligence agency. And if civil liberties might sometimes need to be temporarily suspended in the interest of national security, then it was surely worth the price. McCloy was developing the opinion that some measures were unpleasant but necessary in the pursuit of grand objectives.

A Dutiful Wife

By February of 1942, anxiety over Japanese spies inside America had spread to the mainstream. Two prominent media figures inflamed anxieties with their syndicated columns. On February 12, the journalist Walter Lippman amplified California Attorney General Earl Warren's claims that west coast Japanese were sending signals to Japanese warships off the coast. There was no evidence of such activity, but Lippman stoked the public's fears. The next day the popular cartoonist Theodore Geisel published in *PM*, a Left-leaning New York newspaper, a cartoon depicting caricatures of buck-toothed Japanese men converging on a TNT supplier while another looks out to sea. The caption read, "Waiting for the signal from home."[52] Geisel, known to most as the loveable Dr. Seuss, on this occasion used his artistic skills to fuel racial fears.

Someone needed to break the momentum toward mass internment. But with McCloy actively working in support of it, and with Stimson and Biddle sidelined, there was no one left who could intervene to block the President's imminent order – except, of course, his wife. Eleanor Roosevelt has long been thought of as the conscience of a nation. She fought valiantly to keep America true to its principles. And while this was often true, in this case she failed to speak out against the injustice to Japanese Americans. In fact, she publicly supported her husband's relocation directive on the grounds of national security, though this was never her true position.

The previous October, as war between America and Japan seemed ever more likely, Japanese Americans were growing increasingly anxious about their safety if war should break out. The President of the

Central California Japanese Association, along with a leading Japanese-American journalist, traveled to Washington to meet with Attorney General Biddle, who assured them that the Fourteenth Amendment guaranteed their security. He had no reason to believe it wouldn't. The two representatives then met with Eleanor Roosevelt, who made a public statement in support of the community's loyalty.[53] On January 11, 1942, she spoke in support of civil liberties for all Americans, and though she did not mention Japanese Americans directly, the implications were clear.[54] On a tour of the west coast, she was photographed with a group of Japanese Americans and wrote that the country must reject the hysteria against minorities. She stressed that the country must build up their loyalties and not shake them by treating them with unwarranted suspicion.[55]

Also in January, Mrs. Roosevelt was approached by *Common Ground*, a magazine that focused on immigrants and minorities. The editor asked the First Lady if she would contribute a piece on the Japanese Americans. She quickly agreed. Her drafts of that essay reveal her genuine sentiments at the time, but scarcely one month later she publicly supported her husband's plan for evacuation and internment.

On February 15, 1942, Eleanor Roosevelt held one of her regular radio interviews, then being sponsored by the Pan-American Coffee Association. The man who introduced the First Lady began by encouraging Americans to drink more coffee throughout the day, as it steadies the nerves. It was a discordant contrast between a cheerful advertisement and a call to force thousands from their homes. Mrs. Roosevelt squarely addressed the topic on millions of Americans' minds. We know that enemy aliens do exist in the country, she told her listeners, and they must be apprehended, but we "also know that we have innumerable friends who are aliens, who have taken refuge in the United States and whose whole hope for the future lies in the justice and the freedom which this country offers." This would have been a strong starting point from which to calm fears and shape opinions against forcing law-abiding Americans into concentration camps. But she could not oppose her husband so directly on a matter of national policy: "It is obvious," she continued, "that many people who are friendly aliens may have to suffer temporarily in order to ensure the safety of the vital interests of this country while at war."

Eleanor Roosevelt spoke with the precise manner of one who had received elocution lessons in her youth. Today, her accent might sound affected, false, as if she were attempting to pass as English. In her day, that tone and style made her seem both refined and authoritative. She warned against vigilantism by stressing that the government was fully in control of the situation. She urged angry Americans not to take justice into their own hands, as many had been doing. Her reasons for discouraging vigilantism were not because it was wrong to attack innocent citizens. Instead, she argued that although such actions may be inspired by the highest sense of patriotism, those actions could bring retribution against American nationals in the Far East. She asked Americans to report any suspicious activity to the proper authorities.

The First Lady assured her listeners that the relocation was a matter of national security: "We are going to move the Japanese population out of strategic areas on the west coast as soon as possible, but it is going to be done so that they will not waste their skills." The Japanese must not be allowed to plant their gardens where they currently reside, she explained, but must instead plant gardens in their new areas in the nation's interior. This would allow them to provide an important food source for the nation. She made absolutely no mention of the harm that this policy would do to these thousands of families. Her focus remained almost entirely on how relocation would affect everyone else.

At the close of her remarks, Mrs. Roosevelt obliquely spoke against racial hatred. We will try to deal with the problem of the alien with all due regard to the safety of the nation. We must never forget, she cautioned, that "the things for which we fight, such as freedom and justice, must be guaranteed to all people and not just a select few."[56] And though she emphasized the word "all," this final sentence could not mitigate the damage that was about to unfold.[57]

Eleanor Roosevelt's position on relocation at this time had to be a bitter pill for Japanese Americans to swallow. If anyone could move public opinion in support of this minority, the First Lady had both the gravitas and the platform from which to do it. If she had privately tried and failed to change her husband's mind on the subject, she could at least have remained silent on the matter. Instead, she took a public role in supporting FDR's directive with only a half-hearted message of support for their rights as citizens. It must have been equally bitter for Mrs. Roosevelt to make such a statement, as it went against everything she had previously and consistently advocated.[58] She was an ardent defender of civil liberties and civil rights. She always tried to see people as individuals and not stereotype them into specious and shallow categories. It is hard to imagine that she herself believed that forcing thousands of families out of their homes and into barbed wire concentration camps was either necessary or acceptable. But what was she to do? Speaking out against her husband's policy would have opened her to charges of disloyalty at best, treason at worst. She would have been branded as a disloyal wife, which would have sapped her ability to shape public opinion. And there was another complication. At the same time that the internment order was being formulated, she had also come under heated attack in Congress for her role in the Office of Civil Defense. Congressmen criticized her nomination of personal friends to fill high-level positions, and the public kerfuffle convinced her to step down from her involvement in the agency.[59] Given the circumstances and timing, Eleanor likely reasoned that her least unpalatable option was to go along with the relocation policy, and to try to soften its roughest edges.

While Eleanor Roosevelt was hamstrung in her ability to mobilize public opinion against internment, private citizens took up the charge. The Fair Play Committee organized to help counter the racist groups that had been fomenting hatred against people of Japanese ancestry. Founded by a former president of the University of California, David Prescott Barrows, and joined by prominent scholars, businesspeople, clergy, and labor leaders, the Committee compiled anti-racist materials, which it then disseminated to influential figures, from journalists to politicians and more. Their ranks included the California Governor Culbert Olson, a former California governor C. C. Young, the Chancellor of Stanford University, the Episcopal Bishop of California, and many other leaders along the west coast. Three weeks after Pearl Harbor, the Committee proudly announced that, on the whole, Japanese Americans have retained their civil liberties. Americans had "kept their heads," they proclaimed. "The American tradition of fair play has been observed."[60] Their declaration of victory proved premature.[61]

The noble-minded members of the Fair Play Committee did their best to counter racist views, but John McCloy was in a stronger position to manipulate public opinion. OFF had been finding that the overwhelming majority of Americans on the west coast did not approve of the internment of Japanese Americans. McCloy almost certainly knew of their findings because he was in frequent, sometimes daily contact with OFF and its head, his old Harvard Law classmate Archibald MacLeish. McCloy's diaries show his consistent involvement in the deliberations over how to censor and present information to the American people. Even before Pearl Harbor, McCloy was actively involved with OFF in shaping the nation's official narratives, particularly surrounding Japanese aliens from the west coast. For example, on December 1, 1941, he called General Sherman Miles, chief of the Army's Military Intelligence Division, to discuss the upcoming meeting with Carter and Munson about the situation of west coast Japanese aliens. That meeting occurred scarcely more than an hour later, and at 4:20 pm McCloy phoned General Miles again, and both men agreed that the meeting with Carter and Munson had been "unsatisfactory." Presumably, Carter and Munson had presented their findings that the Japanese community posed no threat at all, and this is what McCloy found unsatisfactory. At 5:30 pm, McCloy left his office for a meeting at OFF to review public statements on Japanese aliens and related matters. Among those matters was a discussion of opinion polls.[62] Based on his steady contact with OFF and his phone calls with MacLeish, it is likely that McCloy knew precisely how unpopular the idea of a forcible internment order was with the majority of west coast Americans. Part of McCloy's job, as he saw it, was to help make public perceptions conform to government policy – the policies that he, himself, was largely creating.

McCloy had to be concerned about public support for internment. Based on the demands of racist media figures, along with the calls from west coast politicians and congressmen to remove all those of Japanese descent, McCloy might reasonably have assumed that most west coast residents shared those angry sentiments, but the OFF's polls cast some doubt on that assumption. There was indeed one startling survey by the National Opinion Research Center, which showed ninety-three percent of Americans supporting the internment of Japanese aliens and fifty-nine percent supporting it for Japanese Americans.[63] This survey is frequently cited in scholarly literature and popular representations of the period as proof of American's intensely anti-Japanese sentiments.[64] However, this oft-cited poll showing overwhelming support for internment was conducted five weeks after the President issued the internment order, once Japanese Americans had been officially deemed as dangerous. In sharp contrast, a poll taken between February 7 and 13, 1942, prior to the executive order, indicated that most west coast residents opposed internment.[65]

In addition to that early February poll, a separate OFF survey found support for interning Japanese Americans at nineteen percent. Still another indicated support for internment at just 10.5 percent.[66] All of this suggests that, at least from a few OFF surveys in early 1942, there was no majority of west coast residents insisting on internment. None of this could have been good news for McCloy.

Given the rudimentary nature of these surveys, we cannot make any definitive claims about what most Americans or even west coast Americans believed with regard to internment. Perhaps a majority actually did support it, or perhaps most west coast citizens were not as virulently racist as has been believed. Either way, we do know that once the President issued his executive order, two powerful trends emerged. The first came from angry Americans demanding harsher measures against all those of Japanese descent. Curiously, those calls had remained largely muted in the months after Pearl Harbor. The historian Greg Robinson, arguably the leading expert on the internment, found that prior to the executive order, remarkably few letters arrived at the White House demanding action against Japanese Americans. Only after FDR's executive order on February 19, which framed Japanese Americans as dangerous enemies, did the flood of demands begin.[67] This suggests that the OFF surveys cited previously may have accurately reflected the public's limited support for internment. But once the President sanctioned mass removal, most Americans got on board. The second trend sought to counter the first, as Americans across racial and religious backgrounds began disparate acts of resistance.

Although an active minority of the American public supported the harshest treatment of Japanese Americans, there were many others who tried to restore civility. Some were driven by Christian convictions of charity and goodwill. Others were propelled by liberal notions of equality, fairness, and racial justice. These men and women worked to ameliorate the wrongs being perpetrated against an entire racial minority. Though their odds of success were long, they never wavered in their conviction that the government's policy was unjust. If the defenders of American ideals – those values that Francis Biddle had so loftily espoused – had only coordinated their actions, they might have managed to prevent, or at least have reduced, the damage done to innocent citizens. Even despite their disorganized efforts, they might still have succeeded in limiting the internment, but they could not counteract the orchestrated actions of a few internment supporters or the influence of one man's quiet role.

3   COORDINATE

At age eight, Atsushi Tashima thought that the family trip to a camp in Arizona was a great adventure. He learned to fish and swim and do the kinds of things he never got to do when living in the urban confines of East Los Angeles. Life at camp made him forget that he was poor. Back home, his family didn't have the things that other families had. But in camp everyone was equal because no one had anything. Sometimes, after returning to camp from a kids' outing to the Colorado River, he would tell his mother that he had just been back to California. She would smile at him and say nothing. Only much later, as an adult, could he recognize the sorrow behind her silence.[68]

Donald Nakahata was twelve years old and excited when the evacuation came. He thought he was going to get a pair of cowboy boots because they were going to the desert. Donald grew up on Pine Street in San Francisco. His father was working as a journalist for a local Japanese-American newspaper. After Pearl Harbor, his father decided to help out covering the news of the community in San Jose, but as a journalist, he was considered suspect. Donald walked his father down Pine Street to Fillmore to catch the number twenty-two streetcar on his way to work. They said goodbye, and that was the last time that Donald ever saw his father.[69]

Mary Tsukamoto refused to believe that her family would be forced to move. As she learned of other communities being relocated, she realized that might happen to her, but it still seemed impossible to imagine. She had joined her local chapter of the Japanese American Citizens League in an effort to help others integrate. When the FBI began taking people's husbands away, she tried to get welfare assistance for the wives and children left behind. The entire evacuation was occurring so quickly that no one had thought about the full range of effects it would have on families, especially those family members with disabilities. One of the women whom Mary tried to assist had a grown son who was intellectually disabled. The woman had always cared for him at home. When her family was evacuated, the authorities forbade her to take her son. They insisted that he had to be placed in an institution. Both Mary and the mother wept when they heard the news, but there was nothing that either could do. While the mother was still at an assembly center in Fresno waiting to be moved west, she received a letter that her son had died.

When Mary's time came, she boarded the train with her family. As they slowly approached the camp, the passengers were told not to look out the windows, but naturally, they couldn't help it. They saw people, so many of them, covered in dust, just staring out from behind a fence. They looked to Mary like animals in a cage. And then Mary realized that soon she and her family would be among them, and that she would look the same as the ones behind the fence.

The inmates stared at the new arrivals dragging their suitcases behind them. Soon they learned what it was like to wait: waiting in line to eat, waiting in line to bathe, waiting in line to use the latrine. There was dirt in the showers, dirt everywhere. Many became ill. There were so many people crammed together all the time that they were almost always pressed against each other.

One night early on, the inmates held a variety show. Five young boys made a skit dramatizing what it was like to have to use the latrine when there was hardly any privacy, when everyone could hear you. In a camp where she found little to laugh about, the boys had managed to find the humor in their circumstances. Everyone started laughing. Soon the hall erupted with raucous, belly-aching laughter. Mary found herself laughing so hard that it hurt.

No one knows exactly why the first riot began. Maybe it was the baking desert heat combined with the lack of mosquito netting that had been promised but never arrived. It could have been the tight, unhygienic conditions, the primitive medical care, the spoiled meats or the oatmeal that was saturated in small black bugs. Maybe it was the barbed wire fences, searchlights, and armed guards with machine guns. Or maybe it was when an old man wandered too close to the fence, and

Figure 3.1 Japanese Americans interned at Santa Anita, 1942. Photo by Library of Congress/Corbis/VCG via Getty Images.

a guard shot him dead. Most likely it was the combination of all these factors and the slow realization that they might be interned in these concentration camps forever.

The Worst Job of His Life

Four days after Eleanor Roosevelt addressed the nation to explain the need for internment, FDR signed Executive Order 9066 authorizing the forced removal of all Japanese and Japanese Americans from the west coast. Immediately the thorny question arose of what to do with their property. Should the evacuees' property be held by the government for the duration of the war, or should banks hold it, or should it be sold to the highest bidders, who would offer rock-bottom prices. Stimson continued to be frustrated by Roosevelt's failure to think through the complexities of his own orders. Biddle, too, found FDR's executive order ill-conceived and based on a slender hope that it might help secure the nation.[70] It was left to the President's subordinates to square his unsquareable circles.

FDR tried to task his Treasury secretary, Henry Morgenthau Jr., with the matter, but Morgenthau resisted. Morgenthau opposed the idea of internment, viewing it as an overreaction to a nonexistent threat.[71] Some of his own staff had proposed the seizing of thousands of Japanese-American-owned businesses, but Morgenthau rejected their plan. He saw the entire relocation policy as "hysterical and impractical."[72] He did not wish to be involved in the seizure of property, unless it involved the property of Japanese-owned large businesses. He felt that on principle the Japanese and Japanese Americans should not be victimized.[73] Together with McCloy, the two worked out a deal that ultimately did little to safeguard anyone's personal property.

The evacuees were told to sell whatever they could and to bring with them only what they could carry.[74] The result was a debacle of governmental mismanagement in which American citizens were stripped of their possessions, homes, and businesses, seldom to reclaim them after the war. White people looted the warehouses where the Army stored their belongings as guards overlooked these crimes. The evacuees were forced to sell their land, cars, memorabilia, and nearly everything they had accumulated over a lifetime of hard work and prudent saving. The community's losses totaled around $400 million, the rough equivalent of more than $5 billion in 2020.[75] But for Japanese Americans, the material losses were merely the beginning of a multi-year ordeal.

As the Army took control of removing thousands of Americans from the coast, it also had to erect camps deep in the country's interior, complete with schools and other essential facilities. This was not a job for which the Army was trained, and their activities took resources away from the war effort. As expected, the conditions within these concentration camps were often bleak, dirty, and cruel.

The Army forbade the use of the term "concentration camps," instead insisting on the euphemism "War Duration Relocation Centers."[76] The Orwellian label notwithstanding, there was no denying that these were in fact concentration camps: confined areas guarded by armed soldiers, comprising makeshift facilities from which the inmates were forbidden to leave at their own will. Soon the defense of this forced concentration of American citizens was reframed as a means of protecting Japanese Americans from the hostility of violent whites. Even the First Lady attempted to spin the situation. In her syndicated column, she wrote that she was happy that a War Relocation Authority would be taking charge of evacuees. "Unfortunately," she lamented, "in a war, many innocent people must suffer hardships to safeguard the nation." And then she added that the evacuees will be given work projects, which "is certainly better than having nothing to do."[77] For those suddenly trapped behind barbed wire, the First Lady's comments could hardly have been much solace.

The Fair Play Committee, which had been founded specifically to combat anti-Japanese-American actions, also decided to support the President's internment order, believing it a sensible solution to a wartime crisis.[78] Once the President had issued the order and the First Lady had publicly backed it, opposing internment risked marginalizing the Committee, limiting its influence. Its members realized that the organization needed a name change. Not wanting to appear indifferent to widespread fears of sabotage and future attacks, the group changed its title to the Committee on National Security and Fair Play. The group insisted, however, that Americans would be traitors if they "flouted democratic principles of justice and humanity" in their treatment of Japanese aliens or Japanese Americans, despite the frenzy of wartime.[79] The Committee was trying to tread the fine line between popularity and principles.

In March, McCloy and Biddle, along with one of FDR's close advisors, drew up a plan to create an independent agency to oversee the evacuation. On March 18, Roosevelt signed another executive order, officially establishing the War Relocation Authority. As its head, FDR chose a staff member in the Department of Agriculture, Milton Eisenhower, who came with a strong endorsement from his brother, Dwight Eisenhower, the assistant Army chief of staff. Milton Eisenhower would later refer to his time in this role as the worst assignment of his life.[80] A few months later he resigned, hoping to work instead in the newly established Office of War Information, the successor to the Office of Facts and Figures. He felt sickened both by the treatment of evacuees and by the racism of white west coast politicians.

With Eisenhower having soured on relocation, and with the government's own commissioned surveys showing limited public support for internment, McCloy needed to ensure that the public would not actively oppose the policy. Fortunately for McCloy, he had another asset in the popular conservative radio journalist Fulton Lewis Jr. Lewis hosted a nightly prime-time broadcast heard by millions of

Americans across the country. On the afternoon of April 6, 1942, McCloy spoke with Lewis about the latter's upcoming broadcast that evening. Lewis asked whether he should discuss the internment issue or ignore it altogether. McCloy advised the journalist to confront the matter head on, urging him to describe the humane manner in which the government was handling it, despite exceptional difficulties. He wanted Lewis to say how effective the government had been in dealing with the mass evacuation.[81] This was just one of the many ways in which McCloy was quietly working to craft public perceptions of an unjust affair, for there was much about internment that, if fully known and fairly understood, would hardly have been supported.

Although racism against Japanese Americans remained real, those hateful sentiments did not automatically produce a demand for internment among most Americans. That support had to be manufactured, and government-made propaganda films could help. Despite his deep revulsion to internment, Milton Eisenhower needed to tell the American people why the Japanese-American population was being uprooted. In a roughly ten-minute film prepared for newsreels in January 1943, Eisenhower described the decision in the most positive light he could muster. Seated at a desk in a spacious wood-paneled room, a massive American flag behind him and a handkerchief neatly tucked into his breast pocket, he explained to viewers that when the Japanese attacked Pearl Harbor, we knew that some among the west coast Japanese population were potentially dangerous, and most were loyal. But no one knew what would happen to them if Japan invaded. And so the Army decided to relocate them to the interior. Eisenhower avoided any discussion of what he meant by "no one knew what would happen." The audience was left to assume that either the relocation was for their own protection, or a significant number of Japanese Americans would rally in support of invading forces, acting as a fifth column, an enemy from within. Eisenhower was at pains to stress the humaneness with which the government conducted the internment, and his own discomfort seeped through in the words he chose:

> Neither the military nor the War Relocation Authority relished
> the idea of taking men, women, and children from their homes,
> shops, and their farms, so the military and civilian authorities

determined to do the job as a democracy should, with real consideration for the people involved.

But Eisenhower could only spin the operation to a point before the truth was stretched to its breaking point. He admitted that the relocation involved financial loss for these Americans, and he added that this was a sacrifice that the loyal ones felt they could make for the war effort. He glossed over the unhygienic conditions in both the temporary facilities (often the stables at racetracks) and in the camps themselves. He referred to the barren landscapes to which these families were sent as places where "the land was raw, untamed, and full of opportunity." And he inaccurately claimed (though he may have believed it to be true) that the Army "provided plenty of healthy, nourishing food for all." He concluded by asserting: "We are protecting ourselves without violating the principles of Christian decency."[82] Apparently, that was not what he truly believed. Within one year, Eisenhower would leave government service for good, retreating to the cloistered confines of academia.

Dillon S. Myer succeeded Eisenhower as director of the War Relocation Authority, and he may have found the job almost as odious as Eisenhower had. Remaining in the position for the duration of the war, he defended the internment in tortured talks, speeches to civic groups, and public testimony to Congress. In July 1943, Myer addressed the nation over NBC Radio and revealed his own extreme ambivalence about the camps.

> In spite of the fact that the War Relocation Authority is respon-
> sible for managing the ten relocation centers – we don't feel that
> they are desirable institutions or anything in which the people of
> the United States can take pride. It isn't the American way to
> have children grow up behind barbed wire. It may be possible to
> make good Americans out of them – but the very surroundings
> make a mockery out of principles we have always cherished and
> respected. It's difficult to reconcile democracy with barbed
> wire – freedom with armed sentries – liberty with searchlights.[83]

Myer maintained that the inmates were becoming increasingly loyal Americans, thanks to the inculcation of American values through camp branches of the Boy Scouts, 4-H Clubs, and Future Farmers of America, but his ambivalence persisted. In a speech to a Rotary Club in

Lawrence, Kansas, he argued outright for the end of the system he oversaw. He explained that the camps were a burden on taxpayers, that the children would become more American outside of the camps rather than in them, and that all of the inmates would be better able to aid the war effort once they were back in their communities. But his most compelling argument for closing the camps rested on his belief that incarcerating citizens on the basis of ancestry was "in no way consistent with American principles." The sooner the camps could be emptied, he insisted, "the quicker our nation will be living up to the objectives for which we are fighting."[84] Myer was echoing the sentiments that Francis Biddle had expressed on Pearl Harbor Day. Both men recoiled at how the internment contradicted the American ideal of equal justice for all, and neither could undo the injustice of their government, despite being principal players in the system.

A few months after Myer's national address, in November 1943, a riot erupted at the Tule Lake camp. A guard was badly beaten, which led the Army to send in tanks and take control of the facility for the following two months. Of the ten concentration camps spread across seven states, Tule Lake was the only one specifically designed to hold the Japanese Americans and Japanese aliens who were deemed either disloyal or labeled as troublemakers. Before the camp was converted into a distinct facility, it received a semi-famous inmate in 1942. Raymond Muramoto[85] was the co-star of a popular radio broadcast, *The Green Hornet*. He played the Hornet's sidekick, Kato. Kato possessed superior martial arts skills, which he used to fight criminals. After Pearl Harbor, the nationality of his character changed, varying from Chinese to Korean to Filipino, though the obvious Japanese name remained. Muramoto's celebrity did nothing to save him from internment in the most notorious relocation center. Of all the concentration camps, Tule Lake most resembled a prison, especially when more than 300 inmates were confined in a stockade. After nearly 200 began a hunger strike, eventually conditions improved.[86]

Resist

Long before the riots began, another group of Americans saw clearly the unfairness of forced relocation and its likely effects. The Quakers, through their organization the American Friends Service

Committee, set about ameliorating the suffering of Japanese Americans. Even before Clarence Pickett, a remarkably progressive leader, assumed the top position at the AFSC, the Quakers had been focused on combatting racism. Soon after FDR issued his executive order authorizing relocation, the Friends took action.

Word had spread rapidly that whites were pilfering Japanese-Americans' property and threatening them with violence. The Friends sent two representatives to its California office and found that it was a "madhouse" of activity, overwhelmed by the myriad problems it was attempting to sort through. Quakers immediately began collecting food for hungry families and working with Army officials to gain access to the temporary holding areas, whose living conditions they felt came close to that of German concentration camps. They felt strongly that this was not the American way of justice.[87]

The AFSC took special interest in helping college students leave the camps and reintegrate into universities. Eleanor Roosevelt had been pressing her husband to do more to lessen the plight of innocent internees. Probably as a result of her insistence, on May 25, FDR at last stated that he hoped Americans would distinguish between loyal Japanese Americans and the Japanese enemy.[88] His internment order certainly undermined that sentiment. Nonetheless, because of their forward-leaning actions, in May 1942, Milton Eisenhower, as head of the War Relocation Authority, officially charged the Friends with responsibility for overseeing the effort to get college students back in school. Clarence Pickett supervised the program, and the President of Swarthmore College assumed leadership of the new National Japanese-American Student Relocation Council. Their efforts enabled more than 3,700 students to leave the camps and pursue college degrees.[89] Quakers also tried to get work inside the camps to help improve conditions and assist with the teaching of children.

The Friends did more than just educate those within the camps. They also tried to educate the general public by denouncing wartime propaganda, which unjustly painted all Japanese Americans as traitors. One film in particular, *Little Tokyo*, stood out as especially damaging. Its plot suggested that all Japanese Americans sought to conduct or assist sabotage within the United States. The film's producer, 20th Century Fox, flatly rejected Quaker criticisms, stating that everyone knows that the Japanese were engaged in spying.[90]

Figure 3.2 A white American gives a baseball bat to an interned Japanese American, through a wire fence, at the "evacuation assembly center" in Santa Anita, 1942. Photo by Library of Congress/Corbis/VCG via Getty Images.

The Friends held true to their guiding principles, but it must have felt as though the most powerful people in the country did not stand with them. The nation's best-known Quaker shared their objections to internment, but even he remained largely silent. Although Herbert Hoover did not publicly attack the Roosevelt administration for its actions, privately the former president expressed genuine dismay. On June 28, 1943, a journalist wrote to Hoover, asking for his opinion of a pamphlet the writer was preparing, which criticized the internment. Three days later Hoover replied. "I do feel uneasy over the treatment of American born Japanese except for cases of specific charges."[91] There are at least two reasons why Hoover would have objected to FDR's decision. First, Hoover was wary of the overreach of presidential power, especially regarding individual freedoms. Roosevelt's executive order smacked of the type of authoritarian abuse that he often warned against. Second, the mistreatment of an entire ethnic group ran contrary to his moral code, and Hoover was a man who tried to make his morals drive his actions. But at this critical moment, Hoover held his peace.

While many Quakers were pursuing nonviolent resistance to Roosevelt's executive order, a handful of Japanese Americans engaged in civil disobedience, some based on principles, others from more self-serving motives.[92] Gordon Hirabayashi believed in principles. An idealistic twenty-four-year-old Quaker college student, Hirabayashi felt deeply that Christianity required pacifism and justice demanded equality under the law. On May 4, 1942, Hirabayashi took the most principled stand of his life. He began actively defying the curfew. In the wake of FDR's Executive Order 9066, all Japanese Americans were subjected to a curfew. They could not be outside after eight o'clock at night. Hirabayashi knowingly, intentionally broke that rule. On May 16, he walked into a police station in Seattle and submitted himself for arrest.

Hirabayashi had the backing of the American Civil Liberties Union (ACLU). With the aid of ACLU attorneys, Hirabayashi's case eventually landed in the Supreme Court. It was the first test case of the internment order, and it had a strong chance of being decided in favor of Japanese Americans.

Fred Korematsu's motives for resisting relocation differed from those of Gordon Hirabayashi. Hirabayashi acted solely on principle. Korematsu had fallen in love. A shy young man standing five feet eight inches tall with a slender frame, square jaw, and handsome face, Korematsu had a distinctive way of clasping his hands behind his back and leaning slightly forward as he listened. With his right eyebrow higher than his left, the overall effect was of a young man deeply curious about the world around him. At the time of the internment, his attention was focused on someone in particular. Korematsu had fallen for an Italian-American woman, and he did not want to be apart from her. Unlike the vast majority of Japanese Americans, he decided to flout the evacuation order. He was twenty-one years old.[93]

Korematsu had grown up in San Leandro, California. Knowing he would need to leave his family home to hide, he rented a room in the Fruitvale section of Oakland, unrealistically hoping he could evade authorities. The year before, he had purchased a 1938 Pontiac for $800. When he tried to sell it, the most he could get was $200. Though he felt he was being taken advantage of, he had little choice. He then made the imprudent decision to get plastic surgery to make him look Caucasian. Something about the white Victorian house in San Francisco gave him pause. The doctor's office did not look like a clinic or hospital. He walked up the ten steps to the front door, and then walked down again. He was teetering on the edge of his future, and chose the surgery. It did not go well. Beyond correcting his broken nose, the procedure had no noticeable effects other than costing him $100.

Korematsu found work as a welder in Berkeley. On buses or in public no one seemed to pay him much attention. When he learned in early May that his family was being sent to an internment camp, he naturally felt a stab of guilt, but he could not bring himself to join them. On Memorial Day, May 30, he and his girlfriend were walking on the street in San Leandro when the police stopped him. He gave them his assumed name, but the police were not convinced. They booked him and put him in jail.

The headline read, "Oakland Jap Held for F.B.I."[94] Korematsu was transferred to a stockade in the Presidio in San Francisco, where he soon received a visit from an attorney from the American Civil Liberties Union. The ACLU needed a test case to challenge the evacuation orders, and Korematsu appeared to be the only one they could find. The attorney explained that the odds of winning a suit against the government were slim and that Korematsu would be subjected to intense media scrutiny. Not seeing any better option, Korematsu agreed. What had begun as a young man's defiant act of love was about to transform into a landmark test of America's loyalty to its ideals.

An Inside Job

While Hirabayashi and Korematsu were beginning their separate legal challenges to internment, three influential Americans, each acting independently, stepped up their efforts to shift public opinion. Eleanor Roosevelt's article in *Common Ground* appeared in the spring issue. In it she tackled prejudice head on. She told of people being fired from their jobs or denied the chance to aid in local civil defense activities, simply because they were not citizens or had foreign-sounding names. Appealing to Americans' sense of patriotism, she insisted that this behavior would not help us win the war.

The First Lady noted that German Americans, Italian Americans, and Japanese Americans are on the defensive because a few disloyal ones have made the entire group suspect. She urged everyone to view people as individuals: "The same Bill of Rights covers all our citizens, regardless of the country of origin." She stressed that unity is essential if we are going to win the war.[95] But in words that must have stung her as she read it months after having supported the forced evacuation and internment plan, she implored Americans never to judge loyalty by race: "We must remember that we cannot tell the difference between a loyal and a disloyal citizen or between a citizen and a non-citizen just by looking at him or his name, by seeing the color of his skin, or by hearing him talk." This was, of course, precisely the basis for internment. Citing Walt Whitman's praise that America was a nation of nations, Eleanor Roosevelt warned that if we do not want to create nations within a nation, then we must rely on the true tests of loyalty: usefulness and love of America.

A second important figure soon joined the defense of Japanese Americans. He had just returned to America after a very long absence. Joseph Grew had spent the preceding ten years as the American ambassador to Tokyo. In that decade he had witnessed Japan's steady descent from democracy to dictatorship. He was there in 1931, when a wave of political assassinations by Right-wing militarists shook the nation's stability. He watched as militarism took root and altered Japan's political culture. He was there in 1937, when the Japanese Army began a full-scale escalation into Chinese territory, embroiling Japan ever deeper in a war it could not win, but would not end. He was there in 1940, when Hitler brought a willing Japanese government into the Axis fold. And he was there in 1941, on the date that will live in infamy.

Immediately after the attacks on Pearl Harbor, Grew and his coterie of diplomats were placed under house arrest, forbidden to leave the American compound. The diplomats were not mistreated, but this was not true of many other Americans – the businessmen, journalists, teachers, and missionaries who happened to be in Japan when the war began. After six months of confinement, Grew and the others were at last placed aboard a ship called the *Gripsholm*, where they waited seven anxious days anchored in the port of Yokohama while the details of their release were negotiated. At last the ship was permitted to return to the United States. When the Ambassador disembarked on American shores, he had a message for his country.

On August 30, Grew addressed the nation over CBS radio. He spoke of the treatment that many of his countrymen received at the hands of the Japanese. These were the stories told to him by his fellow passengers aboard the *Gripsholm*, and he could see for himself the evidence borne on the bodies of these survivors. Many had been placed in solitary confinement with little food or clothing in bitterly cold prison cells. And then, though insisting that he would not describe "the most cruel and barbaric tortures" inflicted upon them, Grew did describe the waterboarding used on several elderly Americans, one of them over seventy.

The eldest missionary had his hands bound behind his back while another cord around his neck drew his knees up to his chin. The rope was tied so tightly that it pierced the skin. Rolling him on the ground face up, Japanese police poured water down his nose and mouth until he lost consciousness. They then brought him back, only to repeat the process over and over again. On one occasion while he was on the ground a policeman kicked him so brutally that he cracked a rib. The policeman then felt with his hands to locate the cracked rib, raised up his fist, and smashed it against the bone. Another American had suffered gangrene from the treatment he received in his cell. Grew had known the man before the imprisonment, but when he saw the man aboard the ship, he could not believe the horrific transformation. A woman on board told Grew of the agonizing shrieks she heard from her own cell of Hong Kong Chinese prisoners being bayonetted to death. While they waited in Yokohama for word of their release, several of the passengers told Grew that if the negotiations failed and they were to be sent back to prison, they intended to commit suicide.

What must it have been like at that moment for Americans listening to the Ambassador's address? Families gathered around their radios, riveted by the speaker's tales. Many must have seethed with hatred toward all Japanese. Understanding and expecting this reaction, Grew then took a few minutes to speak on behalf of the average Japanese. He told Americans that he had spent the past ten years in that country. He had forged friendships with Japanese people whom he came to respect, admire, and love: "They are not the people who brought on this war. As patriots they will fight for their Emperor and country, to the last ditch if necessary, but they did not want this war and it was not they who began it." He spoke of the Japanese people who endangered themselves to smuggle food to imprisoned Americans, sometimes even managing to get a little meat beyond the guards. This was an especially valued gift, as meat was difficult for the Japanese, themselves, to come by.

There was a nobility to Grew's remarks. He did not want Americans to turn their anger against all Japanese, even at the height of war and in the wake of Japanese war crimes. It was the Japanese military caste, with its utterly bestial and ruthless military system, that must be crushed. Its predominance, he told Americans, must be broken for the future safety of all humanity.[96]

Grew's prominence and long experience in Japan afforded him considerable credibility with the American public, but fear and hatred of Japanese Americans among a sizable segment of the white populace still remained. Shortly after Grew's radio address, a third expert added his voice to the small but vocal chorus calling for tolerance. In the October 1, 1942 issue of *Harper's* magazine, an anonymous author, claiming to be an expert on the Japanese-American population, attested to the overwhelming loyalty of this minority.

The author seemed to have a sense for what could move the public, if enough Americans would listen. He did not simply recite facts and figures concerning the loyalty of Japanese Americans. Instead, he told stories about real people he knew in order to explain what made them so loyal. Most Japanese-American women enjoyed far greater freedom in their personal lives than their mothers had in Japan, he told his readers. Most mothers wanted their daughters to have opportunities to study and work and experience the greater equality that American society afforded them. When Japanese-American youth were sent back to Japan to study, they typically could not integrate into such a restrictive social order.

The author related the story of his own maid, whose parents took her at age sixteen to a small farming village in Japan. The young woman could not fit in. She barely spoke Japanese, which was typical for many of the second generation. She was ridiculed by the village for her American ways of thinking and behaving. The young woman was so despondent that she pleaded with her parents to let her return to the United States. The parents relented, and she went to live with an aunt in California. But now, at the time of this article's writing in May 1942, the young woman and her aunt were languishing in an assembly center, soon to be shipped off to an internment camp.

Only someone with an intimate knowledge of the Japanese-American community could have written so persuasive a piece. Had

Harper's revealed the author's identity, the publication almost certainly would have cost him his job and probably his career. The author was Lieutenant Commander Kenneth Ringle, formerly of the Office of Naval Intelligence. It was Ringle who had submitted a confidential report to FDR prior to the executive order insisting that on the whole Japanese Americans posed no threat. A year and a half later, he had been transferred to the War Relocation Authority to work for Milton Eisenhower. Both men were in a difficult position. Neither supported the internment of innocent American citizens.

Ringle's article reiterated some of the same points he had previously made to the President. Though he felt impelled to conceal his identity, Ringle did not conceal his opinion. As he saw it, the internment was based on prejudice. The camps treated the vast majority of loyal citizens the same as the few disloyal. This treatment could not be justified.[97]

Ringle revealed that he was not naïve to the possible dangers from within the community. He took a hard line against Kibei, Japanese Americans who had traveled to Japan at an early age for education and possible military service. Ringle considered this group a threat, assuming that they were loyal to Japan and may have been sent back to America as saboteurs. He insisted that the Kibei should be presumed guilty until proven innocent. Their parents should be equally suspect. In contrast, he argued that second-generation Japanese Americans aged seventeen and older were too steeped in American ways to feel part of Japanese society. The gulf between the two cultures was simply too vast. Ringle advocated separating out the Kibei from the rest of the Japanese-American population, keeping the Kibei in detention centers, and allowing the overwhelming mass of Japanese Americans to return home to the west coast. Ambassador Grew shared Ringle's view. Grew told a Senate subcommittee that loyal Japanese-American citizens should be separated in the camps from Japanese aliens. He did not oppose the existence of the camps themselves. He urged greater surveillance of the ones who had been released for outside employment, insisting that "We simply can't afford to take chances in wartime."[98]

Ringle never based his arguments on matters of civil liberties. He presented his solutions as being in the national interest in wartime. Allowing the vast number of loyal Japanese Americans to return to their homes would benefit the nation. These people could then join the workforce either harvesting crops for the war effort or working in war production facilities, though subject to more stringent security assessments. If the government would undertake a public relations campaign to reassure white citizens of this community's loyalty, then white employers could be induced to hire them. To Ringle, it just made sense. But Ringle was offering sensible solutions to a senseless system. Although only a minority of the west coast white population supported the forcible removal of Japanese Americans from their homes and into concentration camps, this did not mean that anti-Japanese prejudices were any less real. A Gallup poll published just days after Christmas 1942 revealed that nearly seventy percent of west coast residents would refuse to hire Japanese servants after the war.[99] Given the state of uncertainty about Japanese-American loyalties, overturning or even altering the current status of interned Americans was going to require concerted action.

Ringle, Grew, and Eleanor Roosevelt never coordinated their efforts. Similarly, the Quakers, the Fair Play Committee, and the American Civil Liberties Union operated independent of each other, though each organization was working toward similar goals. Similar, but not identical. Each of these figures and groups wanted America to live up to its stated values, but each was conflicted or constrained in their own way.[100] Despite all their efforts to shift public opinion, the net effect was scattershot at best, and the President's relocation order remained in place. There was, however, still one last hope of overturning it. The Supreme Court could strike down the President's decree, and given the justices' inclinations, the odds of that occurring seemed high.

4 COVER-UP

While Roosevelt was unifying the Allied war efforts and the postwar relief, his relocation order was dividing his own administration. By early 1943, the internment issue had not only created rifts among government agencies, particularly between the War and Justice Departments, but was also revealing fault lines within the Justice Department itself. On one side, Attorney General Francis Biddle opposed the policy, convinced it was a violation of civil liberties and of dubious constitutionality. Internment contradicted not only the spirit of his impassioned speech on December 7, 1941, it also revealed the emptiness of his pledge to protect the rights of all Americans regardless of their backgrounds.

In contrast to Biddle, Solicitor General Charles Fahy viewed the War Department as his client. He saw his role as the War Department's representative before the Court. Supporting Fahy was a younger lawyer named Arnold Raum, who, like McCloy, had worked on the legal aspects of the Black Tom case in the 1930s. Raum felt that the government was fully justified in its actions because wartime exigencies elevated public safety over personal freedoms. Believing that individual loyalties were impossible to determine, safety required that the entire Japanese-American community be removed from the coast.[101]

Opposing Fahy and Raum were two highly energetic younger lawyers within the Office of the Solicitor General: Edward Ennis and John Burling. These two men found the internment intolerable. Together they mounted an impressive rear-guard action to bring the full facts before the Court. Gordon Hirabayashi, the principled college student who had turned himself in to police for violating the curfew, was the first Japanese American to have his case come before the Supreme Court. As Ennis and Burling prepared the government's brief for the Hirabayashi case in early 1943, they became increasingly skeptical of the War Department's claims about military necessity. The arguments for internment rested on assertions that Japanese Americans on the west coast had engaged in signaling to Japanese ships. Ennis and Burling realized that they needed to get to the source of these allegations. The reports had been advanced by the War Department, but the two young lawyers decided it made more sense to obtain the original reports on this supposed signaling. In a classic Washington end-around, they bypassed the War Department's records of the Federal Communications Commission (FCC) reports and instead requested the original reports on signaling directly from the FCC, which was charged with monitoring such activities. What they discovered left them flabbergasted.

Not only had the FCC investigations found no evidence of signaling, the original reports actually debunked such claims by the Army. Ennis and Burling were able to show that General Dewitt had altered the FCC's reports to make it appear that they had drawn the opposite conclusion. The Army's insistence on internment, therefore, rested on faked records. But that was just the beginning of what they soon realized was an orchestrated cover-up.

Ennis and Burling also read the anonymous piece in *Harper's* from the previous October. Through some sleuthing, they were able to learn that Lieutenant Commander Ringle was the article's author, and that he had provided an intelligence report stating in strong terms that Japanese Americans represented no threat to public safety. The Army's argument for internment therefore contradicted the findings of the Navy. Arnold Raum pushed back. Raum cited Ringle's assertion in the *Harper's* piece that the Kibei posed a grave danger. He ignored Ringle's assurance that the identities of disloyal Kibei could easily be determined, as they constituted fewer than 10,000 individuals. Ennis's objections were brushed aside.[102]

Meanwhile, as disputes unfolded within the Solicitor General's office, on April 19, 1943, Ennis phoned the War Department to request a copy of General DeWitt's final report on the evacuation. That copy never reached Ennis because McCloy ordered all ten copies of it destroyed. When McCloy read DeWitt's report with his characteristic scrupulousness, he immediately spotted an incriminating admission.

The evacuation policy had been based largely on the claim that time did not permit a careful vetting of Japanese Americans, and therefore the entire community needed to be interned. But DeWitt's report stated that time was not a factor in the decision. Instead, it maintained that it was simply not possible to distinguish the loyal from the disloyal. McCloy knew that it would be difficult to defend the claim that individual loyalties could not be determined. Since the War Department had justified the relocation as necessary because public safety demanded a speedy evacuation from the coast, McCloy was put in a bind. If the Supreme Court justices saw this, it would expose a significant chink in the War Department's defense, one that Justice Department lawyers would easily exploit.

There was indeed a time pressure, but it was on McCloy. The Court would soon be hearing the Hirabayashi case, and he needed to produce the Army's report for Justice Department lawyers to review. Working late that evening, McCloy rang Colonel Bendetsen in California to complain about the draft. The solution was simple. Destroy all copies of the original and replace them with a revised version with more acceptable wording. War Department officials also erased all evidence that the original final report had ever been sent.[103]

With what now seemed a much stronger position for McCloy and the War Department, the government's briefs could safely reach the High Court. Despite this cleansing of the records, the evacuation decision still faced a serious challenge. Following the arguments of ACLU and Justice Department lawyers, the justices retired to make their decision, and the outcome looked very bad for the government. A majority of five justices opposed the internment, and that should have resulted in the overturning of Roosevelt's Executive Order. If the Court had ruled in favor of Hirabayashi, as seemed likely, then the government would have been holding more than 120,000 individuals illegally. It is impossible to know what would have happened at that point. The President might have refused to release the inmates, but more likely he would have found some moderately face-saving solution, probably by announcing a stringent vetting system whereby those with unquestioned loyalty to America would be returned home. And then the vast majority of evacuees would have been released. But as we know, that never happened. Instead, the majority of justices opposed to internment changed their minds, thanks to the influence of one of their colleagues.

Full Court Press

Seven of the High Court's nine members had been appointed by Franklin Roosevelt. The eighth, the chief justice, Harlan Stone, was a Calvin Coolidge appointee, and the ninth, Owen Roberts, had been appointed by Herbert Hoover. Although FDR no doubt hoped that his own appointees would support the legality of his executive order issued in a time of war, the internment issue created a deep rift in the Court. To some the key issue was one of civil liberties and equal protection under the law, but others felt strongly that the courts should not unduly limit Executive authority. No one held this latter view more intensely than Felix Frankfurter, which surprised many in the country who had backed his appointment to the Court.

If any member of the Court could have been expected to defend the rights of a minority, Felix Frankfurter should have been the one. Born to Jewish parents in Vienna, Frankfurter immigrated to New York as a child. Early on his intellectual gifts were apparent, but the moment he arrived at Harvard Law School, he felt intimidated. Standing only five feet five inches tall, everyone else seemed like a giant, and many of his classmates came from elite backgrounds. They were articulate, cultured, and rich. He felt overshadowed and worried that he might be out of his depth, but his mother told him he would simply have to outperform the goyem. And he did, brilliantly. His papers dazzled the professors with their insight and clarity. One of these essays was so remarkable that his professor read it aloud to future generations of law students. Frankfurter remained the top student in his class for all three years of the program. He became editor of the *Harvard Law Review*. He had indeed outperformed his peers, but while he outshined others, his affability helped him to soften jealousies and make friends easily, a skill that greatly aided his career.

After graduating, Frankfurter found a job with a New York corporate law firm, but the work did not engage him. It was not sufficiently challenging, and he yearned for a larger stage. What he really wanted was to influence public policy, to be a mover and shaker. He soon moved to the US Attorney's office, where he prosecuted corporations which harmed the public good. After a period in government, Harvard Law School persuaded Frankfurter to return to campus to teach. Frankfurter's empathy for the working man seeped into his legal activities. His reputation spread as an advocate of progressive causes such as a minimum wage and limited working hours per day. During WWI, President Wilson tasked Frankfurter with mediating strikes across the country. This experience brought him into close contact with the oppressive tactics that some companies used to threaten and frighten their workers.

During the war, Frankfurter opposed the infamous Palmer Raids – the rounding up, imprisoning, and deporting of suspected communists, typically without due process of any kind. He published a devastatingly critical exposé of the Justice Department's illegal practices, cementing his reputation as an unwavering defender of civil liberties even in a time of war.

To help shape public opinion on crucial issues of the day, Frankfurter co-founded *The New Republic*. Animated by the frequent mistreatment of the most vulnerable citizens, in 1920, he co-founded the ACLU to serve as a bulwark against discrimination. The following year, he defended the infamous duo, Sacco and Vanzetti, two Italian-born immigrants accused of murder. After this unpopular stand, Frankfurter became seen by some as a dangerous radical.[104]

In 1924, never shying from unpopular political positions and loudly proclaiming them, he threw his support behind the dark horse third-party candidate for president, Robert La Follette of Wisconsin. Frankfurter felt strongly that neither the Republican nominee, Calvin Coolidge, nor his Democratic opponent, John Davis, was likely to enact the reforms that America desperately needed to address the country's most pressing problem: the growing wealth gap between the richest handful and the working masses. For a third-party candidate, La Follette performed well, receiving 4.8 million votes, sixteen percent of votes cast. Frankfurter's vote was a statement. The vulnerable must be defended.

From his position at Harvard, the dynamic, tireless professor cultivated relationships with influential figures, including the newly elected governor of New York in 1928, Franklin Roosevelt. FDR found Frankfurter among the most stimulating of conversation partners, noting that the professor's mind clicks so fast that it made Roosevelt's head spin. Increasingly Roosevelt relied on Frankfurter for policy advice. After FDR won the presidency, Frankfurter helped draft the legislation that formed the Securities and Exchange Commission. He always had the name of a young lawyer ready to recommend to Roosevelt for placement in his administration, and FDR usually accepted Frankfurter's selections, which of course gave Frankfurter a small army of associates scattered throughout the government. These bright, ambitious young men became so prominent and plentiful that they were dubbed Frankfurter's "happy hot dogs." Among them was his former pupil at Harvard Law School, Dean Acheson, the future secretary of state.

Frankfurter's progressive activism engendered fear and resentment among some Republicans, who believed he held pro-communist sympathies. When FDR nominated him to the High Court in 1937, his opponents drew their knives. But once his nomination was confirmed, the Court's leading liberals rejoiced. Frank Murphy and William O. Douglas believed that together they would guide the nation toward stronger protections for the downtrodden and greater freedom for all. They would soon discover that they had grossly misread their new colleague.

Frankfurter revealed his true colors with the now infamous *Minersville School District v. Gobitis* case. When a school in Pennsylvania expelled two young pupils, Lillian and William Gobitis, for refusing to salute the flag, their father, a Jehovah's Witness, sued the district. Given his background as a founder of the ACLU, Frankfurter should have been the most ardent advocate of religious freedom. But Frankfurter had another side. He also viewed overt shows of patriotism as essential to the American experiment. As an immigrant Jew who had ascended to the height of power within the government's judicial branch, he felt such devotion to the idea of America that he wanted all citizens to engage in ritual practices of patriotism. He couched this belief in the theory of judicial restraint, the idea that the courts should not limit the powers of the executive or legislative branches. In a break with standard practice, Frankfurter read his opinion aloud for the record. A few weeks later, Eleanor Roosevelt listened as her husband and Frankfurter discussed the Gobitis decision over drinks at Hyde Park. FDR acknowledged that the school district had acted foolishly, but he concurred with Frankfurter's allegedly patriotic position. Unable to contain herself, Mrs. Roosevelt interjected that she found it distressing that a school district could force children to act against their religious beliefs. She worried that the decision at such a high level could embolden intolerance among the masses.[105] She was right.

Frankfurter's passionate defense of flag saluting had the inflammatory effect of unleashing a wave of hate crimes against Jehovah's

Witnesses across the country. From Maine to Maryland, and Texas to California, mobs beat Jehovah's Witnesses and burned their property. Perhaps the hate crimes had some impact on the other justices. Three years later, in March 1943, they reversed themselves in a similar case, *West Virginia Board of Education v. Barnette*, declaring that a government cannot enforce any dogma or require adherence to it. Only Frankfurter still clung zealously to his previous position.

A Show of Unity

According to the historian Peter Irons, the Hirabayashi case, following shortly after Barnette, threatened to split the Court wide open over civil liberties. Chief Justice Stone had a particular sensitivity to the mistreatment of racial minorities. In an earlier case five years before, Stone had asserted that the courts had a responsibility to give extra scrutiny to laws discriminating against minorities who had a history of suffering prejudice. When Stone considered the Hirabayashi case, he understood that Japanese Americans clearly fell into the category of those who had experienced prejudice from the legal system. William O. Douglas had his own reasons for objecting to evacuation. Douglas had grown up in Washington State, the only Court member from the west coast. He had known Japanese Americans, attended school with them, and saw the War Department's policy as based on racial discrimination. Three other justices harbored serious reservations as well. The strongest opponent was Frank Murphy, the Court's only Catholic. Murphy had enjoyed long and close interactions with nonwhite citizens. As a politician who had won elections for mayor of Detroit and governor of Michigan, he had forged coalitions with various ethnic and racial groups. Like Henry Stimson, Murphy had worked as a US attorney, and like Stimson, he had served as governor-general of the Philippines. In 1935, his position was abolished under the terms of an agreement granting the Philippines a transition period to independence, but he remained on in the newly created role of high commissioner. While in the islands, he recognized the need to improve social justice for Filipinos. From Murphy's vantage point, the internment of Japanese Americans smacked plainly of racism.

With five of the nine justices expressing a range of reservations about internment, it was possible that the Court would decide against the executive order, but that was not how the case concluded.

Historian Peter Irons has argued that Felix Frankfurter deployed an impressive barrage of tactics, from flattery to cajolery, and from blaming to shaming, in order to bring his recalcitrant colleagues around. The final holdout was Frank Murphy. Initially Murphy dissented, and in his dissent, the draft of which he shared with his colleagues, he implied that his peers were undermining democracy. That was when Frankfurter truly went to work on Murphy, appealing to his sense of pride in the Court's reputation. On such an important matter as this, wouldn't it be best if the Court could demonstrate its unity? Surely Murphy could see the value in presenting a unanimous decision. The Court's unity could reflect the nation's unity, and wasn't that the most vital need in a time of war? Yielding to Frankfurter's seemingly noble plea, Murphy altered his draft, rewrote his opinion, and concurred with the majority.

On June 21, 1943, the Court issued its decision. Hirabayashi was guilty. The ruling was unanimous. But the Court only upheld the curfew orders, which Hirabayashi had violated. The larger issue of the internment's legality remained unsettled.

We cannot know for certain whether the Court would still have upheld FDR's executive order, if Frankfurter had not pressed his colleagues in that direction, but we can see that despite their show of unity in the Hirabayashi case, several of the justices still harbored nagging qualms about what they had done. Their misgivings slowly simmered, and one year later they percolated to the surface when Fred Korematsu's case came before them. But for now, Gordon Hirabayashi was sent back to a concentration camp to join the thousands of others in detention, and the President's orders still stood.

Thwarted Efforts

A high-ranking naval intelligence officer could not prevent it. A US ambassador could not halt it. The Attorney General failed to block it. The First Lady could not even soften the edges of it. The Quakers had too little influence to affect it. Even the reluctant justices of the Supreme Court could not bring themselves to overturn it. Each of these groups and individuals tried and failed. They did not lack power; they lacked organization. Acting separately, there was little they could accomplish. Had they been aware of each other's intentions and coordinated their energies, they might have countered the War Department. By mobilizing a public relations campaign, they might have succeeded in shifting opinions enough to lessen the severity of internment. Perhaps they could have pressured the War Department to adopt Lieutenant Commander Ringle's solutions, allowing the more than three-fourths of Japanese Americans whose loyalty was not in doubt to begin returning home in 1943. It would certainly not have been the first time that a president's policy was abandoned or mitigated by a vocal public outcry. But the voices defending the innocent were muted by an organized opposition.

The forced relocation of Japanese Americans resulted primarily from the actions of three men: John McCloy's insistence, Henry Stimson's weakness, and Franklin Roosevelt's indifference. McCloy's insistence, however, originated with General DeWitt's demands, which in turn were incited by Colonel Bendetsen. Bendetsen played on the General's racist inclinations and helped to foment the drive toward internment. Obviously, no one person was solely responsible for the chain of events that led to Roosevelt's executive order. Undergirding the high-level actions within the government was some public pressure. A vocal segment of west coast politicians demanded action against the Japanese for Pearl Harbor, but they could not distinguish between Japanese subjects and American citizens of Japanese descent. As General DeWitt infamously put it, "A Jap is a Jap," and his racist refrain echoed through thousands of vacant homes.[106] But if McCloy, Stimson, and Roosevelt share the greatest blame for enacting the internment, Felix Frankfurter and his Supreme Court colleagues enabled the internment to continue for several years longer than it should have. The combined actions of these key leaders, backed by an angry, ignorant portion of the public, caused 120,000 innocent civilians to suffer needlessly because the political and legal systems failed to protect them. Thousands of loyal Americans saw their lives uprooted, their homes and property essentially stolen, and their civil liberties denied.

Internment occurred because a minority of officials outmaneuvered the majority of leaders who opposed it. Colonel Bendetsen, General DeWitt, and Assistant Secretary McCloy were all outranked by Secretary of War Stimson. Stimson could have, and should have, ordered them to drop their internment efforts, but as with many pivotal decisions, he wrestled with deep ambivalence. Attorney General Biddle, though new to the Cabinet and lacking Stimson's weight, had J. Edgar Hoover of the FBI, Lt. Commander Kenneth Ringle of the Office of Naval Intelligence, and the President's own personal investigator, Curtis Munson, to support him. He also had Treasury Secretary Henry

Morgenthau, who saw little sense to the internment. And then there was Eleanor Roosevelt. The influential opponents of internment simply outnumbered its proponents, but Bendetsen, DeWitt, and McCloy were better organized, more tenacious, and much more willing to engage in subterfuge. They coordinated their activities while the majority did not. If the majority of advisors had in unison voiced their objections to the President, it is entirely possible that FDR would have relented and the internment would never have happened.

The struggle against internment did not end with Hirabayashi. The case of *Korematsu v. United States* would slowly work its way through the justice system, finally landing in the Supreme Court in the fall of 1944, just as another vexing question of how to treat an enemy was coming to the fore. Although the problem of Japanese-American internment consumed more of John McCloy's time than any other single issue,[107] another matter was about to compete for his and Stimson's attention. At stake hinged the future of Europe and the hope of America's global leadership, the grand prize for which he and his coterie had been striving. They simply could not afford to lose this next battle, but the fight would be even more bitterly contested than the internment case. This time, however, the script would flip, as McCloy and Stimson found themselves on the side of mercy, not revenge. Suddenly they were forced to defend America's perceived enemies, rather than punish them. And their principal adversary in this new battle proved to be a far more skillful rival than any who had opposed them thus far.

5 DISINTEGRATE

What should be done with Germany after the war? The problem of how to handle a defeated Germany spawned intense and bitter debate within the highest levels of American government. The divisions only intensified as victory came into view. The problem was that Roosevelt failed to consider the matter seriously until Germany's surrender seemed imminent. Even after D-Day on June 6, 1944, as Allied forces battled their way toward Berlin, General Eisenhower had no concrete instructions for how to govern the defeated Germans once victory had been achieved. This left a policy vacuum, and Washington abhors a vacuum. As they say within the Beltway, a bad plan trumps no plan every time. And just such a plan was being hatched in the mind of one of Roosevelt's closest advisors.

Standing over six feet tall with a broad forehead and pronounced New Yorker's tone, Henry Morgenthau Jr. was one of the most powerful men in Roosevelt's administration, an impressive achievement for a Jew in America, regardless of his privileged background. In the 1930s, Morgenthau skillfully led the Treasury Department through the Depression years. When the war came, Morgenthau spearheaded the campaign to sell war bonds. Though his face and voice were familiar to average Americans, within government circles, Morgenthau was an enigma. Because of his intense shyness and suspicious nature, many in government mistook him as dim. Most found him autocratic and cold. FDR even dubbed him "Henry the Morgue."[108] In stark contrast, others saw him as passionate, "the most dynamic character in Washington."[109] His ability to fixate single-mindedly on a given problem and relentlessly drive his prescriptions through to the finish made him both an attractive ally and a frustrating foe. More than any other trait, it was Morgenthau's genius for playing the Washington policy game that gave him so much influence over the President.

Morgenthau's plan was to remove all heavy manufacturing capabilities from the defeated nation. The Germans had launched two world wars, and it was time to ensure that they could never trouble their neighbors again. But given the widespread food shortages expected to come after the war, stripping the country of its factories and machinery would almost certainly lead to mass starvation, and everyone knew it. Morgenthau's plan could only seem cruel. It was a modern-day version of a Carthaginian peace, and at the Treasury Secretary's urging, President Roosevelt signed on.

Morgenthau hoped to return Germany to an agrarian state, to the way it might have looked in the pre-modern era. To ensure that the country would remain weak, his plan forbade the occupying troops to assist German economic revitalization. Section eight of his plan restricted the Allied military government from playing any role in maintaining or strengthening the German economy or in solving any economic problems, unless essential to Allied military operations: "The responsibility for sustaining the German economy and people rests with the German people with such facilities as may be available under the circumstances."[110]

The phrase "with such facilities as may be available" had to seem ironic. Given the devastation wrought by the war, there were few facilities. Without substantial assistance, the German people would starve. Morgenthau had a solution. He contended that the German people could feed themselves by returning to the land and focusing their labor force on farming. Morgenthau had made a detailed study of Germany's amount of arable land, its potential crop yields, and its manpower. He believed that the process of converting the country to an agrarian nation would indeed be painful and would take many years, but in the end, he insisted that the transition could be achieved. As he would write in his published defense of the plan: "The main consideration, however, is not discomfort and toil for Germany but peace for the world."[111]

Looking back, it might seem hard to imagine how such a draconian policy could ever have been proposed, much less adopted, but anger at the German enemy ran remarkably high in wartime. Pearl

Harbor had focused Americans' intense desire for revenge against the Empire of Japan, which unjustly affected Japanese Americans. But German aggression in both world wars fueled resentments as well, and Henry Morgenthau translated that anger into policy – a policy that, much like the incarceration of Japanese Americans, would inflict great suffering on innocent civilians.

As Morgenthau was developing his postwar scheme for Germany, the relief organization that Roosevelt had set in motion was just getting off the ground. Top representatives from the United States, Britain, China, and the Soviet Union – the four powers that FDR envisioned would police the postwar world order – had been hammering out an agreement to form an international relief body. Ambassador Maxim Litvinov represented the Soviets in these negotiations. Litvinov had been the Soviet foreign minister in 1939, prior to the signing of the infamous Nazi–Soviet Pact, which carved up Eastern Europe and enabled Hitler to launch the war. Litvinov, who was Jewish, had been a target of the Nazis' anti-Bolshevik propaganda. They had dubbed him Maxim Finkelstein.[112] Eager to reach an accord with Hitler, Stalin removed Litvinov and replaced him with Vyacheslav Molotov, hoping that this would ease the way for a pact between the two regimes. Now that the Soviets were at war with Germany, Litvinov was serving as ambassador to the United States, and with typical Soviet adamance, he insisted on limits to the ability of any relief organization to enter other nations. But because the Russians were clearly in need of aid themselves, Litvinov consented on enough points that the four powers were able to establish a workable arrangement.

The United Nations Relief and Rehabilitation Administration (UNRRA) was officially created on November 9, 1943, when Roosevelt signed the document authorizing it. The following day officials from forty-four countries met in Atlantic City to begin the arduous task of preparing for large-scale humanitarian interventions once the war was won. UNRRA's director general, the Jewish executive of New York's investment firm, Lehman Brothers, had been governor of New York after Roosevelt, and he had wholeheartedly supported the New Deal. In assuring Lehman's appointment, FDR supposedly explained, "I want to see some of those goddamned fascists begging for subsistence from a Jew."[113] It was not to be, for while UNRRA was erecting the first system of international food relief, Morgenthau was pushing the President in the opposite direction on Germany's postwar fate.

Mixed Message

While diplomats assembled privately to begin planning for postwar relief, another leading diplomat undertook a much more public campaign. Ambassador Joseph Grew launched a speaking tour to educate Americans about a postwar peace with Japan. He wanted to combat the widespread hatred that had taken hold of so many Americans ever since Pearl Harbor. He tried to persuade the public that not all Japanese people were evil. It was not an easy sell.

Speaking in Chicago at the close of 1943, Grew acknowledged the "Attilalike aggressions" of Japan's military, but he urged Americans not to conclude that the military reflected the Japanese character. Just as Attorney General Biddle had done in 1941, he reminded his audience of the prejudice against German Americans during WWI, and he noted that today most Americans can distinguish between Nazis and the German people as a whole. Unfortunately, he lamented, most Americans have adopted an all-encompassing hatred of the Japanese.

Grew related an experience he had after speaking to a group somewhere in the South. He likely intentionally concealed the location so as not to offend anyone with ties to that city. After his presentation, a prominent businessman approached him to say that while he had enjoyed the Ambassador's speech, he had not changed the man's mind in the least. "The only good Jap is a dead Jap," the man declared. When Grew asked if the man had ever lived in Japan, he said he had not, but "I know that they are all a barbarous, tricky, brutal mass that we can have no truck with, ever again." This was precisely the kind of thinking that Grew desperately sought to counteract. He did it by appealing to Americans' sense of who they truly are: "We Americans are generally fair-minded," he told the Chicago crowd. "We are not prone to condemn the innocent because they are helplessly associated with the guilty."[114] But Grew's exchange with that angry man encapsulated the rift within the American public. One segment of Americans recognized that all groups of people contain a mix of good and bad. The other segment viewed groups in sweeping stereotypes, unable to see distinctions among them. And the clash between those two opposing outlooks was shaping US policy at the highest levels.

Back in 1937, several years before the United States was at war with Japan, Japanese pilots bombed and sank an American naval vessel, the *Panay*, on China's Yangtze River. The pilots then circled back and fired machine guns at the American sailors floating in the water. Japan's government claimed that it was purely accidental and agreed to pay indemnities. Most Americans remembered this incident, but what they did not know, Grew explained, was how the average Japanese person responded to this attack. A deep outpouring of shame and regret flooded the American Embassy. From across all classes of Japanese society, people sent letters of apology. Many contributed money to help pay for the maintenance of the sailors' graves. But Grew could not forget one young Japanese woman's surprising act. She entered the Embassy and asked his secretary for scissors. She then let down her long and beautiful hair and cut its entire length from the neck. She wrapped the bundle in a parcel, placed a carnation atop the package, and asked the secretary to deliver it to Ambassador Grew as her own apology for the sinking of the *Panay*.

The Ambassador had more than one aim on his speaking tour across the nation. He was not simply attempting to humanize the Japanese people to an angry American public. Grew also wanted to lay the groundwork for a soft postwar peace. Many Americans spoke of walling off Japan, cutting it off from foreign trade and foreign investment. "Let them stew in their own juices" was the feeling among many Americans. Grew tried to educate the public on the dangers in that approach. Japan's population depended on trade with other nations for basic goods: fertilizers from Manchuria, sugar from Formosa, and even rice from Korea to supplement their own production. If Japan were cut off, only one result could follow. Millions of innocent Japanese civilians would starve to death. By forbidding Japan to rebuild in ways sufficient to support a modern, industrialized nation, America would be dealing a death sentence to millions: "I doubt if even the most bloodthirsty of our fellow citizens could with equanimity countenance such a situation." Grew implored Americans to remember the principles they were fighting for and not to succumb to the intoxicating thirst for retribution. "To allow our attitude as victors to be dominated by a desire to wreak vengeance on entire populations" would do nothing to retard future conflicts.

Grew had a hopeful belief in the basic goodness of Americans. There were just two problems with his conviction. The first was that he had undercut his own message. Grew narrated a twenty-minute propaganda film produced by the Office of War Information and released in the same year of his speaking tour. In *Our Enemy – The Japanese*, Grew peddled flagrant falsehoods and specious stereotypes about Japanese people and culture. Grew appeared on camera at the film's opening scene to explain that he had lived among the Japanese for a decade and knew them well. For many Americans, it was the first time they saw the venerable Ambassador, with his bushy mustache, swept eyebrows, and striking widow's peak. His precise elocution bore the marks of an upper-crust education. He pronounced the word "again" as two separate words, "a gain," sounding not unlike Eleanor Roosevelt in manner, if not in pitch or tone. In his narration, Grew declared that the Japanese have never been a creative or inventive people. He told Americans that Japan had been a totalitarian state throughout its modern history, not mentioning the democratic reforms that had been underway since the Meiji Restoration of 1868. And he concluded that this enemy is primitive, murderous, and fanatical.[115] While there was no doubt that Japanese soldiers often fought with ferocity, and many fought fanatically, the film depicted all Japanese people in this light. It was an image of the Japanese people antithetical to the one he was trying to promote in his speaking tours across the nation.

The second problem was that while Grew sought to dampen Americans' demands for revenge against the Japanese, he did not know that the greater threat to a stable peace came not from an angry American public, but from the highest reaches of their government. Just as Americans were debating how best to punish Japan for its "deviltry," Henry Morgenthau was devising a strikingly similar starvation plan for Germany, and the President appeared to be on board.

Tug of War

Morgenthau was not alone in his zeal to cripple Germany's revival. The President himself appeared an enthusiastic supporter – at least much of the time. Franklin Roosevelt and Henry Morgenthau had been friends for many years, having estates close enough to make them neighbors. Morgenthau's father, Henry Senior, a successful businessman who had served as President Wilson's ambassador to the Ottoman Empire, was also a generous donor to the Democratic Party. His son, Henry Junior, had not distinguished himself in any endeavor. He had some background in agricultural and conservation issues, and he ran his own apple farm. Roosevelt's friendship with Morgenthau Jr. was likely strengthened by the closeness of their wives, with each coming to the other's aid in times of crisis. When FDR's first Treasury secretary suddenly died in 1933, Roosevelt appointed his old friend over the objections of Republicans and Democrats alike. Though there were others more qualified, Morgenthau remained in that post for the rest of Roosevelt's unprecedented twelve-year administration. What Morgenthau may have lacked in expertise, he more than made up for in loyalty. Roosevelt trusted him, and on the subject of Germany they were of similar mind. As FDR quipped, "We either have to castrate the German people or you have got to treat them in such manner so they can't just go on reproducing people who want to continue the way they have in the past."[116]

The problem with quoting FDR for clues to his beliefs is that he often expressed conflicting sentiments to different people on the same subject. Roosevelt had a frustrating tendency to tell people what they wanted to hear. He would charm them with wit, and ramble on at length about tangential topics. Visitors would leave his office warmed by the glow of his chummy demeanor, but without the firm commitment they had hoped to secure. The President's habit of repeated flip-flopping made policy formation a sometimes maddening affair. It caused his Cabinet members to battle for his approval and then rush through policy decisions before the President had a chance to change his mind. Roosevelt kept his cards so close to his chest that they practically left an imprint on his skin. Ever the cunning strategist, his words and deeds seldom meant what they seemed at first glance. Below the surface lay levels of calculations: emotional, political, and geostrategic. He once admitted as much to Morgenthau, referring to himself as a juggler whose right arm never knows what the left is up to. Divining FDR's true intentions requires detective-caliber sleuthing. Taking together all of his conflicting words and actions, it seems that throughout the final year of his presidency, Roosevelt generally favored a harsh peace for Germany.

In early August 1944, Morgenthau traveled to England to meet with Eisenhower and press for a punitive peace. The Army had recently drafted a handbook outlining guidance on the future occupation of Germany. Anticipating the coming chaos, it called for the restoration of German civilian government and industry, precisely the opposite of what Morgenthau believed should be done. It ordered that every German adult should have 2,000 calories per day. To Morgenthau these instructions seemed outrageously lenient. To his delight, he found the General receptive. Ike had been hardening toward the enemy as the war continued. He told Morgenthau that he saw the German people as accomplices to Hitler's deeds, and they must be treated that way.[117] Morgenthau rejoiced, having found a powerful ally, but his ebullience was to be short-lived as he soon discovered an even more daunting opponent in Eisenhower's boss.

In late August, Secretary of War Henry Stimson went to see the President. Stimson was deeply concerned by the lack of postwar planning to date. He urged Roosevelt to convene a working group. Roosevelt consented and tasked Stimson, Morgenthau, Secretary of State Cordell Hull, and FDR's close personal advisor Harry Hopkins to craft a policy for the postwar occupation of Germany. When Stimson and Morgenthau met separately in Stimson's office at the Pentagon to exchange views, it quickly became clear that the distance between their attitudes was unbridgeable. Stimson had been raised a Christian, descended from a long line of clergymen. He espoused the importance of truthfulness, frankness, and strong moral character. His Christian virtues often asserted themselves into his political decisions, as the debate over Germany would reveal. Morgenthau respected the elderly War Secretary, but he could not accept Stimson's apparent softness toward the Germans. He had to ensure that the President would not be poisoned by Stimson's forgiving nature.

On Saturday, September 2, Morgenthau and his wife invited Franklin and Eleanor to their nearby estate, Fishkill Farms. Morgenthau argued hard for his plan, and as usual, FDR told his friend exactly what he hoped to hear. The day concluded with Morgenthau convinced that the President was firmly on his side. Germans would be in for a rough go of things under American control. The President even spoke of letting them survive on soup kitchens.[118] Morgenthau felt confident that his plans for postwar Europe would prevail.

Still hoping to win Stimson to his cause, two days later, the night before a crucial Cabinet meeting to discuss the matter, Morgenthau dined with Stimson, along with each of their deputies, Harry Dexter White and John McCloy. Though Morgenthau had disagreed with the War Department about Japanese internment, their differences had not been bitter. This time, however, the divergence of views regarding Germany was pronounced.

Over dinner, Morgenthau stated his absolute certainty that only the toughest punishment of the Germans would keep the future peace. Morgenthau appeared absolutely, single-mindedly intent on seeing the German people suffer for what they had done. Stimson saw it differently. This time drawing on his faith, he advocated instead for a policy of "kindness and Christianity."[119] Again, the divergence of views was conspicuous and profound. Beneath the veneer of cordiality, their heated conversation showed that compromise was impossible. Each man would thereafter devote himself to persuading the President, by whatever means necessary.

At the Cabinet meeting the next day, Stimson was caught off-guard. He discovered that Morgenthau had drawn others to his side. To Stimson's shock, Cordell Hull, the normally sober-minded secretary of state, ardently defended Morgenthau's ideas, though he would later moderate his position.[120] Hopkins added his voice, arguing that Germany should be prevented from producing steel, which would preclude its ability to revive its industrial might. Stimson again stressed the need for kindness and Christianity, but he found himself alone. Passions flared, as his colleagues' bitterness toward Germany exposed itself, but Stimson held his ground: "In all the four years I have been here I have not had such a difficult and unpleasant meeting."[121] As Stimson put it, they were "irreconcilably divided."[122] Instead of settling on a joint decision, they agreed to send separate memoranda to the President.

To say that Stimson carried weight in the shaping of American foreign policy would be an understatement. And although even he was struggling to soften the edge of America's postwar plans, the elder statesman was not too old to learn some new tricks from his wily rival. The battle over how to treat the defeated German people was about to heat up.

6 COLLUDE

In mid-September 1944, at a series of secret meetings in Quebec code-named "Octagon," Roosevelt and Churchill met along with top military advisors to discuss postwar planning. The Secretary of War would have been a natural choice to accompany the President at such a conference. To Morgenthau's delight, and Stimson's utter dismay, the President summoned his Treasury Secretary to join them. Stimson was not invited.

Initially it was unclear whether Churchill could be persuaded to support the scheme, but Morgenthau was able to demonstrate to Roosevelt that Britain had little power to object. Britain was broke. It desperately needed American financial support to rebuild. FDR knew that America's financial dominance gave it outsized leverage over Britain. Roosevelt assured the Prime Minister that American largesse toward Britain would be plentiful – if he would accept the Morgenthau arrangement for Germany. It was a threat, and Churchill understood who had the upper hand. The Prime Minister asked, "What do you want me to do, get on my hind legs and beg like Fala?" – a reference to FDR's dog.[123]

Some historians suggest that Churchill felt compelled to accept the Morgenthau solution, but other scholars argue that the Prime Minister was in fact an enthusiastic supporter of the plan.[124] If German industry were dismantled, Britain might plausibly profit by emerging as Europe's industrial leader. It seems unlikely that Churchill would have wanted a prostrate Germany for several reasons. He fully grasped the balance of power logic that a weak Germany would only heighten Russia's influence, and the Prime Minister had been a consistent, vocal anti-communist for decades. Churchill also recognized Stalin as the heartless butcher he was. Unlike FDR, Churchill held little hope of sustained postwar collaboration with the Soviets. Like Roosevelt, however, he may have seen the tactical value of agreeing to the Morgenthau Plan at that moment. From Morgenthau's perspective at least, both Roosevelt and Churchill agreed with the principle that Germany should be converted into an agrarian nation.[125]

FDR probably saw the need to reassure Stalin that America and Britain were wedded to a harsh peace. Since Stalin was unable to attend the Quebec conference, Roosevelt and Churchill may have wanted to signal that the United States and Britain would not sign a separate peace with Germany, something Stalin had long feared.[126] The Morgenthau Plan served this purpose perfectly. It looked tailor-made to appeal to the Soviet leader.

Breaking up Germany into separate sectors, confiscating its factories, eliminating its industrial power, and leaving its people impoverished was precisely the kind of peace that Stalin applauded. In fact, the man who drafted much of the Morgenthau Plan was not Morgenthau, but his deputy, Harry Dexter White, arguably the most influential American of postwar global economic agreements – and a Soviet source. White had sparkled as a student of economics while at Columbia and Stanford. His Harvard Ph.D. thesis won him awards and attention. After several years of teaching, he was offered a job at the Treasury Department, eventually becoming Morgenthau's right-hand man. Like Morgenthau, White was also Jewish. Brilliant, arrogant, highly placed, and largely a loner, White presented exactly the type of target that foreign intelligence services find irresistible. Historians still debate whether and to what extent White was working for Stalin, but we do know that he repeatedly passed information to Soviet agents. He died of a heart attack in 1948, just after being publicly charged with aiding the Russians.

Soon after Octagon, news that Roosevelt and Churchill had agreed to the Morgenthau Plan was leaked to the press, possibly by White himself in order to signal the President's approval. If in fact it had been leaked by any of Morgenthau's staff, the ploy backfired. A public outcry ensued. Even in the midst of a tough and protracted war, Morgenthau's treatment of the Germans seemed too cruel, at least to some. The *Washington Post* came out strongly against it, calling it "the

product of a fevered mind from which all sense of the realities has fled."
Morgenthau's scheme, the paper declared, would make the German
problem permanent: "a festering sore would be implanted in the heart
of Europe, and there would be installed a chaos which would assuredly
end in war."[127] Beyond the nation's capitol, in the heartland of
Missouri, the *Louisville Courier-Journal* concurred. A peace plan
"must put a realistic justice before more vengeance, which would
degrade us and make martyrs of the Germans." Average citizens sent
letters to the editor expressing deep concern over the plan: "we should
see to it that Germany is completely industrialized. We should arrange
to have no unemployment in Germany. Have everyone working to make
greater contributions to exports." The author continued: "If full
employment and ample compensation to every German is guaranteed
we may feel more confident that they will never again wish to turn to
a future Hitler to improve their status and well-being."[128] Others voiced
similar fears: "Such a plan as Morgenthau's can only lead to ruin not
alone for Europe but for the world. Europe and the world need German
industry; this is a matter of self-interest."[129]

Naturally, not all Americans agreed. There were some who saw
all Germans as criminals needing to be punished, referring to "bestial
Germans" who "happen to resemble a human being." One citizen did
not mince words: "You can't trust a snake! Have we not seen enough?
Haven't we endured sufficiently to learn our lesson?"[130] Clearly, the
public divide over how to treat a defeated foe mirrored the debate
occurring at the pinnacle of government.

The leak to the press of Morgenthau's plan handed Joseph
Goebbels a propaganda coup. Hitler's propaganda minister exploited
it as proof of a Jewish conspiracy to starve and enslave the German
people. The fallout also risked serious repercussions at home. The
election was less than two months away, and Roosevelt worried that
it could be close. His challenger, Governor Thomas Dewey, claimed
that the Morgenthau Plan had stiffened German resistance, charging
that it made the Germans fight with "the frenzy of despair."[131] Ever
the astute politician, Roosevelt promptly disavowed the entire
scheme, essentially ducking for cover. Years later, Eleanor
Roosevelt attested that her husband never truly abandoned the
Morgenthau Plan; he merely wanted to avoid the bad publicity that
surrounded it. She believed that FDR remained committed to the
plan until his death.[132]

The public kerfuffle over the leak notwithstanding, inside the administration it looked as though Morgenthau's views had triumphed. Stimson felt deeply depressed that a plan he thought was madness had been adopted at Quebec. He fumed to his diary that Morgenthau had pushed his insane scheme on the President: "It is Semitism gone wild for vengeance." Stimson could not believe that such a foolish and brutal plan would be implemented by America. He fretted that if it were, it would plant the seeds of a future war: "And yet these two men [Roosevelt and Churchill] in a brief conference at Quebec, with nobody to advise them except 'yes-men', with no Cabinet officer with the President except Morgenthau, have taken this step and given directions for it to be carried out."[133]

Despite his intense opposition to Morgenthau's plan, Stimson never treated Morgenthau with anything other than courtesy and respect. In fact, after Morgenthau received a drubbing in the press when the details of his plan leaked to the public, Stimson sent the Treasury Secretary a consoling note. Responding to Dewey's claims that the Morgenthau Plan had inspired the Germans to fight with greater vigor and that this had cost American lives, Stimson assured Morgenthau that this was not the case: "I am very sorry that you should have been troubled by such a criticism."[134] True to his values, Stimson behaved with characteristic kindness and grace. His actions toward Morgenthau the man were one thing; his actions toward the Morgenthau Plan were quite another.

Something had to be done to counteract Morgenthau's meddling. As the weeks and months unfolded, the battle over Germany's fate rumbled on. Stimson appealed to Roosevelt's humanity, reminding him of the Atlantic Charter and his pledge that no one should suffer from privation. Hearing of FDR's backsliding, Morgenthau countered with tactics of his own. When Roosevelt seemed moved by Stimson's arguments, Morgenthau labeled Stimson's views as appeasement. Aware of the President's affinity for Churchill and the British, he stressed that his plan would benefit Britain's economic revival. Stimson responded by arguing that eliminating a rival rarely benefits economic development, as competition is the key to progress. Memos met with counter memos. Each man lobbied for allies within the administration, but Morgenthau could always play his trump card – his close friendship with the President. Back and forth the tug-of-war continued in the effort to pull the President toward one side or the other.

On October 3, Stimson lunched with the President in the White House and tried to reinforce his views. Roosevelt was obviously unwell. Stimson did not want to tax or distress his chief, seeing that he was in discomfort, but the War Secretary felt impelled to speak frankly. Roosevelt flatly denied having ever signed any document calling for the total dismantling of German industry and returning the country to an agrarian state. Stimson then produced a copy of the agreement that the President had just signed in Quebec. Roosevelt claimed he had no recollection of that document. The President's health had been rapidly deteriorating, but the idea that the President could have so quickly forgotten the basis of a hallmark postwar plan signed scarcely three weeks previously, and over which there had been such heated debate, challenged credulity. Stimson retraced some of the previously trodden ground, and then he added a pointed remark. He said that we were after "preventive punishment, even educative punishment, but not vengeance."[135]

Stimson did not object to Morgenthau's plans for demilitarization or de-Nazification. He naturally wanted to see Nazis punished for their crimes. His objections centered on Morgenthau's idea that Germany must be reduced to an agrarian state. Stimson argued that German exports had benefitted much of Europe, and its imports of other countries' goods had greatly increased European prosperity as well. It struck Stimson as foolhardy to dismantle some of the most productive regions of the continent precisely when their productivity would be most needed. But his arguments did not rest on economics alone. He also vehemently rejected the plan to hold Germans to a subsistence level on the brink of poverty. He believed that this would mean "condemning the German people to a condition of servitude." Through such a policy, Stimson warned, America would be "poisoning the springs out of which we hope that the future peace of the world can be maintained." Ultimately, his convictions rested not simply on mercy, but also on the logic of blowback. As he saw it, policies that are overly harsh do not prevent war, they breed it.[136]

Therein lay the root of this debate between the two men, between advocates of a harsh or soft peace. Both sides shared the same ultimate objective: to reduce the likelihood of another world war. The question was how to achieve it. Both sides could make compelling cases. In Morgenthau's view, future peace required the dismantling of Germany's capacity to wage war. It was that simple.

Remove their means of manufacturing the weapons of modern war, and the Germans could not threaten the peace. By contrast, Stimson believed that peace required prosperity, and by forcing Germany to subsist at artificially low living standards, the Allies would breed resentments that would undermine stability. Morgenthau's view was a negative conception of world order: disintegrate Germany from the calculus of great power politics, and the result would equal peace. Stimson's view was more positive: reintegrate Germany into European recovery, and the Germans would become stakeholders in an interdependent world. Roosevelt's advisors split down this divide. Their position depended in large part on what each believed about the German people themselves.

Weighting the Scales

Throughout the fall of 1944, as McCloy and Stimson struggled to keep Morgenthau's machinations from sabotaging postwar peace, the problem of Japanese-American internment reached a climax as the Korematsu case approached the court of public opinion. Hoping to change attitudes toward Japanese Americans, Eleanor Roosevelt published an article in the popular magazine *Colliers*, in which she defended the government's decision and its handling of relocation but at last spoke out directly against anti-Japanese-American hatreds. She acknowledged the anger that many white Americans felt toward the Japanese military for its cruelty, but she rejected the extension of this anger to loyal citizens. Those Japanese Americans who had been carefully vetted and found loyal were being gradually reabsorbed into society, she told readers. And then she retraced the history of anti-Asian laws that prevented Japanese Americans from becoming citizens. This time she did not mince words.

Californians and others along the west coast, she charged, viewed the Japanese as economic competitors, and their resentments were fueled by fear. After Pearl Harbor emotions ran too high. Many wanted to "wreak vengeance on Oriental-looking people." Though guilty of no crimes at all, Japanese Americans were sent off to detention camps. Now it was time, the First Lady implored, to allow them to reenter society. If you should meet one of these families in your neighborhood, she advised, do not condemn them before giving them a fair chance to prove themselves in the community. She concluded with an appeal to the noble principles in which she had always believed, though not always advanced as she might have wished:

> We have no common race in this country, but we have an ideal to which all of us are loyal. It is our ideal which we want to have live. It is an ideal which can grow with our people, but we cannot progress if we look down upon any group of people among us because of race or religion. Every citizen in this country has a right to our basic freedoms, to justice and to equality of opportunity, and we retain the right to lead our individual lives as we please, but we can only do so if we grant to others the freedoms that we wish for ourselves.[137]

Eleanor Roosevelt's efforts to mollify American racial fears may have helped with reintegration, but what Japanese Americans needed most was a legal victory in the High Court. The battle over Japanese Americans' civil liberties in a time of war had been waged by attorneys in several related cases, but the Korematsu case marked the final attempt to restore justice to thousands of wrongly persecuted citizens. McCloy's biographer has argued that as the presidential election drew closer, McCloy "almost single-handedly blocked every step" to end their imprisonment.[138] From McCloy's perspective, if the Supreme Court ruled against the government, it would not only tarnish the War Department's reputation but his own as well, since he was the person most tightly tied to the evacuation order. He had to prevent Korematsu's lawyers from swaying the Court, whatever it took.

On a Saturday morning at the end of September 1944, McCloy was reviewing the Justice Department's brief on the Korematsu case when he came across a curious footnote. McCloy's legal training had been solid, and his attention to detail was never lacking. He was not a man to overlook a footnote, as the Justice Department lawyers had hoped he would. They clearly did not know whom they were up against or how badly he needed to win this case.

The two most tenacious Justice Department attorneys, Ennis and Burling, had slipped into a footnote a request that the Court not admit the General DeWitt report, the Army's report on Japanese-American sabotage. The Justice Department lawyers noted that the report was based on outright falsehoods, fabricated assertions of treason for which there was no evidence. If the Court learned that the report contained lies, then the justices would hardly be able to support the government's position that removing Japanese Americans was a military necessity. McCloy immediately rang the Justice Department and was told that he was too late to have the footnote removed. The brief was being printed at that moment. Undeterred, McCloy contacted the printer and had them literally stop the presses. The Justice Department refused to budge, and it ordered their brief reprinted. Again McCloy blocked the printing. After five days of wrangling, a more senior-level Justice Department official negotiated a compromise with the War Department. The DeWitt report would be admitted. The battle over evidence was over, and Justice had lost.

Whether McCloy ever needed to take such extreme measures on the DeWitt report is impossible to know for certain. He might not even have needed to suppress the original Ringle report of 1941, in which the Office of Naval Intelligence concluded that Japanese Americans represented no threat. Perhaps it did not matter that Ringle's report was never introduced as evidence in 1944, because McCloy possessed a secret weapon of sorts: a close contact and confidant, a man perfectly placed for shifting the Court in his favor. He was always able to call on his good friend, neighbor, and former law professor, Supreme Court Justice Felix Frankfurter.

The friendship between these two men made sense. Both were outsiders. The gates of Harvard had not swung open for them with the ease that they had for Biddle, Grew, or Stimson. Instead, McCloy and Frankfurter had to hurdle over those gates: McCloy through brute determination, Frankfurter by dint of his undeniable intellect, and both by the sheer strength of their ambition. No longer were they pupil and professor. That relationship had been transformed long ago. For McCloy wielded tremendous power – the power to shape the course of armies or imprison whole peoples. It was the type of power that Frankfurter lacked. But the Justice wielded something even greater than his vote on the High Court. He held the intoxicating reins of influence. Ensconced in Washington at last, their ambition having lifted them as high as each could hope, they now combined their forces to pull the strings of policy that would make their country rise.

Scarcely a week went by when McCloy and Frankfurter did not meet or speak. Living just around the corner from each other in the Georgetown neighborhood, they frequently took walks together in the evenings. Their wives spent time together as well. Frankfurter advised McCloy on all matters, domestic and foreign.[139] McCloy kept meticulous records of his daily activities, down to the minute, and the frequency of his contact with Justice Frankfurter is revealing. Even prior to Pearl Harbor, McCloy consulted with Frankfurter consistently. On December 1, 1941, for example, McCloy noted that at midday he conferred with the Justice, cryptically referring to their topics as "personal matters."[140] On December 7, at 11:30 in the morning Washington time, before the bombs fell on Pearl Harbor, McCloy telephoned Frankfurter on other matters.[141] But at 3:15 pm, McCloy called the Justice Department to order the arrest of every member on his A and B lists of suspicious Japanese aliens on the west coast. At 3:49 pm, he rang Justice again to urge that the arrests begin immediately. At 4:30, Secretary Stimson called him into his office to discuss the general situation and stress that the war must be about "much more than revenge against Japan."[142] Stimson had already grasped that others would be driven by the thirst for vengeance, and the wiser, elder statesman hoped he could head off his deputy's dangerous predilection. At 11:50 that evening, McCloy rang Attorney General Biddle to ensure that the arrest of Japanese suspects, some 750 people, had begun.[143] Just three days later, McCloy stopped off at Frankfurter's home at 8 am to discuss the Allied War Council. It is unclear if there were any issues at all on which McCloy did not seek Frankfurter's advice. We will likely never know how much McCloy revealed to Frankfurter about the Korematsu case. Neither would have been so foolish as to have made written records of such discussions.

The Court heard the case of *Fred Korematsu v. United States* on October 11 and 12, 1944, and as expected, the simmering resentments that had been brewing since the Gobitis case in 1940 erupted at last. But the standard liberal–conservative divide did not form as anticipated.

Frankfurter, no longer surprisingly, came down on the side of the Roosevelt administration. He stressed the crucial importance of allowing the military to take measures in wartime to safeguard the nation. This was precisely McCloy's view of the matter.

> To recognize that military orders are "reasonably expedient military precautions" in time of war, and yet to deny them constitutional legitimacy, makes of the Constitution an instrument for dialectic subtleties not reasonably to be attributed to the hard-headed Framers, of whom a majority had had actual participation in war.[144]

In other words, the constitutionally guaranteed rights of citizens can be abrogated in wartime, if the government deems it necessary, and the Founding Fathers would agree.

The deepest, most acrimonious divide in the Court ran along the fault line of civil liberties, and no two justices exemplified the dispute more than Felix Frankfurter and Hugo Black. These two intensely acerbic wits clashed repeatedly throughout their tenure on the bench. Both possessed commanding egos, and each led a wing of the Court, ever jockeying for swing votes. Each was intent on making his mark on history and bending the Court to his will. Frankfurter looked down at Black, who lacked a Harvard pedigree. As Frankfurter saw it, Black piously made himself out to be the champion of justice and decency, while all others were the "oppressors of the people and the supporters of some exploiting interest."[145] Black, in turn, ridiculed Frankfurter's typical stance by making faces and parodying Frankfurter's voice: "Felix said, 'Hugo, the trains have to run,' and I said, 'Yes, Felix, but they don't have to run over people's legs.'"[146]

Frankfurter came to view Black as the ring leader of two other liberal justices, William O. Douglas and Frank Murphy, the three of whom Frankfurter jointly referred to as the Axis. It was rare for Black and Frankfurter to be on the same side of any issue, but over Korematsu, their perspectives, or their interests, aligned.

It was undeniably odd to see the liberal Justice Hugo Black writing the majority opinion in support of internment. What could have possibly caused him to abandon his convictions at this time? One possibility is that his illiberal opinion in Korematsu sprang from his brief military service. Though he had never served in combat, Black did train as an Army captain during WWI, but the war had ended before he was ever sent abroad. Over the internment issue, Black asserted that the Court should not restrict military commanders' ability to act in the national interest. But could a short training period in the Army have truly caused him to elevate military demands over his commitment to civil liberties? There is another possible explanation. Black's curious support for internment may have had much more to do with a purely personal connection to one military commander in particular.

The Korematsu case hinged heavily on the actions of Black's old friend, General John DeWitt. While McCloy orchestrated the internment from behind the scenes, and the President issued the executive order, General DeWitt stood front and center as the internment's public face. A ruling against internment would be a ruling against DeWitt, and Black may have been reluctant to disgrace his comrade, especially given what DeWitt had done for him years before.

DeWitt had stood by Black back in 1937, during the tumult that surrounded Black's appointment to the High Court. If Frankfurter's nomination process had been highly charged, Black's was truly explosive. Black had been serving as the junior Senator from Alabama when Roosevelt put forward his name. Since the Senate approved nominations, he expected the process to glide smoothly. And it would have, if a reporter for the *Pittsburgh Post-Gazette* had not revealed that Black had been an active member of the Ku Klux Klan.

The story immediately raced across the country. Reporters surrounded Black's home, desperate to barrage him with questions. Photographers climbed trees outside his windows, hoping for a lucky shot of the embattled nominee. Black's home life became unlivable. The outing of Hugo Black's hooded past fueled a media frenzy that captivated the nation. Ever sensitive to political firestorms, Roosevelt astutely remained silent as Black received death threats. Amidst the public censure and condemnation, one man held steadfast in support. General DeWitt was then serving as commandant of the Army War College, and he offered Black refuge in an Army barracks there. Black surely never forgot DeWitt's friendship at that difficult moment. Refusing to withdraw his nomination, Black went on the offensive. He agreed to speak to the nation. As more than thirty million Americans sat riveted to their radios, Black admitted that he had indeed been a member of the Klan, but that he resigned his membership in 1925, just prior to joining the Senate. His membership had been more for purposes of political advancement than ideological affinity, though he must have shared at least some of the Klan's views. It was an aggressive gambit, and, as FDR predicted after hearing it, the speech did the trick. Black successfully turned public opinion to his side.

Although Black and Frankfurter and four other justices defended the government's internment policy, the unity forged over Hirabayashi the year before no longer held. Herbert Hoover's appointee, Owen Roberts, voted against Roosevelt's executive order. Two Roosevelt appointees, Robert Jackson and Frank Murphy, also dissented. All three men likely regretted their votes in the Hirabayashi case. Roberts put it plainly, writing: "it is the case of convicting a citizen as a punishment for not submitting to imprisonment in a concentration camp, based on his ancestry, and solely because of his ancestry, without evidence or inquiry concerning his loyalty and good disposition towards the United States." Justice Jackson was more pointed in his dissent: "here is an attempt to make an otherwise innocent act a crime merely because this prisoner is the son of parents as to whom he had no choice, and belongs to a race from which there is no way to resign. If Congress in peace-time legislation should enact such a criminal law, I should suppose this Court would refuse to enforce it." Murphy was the most outspoken. He labeled the internment as "utterly revolting" and called it "the legalization of racism." He cogently asserted:

> All residents of this nation are kin in some way by blood or culture to a foreign land. Yet they are primarily and necessarily a part of the new and distinct civilization of the United States. They must, accordingly, be treated at all times as the heirs of the American experiment, and as entitled to all the rights and freedoms guaranteed by the Constitution.[147]

But what Murphy found most disturbing was that the internment smacked of fascist behavior, similar to that of the dictatorships. Internment looked too much like the Nazis' treatment of the Jews. As Murphy saw it, this was not who we are as Americans – or, at least, it was not who we should be.

Shortly prior to the Court's decision, as the justices deliberated, Dillon Myer traveled to Los Angeles to speak to the Fair Play Committee, which had renamed itself a second time and now operated under the title of the Pacific Coast Committee on American Principles and Fair Play. Myer had continued to head the War Relocation Authority, and he continued to believe that internment could be managed in a humane way. He was, in effect, what his biographer dubbed him, a keeper of concentration camps.[148] In his speech entitled, "Racism and Reason," Myer affirmed the desire to see the Japanese-American "problem" settled in "a Christian spirit." He clearly saw himself as the opponent of racist actions. He took aim at those who expressed hateful views toward Japanese Americans and declared that America still held true to its ideals. "Despite all the clamor of the race baiters and their tawdry appeals to fear and hatred," he told the committee, America's basic decency remains. He assured them that the true American character would rise forth in the coming days.[149] It would take another forty years before the government acknowledged the wrong it had committed. Before that day came, however, McCloy and Stimson still had to battle Morgenthau over what they saw as an even greater wrong, the planned postwar treatment of Germans. And soon they would also have to orchestrate a merciful ending to the brutal war with Japan.

7 DENY

Henry Wallace's ideas seemed nothing short of radical. He believed that women should have all the same rights as men. He believed in total equality for Black Americans. He felt that workers deserved greater pay and stronger unions. He stood for national health insurance even before Britain introduced its own National Health Service. In short, for many Americans, he was decades ahead of his time. Wallace was the standard bearer of nearly every major liberal cause of his era. He was a hero to millions of Americans, who felt that their society had ignored their legitimate needs. And they looked to him as their champion. As Franklin Roosevelt's vice president, Wallace seemed certain to succeed FDR and move America in a distinctly progressive direction. But to those who opposed him, he held one other conviction that was so unforgivable, it made his other fringe positions seem almost tolerable by comparison.

Wallace was "soft on communism," or at least that was the charge, and he did little to shake that image. There is no known evidence that Wallace was working for the Soviets, but he believed to his core in the freedoms of speech and association. If American communists wanted to hold rallies and campaign peacefully for their views, then Wallace insisted that they should have the right to do so, just like any other party. And if they wanted to support him, he would not disavow them. Unfortunately for Wallace, the times were changing in America, and he failed to read them. His failure would set back American progressives for at least the next half-century.

While the battles over Japanese-American internment and the future of postwar Germany were being fought inside the government, a different political battle was occurring within the Democratic Party. As the campaign of 1944 heated up, it was clear to those close to FDR that the President was gravely ill. It seemed likely that Wallace, as vice president, would soon succeed him, and the more conservative power brokers within the Democratic Party could not bear to see this happen. Several of them harbored an additional concern. Some of the southern Democratic leaders feared what Wallace might do regarding racial equality if he held presidential power. And so a backstage movement began to thwart Wallace's bid for reelection as vice president.

Edwin Pauley, secretary of the Democratic National Committee, helped to organize the anti-Wallace effort with the aim of pushing Truman as the replacement. An oil executive from California with a knack for maneuvering toward his goals, Pauley sometimes conducted morning conversations with FDR while the President relaxed in bed. Roosevelt may have felt a bond with Pauley, who had previously been a wheelchair-user, the result of a plane crash. But Pauley was conspiring with FDR's appointment secretary to turn FDR against Wallace by ensuring that the President would receive a steady stream of anti-Wallace visitors, while Wallace supporters would be kept at bay.

As the Democratic National Convention's nomination process neared, Party bosses met with Roosevelt to discuss the matter. Each time FDR floated the name of someone he might consider, the group pointed out the various strikes that man had against them. The President liked Supreme Court Justice William O. Douglas, but the gossip mill said that Douglas had a drinking problem, which could certainly be a liability. Senator James Byrnes, "Jimmy," was keenly interested in the job, but being from the South and given his views on race, he was likely to turn off Black voters. He had also abandoned the Catholic Church, and his prior stance on wages might diminish the labor vote. Senator Alben Barkley of Kentucky had his eye on the position, but he and Roosevelt had disagreed recently on an issue, and his age, sixty-seven, was a detriment, the bosses claimed. The list of running mates was getting thin. The entire discussion was engineered to lead Roosevelt toward the one acceptable candidate: the bosses' choice.

Finally, only Truman, the junior senator from Missouri, remained acceptable to the group. Roosevelt barely knew him. Truman had no experience in foreign affairs and not much in domestic affairs either. He would be unknown to most Americans, but he had the fewest strikes against him. FDR acknowledged that the group wanted

Truman and agreed. And so it was that a closed-door meeting decided the fate of millions.[150]

Wallace, however, had every expectation that he would be re-nominated, and he thought he had the votes to ensure it. In mid-July 1944, at the Democratic National Convention in Chicago, delegates assembled to enthusiastically re-nominate Roosevelt for an unprecedented fourth term. Wallace was the obvious front-runner for vice president and seemed poised to win easily, but his opponents within the Party convinced Senator Harry Truman to run against him. Truman had no ambitions to be president. He was perfectly content to remain a senator. Jimmy Byrnes had asked Truman to nominate him at the convention, and Truman eagerly agreed. When Party bosses told Truman that they wanted him to run for vice president, he allegedly replied, "Go to Hell." He had given his word to Byrnes, and Truman had little more than his word. He certainly did not have experience, education, or money. A failed businessman still paying off the debts of his bankrupt clothing store, Truman, his wife Bess, and their daughter Margaret lived in a modest DC apartment. They were unassuming folks, bred in the midwestern ethos of hard work and simple styles. Truman could scarcely imagine himself succeeding the urbane, Harvard-educated, worldly statesmen who had for so long occupied the White House. Truman was not the only one who could not imagine it; neither could most of those around him.

Truman had not even sought a career in politics. It was his chance connection to the corrupt Democratic Party boss of Kansas City, Tom Pendergast, who convinced Truman to run for local office. With the Party machine behind him, Truman found himself in the US Senate. He developed a reputation as an honest man and a straight-shooter, which for the most part he was. Unfortunately, he had put his wife, Bess, on the payroll of his Senate staff, though she did not actually do much work. If word got out, he would not only be embarrassed and his reputation tarnished, Bess would also be humiliated, a scenario Truman dreaded. But the Party chiefs convinced Truman that plenty of congressmen had their wives on staff, and he had nothing to worry about. After being assured that Roosevelt actually wanted him on the ticket, Truman reluctantly agreed to run.

At the Party convention, Wallace supporters turned out in force. "We want Wallace," the delegates chanted, as a pipe organ played beneath them. They seemed to dominate the convention hall, crowding out all others. On the first ballot, Wallace netted 429 and a half votes to Truman's 319 and a half, with smaller numbers of votes given to other, less viable candidates. Against such a raucous crowd, it looked likely that Wallace would win outright on the next ballot, which was poised to take place. To buy time for a rear-guard action, Party bosses instructed the convention chairman to announce that the second ballot would be delayed until the following day. Seizing on the only plausible tactic, Wallace's opponents convinced enough of the supporters of long-shot candidates to give their votes to Truman. By consolidating those delegates into an anti-Wallace bloc, the conservatives managed to win the nomination for Truman and thereby remove Wallace from the ticket. Had the anti-Wallace movement failed, the course of American history and the Cold War would have been markedly different. Wallace and his many supporters felt that they had been denied the nomination. Given Roosevelt's declining health, many understood that Wallace had actually been denied the presidency.

Having lost the last three presidential races, Republicans were becoming increasingly aggressive in their tactics, desperate for a win. In some ways Thomas E. Dewey seemed like a long shot to defeat FDR. His first attempt came in 1940. A popular New York district attorney, Dewey had made his reputation on busting mob bosses. His successes brought him national acclaim, and his crime-fighting persona made him the subject of several Hollywood films. The downside was his age. Dewey was only thirty-seven when he launched his campaign, leading one of FDR's Cabinet officials to sneer that Dewey had thrown his diaper in the ring.[151] The age issue could be spun as an advantage, but his personality could not. Dewey came across as arrogant. One reporter called Dewey "a self-made man who worshipped his Creator."[152] Though he lost the nomination in 1940 to Wendell Willkie, Dewey captured it four years later, certain he could vanquish Roosevelt and the New Deal Democrats.

As the race intensified, Republicans sought out any hint of scandal. Exactly as Truman had feared, it soon leaked that he had placed his wife on his Senate staff. The witty Republican congresswoman Clare Booth Luce, always ready with a cutting quip, dubbed Mrs. Truman "Payroll Bess." Bess was his highest paid staff member, though she did almost nothing of consequence. Her position was a nepotistic sinecure, and Truman did it because he was poor. Years of debt and meager income made him take advantage of the chance to elevate his family's well-being. It was wrong, and he knew it, but that didn't make the humiliation hurt any less.

Morgenthau had to be concerned about the coming election. Dewey, now the governor of New York, had offered the vice presidential slot to Earl Warren, California's popular governor, who had risen to power partly by demanding the removal of Japanese Americans from the west coast. But Warren was too politically astute to run on a ticket which he felt certain would lose to a popular wartime incumbent. Dewey then turned to a fellow governor, John Bricker of Ohio, as his running mate. Bricker seemed to hold racist views equal to Warren's. While campaigning in April, Bricker stated that local communities on the west coast should be permitted to determine for themselves whether the former Japanese-American residents could return to their homes. He said that the returnees should be closely watched after they were released. Just as military officials had tried to argue that relocation was to protect Japanese Americans, Bricker couched his support for surveillance and local referenda as being in the Japanese Americans' best interest. The Japanese have behaved like beasts against Americans, and this has kindled hatred among our people, he told a crowd: "It is up to us to prevent this hatred from finding expression in revenge against innocent and patriotic Americans."[153] It was a rather mixed message, almost as insidious as his remarks about the Jews.

In another speech Bricker criticized the Roosevelt administration for its lax position on immigration. Referring to European Jews who had entered America, the governor observed that most were not frail women and children, but adult men, suggesting that Jewish immigrants fleeing Nazi-occupied countries should not be admitted. Then he added: "I'm not saying that this group was cleared with Sidney. I don't know."[154]

Bricker was issuing a not-so-subtle dog whistle. Sidney Hillman, a prominent Jewish labor leader, co-founded the American Labor Party and the Congress of Industrial Organizations. Bespectacled and confident, and prone to gesticulation, Hillman controlled a substantial war chest, which afforded him an outsized influence over the labor vote. He rallied support for Roosevelt, and was a target of Republican animus. FDR had reportedly told Party Chair Bob Hannegan to clear Truman's nomination with Sidney before it became official. In response, a national campaign arose with posters asking, "It's your country. Why let Sidney Hillman run it?" Dewey then linked Hillman to the communists, alleging that they were behind the New Deal.[155] There lay an unmistakable undercurrent of anti-Semitism to Dewey's and Bricker's remarks. To his credit, Dewey recognized the ugly aspects of this particular attack and backed off.

As the polls tightened in the final months of the election, Morgenthau had to be concerned. A Roosevelt defeat would not simply mean his own fall from influence. Throughout 1944, much greater issues of concern to Jews were at stake. Lives hinged on secret actions inside the government, and Morgenthau stood at their fulcrum.

Categorical Enemies

In his diary on September 4, Henry Stimson made an offhand and intriguing comment. "Morgenthau," he wrote, "is not unnaturally very bitter and ... it became apparent that he would plunge out for a treatment of Germany which I feel sure would be unwise."[156] Stimson believed, as many others may have also surmised, that Morgenthau's Jewishness gave him a deep-seated animosity toward Germans over their atrocious treatment of the Jews. Although the full horror of the Holocaust was not yet known, the Nuremberg Laws, which made Jews second-class citizens in Germany, as well as *Kristallnacht*, the violent destruction of Jewish property in 1938, were public knowledge. But Morgenthau's awareness of German atrocities went far deeper than what the public knew. Beyond his already overwhelming task of funding the war effort, the Treasury Secretary had spent much of 1944 engaged in an extraordinary effort to save the Jews of Europe. Through this work he was learning daily the gruesome horror of Nazi crimes.

Morgenthau had built a Treasury Department staffed with bright, energetic young men, who shared the Secretary's zeal to defeat Hitler. One of these, Josiah DuBois, had graduated from the University of Pennsylvania at age eighteen and was among the youngest of Morgenthau's inner circle. In December 1943, DuBois was reading over some State Department cables regarding the condition of Jews in Eastern Europe and noticed a curious discrepancy. He saw a reference to an earlier cable without any details or explanation of that other cable. When DuBois requested a copy of the earlier cable from State, the Department refused to provide it. Something didn't feel right. Acting partly on instinct, he contacted a friend who worked at State, and the two men snuck into the Department's file room at night and found the cable in question. What it revealed shocked and disturbed all of Morgenthau's team. Almost a year earlier the State Department had been receiving credible information through its legation in Bern, Switzerland, detailing the organized murder of Jewish men, women, and children. DuBois copied down the chilling facts: 6,000 Jews were being killed in Poland daily; 130,000 Jews were being deported to Transnistria; 60,000 of those were reported dead. And then the instruction followed. The Bern Legation was forbidden to transmit such information back to America. The conclusion seemed inescapable.[157] The State Department was actively attempting to suppress information about the Holocaust. It was denying the government knowledge of this genocide.

DuBois and his colleagues brought a summary of their many discoveries to Morgenthau on January 13, 1944. The title of their report pulled no punches: "Report to the Secretary on the Acquiescence of This Government in the Murder of the Jews." Morgenthau, who had long experience with anti-Semitism and with the attitudes of many elites who staffed the State Department, was less shocked than others. He understood that he would need the President to weigh in. Two days later, Morgenthau and a few trusted colleagues met with Roosevelt in the White House, where they revealed what they knew about both the horrors of Nazi extermination practices and State's efforts to keep it secret. The State Department's anti-Semitism could no longer be denied. They proposed that the President establish a new executive branch office to rescue Jews. This War Refugee Board would be overseen by chiefs of Treasury, State, and the Foreign Economic Administration. Morgenthau's team worried that Roosevelt might quash their plan, but FDR did not hesitate to approve it. He read over their report quickly and made only one change. Instead of assigning the chief of the Foreign Economic Administration to the War Refugee Board, the President wanted someone else. He wanted another person he could trust, possibly as a counterweight to Morgenthau. He wanted Henry Stimson.

Six days later Roosevelt officially approved the Board's creation. From that point onward, Morgenthau oversaw most of the Board's remarkable deeds to rescue Jews from Nazi-occupied nations. They transferred funds to bribe German and other European officials in exchange for the release of Jews. They arranged for ships to ferry Jews to safety. They dispatched clandestine agents to smuggle Jews across borders. In the nearly two years of its operation, it saved an estimated

200,000 lives. And all that while Morgenthau continued to learn how the Nazis were cramming Jews into train cars, starving them in concentration camps, murdering them in gas chambers, and turning their skins into lampshades. Few in the public would believe these reports, for they sounded like the worst fabrications of wartime propaganda. But Morgenthau's sources were numerous and sound, and he knew that it was true.

Roosevelt's insertion of Stimson to the new Board turned out not to be as onerous as Morgenthau might have feared. First, Stimson was sympathetic to the plight of Jews under Nazi rule. He noted in his diary on February 1: "These poor creatures have lost their homes, are being hunted by the German constabulary and are seeking to get out of the German occupied zone into someplace where they can be safe."[158] Second, Stimson's own responsibilities managing the massive War Department were excessive and his health issues kept him from participating to any significant extent in the Refugee Board's activities. Morgenthau's greater concern was with Stimson's assistant, McCloy.

It was around this same time in January 1945, when the embattled Treasury Secretary learned that McCloy had been keeping Treasury out of the discussions over JCS 1067. This Joint Chiefs of Staff directive intended to guide US military occupation policy for Germany after the war. Stimson and McCloy saw it as entirely within their purview; not a matter for Treasury. Morgenthau was incensed. He viewed all postwar plans for Germany as rightly within his domain. Morgenthau again intervened with the President, imploring him to maintain a tough stand in order to root out German militarism. Recognizing that Morgenthau had the upper hand, McCloy decided to work with the Treasury chief to see if some compromise could be found. In March, that pretext unexpectedly arrived.

On March 10, State Department officials exerted their own influence over postwar plans by sending the President a modification of JCS 1067 that omitted any mention of dismembering Germany. Morgenthau was livid. State was trying to undermine the crux of his plan. McCloy saw his opening. If all three departments did not cooperate on this vital and pressing issue, the chaos would continue.[159] With the Allies closing in on Berlin, postwar policy simply had to be hammered out.

After Roosevelt returned from the Yalta Conference, he instructed the relevant officials to reach a definitive agreement on postwar plans. On March 15, he formed the Informal Policy Committee on Germany (IPCOG). It was a group of influential deputies, the movers and drivers of policy within America's most powerful departments. FDR made William Clayton its chair. Clayton, the Assistant Secretary of State for Economic Affairs, had at one time been the world's largest cotton trader. A highly successful businessman, the wealthy entrepreneur wanted to see a postwar world open to free trade. A strong and reformed Germany would serve that end. Morgenthau's deputy, Harry White, the Soviet source, represented Treasury, while McCloy represented Stimson and the War Department. Ralph Bard, undersecretary of the Navy, joined the group, as did a representative of the Foreign Economic Administration.

The battle lines were clear. Stimson and McCloy from War, Clayton from State, and possibly Bard from Navy, saw a centralized Germany as necessary, both for governance during occupation and as a means of encouraging some rebuilding of their economy. Morgenthau and his second-in-command, White, wanted desperately to prevent Germany from rebuilding, and dismemberment seemed like a good way to achieve that end. On March 19, Morgenthau met with the Soviet Ambassador in Washington, who naturally concurred that breaking up Germany was best. Intent on stopping Clayton and State from interfering, Morgenthau played his trump card. The following day he sent Roosevelt a memo outlining the three crucial elements to his vision for postwar Germany. First, he argued that the United States had to avoid assuming responsibility for the German economy. Their economic hardship was Germany's problem, not America's. Second, he said that America must aim to shrink German heavy industry in order to prevent their war potential. If this limited German food production, so be it. "The occupying forces should accept no responsibility for providing the German people with food and supplies beyond preventing starvation, disease, and such unrest as might interfere with purposes of occupation." Third, the United States must decentralize Germany's political structure.[160]

The next day, March 21, IPCOG met to resolve the disagreements, but they failed to find a middle ground. Time was running short as victory was in sight, though there was still enough time for one more Washington power play. On March 22, Joseph Grew, now the acting secretary of state, went to see Roosevelt to make his case for centralization. As usual, it proved extraordinarily difficult to pin down the President on precisely what he wanted. FDR seemed to oppose the State Department's March 10 directive, but he had indicated conflicting sentiments to different audiences for months. The President now appeared willing to moderate Morgenthau's harshest intentions for German industry. Roosevelt allegedly said that he did not want to dismantle all German industry but instead alter its character. He did not want America to be burdened with taking care of the Germans, and that meant a very substantial role for German industry. McCloy was present at this meeting, and in a phone call he informed Morgenthau what had transpired. When McCloy reported this to Morgenthau, rather than being angered over Roosevelt's endless flip-flopping, the Treasury Secretary appeared grateful for the information.[161] McCloy related another bit of surprising news. Clayton was coming around to the Morgenthau view. Morgenthau remarked, "I'm a new man."

Roosevelt clearly needed his administration heads to come together. The process was exasperating, and all those involved were growing weary of the constant back-and-forth. The next day McCloy, Morgenthau, and Clayton, the three key players, met at the Treasury Department and forged a compromise. Clayton had initially opposed the Morgenthau Plan, but he seemed to have had a change of heart. He also knew that, at least for now, he and Grew would have to relent to some degree. McCloy hoped that he could craft a document giving the military some room for maneuver as time passed. Morgenthau ensured that the plan would maintain a low standard of living for the German people. Joint Chiefs of Staff Directive 1067 would become the ultimate document to govern American occupation policy, and after months of plotting, wrangling, and badgering, Morgenthau had succeeded in bending it to his will. The consequences would prove disastrous.

Morgenthau called the compromise "the first step toward a kind of peace which I think will last." He saw 1067 as a "good, tough document." The Treasury Secretary had fought relentlessly to achieve the final product, and though it was not as harsh as he had wished, he felt proud of the spine he showed throughout the bureaucratic battle. The final negotiations had been intense. "I have never been under such pressure in my life to give way on principles, and I didn't," he told his diary. He continued:

> We stand for something worthwhile. . . . It was one of the most
> important conferences that I have ever participated in, and it is

very encouraging that we had the President to back us up . . . . They tried to get him to change, and they couldn't – the State Department crowd. Sooner or later the President just has to clean his house.[162]

Shortly after this meeting, Morgenthau left Washington for a desperately needed vacation to Florida. There his wife Elinor suffered a massive heart attack. He stayed at her side each day until she stabilized.

Morgenthau, himself, had been under immense pressure. He and his team worked six-day weeks, and seven days were not uncommon. Vacations were rare. He was responsible for the ongoing effort to fund the war – the costliest undertaking in modern American history, possibly the costliest ever. Measured in 2022 dollars, the war cost $5.3 trillion. By comparison, the Marshall Plan cost $117 billion. He skillfully oversaw repeated campaigns to sell war bonds, making America's massive war effort feasible, yet he did it while keeping interest rates remarkably low. From 1939 to 1941, he led the drive to increase production of airplanes, from roughly 2,000 aircraft at the start to more than 19,400 two years later. He devised other means of increasing machine tool production, ultimately enabling the expansion of America's air fleet to more than 96,000 by 1944. Without those planes, victory would have been unlikely. He helped to manage and improve the Lend-Lease program to Britain, ensuring that America's crucial ally could keep fighting. Under his supervision, the British received more than $30 billion. All the while that he was directing these and other financial operations, he was the primary official (far more than Hull or Stimson) overseeing the War Refugee Board with its steady stream of gruesome news. Morgenthau was consuming reports of genocide before that word had even entered the lexicon.

The Treasury Secretary's responsibilities were simply enormous, and the strain took its toll. Morgenthau suffered from debilitating migraines, often needing to lie motionless in total darkness for hours at a stretch. At times they were so severe that he required intravenous drugs. By December 1944, he was seeking out expert medical care in New York and Philadelphia. One doctor prescribed potassium chloride pills. The other recommended a teaspoon of bicarbonate soda with two glasses of warm water each morning.[163] He found that the pills gave him some relief, but the episodes continued to recur.

Stimson's health had been declining as well. In September he turned seventy-seven. He had never planned to still be working at this late stage of life, but his duty to country took precedence. Stimson was unavoidably a man of his era. He had a strong sense of what the American character should be, and it was largely Christian and white. He had supported the National Origins Act in the 1920s, which favored immigration from northwestern Europe while excluding Asians. Previously, as governor-general of the Philippines, Stimson sought to uplift the natives whom President Taft had called "our little brown brothers," but he did not believe that the Filipinos were ready to govern themselves. Stimson had once prevented a large donation to Columbia University because he felt that the university had too much Jewish influence.[164] As FDR's war secretary, he opposed the bombing of the Auschwitz concentration camp, even though prominent Jewish leaders urged the action in order to end the suffering of inmates and prevent the camp's further use. Stimson believed that the best policy was to focus on winning the war.

Throughout his battles with Morgenthau over postwar treatment of Germany, Stimson frequently vented to his diary about Morgenthau's Jewishness being at the root of his postwar policy. It was the product of "Semitic grievances," he fumed. On another occasion he wrote what he really believed was driving the policy debate: "Semitism gone wild for vengeance."[165]

If Stimson harbored some of the anti-Jewish sentiments of his era, his opposition toward Morgenthau's plan stemmed not from anti-Semitism, but rather from his belief that a revitalized Germany, reintegrated into the global economy, would help to preserve the postwar peace. In order to defend against charges of anti-Semitism, and to rally supporters to his side, Stimson called on the help of a Jewish friend, a man for whom he had great respect, and someone with whom he had a nearly four-decade relationship. Back in 1906, when Stimson was serving as US attorney in New York, he knew that he needed the best possible aides. He wrote a letter to the dean of Harvard Law School, asking him to name the brightest young men in the current graduating class. The dean replied that one young man stood out from the rest: a gifted son of Jewish immigrants named Felix Frankfurter. Stimson hired the eager graduate, and the two men began a long and productive collaboration, first in fighting corporate corruption, and later in guiding the nation.

Stimson quickly realized he had made a magnificent choice. Frankfurter proved he was indeed the brightest, most able assistant in the US attorney's office. When Stimson ran for governor of New York in 1910, he hired Frankfurter, at age twenty-eight, as his speech writer and strategist. And as Frankfurter's star rose, he never forgot his former mentor. It was Frankfurter who engineered Stimson's return to government. Having cultivated a friendship with FDR years before, in 1940 he advised the President to make Stimson the new war secretary. Frankfurter told the President that Stimson was out of sorts with his own party (the Republicans), that he supported FDR's foreign policy, and that he could be counted on to execute the President's wishes unequivocally: "You couldn't possibly have a more devoted aide in your administration than he would be."[166]

As soon as Stimson took charge of the War Department in 1940, Frankfurter was never far from consultation, whatever the issue. On December 1, 1941, as tensions with Japan crackled with anticipation, Frankfurter telephoned Stimson to argue for a tough stand. He had just come from visiting the ailing Harry Hopkins. He urged Stimson to ensure that Roosevelt did not let "the appeasers pull him back." Both Frankfurter and Hopkins were "anxious to have decisive action taken as soon as possible."[167]

Though an expert on constitutional law, Frankfurter also possessed some firsthand knowledge of foreign affairs, having served as Stimson's aide when the latter was secretary of war under President Taft. The two men traveled on official assignments together, and over time Stimson came to value Frankfurter's judgment on all matters. This was due in part to Frankfurter's undeniable intelligence, and also to their long and close relationship. On December 8, the day after Pearl Harbor, Stimson escorted Mrs. Frankfurter to Congress to hear FDR's declaration of war.[168] On New Year's Day 1942, Stimson and his wife Mabel needed cheering up, given the grim developments in both theaters of war. They chose to spend time with the Frankfurters.[169]

Given their long and close association, when Stimson's feud with Morgenthau escalated, the aging War Secretary naturally turned to Frankfurter for support. Stimson invited his old friend to dine with him at his eighteen-acre estate in northwest Washington. Over dinner the two men discussed world affairs, and naturally Frankfurter sided completely with Stimson on the question of Germany. Frankfurter called Morgenthau "a stupid bootlick," and pledged to help Stimson however he could.[170] Frankfurter's long friendship with Stimson would have been reason enough for him to come to Stimson's aid over the German question. But Frankfurter's zeal to assist in this particular battle might have stemmed from a much older, unpleasant experience with Morgenthau's father, Henry Senior, during WWI.

In June 1917, President Wilson had hoped to separate Turkey from its alliance with the Central Powers. Wresting Turkey away from Germany would be a considerable coup and might help tip the balance in the war. President Wilson tasked Frankfurter to accompany the former ambassador to Turkey, Henry Morgenthau Sr., in the mission to Constantinople. From their first encounter, Frankfurter felt uneasy about Morgenthau. He felt that Morgenthau spoke in grand, vague terms without specifics. "You couldn't get hold of anything," Frankfurter recalled. He assumed that this was just "the froth of the man," until he realized that the froth was the man. On their long journey by boat, Frankfurter's unease blossomed into full-blown distaste. Frankfurter concluded that Morgenthau was simply full of hot air, "incapable of continuity of thought or effort." He found the ambassador's "ego enormous and insatiable." He could not imagine how such a man, who spoke so imprecisely and appeared to know so little, could have risen to an ambassadorship other than by dint of his generous donations to the Democratic Party and the Wilson presidential campaign.[171] Frankfurter's low opinion of Henry Morgenthau Sr. probably predisposed him to look down on the ambassador's son. Whatever his mix of motivations, Frankfurter proved so energetic in his behind-the-scenes lobbying against the Morgenthau Plan that Stimson worried the justice might be too conspicuous. This, however, was the least of Stimson's concerns.

Final Acts

Soon the war in Europe would be over and postwar policies would at last be implemented. On April 11, Morgenthau traveled to see the President at Warm Springs, Georgia. Though the President's poor health had been obvious for more than a year, Roosevelt's condition now looked alarming. He had difficulty hearing. His hands shook, though they steadied a bit after two cocktails. He struggled to transfer himself from his wheelchair to a regular chair. Morgenthau noted that the President did enjoy their meal of veal and noodles, followed by a chocolate waffle with whipped cream and chocolate sauce. It would be his last.

Still trying to lobby the President on postwar Germany, Morgenthau mentioned how appalling the State Department's plans had been before they intervened to correct them. He told Roosevelt that he would have to break the State Department crowd. He suggested making Claude Bowers a political advisor to General Eisenhower. Bowers was a journalist, historian, and passionate liberal who had delivered the keynote address at the Democratic National Convention in 1932. Morgenthau must have believed that Bowers would align with his own views on Germany and could ensure that Eisenhower would not go soft. Morgenthau told the President that he was fighting for future peace: "A weak economy for Germany means that she will be weak politically, and she won't be able to make another war. I have been strong for winning the war, and I want to help win the peace." Roosevelt replied, "Henry, I am with you one hundred percent."[172]

Just how much Roosevelt endorsed Morgenthau's plans can never be known for certain. But Roosevelt's world view strongly suggests a man who was guided by pragmatism, willing to adapt as conditions changed. He once had explained that his government would try whatever worked, and if it did not succeed, it would try something else until it found what did. Had Roosevelt lived into the postwar era, he most likely would have adapted policy toward Germany as prudence required. He probably believed that government works best when led by pragmatists, not ideologues.

On April 12, the day after Morgenthau had dined with him, President Roosevelt suffered a cerebral hemorrhage and died. In the midst of her grief, and with the weight of funeral arrangements upon her, Eleanor Roosevelt maintained the presence of mind to telephone the hospital staff where her friend Elinor Morgenthau was recuperating. The First Lady instructed the staff to remove the radio from her friend's hospital room so that she would not hear the news of FDR's death and suffer any additional stress to her heart.

At just after 5:00 pm, Harry Truman arrived at Sam Rayburn's office in the House of Representatives. Mr. Sam, as the Speaker was affectionately known, invited Truman over for a drink. Handing him a bourbon and water, Rayburn told Truman that he had a call from the

White House. When Truman phoned, he was told to come as quickly as possible. Truman turned pale. When he arrived, he was escorted to Mrs. Roosevelt's private study. The First Lady gently informed him that the President was dead.[173]

As Eleanor Roosevelt observed Truman over the coming months, she found him profoundly ill-suited to the job. She believed that Truman was not used to reading or deep reflection. She felt he was lonely, not at ease, and unprepared. He knew so little of foreign policy, she remarked to a friend, that it made her want to cry: "I was appalled at how little he knew."[174] She was not alone. FDR had occupied the White House for so long, and throughout such tumultuous times, that many struggled to accept that Harry Truman was now the president.

Harry Truman succeeded to the presidency, and the battle between Morgenthau and Stimson entered its final act. Almost immediately, Truman found himself having to think about how the defeated German people should be fed. Just four days after being sworn in, the Secretary of State told Truman of the coming food crisis. Chaos would be likely in the defeated areas, he explained, "without drastic action and the reduction of consumption to essentials." He warned Truman of disastrous political and economic results if America could not meet these basic needs. Americans would literally need to tighten their belts and eat less in order to avoid a humanitarian calamity.[175] Two days later, Churchill cabled to ask for Truman's views on the matter. The Prime Minister specifically wanted to know whether Truman agreed with Churchill's view that the occupying powers should share the food produced within Germany across all four occupation zones. The problem, he noted, was that the Soviets would be controlling the most fertile region in the east, and the one that contained the least number of inhabitants. Churchill wanted the Soviets to share the food grown in their zone with the rest of the country and alleviate the burden on Britain, France, and the United States.[176] But would the Russians agree? If they did one day restrict food supplies, they could easily inflict severe pain on tens of millions. Truman did not think it either sensible or charitable to let the German people suffer, but he also had an extraordinary number of even more immediate matters to address. Ill-informed on most matters and bombarded by pressing problems needing quick decisions, Truman accepted the policies that had already been developed by Roosevelt's officials, including the modified Morgenthau Plan.

On May 8, four long years after America entered the war and nearly six since Germany invaded Poland, the Allies declared victory in Europe. Germany's fate under occupation would now rest on the plans that had been so bitterly contested in Washington. Thanks to Stimson's steady opposition to a punitive peace, on May 10, Truman agreed to sign JCS 1067, a somewhat less severe directive for German occupation, though the directive still preserved the crux of Morgenthau's ideas for preventing German economic recovery. The Treasury Secretary wryly remarked that he hoped "somebody doesn't recognize it as the Morgenthau Plan."[177] But of course that was exactly what he did hope. Morgenthau knew that he had not completely molded the policy in his image, but he had succeeded, with his characteristic tenacity and single-mindedness, to punish Germany for its crimes. To finish the job, he would need to extend his influence over Roosevelt's successor. If he could not move Truman in the right direction, then he would have to move the policy process, as he had so masterfully done for years. And with JCS 1067 firmly in place, Morgenthau could at last turn his attention to the next major task: constructing an equivalent peace plan for Japan.

Morgenthau desperately hoped to make a positive impression on the new President, but Truman did not appear to have much fondness for the Treasury Secretary. Morgenthau secretly yearned to be named secretary of state, believing he had the experience and connections after twelve years at FDR's side. But Truman was preparing to bring in his own team, men less like the Eastern seaboard elites, the Groton and Harvard types whom Roosevelt favored, and more like Truman, Midwesterners and others to whom he could relate. He also had Jimmy Byrnes in mind for secretary of state. Byrnes resented the fact that Truman had received the vice presidency, when Byrnes felt that he, himself, was far more qualified and deserved to be president after Roosevelt's death. Truman, after all, had promised to nominate Byrnes for the vice presidency, yet he ended up running against him. Truman hoped that by giving Byrnes the secretary of state post, it would help to smooth over hurt feelings.[178] Others like Acting Secretary of State Joseph Grew, or Assistant Secretary of War John McCloy, who would have been more qualified, were overlooked. If Truman had not promised to nominate Byrnes for vice president in 1944, he might not have felt obligated to Byrnes in 1945, and the nuclear age might have begun very differently.

There was another consideration that made Morgenthau's appointment as secretary of state exceedingly unlikely. At that time, the presidential line of succession naturally went to the vice president in the event of a president's death. Once Truman succeeded FDR, there was no longer a vice president, and the next in line was the secretary of state. No one in the corridors of power wanted to risk having Morgenthau, a Jew, become president. He simply had to be denied that possibility, no matter how slim the odds. Even as the situation currently stood, Morgenthau, as Treasury secretary, was next in line after the secretary of state. With Truman and Byrnes (the soon-to-be-named secretary of state) traveling together to Potsdam in a still volatile and dangerous Europe, if they should be killed, Morgenthau would become president. Therefore, Truman needed to make some changes within the next two months. Before setting off to Potsdam to determine Germany's and Japan's future, Truman would need to decide Morgenthau's fate as well.

As for Stimson, nearly seventy-eight and constantly battling health issues, he longed to retire as soon as the war was won, but not before completing one final task. Several years earlier President Roosevelt had asked him to perform a highly unusual, supremely secret assignment. On top of managing the mammoth War Department with its thirteen million soldiers, Stimson also oversaw the Manhattan Project. As attention turned to the Pacific theater, and victory seemed in sight, it was Stimson who eventually advocated dropping the atomic bombs. Thus, the man who had repeatedly urged kindness and Christianity toward the Germans was the same man who called for the use of nuclear weapons against the Japanese, resulting in the death and suffering of several hundred thousand innocent civilians. Remarkably, nearly every high-level official advising Truman, including Stimson, initially advocated actions that might very well have made the use of those bombs unnecessary. Each person who pled his case for mercy did so with a mixture of motives, but all of them believed that the mass murder of innocent civilians did not represent who they were as Americans. Harry Truman shared their sentiment, and then he overruled them all.

8 MANEUVER

Emperor Hirohito had good reason for concern. At the start of 1945, Japan's military leaders expected that punishing Allied bombings would continue. Taciturn and tightly self-controlled, the Emperor seldom spoke, except at times of great stress, when others noticed that he was speaking to himself. His slight frame and near-sightedness made him seem unimposing, but the outward appearance belied a surprisingly strong will.[179]

On New Year's Day, the Emperor and his Prime Minister exhorted their subjects to fight on to victory. America and Britain, the Prime Minister declared, "have been driven from Asiatic soil," but these enemies are again attempting to dominate Asia. It was time to "restore Greater East Asia to her true position."[180]

The Prime Minister warned his subjects that attacks from the air could intensify. He told the nation to "give full exercise to your creative thinking in order to improve your livelihood, strengthen the air-defense structure, and maintain your determination to fight through with tenacity until the final victory is won."[181] Creative thinking could do nothing to protect Japan from either the American fire bombings or the extraordinary new weapon that would devastate civilians before the year was out.

As the Japanese braced for attacks from the air, Germans witnessed relentless assaults from all directions. At the close of March, John McCloy boarded a plane to Europe. His mission was to assess conditions in Germany as Allied armies advanced east. He toured several cities and witnessed their near total destruction. It was obvious that economic life would be almost impossible to restore without foreign aid, and that anarchy could easily result if help was not forthcoming. McCloy met with several of the leading American generals, including Eisenhower. He intervened with one of them not to bomb the medieval city of Rothenburg, a town he had visited as a boy. Perhaps because of his intervention, the town was spared.[182] On April 12, McCloy returned to Paris, where he learned that President Roosevelt had died. McCloy felt the loss intensely. He had dealt with FDR since 1940, and had come to admire the President's exceptional gifts. McCloy must have struggled to envision Harry Truman as an adequate replacement for FDR.

Once Truman had been sworn in, it fell to Stimson to inform the new President about the bomb. The Secretary of War took Truman aside and obliquely referenced a new and extraordinarily powerful weapon, but he said no more about it at that time. Stimson wanted to prepare a clear and careful brief for Truman, summarizing the state of research and the bomb's possible impact. Two weeks later on April 25, Stimson met with the new President in the White House to lay out the essential facts. It was good news to Truman, who felt the weight of the war upon him.

This was not, in fact, the first time that the two men had discussed the bomb, though Truman had not known it at the time. As the junior senator from Missouri, Truman had staked out one issue for special focus: combatting governmental waste. Months earlier, he had instructed investigators to find out where the outrageously large expenditures for so-called construction projects were going. He had sent some investigators specifically to Tennessee and Washington state, where scientists were secretly at work on nuclear weapons. Learning of Truman's activities, Stimson came to see Truman in his Senate office. Truman respected Stimson, whose stature towered above most in the capitol. "Senator," Stimson said, "I can't tell you what it is, but it is the greatest project in the history of the world. It is most top secret. Many of the people who are actually engaged in the work have no idea what it is, and we who do would appreciate your not going into those plants."[183] It was a sobering encounter, and Truman called off the investigations.

Recognizing that Truman was greatly out of his depth, Stimson proposed convening a small committee of experts to advise the new President on atomic matters. Stimson christened it the Interim Committee, because he expected that after the war it would become a more permanent, official body, which eventually it did: the Atomic Energy Commission. For now, the Interim Committee's first and most pressing task was to advise the President on how best to use an atomic bomb on Japan.

Stimson convened the first meeting of the Interim Committee on May 9, 1945, just one day after Germany's surrender. The Committee continued to meet and debate the issues surrounding atomic power through July 19. Stimson had to choose the members of the Committee with care. They had to represent key government departments. They had to be men who could be trusted beyond doubt, as the bomb's secrecy remained paramount. And above all they needed to possess sound judgment. Two men proved natural fits. Ralph Bard was the undersecretary of the Navy. A Princeton graduate and former financier, Bard, like Stimson, had a history of successful service in both the private and the public sectors. Will Clayton was another valuable selection. Currently the Assistant Secretary of State for Economic Affairs, Clayton had previously been the largest cotton trader in the world. He brought with him a knowledge of international affairs. Stimson added three scientists intimately involved with the Manhattan Project: James Conant (president of Harvard), Vannevar Bush (president of the Carnegie Institution), and Karl Compton (president of the Massachusetts Institute of Technology). Believing that the President should have a personal representative on the Committee, Stimson suggested adding James Byrnes, the former South Carolina senator and Supreme Court judge, who was widely expected to be soon named secretary of state. Along with George L. Harrison (president of the New York Life Insurance Company and an assistant to Stimson who chaired the Committee when Stimson was absent), these eight men held the greatest influence over Truman's final decisions about the bomb.

With Italy and Germany defeated, the most pressing question facing Washington was how best to compel a Japanese surrender. If the atomic bomb, Plan A, looked attractive to some, it brought with it unprecedented technological and ethical dilemmas. Plan B, blockade and invade, looked even less appealing, as it seemed certain to cost many American lives. Stimson fretted about both options, and he was not alone. From May through July, Stimson and other top leaders began a fervent, sometimes desperate, search for a third way. They needed a Plan C, an approach that would produce Japan's surrender without a terrible cost in lives. By early May, most of Truman's top advisors believed they knew the answer. The challenge lay in convincing Truman to adopt it.

Thanks to the outstanding work of American cryptographers, American intelligence officials had cracked the Japanese government's secret diplomatic and military code in a project dubbed "Magic." For most of the war, US leaders had been reading the cables that key Japanese officials were exchanging. These strongly suggested that unless the Americans relented on their demands for unconditional surrender, the Japanese military intended to fight to the bitter end. No surrender would be accepted if it meant that the Emperor could be dethroned and possibly hanged as a war criminal – the fate that was expected to befall the top Nazis. The Magic intercepts also suggested that at least some within the Japanese leadership were willing to surrender under certain conditions, primary among them being the retention of the Emperor. Remarkably, nearly every top American official believed that the United States should modify its demand for unconditional surrender to allow the Emperor to remain on the throne. They felt strongly that if the Japanese could be induced to surrender, many lives, both Allied and Japanese, would be spared.[184]

Joseph Grew stepped forward as one of the most ardent advocates for Plan C, conditional surrender. Grew, the former ambassador to Japan, had recently been elevated to acting secretary of state, and his views carried substantial weight. After ten eventful years in Tokyo and six months under confinement in the Embassy, Grew returned to America and embarked on a speaking tour across the country to explain why the Emperor should remain on the throne after the war. Given his long experience with and close-hand knowledge of Japanese society and government, his opinion should have proved persuasive to Truman.

Grew, like so many of the men in leading positions within the government, possessed precisely the kind of pedigree that Truman lacked. Born into a wealthy, established Boston family (his great-grandfather had been present during the American Revolution), Grew enjoyed privileges unknown to the new President. While Truman had not traveled outside America until his thirties when he served in WWI, Grew had first toured Europe as a seven-year-old on a family trip.[185] At age twelve he entered Groton, the elite boarding school that FDR attended along with him. Led by the Reverend Endicott Peabody, Groton aimed to instill in young boys a virtuous Christian character. And like FDR, Grew transitioned from Groton to Harvard, where he became a senior editor of the *Crimson*, while FDR served on the staff. After graduating, Grew embarked on an expedition: bear hunting in Kashmir, then on to tiger hunting in China. He later reflected that this adventure infused in him a love of travel and prompted him to join the foreign service.[186] For Grew, Franklin Roosevelt was truly a man of his ilk. The contrast with Truman had to seem jarring.

On May 28, Grew met with Truman to make his case for altering American demands. The Japanese, he explained, would defend their Emperor to the death. It made no sense to keep fighting a war of attrition in which unknown thousands would die, if Japan's surrender could be achieved sooner and without such terrible costs. There was another important advantage to leaving the Emperor in power. After the war, America's occupation would be far easier if the Emperor instructed his people to cooperate with the occupiers. Like Stimson, Grew grasped that mercy and moderation were in America's own best interests. In short, from Grew's perspective, it would be foolhardy to insist on unconditional surrender. Truman implied that he agreed, but he suggested that Grew run his proposal past the Navy and War secretaries. Truman was developing the habit of redirecting awkward proposals elsewhere.

Grew may have had an additional reason for pushing conditional surrender. He deeply disliked communism and detested what the Soviets were doing in Eastern Europe. As a member of the upper class, his opposition to communism was understandable, and as a Christian, his position was even clearer. Grew fully expected that if the war in the Pacific dragged on, the Soviets would enter and extend their influence. He feared that inevitably the Soviets would lure both China and Japan into their orbit. Conditional surrender held the added advantage of potentially ending the war before the Soviets could intervene.[187]

That same day, McCloy made a similar appeal to Stimson. McCloy urged modifying American demands because he did not believe that the United States should impose a Carthaginian peace on Japan. His language harkened back to Stimson's own words and reasoning during the bitter debate with Morgenthau over Germany's fate. McCloy wanted to jettison the unconditional surrender requirement altogether. It struck him as madness to insist on unconditionality if relenting on this point might end the war with America having achieved virtually all of its war aims without further loss of life. Stimson did not need persuading. He fully agreed. The shift in policy could be made even easier by the

Joint Chiefs of Staff, who around this time were also arguing for relaxing the terms of surrender. The major players all agreed that unconditional surrender made no sense. The problem was in convincing Truman to modify his uncompromising stance. But if Grew and others within the government could not convince the President, perhaps an outsider might.

Stimson's Trojan Horse

Hoping to blunt the worst effects of Morgenthau's influence on Germany, Stimson had been scheming to bring former president Herbert Hoover into the decision-making process.[188] The situation in Europe was grim, and the food crisis loomed ominously ahead. Hoover had gained international acclaim for his role in organizing food supplies for Belgium during WWI. A gifted mining engineer, Hoover had a rare talent for logistics. His compassion led him to focus on famine relief. Having become a household name as the savior of Americans seeking to evacuate Europe after the war began, he eventually rode his fame to the White House. Unfortunately, after less than a year, his predecessors' failure to regulate financial markets facilitated the Wall Street crash and subsequent Great Depression, for which Hoover was blamed. With Franklin Roosevelt's victory in 1932, Hoover entered a kind of political exile, almost never being invited back to the White House. Stimson now sought to correct this.

Still smarting over his treatment by Roosevelt, and not wanting to be seen as an interloper, Hoover repeatedly refused to come to Washington unless President Truman extended the invitation himself. Stimson prodded Truman to avail himself of Hoover's talents, but an offer was slow to materialize. Hoover began to doubt that the new administration was any more interested in him than the previous one had been. Finally, Truman made the move that Stimson had been pushing for. Once Truman realized that Hoover's expertise would be invaluable, he extended an invitation. Truman had the political savvy to recognize that some of his staff would object to the unpopular, anti-New Deal Republican being summoned for his counsel. To prevent their sabotaging the invitation, Truman wrote out the letter to Hoover by hand and mailed it himself.[189]

Figure 8.1 President Harry Truman greets former president Herbert Hoover at the White House, 1950. Photo by © CORBIS/Corbis via Getty Images.

On the morning of May 28, Hoover arrived at the White House and spent just under an hour in conversation with Truman, mainly discussing the European food crisis and how America could help to remedy it. Hoover tried to use only simple, one-syllable words when speaking with the new President, evidence of how little he thought of Truman's intellect.[190] Just as Joseph Grew had to marvel at the social distance between himself and Truman, Hoover must have been equally struck by the differences. The contrast between the former president and the current one was striking. Hoover had graduated from Stanford. Truman possessed a high school diploma. Hoover began as a mining engineer who devised breakthrough techniques in his field. Truman tried to run a clothing store in Missouri, which went bankrupt. Hoover was a self-made millionaire. Truman hoped that a government pension would support him and his wife in their retirement. Hoover had been named secretary of commerce because of his sheer brilliance, tenacity, and remarkable ability to get things done. Truman had only entered politics by chance, succeeding thanks to a corrupt party boss and his political machine. Hoover won the presidency because he was a national hero, a great humanitarian who saved millions from starvation in WWI.

Truman became president only because every other plausible Roosevelt running mate had too much baggage, and Truman's relative obscurity made him difficult to attack. Hoover could scarcely believe that such a man as Truman now occupied the presidency.

Stimson, too, could hardly have held Truman in high regard. Stimson, a Yale and Harvard graduate, was arguably the most venerable American statesman alive. He knew that Truman, vastly out of his depth and likely overwhelmed, needed every possible expert to guide him at this crucial moment in the war and thereafter. Stimson was counting on this meeting to convince Truman that America's punitive policy toward Germany, embodied in JCS 1067, would exacerbate the humanitarian disaster on the horizon. As Hoover described the steps that America would need to take, Truman recognized both the urgency of the situation and the moral imperative to act. Hoover was having precisely the impact that Stimson had hoped for. Two weeks earlier, on Sunday, May 13, Hoover and Stimson had met privately to strategize for this meeting, if it should come to pass.[191] Now it looked like their plans might be paying off.

But then Hoover did something surprising. He expanded his talking points far beyond the problem of postwar food relief. In the course of their discussions, Hoover also presented Truman with his ideas for how to end the war with Japan. Hoover suggested that if the Japanese were clearly informed that they could preserve their way of life, including the Emperor, then they might surrender and many lives would be saved. As he saw it, conditional surrender made sense because America will have obtained its objectives, "except perhaps the vengeance of an excited minority of our people." And if America could achieve Japan's surrender under these terms, Hoover reiterated that "We would have saved the lives of 500,000 to one million American boys, the loss of which may be necessary by going on to the end."[192]

Truman asked Hoover to put his suggestions in a memorandum, and when Hoover followed up with it the next day, Truman forwarded it to his top officials, including Grew. Presumably the President wanted the Japan expert's analysis. On June 13, Grew replied that the State Department was largely in agreement with the essence of Hoover's thinking and was in the process of preparing postwar policies along those lines. But just to ensure that Truman got the point, Grew concluded his response by reiterating that "Every evidence, without exception, indicates that [the safety of the Emperor and] the preservation of the institution of the throne comprise irreducible Japanese terms."[193] Grew was backing up Hoover, as Stimson almost certainly knew he would. The proponents of conditional surrender were nudging the new President closer toward their view – or so they thought.

Alternatives to the A-Bomb

A number of top officials shared Stimson's humanitarian concerns. They expressed reservations about the bomb's use without warnings to the populace. On May 31, the Committee talked through the options one by one, and each time someone proposed a less direct attack on civilians, others would oppose it. General George Marshall suggested using it first on a naval installation where few civilians would be harmed, but some felt that this would not make a sufficiently convincing impact on Japanese leaders. Others raised the possibility of announcing where and when the bomb would be detonated, in order that civilians could evacuate the area. This idea was rejected out of the reasonable fear that the Japanese military would assemble American prisoners of war in the area to be bombed. The Committee's objections were not based on cruelty or hatred of the Japanese, though many likely harbored resentment over Japanese atrocities throughout the war, of which there were many. The Committee could not have been entirely immune to the revulsion that most Americans felt as news of the Imperial Army's actions spread.

The American public's animosity toward Japan stemmed not solely from the murder of more than 2,000 sailors at Pearl Harbor. The public also learned of the Rape of Nanking, in which Japanese soldiers tortured, mutilated, raped, and murdered hundreds of thousands of Chinese citizens in an unprovoked orgy of violence that made even some Nazis in China queasy.[194] During the Bataan Death March of 1942, thousands of Filipino prisoners were starved, beaten, and killed in a now infamous forced march through the jungle. Japanese soldiers beheaded American prisoners and took photographs as proof. The US government obtained and released some of these photos to the public. In 1945, the public outrage hardened many Americans toward all Japanese. Only after the war would the world learn of the horrific Japanese medical experiments conducted on prisoners, procedures closely resembling those of Nazi experiments overseen by Dr. Josef Mengele in concentration camps.

Brutal as the Japanese Army's behavior had been, the American military inflicted its own brand of barbarity. Ground combat became ferocious and tinged with racial hatred. Creating their personal war trophies, some soldiers cut off the ears and other body parts of Japanese killed in battle. The practice became sufficiently common that commanders had to officially forbid mutilation. From the air the United States employed devastatingly harsh tactics as well. Arguably the cruelest attacks came on the night of March 9, 1945, when 300 B-29s fire bombed Tokyo. Because Japanese homes were mostly constructed of wood, the city ignited in a firestorm. People were burned alive and reduced to ash. Some tried to escape the heat by leaping into rivers and canals and were boiled to death as the fires spread. Waves of bombers continued their assault at low altitudes, striking buildings with relentless efficiency. In the end, an estimated 87,000 people, most of them civilians, died that night. More than one million were left homeless. Some believe that the death toll was actually over 100,000. Whatever the true figure, the Americans had made their point: civilians will be treated as combatants. This was total war, and the population would not be spared. The aim was to break the Japanese will to fight, but one has to wonder whether the average Japanese survivor of the fire bombings would have reached the opposite conclusion. Perhaps the Americans seemed so cruel that many Japanese people reasoned it would be better to die fighting than to suffer under American occupation.[195]

The Interim Committee hoped that the atomic bomb would shock Japanese leaders into recognizing the futility of continuing the war. The bomb was intended more as a psychological operation than a military attack. Striking a naval base was seen as lessening the bomb's effectiveness. Stimson concluded the meeting with the general agreement that no warning would be given, that the bomb would not be used on a civilian area, but that it should attempt to make a profound psychological impact on the Japanese people. Conant suggested striking a military base that was close to workers' homes. Of course, it would hardly be possible to avoid harming civilians if the bomb was used against a military base surrounded by houses. Historians have noted this contradiction between not wanting to harm civilians and yet hoping to make a deep psychological impression on the population. Scholars have assumed that American officials were simply deceiving themselves, not wishing to face the true horror of what they were planning. This is possible, but another possibility is that American leaders were caught between two conflicting aims and simply did their best to find a middle ground: impress the population with the power of the bomb, but do it in a way that at least sought to limit the number of civilian casualties.

At this point in the war, no one knew for certain if the A-bomb would even work. American leaders had to plan for a ground assault on Japan as one possible option for ending the war. Naturally, the new President wanted to minimize American casualties in the final push for Japan's surrender. Hoover's memorandum to Truman suggesting that an invasion could cost between five hundred thousand and one million American lives had its intended effect. It prompted the President to request a meeting with his top military leaders to discuss the invasion plan. On June 17, the night before that meeting, McCloy stopped by Stimson's home to debate the surrender question again. It was not their practice to overrule or overtly disagree with military commanders. They believed in showing deference to military expertise. Stimson saw his role as providing the President with political analysis of military decisions. Both men seemed frustrated that they could not prevent the Army's invasion plans. Both Stimson and McCloy realized that surrender might be achieved without an invasion, and Stimson hoped it could occur without use of the bomb. The next day's meeting would be crucial.

McCloy wanted the President to assure the Japanese Emperor that he could remain, and to threaten use of a dreadful new weapon if they did not surrender. Stimson agreed. But later that night Stimson phoned McCloy to say that he was too ill to attend. His migraines had become debilitating. He asked McCloy to be at the White House in his place.

The following afternoon when McCloy arrived at the meeting, he found that Stimson had dragged himself out of bed, a testament to both the meeting's significance and Stimson's willpower. Truman asked about casualties, and General Marshall did not give any direct answer, though he did say that the initial phase would likely cost 31,000 men. Stimson said little throughout, but he suggested that a submerged class of Japanese liberals still existed and we should try to encourage them. He was attempting to say, indirectly, that the demand for unconditional surrender would weaken this liberal faction. Admiral William Leahy was more direct. He stated that demanding unconditional surrender would only intensify the Japanese intention to fight harder, which would increase casualties. He found unconditional surrender unnecessary and unwise.

Thinking politically, Truman replied that it was too early to change public opinion on this point.[196]

Much of the historical scholarship about this crucial White House discussion relates a curious anecdote.[197] Allegedly, as the meeting was about to adjourn, Truman abruptly turned to McCloy and said that nobody leaves this room without stating his view. The President wanted to know what McCloy thought of the invasion plan. It was a remarkably democratic impulse on Truman's part. McCloy looked over at Stimson, who said that he should say what he thinks, knowing precisely what McCloy would say: "Well, I do think you've got an alternative, and I think it is an alternative that ought to be explored." Then, with disarming frankness, unable to conceal his frustration with the invasion plan, McCloy added that "really, we ought to have our heads examined if we don't explore some other method by which we can terminate this war than by just another conventional attack and landing." Truman seemed receptive, but he recommended that McCloy discuss it with Byrnes.[198] With the President's apparent approval, the momentum toward conditional surrender seemed unstoppable. The momentum aspect is apparent, but the exchange between Truman and McCloy does not appear in the minutes for this meeting. Instead, that aspect of the story was related by McCloy in an interview in the 1960s. Because McCloy depicts himself as central to the event, and since his is the only source describing it, the account must be taken with some skepticism.

The next morning the three national security departments, War, State, and Navy, met to begin drafting the surrender policy for Japan. Over the next few weeks they crafted the language for the Potsdam Declaration, a message to Japan outlining the terms of surrender. With McCloy spearheading the project, the terms clearly stated that Japan could have a constitutional monarchy with the Emperor at its head. This was Plan C, and it looked like it might succeed. But even if it failed, even if the Japanese leadership rejected it outright, it felt to its supporters as the ethical and sensible plan to pursue. It offered the possibility of ending the war without either invasion or atomic attack, both of which would inflict great suffering. Conditional surrender did contain some risk. The Emperor's mere existence served as a rallying point for Japanese militarists. There could be no guarantee that fanatical warriors would not continue fighting Americans during occupation, in the name of their Emperor. But the odds of stifling an insurgency had to appear far greater if the Emperor commanded his people to cooperate with the occupiers than if the Emperor were tried as a war criminal or hanged. As the overwhelming majority of key civilian and military advisors saw it, Plan C simply had to be pursued, even if its odds of success were small. And since the Magic intercepts indicated signs that some within the Japanese leadership were receptive to conditional surrender, the prospects appeared promising.

Stimson clearly wanted to avoid the needless suffering of innocent civilians. His behavior mirrored the same principles he followed in his battles with Morgenthau over the postwar treatment of Germany. He objected to purely punitive measures. While one survey of American GIs serving in the Pacific showed that forty-two percent favored annihilating the entire Japanese race,[199] the War Secretary harbored no such hatred. In fact he went to unusual lengths to save the city of Kyoto from attack. His compassion extended beyond the nuclear issue. He also tried to halt the Army Air Corps' indiscriminate use of fire bombing. On May 16, Stimson told Truman that he wanted to hold the Air Force to precision bombing in Japan because "the reputation of the United States for fair play and humanitarianism is the world's biggest asset for peace in the coming decades." And he added, "I believe the same rule sparing the civilian population should be applied as far as possible to the use of any new weapon."[200] But with fire bombings, as with so many other crucial issues, Stimson could not stop his generals from implementing their most brutal plans.

9 REGRET

Truman's military and civilian advisors were not the only ones to press for some kind of warning before dropping the bomb. Nearly 150 of the scientists in the Manhattan Project came to have second thoughts about the bomb's use. Several of the most outspoken of these tried to reach Truman directly. Leo Szilard, a Hungarian-born physicist, was the loudest of the concerned scientists. Ironically, he was the man most responsible for the bomb's creation. One day in 1938, Szilard was crossing the street in London when an unexpected flash of insight struck him dumb. In the few short steps it took to cross over, Szilard saw in his mind's eye exactly how a nuclear chain reaction could be achieved. Suddenly the seemingly impossible problem of releasing nuclear energy seemed plausible. It was one of those rare moments of understanding that would change the world forever.

Szilard quickly worked out his calculations and published his findings. The greatest source of energy ever known could be unlocked and harnessed for humanity. It could also, he realized, be twisted toward use as a weapon of mass destruction. As a refugee fleeing Nazi control of Europe, Szilard had every reason to fear that German scientists would be hard at work on exactly that evil end. Word within the scientific community spread that German physicists had made advances in this direction in 1939. If free peoples did not beat the Nazis in the race for discovery, humanity's fate looked grim. Szilard understood that he had a responsibility to mobilize the governments of Britain and America toward winning that race.

At the start of August 1939, just one month before the outbreak of WWII, Albert Einstein sent President Roosevelt a now famous letter. The most renowned scientist in the world informed the President that in the past four months there had been breakthroughs in creating a nuclear chain reaction. Uranium could be harnessed to release vast amounts of energy. This meant that it might be possible to produce a weapon more powerful than any ever created – and the Germans were hard at work on the problem.[201] Roosevelt took notice. Perhaps he might not have done, if he had known that Einstein was not the letter's true author. The real writer was Szilard, who had persuaded his older colleague Einstein to contact the American president and implore him to develop the weapon before the Nazis got there first.

Roosevelt immediately grasped what Einstein's letter implied. If enough money and know-how were focused on the quest, America might develop a weapon that could end the war. He ordered leading experts to begin exploring the possibility of an atomic bomb. The race was on, a race to discover nature's most awesome force. Much later, long after Hiroshima and Nagasaki, Einstein looked back on his letter to Roosevelt as the greatest regret of his life.[202]

Despite their initial enthusiasm, once Germany had surrendered and America had the ability to deploy the bomb against Japanese civilians, many of the leading scientists working on the Manhattan Project began having second thoughts. A full six years, two billion dollars, and an incalculable measure of human effort later, Szilard's flash of insight on a London street had crossed over into its dreadful reality. Rather than being used to deter Hitler, which was no longer necessary, the first atomic bombs were targeting Japanese civilians. Szilard felt impelled to stuff the genie, the one whom he, himself, had conjured, back into its bottle – if it was not already too late. Although his gifts lay in science, not politics, Szilard did possess enough political acumen to know that he could not solve this problem alone.

James Franck had been one of Germany's most prominent physicists. A professor at the University of Göttingen, Franck's research into the behavior of electrons had earned him the Nobel Prize for Physics in 1925. But when the Nazi Party came to power in 1933, Franck's career, like that of so many Jewish German professionals, took a traumatic turn. In April of that year the Nazis passed a law banning Jews from civil service. Because Franck had fought in WWI, he could have remained in his position, at least for the time being. But Franck resigned in protest and wisely left Germany for Denmark in November. In 1935, he emigrated to America to assume a position at the Johns Hopkins University, and three years later moved to the University of Chicago. There he collaborated on research with Edward Teller. When the Manhattan Project began, Franck was a natural fit to head its metallurgical research section. What Teller did not expect was Franck's subsequent change of heart regarding the bomb's use.

In the summer of 1945, as scientists earnestly debated the bomb's humanitarian and postwar political implications, Arthur Compton appointed Franck to head a subcommittee on the social and political dimensions of their work. Gathering at night, a group of seven scientists, including Leo Szilard, drafted what would become known as "The Franck Report."

Breaking with many of their fellow scientists, Franck, Szilard, and the others called on Stimson not to let America use the bomb on Japan without first providing a demonstration of its power on an uninhabited island. Only if this failed to convince Japanese leaders to surrender, the group insisted, should the United States consider actually detonating the bomb over a military target where civilians would not be killed. Part of their rationale had a political as well as a humanitarian aspect. The Franck group believed that using the bomb on Japan would cause the Soviets to fear and distrust America, which would then automatically trigger an arms race. Russia and China, they explained, were the only two nations that could survive a nuclear attack, given their immense population and vast territory over which they could disperse their vital industries. The scientists claimed that "even though these countries value human life less than the peoples of Western Europe and America," they would still shudder at the losses that nuclear strikes would inflict. If the United States used the bomb on Japan, then Russia and China would conclude that their security rested on their independent control of an atomic arsenal. The Franck group was convinced that international control was vital for world peace.

There was a sadness around Franck's eyes, as if he bore the sorrows of many others, not simply his own. Though his mustache remained thick, his hair had severely receded and age spots marked his face. On June 11, Franck traveled to Washington to hand deliver the report to Stimson. He was met by an aide who informed the scientist that the Secretary was out of town. The aide was lying, but there was little more that Franck could do. The scientists had tried to influence a political and military process, and they hit an unbreakable bureaucratic wall. We don't know if Stimson ever read or even saw their report.

At the close of their sixteen-page analysis, the scientists predicted that if America used the bombs without first demonstrating their power on a barren island, then the United States would "sacrifice public support throughout the world, precipitate the race of armaments, and prejudice the possibility of reaching an international agreement on the future control of such weapons."[203] Franck and his colleagues were proved right with their second and third predictions. The Soviets began an arms race, and hopes of international control over nuclear energy quickly evaporated. But they were wrong that America would lose the world's support. On the contrary, after the war America emerged as a flawed but still admirable defender of international human rights.

The outspoken scientists could be dismissed as too far from the mainstream. After all, they represented only a faction within the Manhattan Project's scientific community. Robert Oppenheimer, the Manhattan Project's brilliant, Jewish, chain-smoking chief scientist, urged the bomb's use as soon as possible. But a different voice, very much from within the establishment, strongly dissented, and this voice could not be as easily discounted.

As undersecretary of the Navy, Ralph Bard was a member of the Interim Committee. He was therefore privy to the discussions over the use of nuclear weapons. He had sat and listened to the debates. He had heard his colleagues call for the destruction of entire cities and the murder of Japanese civilians with this wholly new weapon equivalent to 20,000 tons of TNT. And as the days and weeks passed, the prospect of it gnawed at him. It just didn't feel right. At last, on June 27, Bard took a brave stand. Alone on the Interim Committee, Bard proposed what all others on the Committee had rejected: Plan D, a demonstration. He typed a one-page note to Stimson outlining his minority view. These three short paragraphs are worth quoting in full, because they represent a remarkably courageous stand against his colleagues' recommendations.

> Ever since I have been in touch with this program I have had a feeling that before the bomb is actually used against Japan that Japan should have some preliminary warning for say two or three days in advance of use. The position of the United States as

a great humanitarian nation and the fair play attitude of our people generally is responsible in the main for this feeling.

In other words, Americans are good people, and we should not use this weapon without fair warning.

During recent weeks I have also had the feeling very definitely that the Japanese government may be searching for some opportunity which they could use as a medium of surrender. Following the three-power conference, emissaries from this country could contact representatives from Japan somewhere on the China Coast and make representations with regard to Russia's position and at the same time give them some information regarding the proposed use of atomic power, together with whatever assurances the President might care to make with regard to the Emperor of Japan and the treatment of the Japanese nation following unconditional surrender. It seems quite possible to me that this presents the opportunity which the Japanese are looking for.

Bard was arguing that if the United States explained to Japanese leaders exactly what was in store for them, there was a chance they might surrender. A combination of Plans C and D, conditional surrender plus a demonstration, might just do the trick.

I don't see that we have anything particular to lose in following such a program. The stakes are so tremendous that it is my opinion very real consideration should be given to some plan of this kind. I do not believe under present circumstances existing that there is anyone in this country whose evaluation of the chances of the success of such a program is worth a great deal. The only way to find out is to try it out.

In other words, no one has any idea whether a demonstration will work. We have nothing to lose by trying, and will inflict great cruelty on the innocent if we don't.

The following day, June 28, Stimson received Bard's memo. Apparently, it did not persuade the War Secretary to press for a warning as Bard suggested. But Bard felt strongly enough about the matter that he went to see the President. After the war, Bard told an interviewer that he urged Truman to issue a warning first, and the President told him that the matter had been carefully considered.[204] Truman thanked Bard for his input, and sent him on his way. Strangely, there are no known records of this meeting. The President's calendar shows no entries concerning conversations with Bard at this time.[205]

We are left to imagine what Bard said to the President. If this meeting actually occurred, was it heated? Was Bard impassioned in his plea for a demonstration? Was Truman adamant in his refusal? We may never know. But we do know that three days later, Bard resigned.[206]

Why would a man near the pinnacle of power suddenly step down? Ralph Bard had been a successful financial investor in Chicago when his old friend Frank Knox, secretary of the Navy, asked him to serve as assistant secretary in 1941, roughly nine months before Pearl Harbor. He quickly took to the position, demonstrating confidence and competence. In April 1943, Bard traveled to Pearl Harbor to inspect the naval base. He even engaged in target practice. Looking dapper in his

Figure 9.1 Assistant Secretary of the Navy Ralph Austin Bard shoots a pistol on a target range during an inspection of the Pacific Fleet base at Pearl Harbor in Hawaii in April 1943. Photo by Paul Popper/Popperfoto via Getty Images/Getty Images.

suit and hat, as if he had just been sipping martinis over lunch, Bard casually fired off a shot as if he did that every day. A photo of his inspection tour shows him staring down the barrel of his gun, aiming at something in the distance, with one eye squinting and his left fist resting comfortably on his hip, as Admiral Chester Nimitz peers through field glasses toward the target. Bard seemed every bit the civilian in charge. The lines that curved downward from his nose to his mouth cut a distinctive chasm in his face. At a time when conformity was prized, there was something different about him, beyond the outward appearance. In June 1944, he was promoted to undersecretary, the Navy's second in command. Even then, Bard stood out. Posing with Secretary Forrestal, Bard sported a bow tie, an unusual accoutrement for the occasion.

During WWII, the Department of Defense did not yet exist. America's national security establishment consisted of the "Big Three": the State Department, the War Department (which contained the Army and its air corps), and the Navy. As the number two man at the Navy, Bard wielded substantial authority. Why would he have stepped down from such a powerful position before the war was won? Even Stimson, seventy-seven and in failing health, willed himself to stay on until the war's conclusion. What impelled Bard to resign just when victory was in sight?

Bard had asked President Roosevelt permission to resign one year earlier, but FDR had insisted he remain. It is entirely plausible that his resignation in 1945 was simply the result of overwork, though the timing does seem peculiar. Perhaps Bard intended to step down at the earliest possible opportunity, but his meeting with Truman and the break with the Committee over the bomb may have convinced him that he could no longer serve in good conscience. Perhaps unable to accept the President's decision, and unwilling to be associated with a nuclear strike on innocent civilians when, in his view, it was not yet necessary, he chose to walk away. But this is merely speculation. Bard did not voice such qualms about the bomb, but he did confess to being extremely anxious that no one should think his resignation had resulted from a dispute with the President. In fact, Bard went to considerable lengths to shape the narrative surrounding his resignation. He sent dozens of letters to colleagues, friends, and journalists, each containing essentially the same wording. He parted with Truman on amicable terms. He would be consulting for the Navy in future. And everything was perfectly fine. Among the first he contacted was the journalist Walter Lippmann. Possibly attempting to head off any rumors, Bard wrote: "I am particularly anxious to have you know the background of this whole matter which was explained in my letter to the President and his reply." And in each of these several dozen such letters, Bard included copies of his official resignation letter to Truman along with the President's gracious reply.[207] Naturally, Bard would not, and indeed could not, mention to anyone his disagreement over the use of the atomic bomb, because no one in the public could know about the bomb.

It was not surprising that Bard chose to notify Lippmann, as Lippmann was one of the foremost journalists and influencers of the day. Throughout much of the twentieth century, Lippmann made a powerful mark. He worked on President Wilson's "Fourteen Points" speech to Congress. He popularized the term "Cold War." And he received two Pulitzer Prizes for his reporting. In the 1940s, Lippmann had already established himself as a leading public intellectual, but his views did not emerge in a vacuum. His thinking was shaped early in his career by a close friend with whom he shared a two-story red brick house in Washington's Dupont Circle in the 1910s and early 1920s. Their home became known among the intellectual elite for its salons, where crucial issues were debated and bonds of friendship were forged. In time their shabby bachelor pad was dubbed the "House of Truth." It was in fact a crucible of modern American liberalism. Out of those conversations the *New Republic* was born, a magazine that would articulate their ideals and bring them to a wider audience. Lippmann's close friend and housemate, the one who greatly influenced his views, was the same man who seemed always to be intimately connected to every major player in the Washington elite: Felix Frankfurter.[208]

Should Bard's proposal have been adopted? The idea of a demonstration had been discussed previously within the Interim Committee. The group rejected the suggestion for fear that the bomb might not work. But the Committee may have been unwise to dismiss the idea for that reason. If the bomb had failed to detonate during a demonstration, the United States would still have another to use if necessary. The momentary embarrassment of a failed detonation had to be weighed against the possibility of saving several hundred thousand innocent lives.

The other reason for rejecting the idea involved the shock factor. The Committee believed that the bomb's greatest value would be its psychological impact on the Japanese people and its leaders. The Committee felt that a demonstration would not have had as powerful an effect as its use on the population. But this, too, may have been an inaccurate assumption. The impact from a demonstration might have been even greater than that from the bomb's actual use. It would have allowed Japanese representatives to witness the mushroom cloud for themselves, rather than simply hearing about it second-hand. Cruel as it would be to place animals on that island, for Japanese representatives witnessing the aftereffects on those sacrificial creatures, the impression would have been profound. A demonstration over an uninhabited island would have left the bomb's true impact on cities and civilians to the imagination.

Perhaps the most compelling reason for a demonstration comes, inadvertently, from one of the most forceful defenders of the bomb's use on Japanese civilians. Historian Richard Frank has argued that the use of the bombs convinced Japanese leaders that the United States would not need to invade the Japanese homeland, and postwar interviews with Japanese leaders bear this out. Given that their only hope of avoiding total defeat had been to grind down the invading armies in a battle of attrition, the bombs removed that last hope. The A-bombs made invasion unnecessary.[209] But if Frank is correct that the bombs made the crucial difference in their decision to surrender, then it was merely the existence of the bombs, and not their use, which made the difference. The demonstration of the bombs' existence was all that was needed to convince them that the Allies had no need to invade.[210]

The United States was bluffing by claiming that it would continue to use atomic bombs until Japan either surrendered or was utterly destroyed. After the test of a nuclear device in the New Mexico desert, the United States only possessed two remaining A-bombs, although more were in production. Given that they were already bluffing, American officials could have told Japanese representatives that the demonstration bomb was merely a smaller version of the actual A-bomb. The psychological impact of this claim might well have proved decisive.

Ralph Bard was correct about one thing. It was impossible to know what the effect of a demonstration would be, but that was not the point. The aim of a demonstration would have been to make the use of the bombs on innocent civilians unnecessary. As he put it, the odds of success were probably small, but given the cost in lives, it was a chance worth taking.

Undermine

Back in 1944, as President Roosevelt's administration began more serious policy planning for postwar Japan, Morgenthau had been too occupied with his bureaucratic battles over postwar Germany and his oversight of the efforts to rescue Jews from Europe to focus on other issues. But by May 1945, he was finally able to turn some of his attention to the Far East. The Departments of State, War, and Navy were entrenching their control over Japan policy, and Morgenthau wanted in. He hoped to have the same influence over the treatment of Japan that he was exerting over Germany. This time, Morgenthau's bureaucratic opponents had the upper hand. Key State Department officials had no intention of allowing him to hinder Japan's economic recovery as he had been trying to do with Germany. They shuddered at the idea of returning Japan to an agrarian society, as a strong, democratic Japan would be central to their vision of a stable postwar world. State Department officials could not stomach Morgenthau's meddling in an area where they felt that the Treasury Secretary had neither any right to intercede nor any knowledge of the situation. It proved especially irksome to Joseph Grew, the acting secretary of state.

On June 25, 1945, Morgenthau called Grew at the State Department to discuss the Treasury's interest in the shaping of postwar policy for Japan. According to Grew's notes of the conversation, Morgenthau sounded frustrated that he was being excluded. He argued that he had input over policy toward Germany and Austria, and since there were financial matters at stake, he should be involved in Japan's policy as well. Grew parried Morgenthau's assertions by explaining that a knowledge of Japan was necessary. Morgenthau asked to be given access to the report that the State was preparing, and Grew blithely informed him that nothing was crystallized yet, that the report was still in development, and that he would be given a copy "in due course."[211] This was a classic Washington brush-off, and Morgenthau, for once, was stymied.

Morgenthau's days in government were numbered, though he could not know precisely how his enemies were outflanking him.

While Grew was blocking him from meddling in Japan policy, Stimson tightened the screws. On July 3, 1945, Stimson met with Truman to advise the President on his own vision for a postwar peace. The War Secretary cautioned that America was about to undertake the largest occupation and rehabilitation program in its history. It could only succeed by not allowing "the element of vengeance" to muddy their plans. As Stimson saw it, the war criminals must be punished, but the rest of the German population and nation must be rehabilitated. Truman agreed.

Stimson then filled Truman in on the debate over postwar plans and Morgenthau's meddling at Quebec. Truman said that he had heard about this and laughed. Stimson presented the episode as having backfired on the Treasury, once the Morgenthau Plan leaked to the press and caused an uproar, forcing Roosevelt to distance himself from it. Stimson then related his lunch meeting with Roosevelt at that time, when they discussed the idea of deindustrializing Germany to convert it to a pastoral country and Stimson's opposition to such a scheme. Morgenthau had always held the upper hand while FDR was president, but now Roosevelt was gone, and so too was Morgenthau's advantage. At last, Stimson could exert some sway over the President. He told Truman that the idea of creating a pastoral Germany had not passed and noted recent comments by the influential financier Bernard Baruch on the subject. Truman retorted that "they were all alike – they couldn't keep from meddling in it." By "they," Truman presumably meant the Jews.[212]

Two days later on July 5, Truman told Morgenthau that he was considering appointing a new Treasury secretary but that he had not yet reached a final decision. The President would be taking his new secretary of state, James Byrnes, to the Potsdam Conference, but Morgenthau would not be accompanying them. It was an especially crushing blow for Morgenthau, who coveted the secretary of state post for himself. He also deeply disliked Byrnes. It was clear that Truman did not desire Morgenthau's services. With Roosevelt gone, Morgenthau had lost his link to power within the administration, and shortly after this meeting he submitted his resignation. The longest-serving secretary of the Treasury, the man who had for twelve years repeatedly bent the policy process to his will, finally found himself unceremoniously removed from power.

Figure 9.2 American general George Patton (left), known as "Old Blood And Guts," inspecting the 2nd Armored Division in Berlin with Assistant Secretary of War John McCloy (middle), and American Secretary of War Henry Stimson, July 23, 1945. Photo by Keystone/Getty Images.

With Morgenthau seemingly defeated, Stimson was free to thwart the harsh peace for Germany, but the Presidential Directive made any softening of occupation policy unlikely. While the Potsdam Conference was underway in July, Stimson lunched with General Eisenhower, who was then commanding the American-occupied zone of Germany, and Eisenhower's deputy, General Lucius Clay. Stimson told the generals about his time as governor-general of the Philippines. He believed that the current harsh peace against Germany failed to learn from America's experience in that earlier occupation.[213] The same was true of the post-WWI settlement, he explained. Still hoping to blunt the impact of Morgenthau's intentions, Stimson took the astonishing step of advising his military commanders to disregard official US policy. "Don't put too much effort in carrying out [your orders] the way they're written."[214] After years of battling Morgenthau and losing, Stimson had finally learned, rather late in the game, that his nineteenth-century etiquette did not and could not succeed in modern-day, cut-throat

Washington politics. At last he began employing some of Morgenthau's backdoor maneuvers. Unfortunately for Stimson, he probably did not realize that Eisenhower favored the punishing peace.

By the time of Potsdam, it became painfully clear to Stimson that his influence, like Morgenthau's, had greatly diminished. Truman had not even intended to bring the War Secretary with him to the conference. When Stimson asked the new President whether he wanted him to attend, Truman realized the gravity of the insult of excluding the elder statesman who had sacrificed so much throughout the war. Truman deftly explained that he had not wanted to burden Stimson with the trip, given his poor health. It was an obvious face-saving excuse for the snub. Stimson assured the President that he could manage, and quickly prepared for departure. But at the conference Truman barely consulted the War Secretary. Stimson served mainly as a messenger, relating the news of greatest import, including the results of Trinity, the test of an atomic bomb in the New Mexico desert. The test took place on July 16, and two days later a fourteen-page report arrived by personal courier to Stimson at Potsdam. It was a message that none could forget.

The observers lay facedown on the earth with their feet pointed toward the site. They had to be at least 51,000 feet from the blast. They were instructed to shield their eyes, despite the dark sunglasses that every person had been issued. It made little difference. The light seemed equivalent to several suns at midday. It was seen 180 miles away. The light appeared golden, purple, violet, gray, and blue. After the flash came a gigantic ball of fire for several seconds, which mushroomed to over 10,000 feet. The roar was heard roughly a hundred miles away. The mushroom cloud kept climbing to the heavens, eventually reaching 41,000 feet.

But these were just the immediate effects – the awesome, terrifying sensory spectacle. The scientists also needed to know what the bomb would do to physical structures, and that answer was self-evident. Fifteen hundred feet from the blast stood a four-inch thick iron pipe, sixteen feet high, set in concrete and strongly planted. It disappeared completely. It had simply ceased to be.

Beyond that stood a massive steel cylinder weighing 220 tons. Its base was solidly encased in concrete. It was surrounded by a steel tower some seventy feet high and firmly anchored to concrete foundations. The engineers had used forty tons of steel to create the tower, making it replicate the height of a six-story building. Unlike a standard structure, they reinforced the tower with cross-bracing far stronger than what would normally be used. The blast tore the tower from its foundations, twisted it, ripped it apart, and left it flat on the ground. The psychological effect on the observers was profound, as no one had expected it to be damaged. General Leslie Groves, the top military official overseeing the Manhattan Project, imagined what it would be like as the victim of such a weapon. He commented, "I no longer consider the Pentagon a safe shelter from such a bomb." Even General Groves was considering the effect of this weapon on human beings.

One of the military observers that day was a brigadier general. He made detailed notes on the experience. He referred to the explosion as having an "awesome roar which warned of doomsday." It "made us feel blasphemous for tampering with the power of the Almighty." He concluded that among the people present and responsible for unleashing this new power, there was a feeling that they should dedicate their lives to ensuring "that it would always be used for good and never for evil." Stimson hurriedly delivered the report to Truman, who thereafter felt emboldened to take charge at the conference.

With all these knowledgeable and persuasive voices aligned in support of softening American war aims, what led Truman to override them all? There was one advisor who objected strongly to a soft peace: James Byrnes, the prominent former senator from South Carolina and newly appointed secretary of state. Truman looked to Byrnes for guidance in foreign affairs, a realm in which Byrnes was said to be knowledgeable and where Truman was severely deficient. During FDR's administration, some even referred to Byrnes as the "Assistant President."

Most scholars assume that Byrnes was the prime source of Truman's hard line on unconditional surrender. The records show that Byrnes was opposed to any softening toward Japan, and he is believed to have rewritten the Potsdam Declaration issued on July 26. Although this critical document issued at the close of the Big Three's final wartime conference contained language reassuring the Japanese people that they would be free to choose their own form of government, the final version reverted to a demand for unconditional surrender of all military forces. The declaration contained no assurance that the Emperor could be retained. On the contrary, one part read: "There must be eliminated for all time the authority and influence of those who have deceived and misled the people of Japan into embarking on world conquest." This language could easily have been interpreted to mean that the Emperor would be among those who misled Japan. He would therefore be, according to the cryptic wording, "eliminated." The declaration meant that Plan C had effectively been abandoned. With invasion being the least appealing option, and with the bomb now ready for use, the refusal to extend conditional surrender terms meant that the world's first nuclear attack was imminent.

When President Truman announced to the world that the first atomic bomb had been dropped on Hiroshima, he made it plain that this was an act of retribution: "The Japanese began the war from the air at Pearl Harbor. They have been repaid many fold." His words were not a spontaneous expression of anger; they had been drafted over several months.[215] "The force from which the sun draws its power has been loosed against those who brought war to the Far East," Truman declared. Millions of Americans and their allies, along with millions of Asians who had suffered under Japanese soldiers' savagery, rejoiced at the news. A palpable sense of payback felt justified given the extreme cruelty that the Japanese military had inflicted on so many for so long. But in time, and in not so short a time, Americans would begin to grapple with the true horror of what the bombs had done.

10 FALLOUT

At 8:15 on the morning of August 6, 1945, five-year-old Ikuko Wakasa was playing outside her home. Her mother was washing dishes in the kitchen, cleaning up after breakfast. Her father was still at home. He had not yet left for work. Ikuko was playing in the garden when she heard an airplane overhead. She saw a flash of white light and then felt an ear-splitting boom. Shattered glass struck her face as bookcases tumbled down inside the home. Blood gushed from her ears and would not cease. Her mother's body was pierced by glass. Her father pulled out the largest shard from her mother's back and poured an entire bottle of iodine over the wound. But there was little he could do for Ikuko. The child's wounds kept bleeding.

Ikuko's father carried her to a military hospital, but the lines were so long that they realized no doctors would be able to treat her. Too many others were in worse condition, naked, bloody, burned, and groaning in agony. They had no choice but to leave.

Ikuko was terrified by the things she saw that day. Fires were burning across the city. There was a strange and awful smell in the air. Many residents of Hiroshima saw processions of naked, blackened people walking like scarecrows with their arms at odd angles as they headed toward the river. They were trying to keep their limbs from rubbing against their other burns. Many had their flesh melted and falling from their bodies in slimy chunks. Ikuko's family came upon a man so badly burned that they could not tell if he was young or old. They placed him on the floor of their home and put a pillow under his head. As they watched, the man changed. His body seemed to swell and darken. Flies gathered on him, and his body gave off a terrible stench. He could only call out for water. Holding her breath, Ikuko brought him several cups, but she was powerless to do more.

Etsuko Fujioka was in the eleventh grade. When she saw the flash, she ran for cover in her bedroom, but a moment later she was buried under broken glass and fallen objects. Etsuko blacked out. When she came to, she realized that she could not move. Her legs were pinned beneath a pillar. Fortunately, a neighbor helped to free her. In the hospital she listened to the groans of people dying around her. Each one seemed to call out a loved one's name. Although she survived, she was left with permanent scars. In June 1946, her family returned to Hiroshima after a period in the countryside. Other children in school called her "A-bomb scar face." She knew she would have to live with this disfigurement for the rest of her life. She could not understand why Japanese people teased her so badly. She wished that she had died when the bomb exploded.

Naoko Masuoka was in the eighth grade and outside with her classmates when the bomb fell. The force of the blast knocked her down. She was shocked to look up and see her friends bloody and red with burns. Then she looked down at her own hands and saw that they were black and dripping with a yellowish liquid. Her hands gave off a strange smell. People were screaming all around her. She ran in the same direction as the others, but nothing looked the same. The streets were suddenly so transformed that she could not tell where she was going. She found her way with the others to Hijiyama Bridge. She saw a badly burned girl near her run into the river screaming, "I want to die quickly."

The next five days were the worst of her life. She was laid on a blanket on a floor with countless others who were dying in relentless succession. She only wanted to see her mother and father, if they had survived. On the second day a little girl near Naoko cried out, "Mother," just before she died. Only minutes later her mother arrived. As the woman held her daughter's corpse to her body, she wept: "You wanted me to come to you sooner, didn't you. I was a little too late, wasn't I." Everyone in the room was weeping with her.

As the days unfolded, the bomb's eerie aftereffects left citizens stunned. Trees were stripped of their leaves, the negative imprint of their shadows burned indelibly onto the facades of remaining walls. Women's bodies bore the patterns of their kimonos, etched into their skin. Sturdy factories, the ones that still stood, were now just hollow shells of twisted metal and shattered concrete. Some 650 yards from the blast, trolley cars had been transporting citizens. The cars ignited. Only jumbled piles of fleshless skulls and bones remained.

A middle school stood just 550 yards from the blast. The children were incinerated at their desks. In some ways, they were fortunate to have died quickly. Other children had their hands or legs burned into blackened char. Some had their mouths burned away, their faces revealing only gums. Children without eyes cried as nurses plucked glass from their flesh with tweezers. Glass had become the A-bomb's shrapnel.[216]

Michihiko Hachiya pulled a shard of glass from his neck. His cheek and hands were bleeding, and he sensed that his home was about to collapse completely. He and his wife Yaeko ran outside and quickly stumbled over a man's severed head. The body had been crushed by a massive gate. The next moment their own home crashed down into ruin. Fires had broken out around them, so they ran toward the hospital,

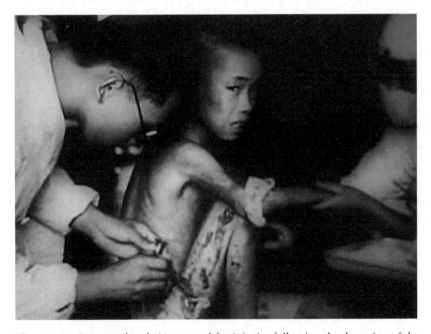

Figure 10.1 Japanese boy being treated for injuries following the dropping of the atomic bombs. Scene captured in footage taken days after the attacks, 1945. National Archives and Records Administration.

which stood only a few hundred meters away. Dr. Hachiya knew the hospital well, as he was its director. Though they were not far, the wound in his thigh was spouting blood and he could not go on. He sent Yaeko ahead without him.

Dr. Hachiya watched as a parade of burned and naked people walked silently toward the hospital. He realized that the facility would be overwhelmed, and his colleagues would need him. Somehow he conjured up a reservoir of strength and staggered to the building.

Recognizing him immediately, the staff carried him into a makeshift examination room. The hospital was in disarray: shattered, cracked, and flooded with patients. No one spoke. They treated his wounds with iodine as he looked out the window at the sloping roof. They had not noticed the smoke and flames just outside. "Fire!" Dr. Hachiya shouted. "The hospital is on fire!" Amidst the chaos, the staff instantly focused on evacuating the patients to the garden. Lying on a stretcher, Dr. Hachiya watched as his hospital disintegrated into a fiery heap. The blaze spread to the buildings around them. He and the others could not stop coughing from the smoke. The temperature was increasing rapidly. He felt certain he would die there, but the staff managed to rescue him. Other patients either escaped on their own or were burned alive.

Dr. Hachiya remembered little of the next two days, but once he recovered enough to think clearly, he began making a diary of each day's events. Part of the hospital had survived, and his staff began treating the injured who were so numerous that they lined the floors, bathrooms, staircases, and any available space. Most had diarrhea, a symptom of radiation sickness, though no one knew that at the time. Quickly the hospital floors became covered in feces. People's skin had been burned away, and now their open wounds were in contact with filth. It was unavoidable. There was nothing they could do.

As Dr. Hachiya slowly recovered, he did his best to examine and treat the patients and to understand what could be causing their peculiar symptoms. News trickled in from visitors to the hospital. One of the doctor's old friends had been living outside of Hiroshima when he saw the flash and heard the thunder. He now told Dr. Hachiya what he had seen as he passed through the city after the attack. There were men who had no faces: "Their eyes, noses, and mouths had been burned away, and it looked like their ears had melted off."[217]

Feuding Values

The day after America's first nuclear attack on Japan, Senator Richard Russell sent an urgent telegram directly to the President imploring him to continue the atomic bombings until Tokyo had been "utterly destroyed." Russell was considered the most powerful man in the Senate. He controlled the votes of southern Democrats who had successfully blocked any civil rights legislation for decades. Russell had a close working relationship with Truman, and his words carried weight:

> Let us carry the war to them until they beg us to accept the unconditional surrender. The foul attack on Pearl Harbor brought us into war and I am unable to see any valid reason why we should be so much more considerate and lenient in dealing with Japan than with Germany.

Russell insisted that "Japan should be dealt with as harshly as Germany." Japan must not receive "a soft peace."

The Senator demanded that atomic bombing continue even if conventional bombs had to be used in the interim while more A-bombs were created: "If we do not have available a sufficient number of atomic bombs with which to finish the job immediately, let us carry on with TNT and fire bombs until we can produce them."

Russell did not want Truman to go soft at this crucial moment. He reminded Truman that Americans had a score to settle with Japan:

> Our people have not forgotten that the Japanese struck us the first blow in this war without the slightest warning. They believe that we should continue to strike the Japanese until they are brought groveling to their knees. We should cease our appeals to Japan to sue for peace. The next plea for peace should come from an utterly destroyed Tokyo.

Truman disagreed. The new president held a very different view of what is justified in war. Whether his humanitarian convictions sprang from his firsthand observation of suffering in WWI, or instead from some deeper wellspring of compassion, Truman had no intention of inflicting any more destruction than was necessary. He replied to Russell on August 9:

> I know that Japan is a terribly cruel and uncivilized nation in warfare but I can't bring myself to believe that, because they are

beasts, we should ourselves act in the same manner. For myself, I certainly regret the necessity of wiping out whole populations because of the "pigheadedness" of the leaders of a nation and, for your information, I am not going to do it unless it is absolutely necessary. It is my opinion that after the Russians enter into war the Japanese will very shortly fold up. My object is to save as many American lives as possible but I also have a humane feeling for the women and children in Japan.[218]

These were the two feuding sides of the American conscience. Russell demanded annihilation; Truman called for mercy.[219] Both men knew they had to answer to the electorate, and each could imagine that the public would support his view. But while Russell felt certain that revenge was in the air, the American public's thirst for retribution was more complex than at first glance.

The American public is assumed to have overwhelmingly supported the use of atomic bombs on Japan, but this impression comes in part from a Gallup poll conducted just days after the bombs destroyed Hiroshima and Nagasaki. The poll found that eighty-five percent of Americans were in favor of the bombs. Only ten percent disapproved, and five percent were unsure.[220] Those figures might suggest a deep current of hatred toward Japan, the depths of which can only be hinted at by polling data. Or, when examined in a different light, they might reveal something else entirely. In November 1944, the Gallup organization asked Americans what should be done with Japan after the war. Some thirteen percent responded that all Japanese people should be killed. Another thirty-three percent said that Japan should be destroyed as a political entity. Only eight percent felt that Japan should be rehabilitated and reeducated. Twenty-eight percent said that Japan should be supervised and controlled.[221] In other words, even at the height of the Pacific War, after nearly four years of bloody, brutal fighting across the Pacific in which savagery became widespread, fewer than half of Americans sought a harsh peace. More than a third expressed a desire for moderation.

Polling data can be misleading, as election forecasters have so often learned. The poll which found that eighty-five percent supported the use of atomic bombs must be considered along with another Gallup poll taken in June 1945, barely two months prior to the nuclear strikes. In this survey Americans were asked if they supported the use of poison gas against the Japanese, if doing so would reduce American casualties. Forty percent said yes, but almost fifty percent said no.[222] As horrible as poison gas undeniably is, a nuclear bomb is vastly worse. This suggests that most Americans simply had no concept of what an atom bomb meant. Because nuclear energy was almost entirely unknown to the average person, the public could not have imagined its effects. At a time when fewer than one in twenty Americans had a college degree, the vast majority would not even have known someone in their social circles who could explain it to them. Most Americans probably assumed that an A-bomb was merely a very powerful conventional bomb. They had no other frame of reference. In fact, to help describe the bomb to the public, President Truman compared it to a conventional bomb, only 200 times more powerful than the largest bomb ever used. When viewed in tandem, these two Gallup polls together suggest that Americans had no idea what an atom bomb entailed, and given their opposition to poison gas, the majority probably would have opposed the atomic bombs by equal or even greater measure. It would take time for any understanding of a nuclear attack and its effects on civilians to enter the public mind, but the dawn of that understanding was soon to begin.

Meanwhile, as Japanese Americans began filtering out of their concentration camps and returning to the west coast, their reception was far from welcoming. Returnees reported cases of violence against them, and many other incidents likely went unreported. Some returnees had their homes burned. Others had shots fired into their farm houses. Roughly seventy-five percent had lost their homes altogether. Many wound up in slums or trailer parks. Most found that the personal possessions they had stored in safekeeping were missing or damaged. Few white employers would hire returnees, their suspicions still lingering.[223]

Unlike all previous First Ladies, Eleanor Roosevelt had no intention of retiring from public life once she was no longer in the White House. Still acting as the conscience of a nation, and possibly still uneasy about her prior public support for internment, she forwarded Truman an article on December 18, 1945, detailing the rash of hate crimes that white Americans were committing against Japanese Americans. The same day Truman responded, stating that he would pass the article on to the Attorney General, instructing him to investigate. The President added, "This disgraceful conduct almost makes you believe that a lot of our Americans have a streak of Nazi in them." Three days later he forwarded the article to Attorney General Tom Clark, remarking that these hate crimes made him ashamed: "Isn't there some way we can shame these people into doing the right thing by these loyal American-Japanese?" The Attorney General recommended, and Truman approved, a nationwide investigation into anti-Japanese-American hate crimes.[224] Truman's compassion reflected a growing segment of the American public that wanted to see themselves as Ralph Bard had seen them – as a good and decent people. Soon, however, Americans would be forced to confront their attacks on the Japanese nation.

Facing Facts

The first significant breach in the wall of public support for the A-bombs came one year after their use.[225] On August 31, 1946, the anniversary of the nuclear attacks, the *New Yorker* published an extraordinary piece of journalism that captivated the country. The magazine devoted the entire issue to John Hersey's graphic descriptions of the bomb from the victims' perspectives. It was the first time that most Americans encountered the full horror of the event, and the effects on them were profound.

Hersey profiled six survivors, detailing what they saw and felt on that day and over the weeks that followed. His descriptions conveyed in gruesome detail the nightmarish nature of what the bomb had wrought. He told of Father Wilhelm Kleinsorge, a German priest, who came upon a group of men who must have been looking up at the airplanes overhead. Their eye sockets were hollow; their faces burned away. They called out for water, but Kleinsorge was unsure how to help them: "Their mouths were mere swollen, pus-covered wounds, which they could not bear to stretch enough to admit the spout of the teapot."[226]

Hersey described how the Reverend Tanimoto, pastor of a local church who had studied theology at Emory College in Atlanta, tried to take one woman's hands, but her skin slipped off in "huge, glovelike pieces." He tried to carry many victims up the river banks, but the waters rose in the night causing many to drown. He could still see some corpses floating in the river the next morning. And Hersey told of a woman who thought she had survived the bomb, but a few weeks later was brushing her hair and noticed large amounts remaining in her brush. Soon she and many others took ill with the beginnings of radiation sickness.

Hersey's article became an instant sensation. Copies sold out and demands for reprinting spread. The American Broadcasting Company read the entire article to radio listeners over four half-hour segments. With the *New Yorker*'s permission, newspapers reprinted the article in full.[227] One of the junior scientists who had worked on the bomb as part of the Manhattan Project read Hersey's piece and wept. He now felt ashamed by his jubilation when the bomb successfully detonated. The true horror of what he had done was sinking in, for him and many others. Hersey's revelations had touched a raw nerve. Awakened by the bitter fruit of knowledge, Americans began a serious bout of soul searching – a process that has continued to the present day.

Part of the public's reassessment came from the dawning realization that this was not simply a more powerful bomb than ones that had come before. The atomic bomb's aftereffects, radiation sickness, meant that this new weapon went on killing long after the initial strike. After reading Hersey's piece, Norman Cousins, editor of the *Saturday Review*, declared that the damage caused to human tissue later on by fallout – the mix of isotopes and radioactive debris that rises in the atmosphere with the explosion and then descends back to earth – may be greater than that caused by the initial detonation.[228] The early signs of radiation sickness include loss of hair, nausea, vomiting, diarrhea, fever, and hemorrhaging due to changes in the blood. The longer-term effects are more serious, as victims often develop leukemia and other types of cancer. As the public's awareness of radiation spread, support for the decision to drop the bombs threatened to erode, and key governmental officials recognized the risks. For that reason, General Leslie Groves, who had played the leading role in directing the Manhattan Project, attempted first to suppress information about radiation sickness, and when that proved impossible, then to downplay its significance. Groves even told a Senate committee in November 1945 that doctors had told him radiation sickness was in fact "a very pleasant way to die."[229]

The historian Sean Malloy delved deeply into the question of what Truman, Stimson, and other key figures knew about radiation. He concluded that while a number of scientists did understand those effects and reported on them, none of the leading decision makers grasped the long-term health effects that the atomic bombs would have. There were simply too many other urgent issues to consider. The health risks to civilians never received more than a fleeting discussion by the Interim Committee.[230] This is perhaps surprising since physicist Karl Compton, one of the eight members of that influential body, had a brother, Arthur Compton, who served as one of four auxiliary scientific advisors to the Committee. Arthur Compton had authored two reports in 1941 on the effects of radiation. Both brothers played significant roles in the bomb's development. Karl Compton had to be familiar with his brother's work on radiation, yet neither man appears to have raised such issues with the Interim Committee. The Committee's focus remained on the bombs' immediate physical and psychological impact. It is doubtful whether this knowledge would have altered Truman's decision, but no one can know this for sure. President Truman clearly felt compassion for the innocent women and children who would be killed by the atomic bombs, and while he seems not to have known about the long-term effects of radiation on those victims, he certainly did not know about its effects on the unborn.

Dr. Yamazaki was staring straight down at a tiny part of a giant puzzle. A Japanese woman had brought her five-year-old son, Toshio, to see the noted pediatrician. She knew that something was clearly wrong. The doctor recognized the first problem instantly. The child's head was much smaller than it should have been, a condition called microcephaly. An examination revealed the serious extent of Toshio's condition. He could not speak. He still needed to be fed. He had no bladder control. His eyes did not maintain focus. His heart did not function properly. And his intellectual development lagged far behind boys of his age. His care would be a challenge for the mother, and she was not alone.

James Yamazaki, a Japanese-American physician, had been sent to Nagasaki soon after Japan's surrender. His mission was to research the effects of radiation on the population. Yamazaki had served in the American Army in Europe, even as his own family had been interned in Camp Jerome, a concentration camp in Arkansas. Yamazaki's father had emigrated from Japan to San Francisco in 1904 to study as a physician. He survived the earthquake of 1906, and later converted to Christianity to be ordained as a minister. Because of his fluency in both Japanese and English, camp authorities made him a translator to assist inmates in completing a controversial loyalty questionnaire. Some inmates vented their anger at the eighty-one-year-old minister, beating him so badly that he had to be hospitalized. Their anger may have stemmed in part from Reverend Yamazaki's patriotism and encouraging of his sons to join the Army. James shared his father's patriotism and enlisted, serving as a combat physician in the European theater.

After the war, James Yamazaki was asked to undertake medical research in Japan. What he found was deeply disturbing. Many pregnant women who had been exposed to the atomic bomb's radiation spontaneously aborted their fetuses. Others who delivered their babies watched helplessly as their children developed severe illnesses, intellectual disabilities, and cancers. The rate of child leukemia in Nagasaki and Hiroshima swelled to thirty times that of the Japanese populace. In time, some of the mothers would find each other and form a support group, the Mushroom Cloud Auxiliary.

Yamazaki was only one of a number of Americans sent to Japan to study the bomb's effects. Karl Compton also traveled to Hiroshima to see for himself what the Manhattan Project had produced. In early October 1945, Compton met with Truman. The President asked him to submit a summary of his observations from Japan, which Compton did on the following day.

Compton first described the damage to Tokyo. The destruction from the conventional bombing campaigns was far worse than aerial reconnaissance had previously suggested. Buildings which seemed intact from the air appeared completely gutted when examined up close. Of the city's nine million inhabitants, only some two million remained. As for Hiroshima and Nagasaki, Compton asserted that the cities were safe. There was no radioactive "burning" near the detonation sites and no authenticated case of anyone dying from radiation sickness after entering the area.[231]

Karl Compton stepped forward as the first prominent official to combat the concerns raised by Hersey's *New Yorker* piece. Given his high-level knowledge of both the decision to use the bomb as well as its impact, he was in a strong position to quell the growing public misgivings. Yet it was a different member of the Interim Committee, James Conant, president of Harvard, who urged Compton to take a prominent stand against the segment of the public that was having doubts. In December 1946, two months after the Hersey sensation, Compton published "If the Atomic Bomb Had Not Been Used" in *The Atlantic*.

Compton did not equivocate. He asserted with complete conviction that the bomb saved hundreds of thousands, possibly millions of lives. If America had not used it, the war would have gone on for many more months. And no one of good conscience could have decided otherwise. Compton assured his readers that the destruction from conventional bombing had been worse than that produced by the atomic bombs – a remarkable argument to make in light of what Hersey had described. It might have been true, if one considered only the physical destruction of buildings and not the effects on human bodies. Beneath his conviction that the atomic bomb was necessary lay the assumption that the United States faced only two options: use the atomic bombs or invade Japan.[232] This stark framing, that the United States had only two choices, has shaped the debate to the present day. Two months later, someone more prominent than Compton would make an even more spirited defense.

James Conant felt that while Compton's essay had been a good first strike, only Henry Stimson could deliver the knockout blow. Other than the President himself, only Stimson possessed the stature and respect necessary to assuage this new bout of public hand-wringing. The fallout from Hersey's article risked contaminating the public mind-set not only toward the past, but also for the future creation of an American nuclear arsenal. Although the Soviet Union had not yet developed an atomic bomb, most officials expected that they would do so within the next few years. Once they achieved that breakthrough, the arms race would be on, and America could not afford to be hamstrung by pacifist guilt. Stimson, now in retirement, was asked to perform one more duty. President Truman encouraged him to set the record straight. The aged Secretary of War needed to present the strongest case possible for the bomb's use during the war, and as always, he came through.[233]

Stimson's *Harper's* piece couched the decision in simple, matter-of-fact terms that anyone could grasp. The enemy's fanatical leaders had to be convinced to surrender in order to avoid an Allied invasion. That invasion, Stimson claimed, would cost up to one million Allied casualties. We had two means of inducing their surrender, Stimson explained: allow the Emperor a role in the future, and impress the leadership with our ability to destroy their country. Stimson told how he advised the President to communicate that the Emperor could be part of a constitutional monarchy and that we envisioned a constructive trading relationship with Japan in time. The aim was to give them hope of a better future. The bomb provided the necessary incentive for surrender. It therefore saved lives.

Stimson's humanity must have resonated with readers. He stated frankly that war is the face of death: "The decision to use the atomic bomb was a decision that brought death to over a hundred thousand Japanese. No explanation can change that fact and I do not wish to gloss over it. But this deliberate, premeditated destruction was our least abhorrent choice." War has grown ever more barbarous and destructive. Now, with the release of atomic energy, mankind can at last destroy itself. The destruction of Hiroshima and Nagasaki shows that humanity must never have another war.

Stimson had struck precisely the right tone. He acknowledged the horror of the atomic bombs without discussing the details of that horror, as Hersey had done. He justified the decision not in terms of retribution, but instead as the least abhorrent option, the one that saved the most lives. And he humanely urged world leaders to ensure that atomic weapons need never be used again. He was a secretary of war calling for world peace. This was Stimson's final major act of public service, and he executed it masterfully.[234]

Unfortunately, the article did more to confuse the issue than it clarified. What played well with the public proved less persuasive to scholars. In time, historians would ask a series of uncomfortable questions. Where exactly did these projected casualty figures, the loss of one million lives, come from? Why wasn't the Japanese government told that it could retain the Emperor before the bombs were dropped, as Stimson had advised? Why was the idea of a demonstration dismissed so swiftly? Why wasn't the Japanese leadership given just a little more time to evaluate the damage to Hiroshima before the second bomb was dropped? These questions, and many others, have led to passionate, divisive debates for decades.

We can never know for certain whether Japan would have surrendered without experiencing a nuclear attack, but America made Japan's surrender less likely with its wording of the Potsdam Declaration. The Declaration proclaimed that the time had come for Japan to cease following its militaristic leaders who had brought the nation to "the brink of annihilation." The leaders of America, Britain, and China stated that their terms for surrender were final; they could not be altered. The first of these declared that the authority and influence of those who had misled Japan into a drive for world conquest must be "eliminated for all time." Point ten of the Declaration stated that the Allies would mete out "stern justice" to all war criminals. It was not difficult for Japan's leaders to recognize that they were among those whom the Allies would seek to punish. They had to assume that they would be killed. In other words, the message that the Potsdam Declaration sent to Japan's leaders was simple: surrender and be hanged, or fight on and be annihilated. This was hardly a choice likely to induce surrender. Not surprisingly, Japanese leaders responded that they would take no notice of the Declaration. It is remarkable that given such an unsavory choice, after Hiroshima three of the Cabinet's six members actually considered accepting the surrender terms. The other three refused until the Emperor at last intervened. But within their official surrender, they included a final demand.

11 RECKONING

Was it truly necessary? Did America really have to use the atomic bombs in order to induce Japan's surrender? Hersey's, Compton's, and Stimson's articles had forced Americans to grapple with the horrific effects of what had been done in their name. If it had been a choice between an invasion or the bomb, as Stimson had framed it, then of course the bomb had to be used. In the cold calculus of war, the loss of two hundred thousand Japanese lives (plus the Korean slaves and American and Allied prisoners killed by the atomic bombs) was preferable to the loss of five hundred thousand to one million American lives expected to be killed in the invasion. If the decision had been that simple, any American leader would have been entirely justified in choosing the nuclear strikes, and any Allied soldier in the Pacific would have been forgiven for thanking God for the atom bomb. But as we now know, it was not that simple.

The controversy around this issue has been unrelenting, and part of the debate has involved the question of casualty estimates.[235] In Stimson's *Harper's* piece, he claimed that the atomic bombs made an invasion of Japan unnecessary, thereby saving more than a million American lives.[236] Some historians have contested this claim, insisting that President Truman was never given any casualty estimates regarding an invasion. At the key meeting on June 18, 1945, the President directly asked for casualty estimates, but General Marshall declined to offer them. Most likely, Marshall did not want to scare Truman off from the invasion. It was in Marshall's interest to low-ball any casualty estimates, or avoid providing them altogether. If Truman thought that the casualties would be politically unacceptable, then he might not have approved of the invasion plan. But in Marshall's defense, it was also extremely difficult to know how high the casualties might climb.

The claim that President Truman never received the extremely large casualty estimates is not entirely correct.[237] Although he does not appear to have obtained them from General Marshall or Secretary Stimson, he did receive estimates of between five hundred thousand and one million, but they came from a very different source. They came from Herbert Hoover. Hoover, in turn, appears to have received them from a group of senior military officers who took it upon themselves to inform Hoover of important intelligence reports. Some in this group periodically visited the ex-president in his Manhattan Waldorf Towers apartment to share top secret matters with him, believing that he would use this information responsibly.[238]

Stimson had worked hard to arrange the meeting between Truman and Hoover, hoping that Truman would employ Hoover's expertise in the coming food crisis, and thereby counteract the worst aspects of Morgenthau's influence on German civilians. But Stimson may have been using Hoover to help shape Japan policy as well. It is hard to imagine that Stimson and Hoover did not discuss what Hoover would say to Truman prior to their White House meeting. After all, Hoover and Stimson had met on a Sunday just two weeks prior to Hoover's White House session with Truman. Stimson had invited Hoover to visit the Stimson home on Long Island. We do not know all the details of what they discussed, but they met for nearly three hours. Stimson noted in his diary only that they agreed on how Europe should be rehabilitated.[239] Given that they held discussions for several hours, Stimson's records are remarkably spare. We do know that Hoover and Stimson had a solid working relationship of mutual respect and trust, dating back to Stimson's service as Hoover's secretary of state. We know that both men had strong reasons to press their views on the new president. Both being highly educated, Harvard and Stanford elites, and knowing that Truman had only a high school degree, they likely doubted Truman's intellectual abilities. As Hoover noted in his diary, he spoke to Truman in simple, one-syllable words.[240] The casualty figures he offered Truman, five hundred thousand to one million men, fit that same mold. They were simple, round numbers, certain to frighten the new president away from Plan B: blockade and invade. They were also extremely un-Hoover-like. Hoover the engineer, the master of detail, the man who built his career on precise calculations, would have been expected to provide precise casualty estimates, not ones that were give or take half a million. And we know one other fact. Three days after Hoover and Stimson met to discuss Hoover's upcoming session with the President, Hoover sent Stimson a draft of his views on Japan. In his diary, Stimson called the Hoover suggestions "very interesting, rather dramatic and radical."[241]

After Truman received Hoover's alarming memo, the President called for a meeting to discuss expected casualties. Truman naturally wanted to minimize them, and Hoover's memo seems to have disturbed him greatly. The battle for Okinawa had been brutal and bloody. Truman wanted to know if an invasion of the Japanese home islands was likely to be even worse. After receiving the Hoover memo, Truman forwarded it to several officials including Stimson. Stimson forwarded it to Marshall, who sent back two reports stating that Hoover's figures were far too high. But Stimson did not forward those reports to Truman.[242] Why not?

The answer is likely that Stimson agonized over Plan A, the use of atomic bombs on innocent civilians, and he wanted to move Truman away from Plan B, blockade and invade the Japanese islands, which he viewed as recklessly unnecessary. He hoped instead to guide Truman toward the far easier, less costly option, Plan C, conditional surrender.

But if Stimson opposed an invasion of Japan, why did he not say so directly? Why should he have encouraged Truman to believe in Hoover's extremely high figures and blocked Marshall's much lower estimates from reaching the President? Seen in the context of Stimson's past four years as war secretary, the explanation is clear. Stimson, the consummate organization man, often found it difficult to contradict his generals, and as a result, the generals typically got their way. But his battles with Morgenthau had taught him how to engage in the scheming, backdoor, end-around world of Washington's policy arena. If Morgenthau had been a nemesis, he was also a role model. Morgenthau had inadvertently shown Stimson the art of political maneuvering, a skill that Stimson clearly needed to enhance. Stimson had been losing policy battles, both with Morgenthau at the Treasury and the generals in his own war department. Just two days after Hoover's meeting with Truman, his simmering frustration at last boiled over.

On May 30, 1945, General Leslie Groves came to Stimson's office to discuss some matters relating to the bomb. Stimson asked if he had finished preparing the target list, and Groves explained that it was not yet ready, but that he would send it to General Marshall the following morning for review. Stimson said he wanted to see it now. Groves demurred, arguing that he wanted to check over the list and make it just right before submitting it. Stimson insisted. Groves said it would take a long time to have the report sent over. Stimson uncharacteristically pointed to his phone and instructed the General to call his office and have the report sent over while they waited. Unable to wriggle out of the jam, Groves did as ordered.[243] As Stimson expected, the list named Kyoto as the prime target. And then, according to Groves, Stimson said something remarkable: "This is one time I'm going to be the final deciding authority. Nobody's going to tell me what to do on this. On this matter I am the kingpin."[244]

Weeks later, General Groves tried to put Kyoto back on the list of preferred targets, believing that destroying such a city would have the greatest psychological impact.[245] This time Stimson intervened directly with the President to insist that Kyoto be spared, and Truman acquiesced.

Why did Stimson take so strong a stand over Kyoto? It was highly unusual for him to override his generals. In 1961, the historian Herbert Feis published his account of the decision to use the atomic bombs, and he advanced a story that stuck. According to Feis, Stimson encountered an American soldier who had spent time in Kyoto. Over dinner at the Stimsons' home, the soldier (whom Feis did not identify) described the great beauty of Japan's ancient capital, which led Stimson to examine old photos of Kyoto and to learn about its charms. As a result of this chance encounter, Feis claimed, Kyoto was spared destruction.[246]

Although it is a compelling story, there are problems with Feis's account. First, Stimson did not need the soldier to inform him of Kyoto's beauty or significance because Stimson had toured the city for himself almost two decades earlier. Second, despite having visited Kyoto, Stimson failed to make any more than a passing reference to it in his diary, suggesting that it did not hold a powerful appeal. While governor-general of the Philippines in the late 1920s, Stimson had visited the ancient capital. On Sunday, March 3, 1929, he and his wife took a brief sightseeing tour before departing for Tokyo. His diary notes only that he stayed overnight and toured the city briefly before moving on to Tokyo for meetings. It would seem odd that if the majestic city had impressed him so profoundly, he made no more than a perfunctory note of his presence there. It seems unlikely that one soldier's report on Kyoto's charms would have caused Stimson to take the highly uncharacteristic step of overruling his generals.

Another explanation for Stimson's strong stand on Kyoto might be that he believed that military considerations must never be devoid of political ones. After the war, the US occupation would be untenable if the Japanese population were not resigned to cooperating with American soldiers and civilian authorities. He may have felt that destroying such a sacred place as Kyoto would harden the Japanese population against American occupiers and severely hamstring the postwar peace. It is unclear though why he would not have thought that the use of an atomic bomb on any other city would not have equally hardened the population against America. Although Kyoto had historic significance and remarkable beauty, the atomic destruction of other cities and the incineration of their inhabitants could just as likely have engendered the same hatred toward American occupiers.

While it is possible that Stimson's uncharacteristic insistence on sparing Kyoto could be explained by his admiration of the city's beauty and his concern for the postwar peace, there is another, more plausible explanation. Stimson's unusual comments to Groves have been interpreted as evidence of Stimson's respect for Kyoto's cultural significance, but his words could be seen in a very different light. Rather than reflecting a deep reverence for Kyoto, his comment might have indicated a frustration over being boxed in by the military. It is peculiar that he would have said, "This is one time I'm going to be the final deciding authority." After all, Stimson should have been the deciding authority every time. As war secretary, he should have always had the final word on all military decisions, second only to the President. His remark, "Nobody's going to tell me what to do on this," strongly suggests that he felt that he was not always in command. Even if Groves had not recalled Stimson's words exactly, the sentiment he conveyed was clear. The elderly War Secretary felt that the military had been circumventing or ignoring his views. And they had been.

This was, of course, what had been happening with the fire bombings of Japan. Stimson had urged his generals to desist from such cruel attacks on civilians, but his pleadings, which should have been orders, were ignored.[247] The same was true with the internment of Japanese Americans in 1942. Stimson objected to the imprisoning of thousands of citizens on the basis of race, but General DeWitt and other military commanders had demanded it, and, given his ambivalence, Stimson failed to stop them. He seemed unaware of the subterfuge that McCloy and DeWitt employed in the Hirabayashi and Korematsu cases. Most likely they kept this information from him knowing that he would never countenance such behavior. As a Harvard-trained attorney, Stimson would have recognized the suppression of evidence and doctoring of documents immediately for what it was: obstruction of justice. If he did not know what his own War Department was doing on an issue twice adjudicated in the Supreme Court, then he was kept in the dark on some critical matters by the department he supposedly led. If, on the other hand, Stimson had caught wind of it, he would have been anguished. His generals' actions violated his every ethical instinct, yet he was not a man to defy his president. Roosevelt's internment orders were on trial, and Stimson was not the type of man to act as a whistleblower, especially in the midst of a world war. He was a loyal public servant, not one to buck the system, publicly defy his commander in chief, or even privately push back against his generals. Instead, he was the kind of man to suffer crippling migraines and sleepless nights.

Now, in the summer of 1945, he was finding that his military was pressing for what could be a bloody and possibly needless invasion, or necessitating the use of an atomic bomb that would kill unknown numbers of innocent civilians. Seen in this light, Stimson's actions surrounding the planning of invasion take on a different hue. The War Secretary may well have found it more effective at times to use others to influence the President and help shape policy as he thought best. Using Hoover to nudge the President away from invasion and toward conditional surrender was a clever method of circumventing the generals while not contradicting them outright. This was no longer the 1920s, when Stimson could nobly declare that gentlemen do not read other gentlemen's mail. America was no longer a rising power. America had risen, and the stakes were the highest they could be. America possessed the power to reshape the world, and soon it would have the power to destroy it. Policy choices mattered more than ever before. Hundreds of thousands of enemy lives hung on what a handful of men in Washington decided. As Stimson saw it, he had no choice but to nudge those decisions toward mercy, whenever and however he could.

Both Stimson and Hoover might have genuinely believed the high casualty figures. No one really had any idea what the casualties would be. Based on the Japanese military's pattern of behavior, the fighting would likely be intense and costly. The US military knew that the Japanese forces were preparing for an invasion by building defenses in Kyushu and assembling some 900,000 troops. On paper, an Allied invasion looked to be a bloody affair. On the other hand, continued aerial bombardment and naval blockade, plus the extreme food shortages that were worsening daily in Japan as a result of extensive bombing, might well have diminished the Japanese ability to fight successfully. Starvation can do much to sap the morale of troops, not just their effectiveness.[248] With so many conflicting possibilities, there was simply no way to estimate with any accuracy how many would die in an invasion.

Because there was no way to know the exact cost of an invasion, Stimson favored the simplest option: to encourage Japan's surrender by permitting them to retain the Emperor. This is what Ambassador Grew had been advocating, and Stimson and most other key officials agreed. The problem was that Truman was equally convinced that unconditional surrender was required. The offer to retain the Emperor seemed to violate that principle, and that was something Truman was reluctant to do.

Reason

Truman thought historically, but in a flawed way. Though his formal education was limited, he was in many ways an autodidact. He once bragged about having read every book in his local library, and while this may have been an exaggeration, he did possess genuine curiosity, having consumed many works on world history. Prior to becoming president, his sole experience abroad came as an enlisted man fighting in France in 1918. He had witnessed the horrors of the First World War, and in Potsdam he saw the even greater devastation wrought by the Second. The last thing he wanted was to be responsible for causing the Third, especially in light of the bomb. Suddenly he found himself in the lonely position of being the only person on earth with the authority to launch a nuclear attack. He knew that he would not be lonely for long. Most estimates expected that the Soviets would possess atomic weapons within four years. In that event, another world war risked the destruction of both societies, and possibly all of human civilization. One thought had to weigh on Truman's mind at this time: do not repeat the mistakes of the past.

As Truman understood it, the Allies of WWI had failed to obtain Germany's unconditional surrender. The result of this failure was WWII. If he softened on Japan at this critical juncture, would he be guilty of sowing the seeds for a third world war? An influential voice probably added to his concern. Eleanor Roosevelt had expressed this very fear. Writing in June 1944, the popular First Lady reflected a belief no doubt held by many Americans: "We gave up unconditional surrender the last time ... and now we have sacrificed thousands of lives because we did not do a thorough job."[249]

In his first address to Congress four days after Roosevelt's death, Truman assured the nation that he would never accept a partial victory. Too many had sacrificed too much. A temporary peace would "jeopardize the future security of all the world." In words that must have given Japanese leaders sobering clarity, Truman declared that America would pursue the war criminals to the end of the earth. And he underscored American war aims against Japan: "Our demand has been, and it *remains*, unconditional surrender!"[250] At the utterance of those words, the combined Congress rose to its feet in applause.[251] The President was not simply reflecting popular sentiment. He genuinely believed in unconditional surrender on principle because of how he reasoned historically.

Truman thought in terms of historical patterns, from which he drew global lessons. In his farewell address in January 1953, he spoke of the causes of WWII with analogical reasoning. "Think back for a moment to the 1930's and you will see the difference," he told Americans.

> The Japanese moved into Manchuria, and free men did not act. The Fascists moved into Ethiopia, and we did not act. The Nazis marched into the Rhineland, into Austria, into Czechoslovakia, and free men were paralyzed for lack of strength and unity and will. Think about those years of weakness and indecision, and World War II which was their evil result. Then think about the speed and courage and decisiveness with which we have moved against the Communist threat since World War II.[252]

Truman saw indecision as weakness. He viewed the failure to forcefully oppose Japanese and German aggression as having emboldened the aggressors. And he felt convinced that the 1930s were sufficiently analogous to the 1950s to merit a policy prescription: do not repeat the mistakes of the past.

Later in that same farewell address, Truman returned to historical lessons, using them to defend his decision to intervene in Korea. Speaking about the day when he first learned of North Korea's invasion of the South, Truman explained:

> I turned the problem over in my mind in many ways, but my thoughts kept coming back to the 1930's – to Manchuria, to Ethiopia, the Rhineland, Austria, and finally to Munich. Here was history repeating itself. Here was another probing action, another testing action. If we let the Republic of Korea go under, some other country would be next, and then another. And all the time, the courage and confidence of the free world would be ebbing away, just as it did in the 1930's.

Truman was correct that many aspects of human affairs repeat themselves. But failure can come not only by repeating the mistakes of the past, but also when we cannot discern the differences between past and present. Japanese society, with its religious devotion to its Emperor, was not analogous to German society under Kaiser Wilhelm II. Hitler's rise resulted from a complex coalescence of extraordinary factors, not merely from the Allies' failure to achieve unconditional surrender at the close of WWI. Truman's historical reasoning failed to recognize the differences between these two distinct countries. If his refusal to permit conditional surrender for Japan was based on this flawed analogy, then the dropping of the atomic bombs on Hiroshima and Nagasaki may have been not just a tragedy of history, but also a tragedy of poor historical reasoning.

James Byrnes may have influenced Truman to take a hard line on unconditional surrender, but Truman made his own decisions and always accepted responsibility. He knew that "the buck stops here," as the sign in his office read. He was the decider, and he based his decision in this case in part on his reasoning about the past. Hoping to avoid the errors that produced WWII, Truman concluded that anything less than unconditional surrender of Japan could lead to a third global war, and the stakes in the nuclear age were simply too high to take that risk. In the opening to the second volume of his memoirs, he revealed how deeply this issue affected him: "In spite of the turmoil and pressure of critical events during the years I was President, the one purpose that dominated me in everything I thought and did was to prevent a third world war."[253]

By refusing to modify American demands on Japan, Truman narrowed his own options. Believing in the highest possible casualty figures from invasion, he was left only with use of the atomic bomb. But even then, he could still have pursued a demonstration, as Bard and the physicists had urged. It is entirely possible that neither a demonstration nor an offer to retain the Emperor would have brought about surrender, yet either option might at least have been worth trying. If either had succeeded, America would have achieved all of its objectives without inflicting the cruelty of a nuclear attack on Ikuko and all the other children who were incinerated on that gruesome August morning.

But in those early years after victory, Americans were not yet able to wrestle with these complexities. Stimson, himself, did grapple with them and never fully resolved them. His article had framed the matter in humane terms: the bomb saved more lives than it cost, but that framing grossly oversimplified the matter and may have been untrue. Perhaps Stimson genuinely believed in this simple calculus. Maybe he had convinced himself that the casualty estimates of five hundred thousand to a million men had been real. But the tragedy of Stimson's final service to his president is that, even in retirement, even at nearly eighty years of age and knowing he was near the close of his life, he still could not speak about how the decision had tormented him. Years later, John McCloy remarked that the decision kept Stimson up at night, imagining what the bomb would do to civilians: "I knew Stimson as well as any man alive. And while after the war he wrote an article for *Harper's* defending his decision, I know in his soul there were doubts."[254]

Hersey's article turned out to be only the first glimpse at the face of death to which Stimson had alluded. Slowly, haltingly, and with great resistance, Americans came to learn more about the nuclear attack and to view the use of the atomic bombs with far less certainty than they had in the rush and thrill of victory. Although the Gallup poll in August 1945 suggested that eighty-five percent of Americans supported the use of atomic bombs, a minority of Americans even at the height of victory fever found the new weapon unacceptable. Catholic and Protestant groups condemned the decision because it targeted civilians. Liberal intellectuals such as Norman Cousins opposed it on moral grounds as well. But the highest profile member of the public who opposed the bomb was a former president. Herbert Hoover was appalled by Truman's decision. Hoover wrote that the bombs' use "revolts my soul." He called it "the most terrible and barbaric weapon that has ever come to the hand of man." Its only purpose was to kill innocent civilians – men, women, and children, and to destroy whole cities.[255] Hoover's Quaker values never wavered. His commitment to caring for all human beings, especially children, made him the perfect candidate for the crucial role he was about to assume.

America's triumph in the war had come with moral as well as material costs. The country had imprisoned its own citizens on the basis of race. It had murdered innocent civilians in the most horrific fashion with the atomic bomb. And it was now exacerbating the starvation of German civilians during occupation. At least in the eyes of some, America's greatness was tarnished by its apparent lack of goodness. If the United States was going to be an attractive alternative to the Soviet Union, America needed its proclaimed values to take center stage once more. Americans believed that they were a good people, a nation whose power is a benevolent force in the world. They saw themselves, in Ralph Bard's words, as a great humanitarian nation and a people committed to fair play, not a people who would allow innocent children to suffer and die. This was not simply what Americans believed about themselves; it was what they wanted the rest of the world to believe about them. America's moral standing had to shine again, and only one statesman possessed an unambiguous international reputation for humane kindness. With his unique credentials as the savior of millions during WWI, Herbert Hoover could embody the message that America was not merely great; it was also good. After WWII, he was the best man alive to organize a global humanitarian campaign. In the process, he would not only save millions from starvation, he would rescue the American narrative as well.

Part II
Saviors

Franklin Roosevelt did not like the flag. His problem was not with the stars and stripes, but instead with the presidential flag and seal. In 1944, FDR intended to elevate the country's top wartime commanders in rank by awarding them a fifth star. No military leader in America had ever been granted such a distinction. The presidential flag and seal depicted four stars, one in each corner, and Roosevelt thought it would be inappropriate for a military commander to have more stars than those on the president's official images. But with only four corners, there was no obvious place for a fifth. They could not displace the eagle from the center. The flag would have to be redesigned.

The solution, it turned out, was simple. Encircle the presidential insignia, a bald eagle, with forty-eight stars. As more states were added to the union, new stars could join the circle without disrupting the symmetry. It was an elegant response that satisfied the President's wish. And while the staff were tinkering with the image, someone had an idea. The eagle held an olive branch in the right claw and a quiver of arrows in the left. The eagle had always faced the arrows. Why not turn the eagle's head in the opposite direction? The aides explained that although the United States was presently engaged in the greatest war in history, in the postwar period America should be focused on the olive branch. This would better reflect American values. FDR fully agreed and approved the new look.

Roosevelt did not live to see the new flag. It became President Truman's honor to unveil it at a ceremony during the christening of a new battleship. When Truman was shown the design, he wanted to include some bolts of lightning among the arrows, symbolizing the power of the atomic bomb. His aides managed to talk him out of this idea, arguing that lightning would look unattractive. Perhaps there was a deeper, unspoken reason for their resistance. Americans who understood what the bomb had done to innocent civilians, especially children, did not want to immortalize that memory on the presidential seal. No one needed a reminder of the bomb that too many would never forget.

The atomic bomb symbolized America's emergence as a superpower, so much so that it could simply be referred to as "the bomb," and everyone would know what that meant. Truman's aides may have understood what Truman did not. The fresh design reflected how Americans saw themselves: not as a nation armed for aggression, but as a people looking toward peace. It was how they wanted others to see them as well.

The postwar period immediately presented a dangerous mix of volatility and crises. Japanese Americans had to be released from concentration camps, but most were not welcomed back home. Starving Germans needed food, but some still wanted them to suffer. And then there was the bomb. A growing segment of Americans believed that America had committed an atrocity in Japan. They felt that their country needed somehow to atone for its crimes against the innocent. On top of these dilemmas loomed the Soviet problem. How should America handle the threat of communism: through accommodation, containment, or still another conflict? Within the first five postwar years, the United States had attempted all three. Surprisingly, much of the country's efforts to make up for its wartime excesses came from the same people who had either helped to create them or failed to stop them – only now they were no longer in power.

After the war, most of the key players involved in some of America's harshest acts – the internment, the starvation, and the bomb – either left office voluntarily or were removed. But they did not quietly fade away. Instead, each took an active role in reshaping America's image as a noble nation, positioning America in stark contrast to the Soviet Union. Some devoted themselves to humanitarian relief, hoping to save the innumerable peoples displaced and battered by the war. Others tried to advance their Christian beliefs and values in the lands of their defeated foes. Still others sought accommodation with the Soviets, convinced that this was the only path to peace. What united them all was a near messianic drive to rekindle the lamp of human kindness that had been so darkened during the war. Among their ranks stood a vilified ambassador, a fired Cabinet member, an excoriated vice president, a former first lady, and a reviled ex-president. As individuals, they had little in common, but seen collectively, they shared a lofty goal. Each remained wedded to the notion that America could only be great if it first became good. Almost immediately after the war was over, they devoted themselves to the quest of making America good again. Not one of them could have foreseen how difficult that would prove.

12 RESCUE

Toward the close of March 1944, a British officer was approached by an old woman on the streets of Naples. She insisted that the officer follow her. She had something to show him. In their desperation for food, it was not unusual to find all manner of middle-class Italians selling their possessions in the streets and town squares. Allied soldiers had the pick of objects to purchase for a pittance: jewelry, old books, clothing – truly anything could be had. But this old woman had nothing apparent to sell. Acquiescing to her pleas, the officer followed her to a single, dimly lit room. In the corner stood a girl of possibly thirteen. The woman explained that this was her daughter, and that her services were for sale. For twenty lire, the girl would reveal her private parts. For more, she would engage in a host of sexual acts. The officer was unnerved. He had been part of the occupation since August 1943, and he had seen the pervasive spread of prostitution that had corrupted Naples. Hunger was driving women to sell themselves for food. But the officer had not until then seen a mother offering her own child. "I could have you arrested," he told the woman. She began to weep, but both knew that his threat was empty. The problems plaguing occupied Italy were far too severe for the Allied authorities to deal with so trivial a matter as this.

Norman Lewis had not intended to join the British Army. He had been a wedding photographer and travel writer, but because of his facility with languages, he was recruited into the intelligence service during the war. His diary of the occupation provides a grim accounting of a city under anarchy. The near total destruction of food distribution networks left millions at risk of starvation. Prostitution became commonplace, from old women to young girls. On a visit to an Italian peasant village where deserters had looted the homes and violated all the women, Lewis could only offer the victims a hollow pledge that he would try to bring the perpetrators to justice, knowing this would be nearly impossible. While on this inspection, he could not help noticing one exceptionally beautiful girl, though her eyes looked puffy and sagging, a familiar feature of the malnourished. The following day the girl arrived at his headquarters with a note from her father, possibly written by the village priest. It implored Lewis to provide the girl with just one meal a day, and in exchange she would stay with him, and "we could come to some mutually satisfactory understanding in due course."[256]

Most offers did not come from parents. On another occasion a skinny, grimy, bedraggled twelve-year-old girl arrived at his headquarters to request a blanket. Lewis regretted that he had no blankets to give. She explained that the previous officer had provided a blanket each day. At first this struck Lewis as implausible. Blankets, along with food and medicine, were among the more highly prized items in postwar-occupied Italy. His Canadian predecessor would not have given a child, and the same child, a blanket so readily and so often. And then Lewis understood. This emaciated orphan was a child prostitute who must have had an arrangement with his predecessor. He offered her some biscuits instead, which she accepted, curtsied, and scampered off.

In the absence of a functioning government, citizens as well as soldiers ran amok. Among the worst offenders, according to Lewis, were the French colonial troops. In numerous cities, he claimed that they raped all the women they could find. When not enough sufficed, they raped the men. He believed that Moroccan troops were known to gang rape women, often by acts of simultaneous vaginal intercourse by one man and anal intercourse by another. Many Italian women were left physically wounded, unable to walk, and in pain, with their rectums, genitals, and uteruses severely damaged. British troops were forced to build compounds to protect Italian women, and doctors were attempting to treat hundreds of these victims. Lewis visited one girl who was so brutally raped by Moroccan troops, as was her mother, that the girl was declared insane. Though she could barely walk, he found her recovering and rational. She would have been admitted to an institution if only a bed were available for her. Lewis wondered, "What is it that turns an ordinary, decent Moroccan peasant boy into the most terrible of sexual psychopaths as soon as he becomes a soldier?"[257]

Prostitution and rape were merely some of the new horrors accompanying postwar occupation. Looting, robbery, vandalism, vendettas, gang violence, and black-market profiteering afflicted the daily lives of most Italians. But above all privations, hunger was the worst. It was hunger that drove most of the crimes. Telephone cables were routinely cut in search of copper for sale. Young boys clambered onto the backs of army food trucks to pilfer whatever they could grab. In defense of precious supplies, soldiers smashed batons down on the children's hands to pry them loose, often severing several fingers in the process.

To Lewis it seemed as though all of Naples had descended into the Middle Ages, as malaria became rampant and medicine was scarce, legless cripples crawled the streets, lunatics roamed freely with no one and no place to care for them, and people held handkerchiefs over their mouths and noses to shield themselves from the stench outside. In one particularly mournful moment, he reflected:

> A year ago we liberated them from the fascist monster, and they still sit doing their best to smile politely at us, as hungry as ever, more disease-ridden than ever before, in the ruins of their beautiful city, where law and order have ceased to exist. And what is the prize that is to be eventually won? The rebirth of democracy, the glorious prospect of being able one day to choose their rulers from a list of powerful men, most of whose corruptions are generally known and accepted with weary resignation. The days of Benito Mussolini must seem like a lost paradise compared to this.[258]

Italy's postwar fate presaged the nightmare that was soon to spread. Once Germany and Japan surrendered and their governments collapsed, the Allies faced the impossible task of bringing order out of chaos. Their challenge was magnified by the millions of displaced persons on the move and the painful shortages of all essential goods, the most vital being food.

Figure 12.1 Two young children at a convent in Rome, where they were cared for by nuns. They were part of a group of children who were abandoned or orphaned during WWII, circa 1945. Photo by Slim Aarons/Getty Images.

Relief

If WWII had brought death and destruction to civilians on a previously unimaginable scale, the postwar peace was seeming scarcely better. Hunger quickly beset Europe, most acutely in the defeated nations. Years of combat had shattered most countries' ability to produce and transport food. A global food shortage ensued.

FDR had prepared for this moment by creating the United Nations Relief and Rehabilitation Administration (UNRRA) in 1943. Roosevelt hoped that genuine international cooperation on efforts such as postwar relief would strengthen ties among nations and contribute toward a lasting peace. He wanted to avoid the failings of the League of Nations, and he saw UNRRA as one means of bolstering the UN's chances of success. America also needed a delegate to UNRRA's governing council, and FDR knew the man for that job: the Undersecretary of State for Economic Affairs, Will Clayton.

Figure 12.2 Citizens of Hamburg queuing among the ruins for their soup rations on March 26, 1946. Photo by Fred Ramage/Keystone Features/Getty Images.

Almost immediately, UNRRA came under fire for its failure to provide services. Critics pointed out that it had delivered very little aid to needy people, that some of that aid had found its way onto the black market, and that its management was chaotic and ineffective. Nearly two years after UNRRA's founding, and shortly after the war ended, Lehman and Clayton appeared on national radio to respond to their critics and explain to the public exactly what the agency was doing. Rather than be forced on the defensive, the two men made a strong case for funding the agency by stressing the dire humanitarian conditions that must be addressed.

Lehman pointed out that UNRRA was handicapped from the start. WWII covered an area hundreds of times larger than in WWI. The weapons used caused far greater devastation, and yet UNRRA's funds were substantially less than those given for relief after the previous war. On top of budgetary constraints, they needed ships to transport food and supplies, but during the war all available vessels had to be used to fight the war. The same was true of staffing. During the war it was nearly impossible to find high-level workers because the most capable people were needed in the war effort. Now that the war was at last over, UNRRA was able to begin bringing medicines, fertilizers, seeds, tools, and essential staples to those most in need.

When the interviewer asked Clayton directly what would happen if UNRRA did not receive the funds it was requesting, Clayton, in his characteristic, straight-talking southern manner, replied that without those funds, "you'll see starvation and suffering worse than anything that happened to civilians during the war."[259]

After some back and forth discussion in which the interviewer, Sterling Eisher, mentioned UNRRA's shortcomings, while Lehman and Clayton parried them, Eisher came to a question on many Americans' minds: "I think many people wonder why Italy would be eligible for UNRRA assistance, as a former enemy country." Clayton explained that President Roosevelt had made an exception for Italy because of the mass starvation across that country. He defended UNRRA assistance, noting that it was limited to pregnant and nursing mothers, children, and the extremely poor. The governing council had decided in August to take on relief in Italy, and the cost was estimated at between $400 and $500 million. UNRRA had extended its activities into countries across Europe and Asia in a massive undertaking for a fledgling organization. Another $600 to $700 million in aid was planned for China, and UNRRA was already shipping eight to ten million tons of used clothing for the coming winter. Soviet Ukraine was in economic chaos, and UNRRA was trying to get aid there as well.

The range of countries in need and the scale of issues to tackle were overwhelming. Lehman had been a successful New York governor, but running UNRRA under frustrating conditions had worn him down. A few months later he resigned. Clayton, too, had lost faith in the UNRRA model, despite his public-facing support for the agency. He felt strongly that there had to be a better way. Americans wanted to act in the world without the fetters of international cooperation. When fighting the war, Americans expected to be the supreme commanders. After the war, they wanted the same unmitigated power to call the shots, even when it came to humanitarian relief. In a poetically symbolic mishap that presaged UNRRA's demise, Clayton found himself stuck in Philadelphia in March 1946. He was due to give a speech at an UNRRA meeting in Atlantic City, but he could not find a taxi to take him there. Having exhausted all other options, he was forced to rent the only vehicle available, a hearse.[260]

The Chief

American food relief efforts sprang from two principal directions. New York City's diminutive and energetic mayor, Fiorello La Guardia, took charge of UNRRA after Herbert Lehman resigned at the end of March 1946. La Guardia used his position atop the international body to urge Americans to reduce their consumption. But a longtime critic of UNRRA was simultaneously called into service. On February 25, 1946, Secretary of Agriculture Clinton Anderson telephoned Hoover to request his assistance. The scale of the crisis was so great that Anderson knew he needed Hoover's unique expertise to tackle it. Hoover was out fishing in Florida when the call came. The following day he dispatched his advice to Washington. True to his logical, organized engineer's training, Hoover laid out the first key steps. As always, he wanted data. What was the exact extent of world food needs and where was the crisis greatest? Where were the surpluses and how much was available? How much surplus did America possess? And in all cases, exactly what kind of food was needed most? Finally, the country had to develop a plan for American housewives to help eliminate food waste so that all excess could be sent abroad.

Secretary Anderson did not delay. He sent a plane to Florida to transport Hoover to Washington on February 28. Hoover met with the newly formed famine committee and with Truman. Again, the contrast between the two men was startling. Truman grinned so broadly that nearly every tooth in his mouth was visible. He looked as though he couldn't be happier to be there, chatting with the ex-president. Hoover stared downward, his expression serious, his hair thinly brushed across his scalp. He looked old and defeated, but that was not at all the case. When his moment in the limelight came, he found his shine. Standing before cameras and reporters on March 1, 1946, the white-haired elder statesman, alongside the President, took the first step in the process of asking Americans for their help.

The famine committee's press conference came against the backdrop of grave warnings issuing from Berlin. The British had just announced that they would be forced to reduce German rations from 1,500 calories per day to just over 1,000. Two thousand calories was considered the minimum necessary for adults' daily needs; 1,500 was already a serious strain on the population. Reducing that amount still further threatened mass starvation. General Lucius Clay, in command of the American zone, expressed doubts that he could maintain his own zone's 1,550 daily calorie level. Soviet General Georgy Zhukov asserted that feeding the German population was a shared responsibility, but American proposals to pool food resources had been rejected by the Control Council.[261] The Allies could not agree on a joint policy, and the German people were bearing the consequences, exactly as Morgenthau had foreseen and counted on.

At 3:15 pm in the East Wing of the White House, Hoover, Truman, Anderson, and Secretary of Commerce Henry Wallace briefly described the unfolding world disaster. Anderson pleaded with Americans to do everything they could, to "strain themselves a little more," in order to prevent millions from starvation and death. Wallace adopted a more guilt-laden tone. He said that once Americans learn the facts of this dire situation, "they will take such action during the next six months that they will not be ashamed of themselves a year hence."[262]

Though his demeanor was solemn, befitting the gravity of the crisis, Hoover looked energized. Reporters noted that in some ways he looked even fitter than he had in the 1920s. Tanned from his fishing off the Florida coast, and dressed in a double-breasted navy blue suit, the ex-president took command of the situation and seized the moment to address the American people.[263] During his WWI relief efforts, people used to say that Hoover knew where every bag of flour in the world was located. Now the reporters noted that he still did. When asked directly if America's former enemies, Germany and Japan, should receive food aid, Hoover was unequivocal. Starving people deserve food. Race, nationality, friend, or foe. It doesn't matter. Those in need must be helped. That was Hoover's world view.

Hoover framed the crisis as a moral imperative. At one moment in the press conference he became visibly angered at the thought of farmers feeding wheat to their animals when people were starving. This was unacceptable. The entire nation had to cut its wheat consumption by at least twenty-five percent in order to create sufficient supplies for export to the worst affected countries.[264] He declared that civilization itself was in jeopardy. Only the United States had the power to arrest the threat of mass starvation. And once again that power had "thrust upon us one of the greatest obligations of these troubled years." Remarkably, the crisis had thrust Hoover back into the spotlight from which he had receded years before.

Hoover assembled a team of men who had worked with him on famine relief during and after WWI, including Hugh Gibson, the former ambassador to Belgium and his former military aide, Captain Ivey Westmoreland. Together they would soon embark on a fact-finding survey of the nations most in need. At age seventy-one, Herbert Hoover was about to begin one of the most grueling and intense journeys of his life. In just under two months he would cover more than 35,000 miles, visit twenty-two countries, deliver two dozen speeches, and offer more than forty press conferences, all while gathering detailed data on food shortages. He viewed his mission as part of a religious duty, and that was how he described it to the American people.

Part of Hoover's plan involved raising the American public's awareness of suffering abroad and inspiring Americans to give what they could to help. After all the collective efforts that Americans had made during the war years, Americans were now being asked to sacrifice still more. It was not an easy sell. On March 14, he spoke to the nation over the radio saying, "I know that the heart of the American people always responds with kindliness to suffering."[265] Two days later he delivered another national address in which he explained his mission and why it mattered:

> Saving of human life is a moral and spiritual duty. If your neighbors and their children were hungry, you would instantly invite them to a seat at your table. These starving women and children are in foreign countries, yet they are hungry human beings – and they are also your neighbors. Could you not imagine one of these helpless women or children as an invisible guest at your table? By following the voluntary rules for saving food you give life to that starving person just as surely as if he sat at your table.[266]

Republican congresswoman Clare Booth Luce, wife of the publishing magnate Henry Luce, joined Hoover on the broadcast. She urged families to reduce food waste, saying that America discards the richest garbage in the world.[267] If every housewife saved two slices of bread per day, we could feed twenty million people. It was rumored that Henry Wallace wanted to enforce mandatory food restrictions, but Hoover insisted that Americans would voluntarily give what was needed.

More than half a billion people in the world were at risk of death by starvation. The challenge was great; the need was immense. Hoover embodied the can-do American ethos of his era, but without the rose-colored spin of more recent times: "To whatever extent we succeed in this task, we shall have given that much help, courage and faith to a despondent and discouraged world."[268] If Hoover could succeed in his mission, he would not only save millions of lives, he might also resurrect his reputation.

Hoover knew exactly what it meant to be despondent and discouraged. He had once been a national hero, admired for his extraordinary rescue of Americans caught in Europe at the outbreak of WWI. He was practically beatified for his single-minded efforts to get food aid into occupied Belgium during the war, thereby saving millions from starvation. He was called "the Great Humanitarian" not only for these acts, but also for his work to feed starving Russians during the famine that followed the war. Brought into the Harding administration to lead the Commerce Department in 1921, he completely reformed and broadened the agency's scope and mission, all the while expanding his power base. As one of his biographers described it, he was always the most capable man in the room, whatever the room, and he knew it. His devoted subordinates simply called him "the Chief." In 1929, his ascendance to the presidency seemed obvious and right. And then, just nine months later, the Great Depression struck on his watch.

The shock of going from revered savior to reviled villain must have been excruciating. It was made all the worse by FDR's treatment of him, bashing him as a cause of the Depression at every reelection campaign. Even leading Republicans kept their distance. Thomas Dewey's campaign advisors warned him against being seen with Hoover, so dark was the stain of his association. Hoover was a pariah of both parties.

The tragedy extended beyond just the man. America lost use of the former president's many talents at a time when every person counted. Hoover possessed matchless know-how when it came to famine relief. Twice during WWII, he had offered his services to President Roosevelt through two separate mutual associates. Each time he was rebuffed. FDR wanted nothing to do with him. It was politically valuable to preserve the fear of a Republican Depression, and Hoover served as its embodiment. When asked if he would consider enlisting Hoover's aid in the coming food crisis, FDR quipped, "I'm not Jesus Christ. I can't resurrect him."[269] On one occasion in 1940, Eleanor Roosevelt persuaded her husband to relent and make Hoover the head of a new relief organization, but Hoover refused, suspecting a political trap.[270] When Truman at last invited Hoover to the White House in May 1945, the force of his emotions nearly overwhelmed him. Returning to the place where he had for four years tried and failed to bring his country out of depression, Hoover needed a moment to compose himself as he fought back the tears.[271] The long public ostracism had clearly been difficult to bear.[272]

Hoover had languished not in political wilderness, but more accurately political purgatory. And then, unexpectedly, after twelve humiliating years, he found himself addressing the nation, called forth out of retirement to once again save the innocent victims of war. His country needed his expertise. Only he could lead such a gargantuan global effort. What yesterday had seemed impossible, today appeared essential. "The Chief" was coming to the rescue. And suddenly, there he was again, standing in the White House, reporters scrambling to take down his remarks, photographers snapping pictures for tomorrow's news. Just days before, few would have believed it possible. Some probably still did not. Herbert Hoover was back.

13 SACRIFICE

On Sunday, March 17, 1946, Hoover and his team boarded a twin-engine DC-54 and took off for Paris. It was the first stop on their grim tour of the postwar world. That same plane carried them across Europe and Asia, and though it proved air-worthy, the initial impression was uninspiring. Their airplane had the unsettling habit of producing a low moaning sound each time it landed, leading the passengers to dub it the "Faithful Cow," a play on FDR's private plane, the "Sacred Cow."[273]

Hoover's ability to assemble a team of professionals so quickly stemmed from his ongoing efforts at food relief since the start of the war. The men he gathered were linked through a social network of charitable organizations and activities, and Hoover knew them well, especially the foreign service officer and former American ambassador to Belgium, Hugh Gibson, with whom Hoover had worked during WWI. Scarcely more than three weeks after WWII began, Hoover created the Commission for Polish Relief, and in December he launched the Finnish Relief Fund, Inc. To boost public support for his relief campaigns, he next formed the National Committee on Food for the Small Democracies, gathering more than 1,400 citizens to participate, including journalists, clergymen, and even former Cabinet members. After America entered the war, he realized that private efforts would not suffice. A strong, centrally organized, government-led operation was needed to address the scale of civilian suffering. He continued to press for such an effort, but he met only recalcitrance from both Roosevelt and Churchill.

Back in January 1941, Hoover had proposed a plan for the Germans to supply some 25,000 tons of cereals to the Belgian distribution centers and the British would permit 20,000 tons of meats, fats, and condensed milk through their blockade. In February he obtained Germany's consent in a signed agreement, but the British ambassador to America, Lord Halifax, informed Hoover that Britain refused to lift its blockade, insisting that the feeding of civilians in occupied territories was the responsibility of the Germans. Roosevelt and Churchill had one aim above all else: to win the war as soon as possible. Anything that distracted from that singular objective they saw as harmful. They had no reason to believe that the Nazis would actually permit food and medicines from the Allies to reach civilians. They assumed that the Nazis would seize it for themselves. The Allies would only be aiding their enemy, and the Nazis were eager to play the Americans for fools.

Hoover disagreed. It was entirely possible, Hoover believed, to get humanitarian relief to innocent civilians, especially children and the elderly, in a time of war. He knew it was possible, because he had done it during the previous war. Even then, Churchill, as First Lord of the Admiralty, had opposed food relief. Hoover's values could never accept Churchill's ice-cold calculus. According to Hoover's ethical code, children could never be permitted to suffer when it was possible to prevent it. From his perspective, Churchill's and Roosevelt's single-minded focus on winning the war at any cost was unconscionable. He called Churchill "a militarist of the extreme school."[274] Hoover's wife and longtime companion, Lou Henry, shared his passionate commitment to rescuing the most vulnerable. According to Hoover, Lou Henry had aged tremendously since the start of the war. On January 7, 1944, she died of heart failure. Hoover believed that she never recovered from the cruelty that FDR and Churchill had inflicted by preventing Europe's children from receiving food aid. "They have never seen children suffer," she told her husband.[275] Mrs. Hoover was not alone in her convictions.

The issue divided America. Hoover's fundraising for humanitarian relief had drawn many religious leaders to his cause. He told British Ambassador Lord Halifax that he could launch a campaign that would be "echoed from 10,000 pulpits."[276] Others opposed him, including prominent Jewish leaders. Rabbi Stephen Wise, president of the World Jewish Congress, supported an embargo on food aid to Jews in occupied countries, believing that such relief would invariably be of aid to the enemy.[277] Clearly, Hoover had stridden once again into controversial terrain. His attempts to move American State Department officials, Undersecretary of State Sumner Welles and Secretary of State Cordell Hull, proved completely futile.[278] As long as Roosevelt remained in office and the war continued, Hoover's relief campaign had no chance.

At last in 1946, Hoover was on the move, trying to assess the continent's food needs now that a new president had charged him with the mission. His team found the mood in Paris worrisome. Hoover's right-hand man, Hugh Gibson, sensed a listlessness among the people. In contrast to Belgium, where the citizens were "busy as bees" attempting to rebuild, the French seemed adrift, quick to complain, and short on hope.[279] The war had taken more than just a physical toll on the nation. The psychic costs appeared just as vast. From their very first stop on this extensive mission, it was clear that food aid would merely serve as the first step in the long journey of recovery. Gibson tried to keep his good humor. At a Paris restaurant he found that there were no choices on the typed menu: barley soup, two small boiled potatoes, and a spoonful of chocolate mousse, "about enough for a robust canary." He didn't mind. Earlier in the day the French Foreign Ministry had served them a rather paltry lunch, and he was relieved. He imagined the press reactions back home if reporters sent back photos of Hoover's food mission dining lavishly while the population wasted away. He knew that the team could not possibly dine well in the coming months of travel, even if good foods were available.

From Paris the team flew to Rome, where Hoover had an audience with the pope, who seemed open to supporting their mission. But any brief hopes were quickly offset by the scene in Warsaw. Children attended makeshift schools amidst rubble and ruins. On March 30, Hoover found himself surrounded by a throng of small children eager to take hold of the famous American ex-president, the hero who brought relief. Outside one orphanage, one little girl took Hoover's hand while another girl placed her hand on Hoover' arm. They seemed to be clinging to him. All of the children were as grimy as the buildings around them.

The adults of Warsaw appeared less enthusiastic about Hoover's presence. Gone were the cheering crowds that had greeted Hoover after WWI. Now the populace scarcely stopped to look, and always with a furtive glance behind their shoulders. From the team's

Figure 13.1 Ex-president Herbert Hoover surrounded by homeless Polish children in Warsaw. Hoover, who was a special representative for President Truman, was touring war-torn Europe to study and help alleviate the critical food shortage. This incident took place when Hoover visited a collection center where homeless children were placed until a new home could be found for them. Photo by Bettmann/Getty Images.

perspective, all around them stood the signs of a growing surveillance state as Soviet domination made its presence felt. The team was warned to watch what they said as buildings were bugged. Armed soldiers throughout the city fired their weapons at the slightest provocation. The team could hear shots being fired throughout the night, sometimes sounding frighteningly close.[280] Gibson observed a carefully concealed reign of terror, though not so well concealed that it escaped the team's notice: "People are taken out of beds at night and disappear into the limbo of forgotten things – not only important people but workmen, bakers, tram conductors, almost anybody who is denounced."[281] A parallel counterterror movement was fighting back against the oppression. Gibson learned that the day before they arrived, a train that was headed into Warsaw had been abruptly stopped. Eleven Russians were removed from the train and shot. The train then rode on.

Gibson had an unexpected shock when a strange man called out to him in the street. The man was shrunken and in rags but smiling. "Your Excellency," he called out, and then Gibson recognized him. It was Mike, his old chauffeur. Gibson greeted him warmly and asked what he could do for him. The chauffeur replied, "I'm doing really well." Gibson noted in his diary that he felt pure admiration for the toughness of the Poles.

After meetings in Helsinki, Oslo, Copenhagen, London, and Belgium, the team landed in Berlin, where General Clay met them at the airport. Clay had been so distraught over the crisis in Germany that he had flown to Brussels several days earlier on April 6 to meet with Hoover, unable to wait for the latter's upcoming arrival in Berlin. The General informed Hoover that Germany was on the brink of mass starvation. Clay said that Allied policies were causing needless unemployment and destitution. Both men agreed that average Germans who had not been responsible for Hitler's crimes should not be punished. They both wanted to see official policies overturned. The only question was how soon they could persuade the policy makers.[282]

Hoover met with German representatives of the three Western Allied occupation zones to learn what types of aid they thought were most needed. At one point in their visit, Gibson went in search of Theodor von Lewald, a former civil servant who had been supportive of Hoover's Commission for the Relief in Belgium during WWI. Lewald had once been a prominent German official and member of the International Olympic Committee. When the Nazis took power in 1933, Lewald was removed from his official positions because his paternal grandmother was Jewish. But due to his prior service, the Nazi regime did allow him a ceremonial role in the 1936 Summer Olympics. Gibson now found the eighty-six-year-old living in a battered house among strangers, surviving on near-starvation rations. Gibson brought him to meet with Hoover and saw to it that he was served sandwiches with their afternoon tea. When the meeting ended, Lewald looked wistfully at Gibson and asked if it would be possible to have just one more sandwich.[283]

In Cairo, Hoover phoned Truman to discuss the situation. Truman wanted Hoover to return to America and deliver a series of speeches aimed at rallying the public behind food aid. Hoover disagreed. He convinced Truman to let him record a speech from Cairo, to be aired in America, while Hoover and his team continued on to assess the crisis in Asia. Both men understood that having an ex-president, the Great Humanitarian, lead the charge against starvation lent weight to the seriousness of the crisis. But the current president himself needed to rally the public's support for Hoover's mission. At 7:00 pm on April 19, Truman broadcast a message on all four national radio networks. His speech was carried on shortwave radio across the globe. First, Secretary Anderson announced that the government would begin paying farmers thirty cents per bushel above the market rate for wheat in order to encourage more production and discourage the feeding of wheat to livestock.[284] When President Truman spoke, he made plain the stakes. Truman insisted that

> we cannot ignore the cry of hungry children. Surely we will not turn our backs on the millions of human beings begging for just a crust of bread. The warm heart of America will respond to the greatest threat of mass starvation in the history of mankind ... . We would not be Americans if we did not wish to share our comparative plenty with suffering people.

Truman described the steps that America was taking to address the crisis, sending one million tons of wheat each month to Europe and Asia. It was drawing down its reserves of wheat still further. He urged all Americans to reduce their own consumption of food, particularly bread, fats, and oils, as these were essential to the effort. He asserted that we would all be better off, not just physically, but spiritually as well, if we ate less. And in a show of solidarity with the suffering peoples around the world, he asked Americans for just two days a week to reduce their consumption to the level of the average person in the famine-stricken lands. In his characteristic straightforward manner, Truman put it simply: "Millions will surely die unless we eat less ... . Every slice of bread, every ounce of fat and oil saved by your voluntary sacrifice, will help keep starving people alive."

Immediately after Truman's remarks, the radio networks played Hoover's address from Cairo. He told Americans of the grave conditions facing people in the lands he had visited thus far. As always, he emphasized the effects of starvation on children and tried to put the problem in perspective. Whereas the average American enjoyed roughly

3,200 calories per day, 2,000 calories was considered the minimum necessary for most adults. Millions of people across Europe and Asia had less than 1,000 to subsist on. While many children would die, the ones who survived would suffer deformities and cognitive impairments. He outlined a six-part plan of action, which he was urging America and the other nations with food surpluses to follow. But he acknowledged that time was against them.[285]

Neither Truman nor Hoover was a gifted orator. Hoover's speaking manner was laconic and flat, some might say dull. His talents lay in mining, management, and logistics. Public speaking had never been his strength. Truman, too, had no natural gifts of persuasion. His voice lacked a sonorous quality and could at times sound squeaky. He never lost his midwestern twang. As speakers, both men stood dwarfed by the imposing shadow of Franklin Roosevelt. FDR's comforting fireside chats had reassured a frightened nation in times of economic upheaval, social unrest, foreign war, and domestic attack. His voice exuded confidence – the certain sound of a man convinced of his own rightful rendezvous with destiny. In contrast, Hoover and Truman had to move a nation not by the way they spoke, but rather by what they said. They had to rely on the force of their words to convey the gravity of the moment. And they hoped that their plain-spoken statements would resonate with average folks. Fortunately for Truman, just two months earlier, Samuel Rosenman, FDR's speechwriter, had resigned. Rosenman had coined the term "New Deal." He had tried to craft speeches for Truman in the way he had done for FDR, but the style did not fit. Once Rosenman was gone, Truman was able to begin finding his own voice.[286]

Truman must have hoped his words would strike a chord when he uttered a remarkable assertion in the midst of his speech on fighting famine. "America cannot remain healthy and happy in the same world where millions of human beings are starving. A sound world order can never be built upon a foundation of human misery."[287] This was not simply an exceedingly altruistic view of world affairs. Both Truman and Hoover grasped that America had a vested interest in mitigating the suffering in foreign lands. They understood that mass suffering can fuel political instability, which in turn can invite revolution, extremism, and war. Both men were guided by their Christian faith. They spoke in Christian terms: mercy, kindness, charity, compassion. And both were moved by the plight of innocent children. The President's assertion was no empty platitude; it reflected his genuine convictions. Unfortunately, it was an aspiration being stymied by his government's own policy.

The German Problem

Stimson's success in bringing Hoover back to prominence had been intended to counteract the worst effects of Morgenthau's influence. It was a clever stroke of political jujitsu. By convincing Truman to enlist Hoover's expertise, Stimson launched his last, best salvo against the Morgenthau Plan. He simultaneously inserted a Republican standard bearer into a position of influence with a Democratic regime and provided his old chief an extraordinary chance to restore his place in history. Unfortunately for Stimson, Morgenthau remained the more skillful master of bureaucratic gamesmanship. Just as Stimson had implanted Hoover as a check against the proponents of the harsh peace for Germany, Morgenthau, too, had embedded his own man deep within the workings of the postwar system. In fact, Morgenthau's ongoing machinations did not end with his fall from power. Instead, he crafted a two-pronged effort to keep his plan in place. His first strike came in an attempt to sway public opinion to his side.

Soon after victory in Europe, Morgenthau laid out the details and rationale for his master plan in *Germany Is Our Problem*. The book was an extended argument in defense of his scheme for postwar peace. In those pages he explained his opinion of the German people, which was neither subtle nor concealed. He saw them, all of them, as hostile. "For longer than living men can remember," Morgenthau opined, "the greatest threat to peace anywhere in the world has been Germany's lust for armed conquest."[288]

Morgenthau did not even accept that including Germany in a new version of the League of Nations could prevent its aggression: "Whether a powerful Germany be excluded from the world organization or admitted to it, the danger to peace would be equally great, until that remote day comes when the rest of the world can be sure that Germany's fervor for war has been eliminated."[289] He was open to the possibility that the Germans might change, but only many decades hence. In a remarkable analogy, he likened the human body to the body politic. Just as limbs can atrophy from disuse, he reasoned, so the Germans might lose their habit of aggression if their sword arm, heavy industry, is left to wither. One day, he mused, they might even lose their taste for it.[290]

Morgenthau's own words make plain that his plan rested on an assumption of innate German aggressiveness. By portraying the German people in this uniform way, Morgenthau fell victim to one of the most widespread human foibles: the lumping of all members of a group into a single category.

Morgenthau may not exactly have wanted the German people to starve. In fact, he paid meticulous attention to German crop yields, labor pools, and other factors that would ensure that much of the population could still survive. He did, however, wish to see them reduced to a vastly lower living standard than they had enjoyed before the war. And if they suffered the pain of privation, then that punishment, as he saw it, was deserved. Morgenthau's view took no account of the fact that even at its peak of popularity, only one-third of the German electorate had voted for the Nazi Party. In holding the entire population responsible for the Nazis' crimes, it disregarded the millions of Germans who opposed the Nazis, including social democrats, communists, Catholics, monarchists, and those of other political and religious backgrounds.[291] And his plan left children to suffer, despite their obvious innocence. Morgenthau might not have seen his plan as vindictive, but others certainly did.

Shortly after Germany's surrender, General Eisenhower began implementing the harsh peace, distributing more than 1,000 free copies of Morgenthau's book, an act that suggests his support for the plan.[292] Only later would he and other US officials recoil at the consequences.

Morgenthau's book was not the only document distributed to American troops. The harshness of Morgenthau's message was contradicted by a different book distributed by the US Army to its occupying forces. *The Pocket Guide to Germany* advised soldiers against mistreatment of the defeated enemy, particularly regarding food. It warned them that the unauthorized rifling of fields and orchards is "contemptable and punishable by court martial." It reminded soldiers that occupied countries will be critically short of food. It is always a strain on our supply lines to feed occupied peoples, the guide explained, so don't strain them any further.

The guide articulated an unquestioned belief in America's basic goodness. It admonished soldiers against belittling the Germans, disrespecting their abilities: "we don't like to kick people when they are down." The Germans under Hitler have been raised to admire force, torture, and fanatical loyalty to the Führer above all else. This, the guide declared, is "the greatest educational crime in the history of the world." The guide reminded the troops of core American values: "One of the things in which we take pride in America is the spirit of sportsmanship, decency, and fair play." You learned as children, the guide proclaimed, to hate a bully. You learned that cheating is wrong, and fairness is right. It concluded that American forces were not to engage in revenge, but instead were there to help the German people "take their place as law-abiding, useful citizens in the family of nations."[293]

And there it was again, a statement of American values: decency and fair play. It was reminiscent of Ralph Bard's plea to Stimson, urging a demonstration of the atom bomb to avoid its use against civilians. It resembled Stimson's plea to the generals to halt the fire bombings. It echoed Joseph Grew's remarks when he urged compassion for ordinary Japanese. And it mirrored Kenneth Ringle's words when he opposed the internment of innocent Japanese Americans. This is who we are, a fair and decent people, they all insisted. It is not who the Germans have become. Our job, the Army told the troops, is to be exemplars of our values, so that Germans can become good again.

Morgenthau's book recommended reducing the German people to a subsistence level. The Army's official guide was somewhat more forgiving. Both books embraced the goal of ensuring that Germany would never again launch another war. But neither book lessened the punishing effects of American occupation policy. The harshness of JCS 1067, the directive governing American occupation, was soon to exacerbate conditions in Germany. But before the German problem could be addressed, the larger global crisis had to be confronted.

The New Horsemen

Hoover returned from an exhausting journey in May, armed with facts, figures, and frightful news. Back in March, Secretary of State Byrnes had recommended that Hoover visit India in order to ensure that Asians did not think that America only cared about European recovery. The situation, he told Truman, was worse in "Asiatic lands."[294] It was sound advice. Hoover's whirlwind trek allowed him to witness the devastation of war, but this was not enough. He wanted to know exactly what prevented food production and distribution. The culprit was not only the war. As he saw it, corruption, inefficiencies, and incompetence were also to blame. Hoover focused on concrete solutions. Blame, he felt, could be left to history. Criticism will not feed the desperate.

At Truman's request, before landing on the mainland, Hoover stopped in Honolulu to meet with Edwin Pauley, now the head of the Japanese Reparations Commission. Hoover urged him to prevent any destruction of Japan's industrial ability for the same reasons that he, Stimson, and McCloy had favored reindustrialization for Germany. A strong Japan, like a strong Germany, would fuel economic recovery regionally and globally. It would serve as a bulwark against the spread of communism. And industrial strength aided food production, essential to prevent starvation. Hoover wrote General MacArthur with the same advice.[295]

On May 16, Hoover returned to the White House to discuss his findings with the President. Hoover recommended taking a tough stand with the Soviets over their refusal to join the United Nations Relief and Rehabilitation Administration. Stalin's obdurate position struck both men as unacceptable. Hoover drafted a letter for Truman to send to Stalin on the matter.[296] Truman and Hoover were beginning to develop a working relationship of trust and respect.

The following day, Hoover again addressed the nation by radio, this time from Chicago. Sounding old and tired, but still in command of the crisis, Hoover laid out for Americans some of what he had learned from his travels. The modern world has added four new horsemen, he said: Destruction, Drought, Fear, and Revolution. On top of war, drought was worsening the situation: "Never have so many evil horse-men come all at one time."

Hoover's chilling imagery described the danger to the most vulnerable. Hunger, he said, hung over more than a third of the earth's population. He called hunger a silent visitor who comes in the night and sits beside every anxious mother three times a day: "He is more destruc-tive than armies, not only in lives, but in morals."

Hoover explained in simple terms that adults need roughly 2,000 calories per day just to survive. Americans typically enjoy far more. If we do not provide any further relief, he implored, millions will sink to ever lower levels, soon dwindling to 900 calories per day, about as much as the Nazis gave their inmates at Buchenwald and Bergen-Belsen. At that point governments will break down and anarchy will follow.

The Food Ambassador spent extra time on the plight of children, describing their caloric needs and his action during WWI to ensure their survival: "Civilization marches forward upon the feet of healthy children." Focusing on children was more than a clever rhetorical ploy. Hoover had always felt a special pang of sympathy for children in need.

After detailing some of the foodstuffs that were needed, such as fats and cereals, Hoover presented his listeners with a stark dichotomy. He pointed directly at the great American divide in world view. "There are Americans," he said, "who believe it right, and a duty, to feed the women and children of a surrendered enemy." These Americans recognize that peace requires the saving of former enemies from starvation in order to rebuild them into cooperative peoples. But there are others who remember the crimes of the enemy and demand an eye for an eye. Hoover's response to those who seek vengeance was direct. To garrison half a million American soldiers amidst starving women and children was unthinkable: "we do not want our flag flying over a nation of Buchenwalds."[297] At these words, his audience, which had been listening in attentive silence, loudly and vigorously applauded. It was the only moment during his address that this occurred.

Anyone who had followed Hoover's career closely might have felt a peculiar sense of déjà vu, for the opinions he was voicing now strikingly resembled the arguments he had made about feeding Germans after WWI. In 1919, while leading relief efforts in Europe, Hoover had to endure the anger of some Americans who did not want their country to be caring for the hated enemy. In response, Hoover issued a press release to address the problem directly. In cogent, succinct prose, he listed the many reasons why feeding the Germans was the wisest course. Hunger breeds anarchy, and anarchy only leads to further conflict. Women and children did not make war on us, and they should not be made to suffer. Food aid is not charity; the Germans are paying for it. And the sooner that country can be productive again, the sooner it can repay its debts to the Allies for the war. And then, in consummate Hooverian fashion, he took the long view on humanitarian missions by concluding: "No matter how deeply we may feel at the present moment, our vision must stretch over the next hundred years and we must write now into history such acts as will stand creditably in the minds of our grandchildren."[298]

Another prominent American lent her voice to the crisis. Though Herbert Hoover and Eleanor Roosevelt stood poles apart in most of their views on the role of government, they shared a common conviction that governments must help to alleviate hunger. In an interview with the popular magazine *Ladies' Home Journal*, the former first lady tried to explain the dire situation of Europeans to comparatively comfortable Americans. She invited reporters into her New York City apartment with its view of Washington Square. To underscore the theme of hunger, she served only tea and buttered brown bread. There were no fancy teacakes or elegant hors d'oeuvres. When asked if Americans truly understood what conditions were like across the Atlantic, she answered, "None of us could understand how terrible things are in Europe, without going and actually seeing them. Even pictures of a bombing remain only pictures to us, unless we have stood among the rubble and destruction ourselves." She had stood there. She had seen the destruction and the suffering. And she hoped to raise more than just awareness. She wanted Americans to eat less.

In order to encourage sacrifice, Eleanor Roosevelt first employed guilt: "We Americans cannot expect to live on a little island of prosperity in a sea of human misery." In case that failed to move her readers, she tried fear of communism: "We cannot make our political system, our view of life, seem appealing to other peoples, if we are withholding friendly help from them in the way of food. That would surely make them our enemies, drive them into the arms of a Russia which appears to have more sympathy for their troubles." If we think we have a better way of life to offer others, she implored, then we must show our "essential friendliness" to them when they are in greatest need.

It was difficult to convey the extent of the food crisis. Although she appeared animated, the former first lady never fidgeted. She was of a certain class, raised in a particular era, when young women learned proper posture and diction. It was not considered ladylike for a woman to gesticulate in public, and so despite her animation at the topic, she remained perfectly composed. She told how, after explaining to a well-fed American woman that Europeans were surviving on 1,500 calories per day, the woman replied that she, herself, often dieted by eating that amount, and it really wasn't bad at all. Mrs. Roosevelt determined that from then on she would not speak of calories, but instead of actual meals. Breakfast consists of a quarter heel of gray bread. Lunch is a bowl of thin soup with a slice of bread. For dinner, there is only a third slice of bread. There are no fruits or fresh vegetables, no fats or butter, no eggs, no milk, and only seldom is there salt. For these starving millions, a food package from America would mean the difference between health and sickness: "it will mean that they regard Americans as their friends and not as insensitive strangers across the sea who gorge themselves while Europeans starve."[299]

In June, Mrs. Roosevelt visited Princeton, New Jersey, where she found Americans heeding the call. She described in her newspaper column, "My Day," how the town's residents were intentionally going hungry in order to support the food drive. They aimed to raise $10,000 for UNRRA's relief efforts, but these citizens were increasing their commitment even further. In conjunction with grocery stores, restaurants, and hotels, they encouraged everyone not to eat any fats on one day per week and to have no bread for four meals per week. Mrs. Roosevelt spotlighted these impressive, voluntary restrictions on behalf of Europe's starving millions. Not all Americans followed Princeton's example, but many did.[300]

While Eleanor Roosevelt was highlighting sacrifices at home, Hoover was continuing his mission overseas. After his intense tour of Europe and Asia, and following his many meetings and speeches back in America, the former president undertook another journey, this time to Latin America. His aim was to urge those countries with food surpluses to increase their exports of essentials to the nations in need. In June he negotiated with Argentina's president, Juan Perón, to ramp up beef exports, but Perón insisted on a quid pro quo. He wanted America to lift its restrictions on Argentina's gold holdings in the United States. Hoover convinced Truman to make the deal.[301] By the end of all this activity, Hoover told friends that every molecule in him cried out for rest. The Great Humanitarian had pushed himself to exhaustion because he understood better than almost anyone else exactly what was at stake, both for humanity and for how it would remember him. And while Hoover was crisscrossing the globe, gathering data and pleading with world leaders to take action, a parallel effort to reverse course was taking place within Germany.

About Face

There were, of course, many American officials who recognized the folly of a harsh peace. Even the notoriously fearsome General Patton wrote to his wife on September 2, 1945 that "What we are doing is to utterly destroy the only semi-modern state in Europe so that Russia can swallow the whole."[302]

Patton was correct. Soviet actions in its own occupation zone quickly revealed how the Russians intended to treat their former enemy. Once the war ended, Stalin immediately began implementing a Morgenthau Plan of his own. In one of the greatest acts of international looting, whole factories in Germany were dismantled, packed onto trains, and sent eastward to Russia. Within the Soviet sector, Russian soldiers engaged in rampant rapes of German women, acts which Stalin tacitly approved. In the American-occupied zone, the situation was less violent,[303] but in accordance with JCS 1067, US forces were to take no steps to rehabilitate, maintain, or strengthen the German economy.[304] Though not exactly a directive to dismantle German industry, given the desperate postwar conditions, forbidding occupation forces to aid German recovery was essentially a death sentence to countless civilians.

Morgenthau's publication of *Germany Is Our Problem* was only one facet of his ongoing effort to shape the postwar peace. His second, less visible maneuver involved the transfer of his own loyalist, Bernard Bernstein, onto General Lucius Clay's staff. Clay, who succeeded Eisenhower as the commander of the American occupation forces in March 1947, had grave qualms about JCS 1067. Bernstein had helped Morgenthau with its drafting. By implanting Bernstein inside Clay's operations, Morgenthau hoped to keep up the pressure to implement as much of the original plan as possible. In addition to handling the myriad crises confronting occupation forces, the General also had to keep Bernstein at bay.

Clay, a chain-smoking, hard-driven soldier, was the son of a US senator and the descendant of another of America's most storied senators of the early 1800s, Henry Clay. That ancestor had earned the moniker "the great compromiser" for his role in the Missouri Compromise, which prohibited slavery in certain states. In contrast, Lucius Clay's unyielding stubbornness earned him the nickname "the Great Uncompromiser." Clay found the scale of German suffering pitiful. At times he had American soldiers give some of their own food to starving Germans. In his memoirs he wrote, "My exultation in victory was diminished as I witnessed this degradation of man. I decided then and there never to forget that we were responsible for the government of human beings."[305] In a 1975 interview, Clay explained that under the restrictions of JCS 1067, reconstruction was impossible: "If you followed it literally you couldn't have done anything to restore the German economy." To circumvent official policy, Clay pursued a strategy of slow and steady subterfuge. By gradually issuing exemptions, he hoped to undermine and eventually defang the worst of a harsh peace.[306]

Lucius Clay longed to command soldiers during the war, but Eisenhower ordered him to Washington. It was not meant as a punishment, though to Clay it must have felt that way. You train all your life for combat, he lamented, and then the greatest war of all time comes along and you can't be a part of it.[307] But Eisenhower needed Clay back in Washington to solve a problem. The Army could not fight without a flow of weapons and supplies, and Clay had a gift for logistics. He was assigned to the Office of War Mobilization and Reconversion, headed by former Supreme Court Justice James Byrnes. The two men came to work well together and respect each other. With some ingenuity and attention to detail, supplies made their way to Europe more efficiently. Clay set aside his personal ambitions and played a vital role in winning the war. Now he had to play an even more important role in rescuing the peace.

On September 6, Secretary of State Byrnes delivered a speech in Stuttgart which marked the first official signs that Morgenthau's legacy would have to be undone. The previous day, America and Britain merged their occupation zones into a single entity. Tensions with the Soviets had made cooperation increasingly fraught, and Germans were caught in the middle. The food crisis had not abated, and the destruction from the war more than a year after surrender still seemed grim. Byrnes took this opportunity to clarify American objectives in occupying Germany.

Byrnes had come to Germany in order to assess the problems of rebuilding that shattered nation. America, he declared, had learned the lesson of WWI, after which it had tried to isolate itself. The United States now understood that isolation was not an option in an intertwined global economy. Though he did not say it directly, the subtext of his remarks implied that a rebuilt German economy was vital to the prosperity of Europe and the United States.

Byrnes laid the blame for Germany's current woes at both the Nazis' feet and Soviet intransigence, though he did not call out the Soviets by name. Instead, he stated that the Control Council was failing to govern. Germany needed policies to be coordinated across the four occupied zones. Germany had to have centralized agencies to implement common financial, industrial, and trade policies. It needed transportation, postal, and communications agencies that worked in harmony throughout the country, rather than at odds with operations in other zones. America and Britain had joined their zones in order to increase efficiency, combat inflation, and promote a unified Germany. Germany urgently needed a central department of agriculture in order to maximize food production. And then Byrnes uttered a crucial sentence, one which revealed that after two long and costly years since Stimson and Morgenthau's clash began, the triumph of Henry Morgenthau would be undone: "It is the view of the American Government that the German people throughout Germany, under proper safeguards, should now be given the primary responsibility for the running of their own affairs." That one sentence led Germans to dub this the "speech of hope."[308]

Byrnes acknowledged that Americans had been divided over how to treat Germany during occupation. Americans, he asserted, "have long since ceased to talk of a hard or a soft peace for Germany. This never has been the real issue. What we want is a lasting peace."[309] Byrnes was speaking hopefully, but his words were not entirely accurate. There were voices in America that still wanted the German people punished. Soon they would make themselves heard by the highest authority.

Eleanor Roosevelt favored the harsh peace devised by her friend Henry Morgenthau. She felt that the Germans deserved further punishment. In her syndicated column she declared that the German people had suffered less than any others in Europe. She implied that Americans would be fools to allow German industry to rebuild. "What are we doing?" she asked. "Are we planning to make them strong again so we can have another war?" We are frightening the Russians with our behavior, and she asked her readers to remember that it was the Germans, not the Russians, who had launched the two world wars.[310]

The former first lady was keeping up the pressure for a Morgenthau-style treatment of the German people, but Truman and Hoover were moving in the opposite direction. Truman was grateful to Hoover for his service as food ambassador. He made a point of acknowledging what the elderly statesman had done. A few weeks before Christmas, Truman wrote him: "You did a magnificent job last year for the welfare of the world."[311] Fortunately for Hoover, he had the holidays to rest. He would need it, because in January, Truman called him into service once more. This time the mission sent the seventy-two-year-old ex-president shivering across the frigid, shattered landscape of America's former foe.

14 REFORM

The old woman awoke suddenly in the night. She didn't hear anything, but she should have. Her husband's steady breathing was missing. She got up and went into the kitchen. Flicking on the light, she saw the crumbs on the tablecloth and, understanding what it meant, quickly looked away. She always cleaned the table before bed.

"I thought there was something here," he told her. It must have been the wind, they both agreed. She thought how old he looked, though only sixty-three, standing there in his nightshirt. He thought the same of her. She beckoned him to come back to bed before he caught a cold. He repeated that he thought he had heard something. She pretended to have heard it, too.

In bed, she kept her breathing steady so he would think she had fallen back to sleep. But she could hear his slow, stealthy chewing, and she pitied him. The next night at dinner she cut him an extra slice of bread, claiming that it did not agree with her. He tried to refuse her portion, knowing he was eating her share, but quickly he relented and ate. She waited a long while before joining him at the table under the lamp, where she would have to see him clearly.

Soon after Germany's surrender, as children died of malnutrition and adults struggled to survive on paltry rations, a young author captured the experience in achingly sparse prose. In Wolfgang Borchert's 1946 short story "The Bread" a woman awakes in the night to discover her husband in the kitchen guiltily consuming a little more bread than his allotted amount – a portion that should have gone to her. When, on the next night, she gives her husband her own share of rations, both silently acknowledge the wife's sacrifice under dire conditions.[312] The year after publishing this story, Borchert, a young author with so much promise, died. He was twenty-six years old.

The years 1945 and 1946 unfolded for Germany much the way it had for occupied Italy, only worse. Hoover's famine relief mission had helped to stave off starvation for millions in Europe and Asia, but Germany posed a special problem. The world food crisis hit Germany especially hard, not simply because the war's destruction had shattered its ability to produce and transport food to cities.[313] Germany's situation was compounded by JCS 1067. Because of Morgenthau's insistence, the directive prevented American occupiers from revitalizing German industry, which greatly exacerbated already grim conditions. Caloric intake plummeted from an average of 2,445 calories per day to a paltry 860.[314] It was becoming painfully apparent to American policy makers that if something did not change soon, the death toll would be unconscionable.

The year 1947 opened with another mission for Herbert Hoover. Truman wrote the ex-president on January 18, asking him to visit the American and British occupation zones of Germany and Austria. On New Year's Day, the United States and Britain formally combined their respective zones to form the awkwardly named Bizonia. It had become clear that cooperation with Soviet officials over Germany was heading toward a rift. As Morgenthau had predicted, Soviet leaders wanted a harsh peace and were intent on thwarting any Western softening in the form of rebuilding the shattered German economy, at least for the time being.

Hoover's assignment was couched as an economic mission, an effort to determine if some of the financial burden on American taxpayers could be lifted. Both Truman and Hoover feared the mounting costs of occupation almost as much as the humanitarian dangers. Maintaining Germany was a strain, to the tune of more than half a billion dollars each year for America and Britain combined, and Truman understood that the current arrangement was not sustainable. This was what President Roosevelt had worried about back in March 1945, and it was what Stimson, McCloy, Grew, Clayton, and many other experts had foreseen long before. Clayton even met with Hoover on January 22, in order to discuss the gravity of Germany's position. Germany, like Britain and France, could not produce sufficient amounts of food and material goods to sustain their populations. Worse still, a historically cold winter stymied production for weeks, leaving snow drifts of twenty feet in some areas. Europe, and especially Germany, needed America's help. Clayton and Hoover had no doubt that the legacy of Morgenthau's plan, as expressed in JCS 1067, no longer made sense, if it ever had.

Truman recognized that he could use Hoover for both fact-finding and for political cover. Hoover could provide the thorough, analytical, evidence-based report to justify the new postwar policy that Truman and others wanted. In February, Hoover and his team found themselves back in Germany, surveying the state of hunger. As in their previous missions, Hoover's close aide, Hugh Gibson, proved adept at ferreting out facts and sizing up the mood of those on the ground. In conversations with American occupation officers, he learned that many lived under the threat of aspersions cast by "the smear brigade," namely, Eleanor Roosevelt and Henry Morgenthau. Both were still pushing for a Morgenthau-style treatment of the German people. Just one month earlier on January 3, Eleanor Roosevelt wrote in her newspaper column, "My Day," that although the Germans would eventually have to run their own country because the occupation could not continue forever, the main aim of occupation must be to ensure that German heavy industry is never permitted to rebuild. Light industry was acceptable, the former first lady explained, but Germany must be prevented from ever again being able to manufacture the weapons of war.[315] It is not clear if Mrs. Roosevelt understood that without heavy industry, average Germans, many of whom had never supported Nazism, would suffer intense privation, especially in the winter of 1947.

Hoover's team began in a demolished Frankfurt, still devastated nearly two years after the end of the war. Snow blanketed the country. This was a bitterly cold winter, made all the more bitter by the lack of coal. The main complaint that Gibson heard from average Germans was their inability ever to get warm. Coal was scarce, because mining and transportation networks remained limited. In Hamburg, the team heard exactly how challenging it had become to get coal from the Ruhr. One official told them that a shipment of 1,000 tons of coal had taken eighteen trains to reach Hamburg. This was partly because the first seventeen had broken down, and partly because when those trains did break down, Germans, desperate for warmth, broke in and looted the coal.[316] Germans were literally freezing to death.

Throughout the trip, Hoover, Gibson, and the entire team, along with the American and British officers with whom they met, constantly shivered inside conference rooms, homes, and buildings. Kerosene heaters seldom sufficed to warm large meeting rooms. But the team carried on, gathering facts and calculating needs. The team's hope was merely to raise the rations of German adults to 1,800 calories per day – a sum still below the 2,000-calorie minimum.

The challenges confronting children were even greater. Europe had approximately twenty to thirty million malnourished children. The death rate of 250 per 1,000 was frighteningly high. For Hoover, the children in every land always came first. Their welfare was his greatest concern. His speeches consistently emphasized the effects of hunger on children, knowing that the gruesome facts of malnutrition would tug at the compassionate hearts of most Americans and prompt them to act. But he also knew that a lasting peace would be endangered if a generation of malnourished, stunted, emotionally and intellectually damaged children grew into unhealthy adults.

Hoover's own childhood had taught him the terrible toll that privation brings. Born in 1874 in a tiny Quaker town on the Iowa prairie, his parents and two siblings lived in a house just twelve by twenty feet in size. Most of the townsfolk were farmers, but Herbert's father worked as a blacksmith. When his father was thirty-six, a typhoid epidemic swept through the town. He did not survive. A few years later, Herbert's mother died of pneumonia. By age ten, Hoover was an orphan.[317]

Hoover's Quaker upbringing reinforced compassion for those in need, and Hoover was a man who put his principles into action. While a partner of an international mining corporation in 1902, another of the firm's partners, A. Stanley Rowe, nearly ruined the company by speculating in the stock market and losing his own savings. In a reckless effort to cover his losses, Rowe forged the company's stock shares and sold nearly a quarter million dollars' worth. When his ruse was discovered just two days before Christmas, he tried to keep his partners from learning about it for as long as possible. During the holidays, Hoover and his wife, Lou Henry, spent an afternoon with the Rowes and their five children. In a cryptic comment, Rowe asked Lou if she would help raise the children if anything ever happened to him. Hoover and Lou left the party assuming that Rowe was suffering from a bout of seasonal depression. A few days later Hoover received a letter from the partner explaining what he had done and asking Hoover to forgive him. Rowe then shaved his mustache as a meager attempt to disguise his appearance, left his wife and children, and disappeared.

Hoover had to pick up the pieces of this man's horrendous judgment. The firm was plunged into crippling debt. Hoover was not legally responsible for the losses, but he wanted the firm to survive. He persuaded the remaining partners to jointly assume the debts incurred in order to salvage the company's reputation. It took years to bring the firm out of the red. After Rowe was caught, he was sentenced to ten years in prison. During the next eight years, Hoover sent money to Rowe's sister, who was raising the five children. In Hoover's view, the children were innocent. He saw no reason why they should suffer for the sins of their father. When Rowe was released from prison after eight years of his sentence, he wrote to Hoover to thank him for his generosity and asked to meet with him. Hoover had no wish to see him again, but he responded that he had no vindictive feelings toward him, despite Rowe costing him years of fruitless labor spent extracting the firm from needless debt. Hoover included some money for the man along with a note: "I shall be only too glad if by your future career you can reestablish your good name, and above all, give your children a proper position in the world."[318]

At times, Hoover exhibited an almost storybook form of kindness. Perhaps his compassion stemmed from firsthand experience with suffering. He understood what it felt like to struggle against the elements, from those harsh Iowa winters. He knew the vagaries of disease, how it can rip through a town, taking lives at random. He knew poverty and privation. He may even have known hunger. And he knew the agony of grief, being orphaned at a young age. His 1940s residence in the Waldorf Astoria Hotel must have seemed an eternity away from that childhood, but those early memories may have felt much closer as he encountered the shattered world he now sought to revive.

Persuade

Given the Allies' near total failure to lessen the misery of most Germans, it was not surprising that the defeated populace found little appealing about democracy under occupation. In fact, for many Germans, their postwar conditions were far worse than they had been under Hitler. In the British zone, Gibson spoke with the chief intelligence officer, whom Gibson probed for information on German attitudes. The Lieutenant Colonel related the intense disenchantment that most Germans felt. They had been bombarded with Allied propaganda about the virtues of democracy, but nearly two years after their surrender, the economy was in shambles. Norman Lewis had observed in Naples that most Italians saw no benefits from democracy since it seemed to bring only dysfunctional government and an increase in suffering. Hoover's team was discovering the same perceptions in Germany. From the viewpoint of average Germans, democracy had nothing to offer, and the occupiers appeared utterly incompetent.

As grim as the situation was under the democracies in Western Europe, life was even worse under communist rule. Across Eastern Europe, Soviets had been brutally suppressing opposition, strangling dissent, and reshaping their sphere of influence by force. Many who had suffered under Nazi control for years initially welcomed their Red Army liberators. Their enthusiasm was short-lived. In just the eastern parts of Poland, the Soviets arrested between 35,000 and 45,000 suspects from 1944 to 1947. Those who fell prey to the NKVD (a forerunner to the KGB) were interrogated by torture.[319] Reflecting Stalin's own paranoia, Eastern European Secret Services eyed their own citizens with deep suspicion. By 1954, the Polish Secret Service had created forty-three separate categories of suspicious elements and swelled its surveillance rolls to six million, one in three adults. That year the total number of imprisoned political opponents reached over 84,000. Similar patterns of repression emerged throughout the Soviet sphere.[320] Soviet-occupied Germany, however, bore a special burden in the early years after Hitler's fall.

If Hoover thought that American occupation policy was vengeful, it was nothing compared to Soviet revenge. Hoover's team was learning that the Soviet zone had been stripped to the bone by rapacious Red Army forces, ordered to dismantle German industry and cart it back to Russia. From Hoover's and Gibson's perspectives, these Soviet actions probably appeared as vengeful. From the Soviet viewpoint, however, the removal of German goods represented compensation for the extraordinary destruction that invading Nazi armies had inflicted on Russia. Gibson's contacts confirmed his impression that within the Soviet occupation zone, the Russians had impoverished the Germans, failed to turn them into communist believers, and "have made themselves so obnoxious that the people look upon any other Zone as a paradise."[321]

Was Gibson seeing only what he wanted to see, filtering information through an anti-communist lens? After all, it was Germans who had impoverished Germany; the Soviets were not yet uplifting their economic condition. Economically, the Americans had fared no better in their own zone, thanks in part to the Morgenthau-influenced occupation plan. As for ideological convictions, could Germans really be expected to be communist true believers after just two years since the war's end? And did the Germans in the Soviet zone all look with longing at the Western zones, when conditions there were scarcely better? The situation was grim across postwar Europe, East and West, but certain aspects of Soviet rule clearly stood out as distinct. Gibson's contacts, old colleagues and acquaintances made in the course of his long diplomatic career, shared chilling stories of what they had experienced in Soviet-ruled areas. Some of his friends had landed in hospitals, where the Russian and Czech Secret Services routinely dragged people out of the facility to beat and torture them. Some did not survive the cruelty. One of Gibson's friends would have died in hospital, but just before the Czech Secret Service came through, a Russian man wrote him a note on a sheet of paper, which he held up to him in his hospital bed, and then took the paper away. The message read, "Pretend to be in worse condition than you are." The man took the stranger's advice. When the Secret Service began taking patients out, he acted as though he was near death, and the Czechs ignored him.[322] He never learned why the Russian saved his life. Perhaps the Russian stranger recoiled at the actions of his compatriots but lacked the power to oppose them in any other manner than this.

Through such stories, Gibson and, by extension, Hoover were gradually gaining a frightening window into the horrors of life under communist rule. The Soviet zone provided a useful mirror on American values. Hoover and Gibson could recoil at what the Soviets were doing and conclude that this was not who Americans should be as occupiers. If the Americans and British could raise the quality of life within their zones, they would not only be achieving humanitarian relief, but would also be undermining the appeal of communism. From the Hoover team's perspective, communist supporters in Eastern Europe were simply victims of the Soviet propaganda they were being fed. Absent actual nourishment, they turned to communist parties in desperate hope that

their situation would improve. But for many East Europeans, communism held genuine appeal as a means of correcting the long-standing
inequities in their societies, especially the unfair access to land.[323]

With his characteristic thoroughness and scrupulous burrowing
into details, Hoover compiled his report on the dire conditions of
Germans. On February 26, he submitted his findings to Truman, noting
that the current circumstances represented something entirely new in
human history. The victors were expending colossal sums to support the
vanquished, rather than the other way around. The situation cannot
change, he observed, until German industry is revived. To those who
preferred seeing the German people suffer, he had only disdain: "But
those who believe in vengeance and the punishment of a great mass of
Germans not concerned in the Nazi conspiracy can now have no misgivings, for all of them – in food, warmth and shelter – have been sunk to
the lowest level known in a hundred years of Western history."[324]
Hoover recognized that the desire to see the German people suffer was
simply another case of misplaced vengeance. The majority of Germans
never even voted for Hitler and the Nazis, and thousands of innocent
children were being forced to suffer for the crimes of guilty adults. Years
later, as Hoover compiled his magnum opus, he titled his section on the
postwar period, "Vengeance Comes to Germany."[325]

Beyond the pure unfairness of the current arrangement, Hoover
also saw the self-defeating aspects of present policy. He argued that
Western civilization could not survive in Europe without it surviving in
Germany. The only hope was to make Germany into a cooperative
partner in that civilization. Absent this, there would be no lasting
peace. Hoover saw it as America's responsibility to ensure that the
German people could again flourish, and not be kept down by
American force: "After all, our flag flies over these people. That flag
means something besides military power."[326]

After reading Hoover's report, Truman issued a statement two
days later. He reminded Americans that Europe was still in desperate
straits, despite Americans' many sacrifices in sending food: "I am sure
that I express the opinion of all Americans in pledging that we will
continue the policy of sharing out of our abundance with those in dire
need. Every additional pound of grain we can export is a contribution to
human welfare, to reconstruction, and to world peace."[327]

Truman and Hoover met again in the White House on March
12, 1947. On March 18, Hoover submitted the third of his three reports,

this one devoted solely to the German and Austrian crisis. Once again, he insisted that both countries must be rebuilt in order to resurrect the rest of Europe, but this time he spoke out as frankly and directly as possible against the legacy of Henry Morgenthau. Hoover specifically cited Quebec, the meeting in September 1944 when Morgenthau persuaded FDR and Churchill to adopt a punitive peace. He exposed the folly of Morgenthau's idea that Germany should be "pastoralized" and returned to an agrarian state. He shredded the idea that destroying German heavy industry could be done without widespread suffering and harm to all of Europe. And he made plain the link between the Morgenthau Plan and its influence on current US policy. He observed that "This idea of a 'pastoral state' partially survived in JCS Order 1067 of April, 1945 for the American zone."

This was no offhand comment, a cheap shot at the former Treasury secretary, conjured up simply to lend weight to his recommendations. Hoover had long been distressed by the harshness with which FDR intended to treat the German people. Hoover had been keeping a thick and growing file on the Morgenthau Plan for his personal records. He planned to write a magnum opus about the war, a history seen from his perspective. The same month that he met with Truman to discuss the last of his three reports on Germany, he also added a substantial magazine article to his Morgenthau file. According to the author, who detailed the development of Morgenthau's plan, as early as April 12, 1943, Morgenthau's anti-German sentiments were on full display. On that day the Treasury Secretary spoke at Carnegie Hall to a crowd of New Yorkers and declared: "Now we are ready to deal a few blows ourselves; and they will be blows, I can promise you, that *will rock Nazi Germany to its rotten blood-stained foundation.*" But the original text of his speech referred solely to Germany, not Nazi Germany. A censor in the Office of War Information insisted that Morgenthau insert the phrase Nazi Germany in order to distinguish between average Germans and Nazis. The OWI censor asserted that most Germans are fine people and it was a shame to speak of them in this way. Although Morgenthau relented, his true feelings about most Germans were seeping through. It appears that Hoover read this article at the time he developed his final report on the need to revise America's occupation policy.[328]

In characteristically Hooverian fashion, the master of relief laid out in precise detail the effects of JCS 1067 by listing the reduction in essential materials in tonnage units. Iron and steel, machine tools, cement, agricultural implements, chemicals such as nitrates for fertilizers, boots and shoes, textiles – in every category, Hoover showed how the drastic fall in production meant that Germany would need to import these goods, and it would not be able to pay for them. The United States would continue to have no choice but to foot the bill if it wanted to avoid even greater chaos than was already the case. And then Hoover turned to the crux of the matter: food.

During the war, Germany had still been able to meet eighty-five percent of its food needs, Hoover stated. Since the war, that level had fallen to sixty-four percent. Its agricultural production was based largely on intensive use of fertilizers. Germany now needed at least 500,000 metric tons of nitrogen and 650,000 tons of phosphoric anhydride to produce the necessary amounts of fertilizers. Among the many restrictions imposed on Germany, the production levels of these chemicals would fall to around 200,000 metric tons of each. Unless it could afford to import the difference, the result would be starvation. Hoover concluded that if America's current policies continue, without large imports of fertilizer, Germany's ability to feed itself will fall to a dangerous level. Worse still, all of Europe desperately needed fertilizers to restore food production. Germany had been a vital exporter, but with its productive capacity crippled, it could neither export fertilizers to the rest of Europe nor reap the profits from those exports, further hamstringing its ability to pay for its own needs.

If none of those arguments sufficed to convince the skeptical, Hoover had still more cards to play in favor of relief. The rest of Europe could not recover without an economically productive Germany. Europe depended on German production of capital goods – construction materials, factory equipment, railway equipment, electrical and heavy machinery – all of which required heavy industry to create. Many countries used German products and needed German-made parts simply to repair what had been destroyed or damaged in the war. Without restoring Germany's ability to produce those capital goods, all of Europe would take far longer to rebuild. Germany had also been a profitable market for the import of goods from other European nations. Greece had sold Germany more than a third of its exports, and Turkey had exported over half of its products there. With the German market unable to purchase imports, those nations would likely experience higher unemployment from depressed demand, loss of revenues, and would then be looking to the United States for aid. The continent had long ago become interconnected, and Germany lay at the heart of that system.

Turning to humanitarian concerns, Hoover argued that Germans needed far more calories per day than they were able to produce under current restrictions. He believed that Germans must have 2,600 calories daily, "if there is to be a will to work, to maintain order and to aspire to peace." But at present, he estimated that Germany would need to import over $1,250 million just in food and animal feed alone. Unless Germans were allowed to starve, he concluded, Germany would be an economic drain on America for years to come. "We can keep Germany in these economic chains," he quipped, "but it will also keep Europe in rags."[329]

The American people were coming around to Hoover's view. The initial anger at Germans had been softening as the extent of German suffering became clear. Hoover's public campaigns began paying dividends, as George Gallup revealed in his opinion surveys. Gallup asked those who had read or heard about Hoover's latest report on the crisis whether they agreed with it or not. Six in ten of those surveyed agreed. As one Chicago minister put it: "We have a moral and humanitarian obligation to feed our former enemies and, besides, if we permit chaos to continue in Germany there's no telling where it might lead." The majority were on Hoover's side, on the side of mercy. But three in ten held the opposite view. A lawyer in San Francisco typified the minority position, which called for continuing the harsh treatment: "I thought Mr. Hoover's report was exaggerated. He wants too much done for the Germans. After all, they made millions suffer from hunger when they were top dogs. We shouldn't give them anything but the barest necessities for a while."[330] It had been two long years since the fall of Hitler's Reich, and the question remained whether the minority who sought vengeance would once again outmaneuver the majority who favored virtue.

Despite Hoover's best efforts to change American policy, and despite having the will of most Americans behind him, his arguments failed to persuade some influential figures around the President. Not everyone was convinced by either Hoover's data or his reasoning. Some officials remained adamant that the United States should maintain the pressure. Edwin W. Pauley, the former US representative on the Allied Commission on Reparations, strenuously objected to Hoover's advice.

Hoping to counteract Hoover's influence over the President, Pauley wrote Truman on April 15: "I feel the deepest kind of apprehension over his proposal for the revival of German heavy industry." He belittled Hoover's ideas, stating that he thinks like an engineer: "He is accustomed to thinking a project through and calculating its probable results."[331] But Pauley did not believe it wise to aid German industry probably for the same reasons that Morgenthau had outlined. And Pauley was not alone.

Two days later, John Steelman, an influential aide to Truman, took an even stronger stand against any softening toward the Germans. Steelman was hardly known for having a combative nature. An open-faced, smiling southerner with a Ph.D., he had taught sociology and economics at Alabama College in the early 1930s. His expertise and aptitude for settling disputes caught the attention of FDR's labor secretary, Frances Perkins, who recruited him into the administration. Within three years he had become the commissioner of conciliation, the branch of the Labor Department charged with mediating management–labor conflicts. In 1946, Truman appointed him as the first White House chief of staff, though at the time this position was more modestly titled assistant to the president.

Despite Steelman's background as a man who worked toward compromise, on the German question he took an uncompromising stance. Steelman left no doubt that Morgenthau's legacy loomed large in his thinking: "The proposal advanced by Mr. Hoover in his third report contemplates a fundamental reversal of American political and economic policy in Europe and run counter to the international commitments of this government undertaken at Quebec, September 15, 1944, and at Potsdam in 1946."[332]

Truman knew all about Quebec. On July 3, 1945, Stimson had informed the new president about the Treasury's triumph at Quebec, when Morgenthau had persuaded both Roosevelt and Churchill to adopt his most punishing peace plan for Germany. As Steelman now conjured the memory of Quebec, Truman had plenty of context to understand what his chief assistant was implying. He meant that America had agreed to a tough policy on Germany, and any relenting of this position would be a serious reversal of President Roosevelt's vision for the postwar world – a vision that Truman had vowed to carry through.

But times had changed, and new information forced Truman to revise his thinking. He had never shared FDR's closeness to Morgenthau. He had agreed to JCS 1067 at a time when he was overwhelmed by the countless weighty decisions demanded of him. Two years on from those daunting first few months as president, Truman could now begin to forge a fresh course of his own, one not only informed by Hoover's analysis, but also by that of another key figure in his government.

15 REVIVE

In March and April 1947, Will Clayton, promoted to the post of undersecretary of state for economic affairs, traveled in Europe for a firsthand look at conditions. Just as McCloy had surveyed Europe's devastation in 1945 as Allied forces pushed toward Berlin, it was now Clayton's turn to witness conditions for himself. Clayton had been part of the 1945 compromise with Morgenthau that had produced JCS 1067. In fact, he had chaired the inter-agency committee that created it. He had initially opposed a harsh peace for Germany, then reportedly (at least according to McCloy) came partly around to Morgenthau's view. But now, forced to confront the effects of that critical restriction, the one forbidding American occupation authorities from aiding German recovery, Clayton experienced a total change of heart. On May 27, Clayton reported his observations in stark detail: "Millions of people in the cities are slowly starving." He described the breakdown of normal economic life, primarily the effects of inflation that led farmers to refuse to bring their goods to cities in exchange for worthless paper money. Clayton asserted unequivocally that if the already dangerously low standard of living should be lowered any further, "there will be revolution."[333]

Clayton might rightly be considered the true father of the Marshall Plan. Though there were many leaders who lent their hands to it, Clayton arguably played the most potent role in crafting it. His memo was a critical step in the Marshall Plan's creation and the final undoing of Morgenthau's punitive peace. While his knowledge of international markets and fear of social upheaval led him to argue for a policy reversal, there was more to his memo than this.

By the time he was drafting his pivotal memo on America's new global role, Will Clayton had already been a key player in some of the most crucial decisions on Europe and Japan. He had served as one of eight members of the Interim Committee, which advised Truman on the use of the atomic bombs. He was at Potsdam with Truman at the conference where the postwar fates of Europe and Japan were formalized. And he was now taking a leading role in rebuilding Europe – at least those areas of Europe that Stalin did not yet control.

Part of the secret to Clayton's rise lay in his remarkable wife, Sue. He first met Susan Vaughn in 1897 when she was just sixteen. He had gone to visit a neighbor when an unfamiliar woman opened the door. She was visiting from Kentucky. There she stood, dressed in a pale blue blouse accented by a pink cameo at her neck. Blond-haired and blue-eyed, quick-witted and charming, Sue Vaughn instantly captivated the young Will Clayton. She stood scarcely over five feet tall, a striking contrast to Will's towering six-foot-two stature, yet the two found themselves instantly compatible. It took barely a moment after setting eyes on her for Will to ask if she would go rowing with him on the river that evening.[334]

In the fall of 1899, after two years of courtship, Will proposed to Sue, but she did not give him an answer. He would have to wait, and worry. For Sue had other suitors. A fellow Kentuckian hoped to win her hand. He was a young man with ambition and talent, a man who was going places. His name was Alben Barkley.[335]

Will did not relent. He wrote letters to Sue from New York, describing to her the scenes of the big city, and especially the homecoming of Admiral Dewey, hero of the Spanish-American War in the Philippines. But he mostly spoke of the lands they both knew back home, the natural beauty of the countryside that he missed. In December, Will traveled to Washington, DC, to meet Sue, who was then a student at Washington College. Over dinner at the Ritz he was struck again by her stunning pale complexion, offset by her black coat and furs. Sue accepted his proposal. It was December 24, and it was the best Christmas gift Will could imagine.[336]

On New Year's Day, Will was back at the office, working all day, alone. It was the first day of a new century. That night he wrote Sue: "I didn't have anything else to do and nowhere to go, so I thought I would work, as I never get sad when I am busy. But I am never going to be sad again because I love you."[337]

Like nearly all of his peers, Clayton was raised as a devout Christian. His mother often quoted Scripture. Inside the Bible she had given him she wrote, "Seek ye first the kingdom of God and his righteousness and all these things shall be added unto you."[338] Later, he read from the Bible to his daughters.[339]

From an early age, Clayton possessed an ability to concentrate on multiple subjects at a time and to dedicate himself to seeing tasks to completion, no matter what got in the way. Once, while undersecretary of state, a subordinate told him of his worries over his inability to get something passed in the Senate. Clayton told him, "Never wrestle with the facts. It isn't your fault that the facts can't be changed. Wrestle with what you can do about them."[340] His can-do attitude enabled him to found and develop a cotton trading firm into a multinational powerhouse, establishing for himself a fortune in the process.

In 1916, Clayton moved from Oklahoma City to Houston. His firm expanded, transporting cotton internationally, trading with Russia, and establishing offices in China and Japan. Soon his firm became the largest of its kind in the world. On August 17, 1936, Clayton appeared on the cover of *Time* magazine. At that time, cotton was America's greatest export, and Clayton's company brought $1 billion of it to market annually. As *Time* observed, the logistics of this feat boggled any onlooker, once you realized that it required the seamless integration of "gins, warehouses, compresses, ships, barges, railroads, trucks, spot markets, futures markets; the services of dealers, bankers, brokers, buyers, factors, graders, merchants."[341] There was a point when his company fell under investigation, but cleared of all charges, Clayton continued to rise in prominence, eventually leading to his inclusion in FDR's administration. He was not at first a natural fit. Like many business executives and entrepreneurs, Clayton viewed FDR's New Deal with a mix of suspicion and fear. But Sue had a way of softening Will's more conservative edges. In 1936, she headed the Women's Division of the National Democratic Committee for Houston. As one of the city's most prominent women, Sue carried weight. She served as an alternate delegate to the Democratic convention that year and was reportedly one of the most generous donors to the President's campaign.[342] Her backing of Roosevelt did not go unnoticed by the consummate politician in the White House. Four years later, she gave speeches in support of FDR and against his Republican opponent,

Wendell Willkie. On September 26, 1940, FDR wrote to thank her for her generous financial support of his campaign.[343]

Clayton's international business expertise made him an asset to Roosevelt's administration. After a stint at the Export-Import Bank acquiring strategic materials, Clayton was named assistant secretary of commerce in 1942. In 1943 his portfolio expanded to include chief of the War Damage Insurance Corporation. He also ran the Committee for Economic Development, which planned for post-war conversion of industry. But Clayton had difficulty working with Vice President Wallace. Their clashes left him frustrated and tired. By the start of 1944, Clayton had decided to leave government.

The President recognized Clayton's unique skills and could not let him go. On January 20, 1944, FDR wrote directly to Sue, deploying that famed FDR charm:

Dear Mrs. Clayton,

Recently Will told me of his desire to leave Washington. I am sure that he was influenced by the very natural desire to comply with your wishes. He has been doing a grand job and I want him to remain here and take over some new duties. However, I know that so far as he is concerned, you are the real Commander-in-Chief, and I am writing to ask you to order him to remain here and undertake the tasks for which I am drafting him.

Please let me know when you have issued the orders.[344]

And then the President added a postscript: "Don't relinquish your authority over him."

FDR's charm masked a shrewd understanding. From long experience, he had learned that governments work best when staffed with the best. The country's institutions needed to attract and retain its most capable citizens. It could not afford to lose anyone over petty infighting or personality clashes. Ideological differences could be over-come in the service to the nation. FDR wisely included Republicans such as Stimson, McCloy, and Bard in his administration. Business tycoons such as Clayton had a place in his government, as long as they harnessed their expertise for the good of the country. It fell to the President, as the head of government, to lift up those around him, ensure they were positioned to succeed, and convince them that they were serving a noble cause. America was fortunate that Roosevelt took this view. His ability to retain the services of Will Clayton paid off substantially after Roosevelt had passed from the scene.

On March 5, 1947, on a plane to Tucson, Will Clayton scribbled down the rough outlines of what became his memorandum to Secretary Marshall several weeks later. In it he laid out a thirteen-point statement of American interests and values, laden with proposals for nothing less than a new world order.

"The reins of world leadership are fast slipping from Britain's competent but now very weak hands," his rough draft began. "Either Russia or the United States will pick up those reins. If it is Russia, there will almost certainly be war in the next decade or so. The United States must assume world leadership, but its people won't allow it unless they are shocked into doing so." Clayton believed that Americans would accept the burden of global leadership if they knew what the Soviets were doing within their sphere, namely, ruthlessly tightening their control over countries that he saw as crucial to America's national interest.[345] In his words, we can hear an early murmur of the domino theory that would produce so much suffering in the decades to come. From his perspective, the Soviets were "feeding on hunger, economic misery, and frustration." He felt passionately that the United States must support those threatened nations with economic and financial aid.[346]

Clayton was articulating what many others in the government had been coming to understand. As they saw it, America's role in the world had to expand. The country could not retreat to its own shores. Hoover's food mission was only a stopgap measure to prevent mass starvation. From Clayton's perspective, people were starving, and communists were preying on their misery. To ensure a genuine quality of life for liberated peoples, communism had to be blocked. If communism continued to feed on the hunger and misery of desperate peoples, they would barter away their freedoms for their daily bread. America, as Clayton and others saw it, was the only nation able to lead a coalition of democratic countries against communist expansion. Military might could not suffice in that effort. It was going to take money on an unprecedented scale – and that implied a degree of involvement in those countries' internal affairs. The United States, he believed, had a vested interest in remaking the free world in its image.

Reverse

Two main factors allowed the much wiser Marshall Plan to supplant the vindictive Morgenthau Plan. The first stemmed from an enlightened self-interest. Occupation was proving exceedingly expensive. The costs would be lessened if the German economy were strong rather than weak. Germany's and Western Europe's vibrant consumer base could provide markets for American exports, but those countries also needed to trade with each other in order to grow their economies. In short, rebuilding Germany made financial sense for Europe and America. This is what Clayton, Secretary of State Acheson, and Director of Policy Planning George Kennan were asserting in their discussions with Marshall, and it was exactly what Stimson had explained to Roosevelt nearly three years before in the fall of 1944.

But the second factor shaping their revised policy toward Germany stemmed from empathy. The scale of child deaths from malnutrition was growing increasingly difficult for American observers to stomach. Elderly Germans as well could scarcely withstand the freezing winters without heat or fuel, nor the near starvation rations that Hoover and his team were struggling to raise. As reports continued to filter in to occupation officials and then worked their way back to Washington, the breadth of suffering demanded a change. And that was a testament to the goodness of American officials from Truman on down through the government and military. Marshall Plan aid was intended to block the spread of communism, and this desire stemmed not solely from economic self-interest, but also from empathy. Given what Americans were learning about Soviet rule in Eastern Europe, there was good reason for concern.

Russian troops in Germany engaged in widespread looting and frequent rapes of German women.[347] Russian forces systematically dismantled German factories and shipped them back to Russia piecemeal on the trains. Western observers knew of those actions, but far fewer knew the extent of Soviet violence against their political opponents occurring across Soviet-occupied territories. Truman, however, did learn of this brutality, thanks to covert reports from the Office of Strategic Services, the forerunner to the CIA. William Donovan, more commonly known as "Wild Bill," headed the OSS. His sources were gathering intelligence on Soviet murders and political oppression in Poland.[348] Owing in part to Donovan's reporting, Truman understood the horror of allowing communist control in any country. There were naturally those who supported communist parties in Eastern Europe, believing that communism would alleviate the social and class inequities that had persisted for centuries. As communist parties gained momentum in Italy, France, and elsewhere, Marshall Plan aid appeared as a possible antidote to communism's appeal. If American leaders genuinely cared about the welfare of those liberated from Nazi rule, many of them who were not long ago viewed as enemies, then they had to do more than just combat communism's advance. They had to actively rebuild a shattered world. The first, most critical step was to reverse course by abandoning the Morgenthau Plan and replacing it with Marshall aid.

Although Hoover had consistently opposed the Morgenthau Plan as both impractical and un-Christian, he harbored deep reservations about its replacement. For Hoover, who held an ideological conviction against dependencies, massive American financial transfers to Europe could not be the answer to recovery. While he believed in giving Europeans a hand up, he wanted to see a definite end date to American subsidies. The goal was to prevent starvation, revitalize German industries, and make Europe self-sufficient so that America could withdraw. The Marshall Plan envisioned a far more extensive American commitment to European recovery and stability than Hoover was prepared to accept. But given Hoover's renown as the world's most famous practitioner of humanitarian relief, his support would add weight to the bipartisan effort to pass the landmark legislation. Someone needed to persuade him to change his mind – someone of equal stature, a Republican whom Hoover would respect, and someone who excelled at building consensus.

On November 4, 1947, the eighty-year-old Stimson wrote to Hoover urging him to join a Citizens Committee for the Marshall Plan. Stimson compiled what he hoped would be the most meaningful arguments. He combined them with superlatives, which should have impressed Hoover, since Stimson had never been prone to hyperbole. He remarked that Americans were facing a challenging opportunity, possibly the greatest ever offered to a single nation. The country had the unique chance to use its full strength for the peace and freedom of the world. Americans could refuse to help rebuild the shattered economies "only if they wish to desert every principle by which they claim to live." Failure to assist "would be the most tragic mistake in our history." He concluded that "The sooner we act, the surer our success and the less it will cost us."[349] But Hoover was unmoved. He seems not to have replied to Stimson's invitation. The man who had made his name as the Great Humanitarian simply could not bring himself to support a plan of endless giving.[350]

During the Great Depression, Hoover had mostly clung to his ideological conviction that government works best when it intervenes least. It was a belief only somewhat altered by context. And his adherence to that principle worsened the lives of Americans living in Hoovervilles, draped in Hoover blankets, and standing in lengthy soup kitchen lines. Now, decades later, he remained wedded to the same principle, unable or unwilling to recognize that the postwar crisis demanded the largest governmental intervention in history. Hoover could not see that principles serve best as guides, not masters. By refusing to endorse the Marshall Plan, Hoover missed a historic chance to rethink his dogmatic position and partake in what many scholars would one day call the single greatest achievement of the United States in the twentieth century.[351]

If Hoover missed his chance to aid the movement for the Marshall Plan, he did not fail to continue his humanitarian relief work. Humanitarianism was for him as strong a conviction as his belief in limited government, and that was fortunate for the many lives he managed to touch. His personal sacrifices on behalf of the world's starving millions deserved recognition, and he was soon to get it. After decades of political ostracism, the aging ex-president was about to have one last chance to resuscitate his reputation, and one more moment to inspire Americans to do good. It came on the brink of a breathtaking national triumph, and a stunning political defeat.

Hoover's reports laid bare Europe's desperate straits and what needed to be done, but Europeans could not survive on memos and reports. They needed food – and fast. Hoover's missions had spotlighted the crisis and helped pave the way for the final overturning of Morgenthau's legacy. But getting the Marshall Plan passed through Congress would take time, and time was in shortest supply. The State Department was reporting that Italy and France were in danger of collapse, which would trigger a cascade of calamities across the continent. Department officials believed that the communists were planning to aggravate the food crisis in the hope of bringing down democratic regimes. The Department warned that a totalitarian Europe would mean the undoing of what America had just fought for: "The spiritual loss would be incalculable."[352] Harry Truman had to find a way to get more food to Europe, and that could only happen if Americans ate less, freeing up a surplus to send abroad. The public would have to be persuaded. The military could not wage this fight. Wall Street could not simply fund it. What Truman needed now was an army of advert-isers. And to lead the charge, he needed the nation's sharpest salesman.

16 HUNGER

In late September 1947, Charles Luckman was touring one of his company's newest plants when he received an unexpected call. President Harry Truman was on the line. The country needed Luckman's special gifts, and millions of lives depended on him. Would he come to Washington immediately to head an emergency committee? Three hours later, Luckman was on his company plane to DC.[353]

To Luckman, it felt like the opportunity of a lifetime – a chance to give back to the country that had made him a stunning success. Luckman had studied architecture in college, but when the Depression hit, construction ceased. The young man pivoted to sales, landing a job in 1931 selling soap for Colgate-Palmolive. Almost instantly his latent knack for salesmanship emerged. He proved so adept that by age twenty-seven *Time* magazine dubbed him a "boy wonder of business." At thirty-three he had been made president of Pepsodent. By thirty-seven he had catapulted to the top of Lever Brothers, the makers of Pepsodent, Rinso, Lux soap, and other leading brands. At last a wealthy man, he could afford the tailored suits to augment his crisp appearance. With sharply arched eyebrows, wavy though receding hair, and a pipe in hand, Luckman looked the part of a young and savvy corporate mogul. But his appearance was not what propelled him upward. Two gifts explained his rapid rise: he possessed an uncanny people sense, and he simply knew how to persuade. Those skills were what Truman needed most if he was going to get Americans behind an intensive voluntary food drive.

As the winter of 1947 approached, millions of Europeans faced the horror of mass starvation. A combination of wartime destruction, postwar drought, and the coldest winter in memory was crippling production. The United States had already sent as much surplus grain as it had available, but Europe needed an additional one hundred million bushels, if it was to avoid an apocalypse. There was simply no more to send – at least, not yet.

Harry Truman could not stomach the idea of allowing millions to starve, if he could possibly prevent it. His deep humanity drove him to act. So much had been sacrificed throughout the war, so many lives had been shattered and lost, and now starvation threatened to destroy the hard-won peace. Mass death, malnutrition, and especially the spread of disease that accompanied the crisis would leave Europe prey to anarchy. Hunger, he knew, drove people to despair. Somehow that extra one hundred million bushels would have to be found. And they would need to find it in less than one hundred days. He had to persuade the nation to sacrifice on behalf of total strangers overseas. Both Truman and Luckman were counting on the American people's sensibleness, goodness, and basic sense of decency. They were not wrong to expect support, but their idealized image of America crashed head first into the reality of a divided nation.

The problem, of course, was that the President had no legal authority to seize grain from farmers. Any additional grain would have to be produced voluntarily. But the country had already sacrificed during four long years to rescue Europeans from fascism. Americans had endured rationing on the home front and lost sons overseas. They now wanted to enjoy the benefits of peace. The question was whether Americans could still be convinced to give.

Luckman had scarcely said yes to the President before ringing up friends in the ad business. He realized that if he would be asking Americans to act entirely of their own volition, he would need the help of professional persuaders. He called on the country's top seven advertising agencies to create their most compelling campaigns, and he gave them only that weekend to work on it. Given the scale of the operation, they could not afford to lose a day. Scores of creatives, from copywriters to layout artists, brainstormed through the weekend, often sleeping in their offices.[354] Luckman had thrown down a challenge, and the "Mad Men" of Madison Avenue responded.

Luckman's decision to enlist ad agencies was not unprecedented. During the war, the US government had frequently employed the services of the Advertising Council and others to create films, broadcasts, posters, and informational campaigns to maintain public support. And the advertising professionals were not alone. Songwriters and musicians did their part as well. Henry Morgenthau, while serving as Treasury secretary, recruited America's most celebrated songwriter to compose a tune to help sell war bonds. Irving Berlin's "Any Bonds Today?" implored Americans to "Scrape up the most you can. Here comes the freedom man, asking you to buy a share of freedom today."[355] The song succeeded brilliantly, and Berlin, in an act that might seem mind-boggling today, assigned all royalties to the government.

Americans had also been asked to ration food so that there would be more available to send to soldiers overseas. The sweet vocals of Peggy Lee, backed by Benny Goodman, spurred the spirit of sacrifice with lyrics that today sound of a distant era.

> *Well there may be a shortage of sugar, of aluminum pots and such.*
> But there won't be a shortage of love, when we love each other so much. . . .
> Let the taxes rise, we'll economize, and cut our budget in two.
> We can trade our car in for a horse or a bicycle built for two.[356]

Getting Americans to accept higher taxes might have worked in wartime, but asking them to go hungry during peacetime was an entirely different demand. The government once again needed the nation's best influencers to sell the notion of giving. And a bit of presidential pressure wouldn't hurt either. Although the Citizens Food Committee was not technically part of the government, Truman assigned Luckman an office in the White House. This symbolic act was intended solely so that Luckman could contact others by having his staff announce, "The White House is calling." It was a shrewd move, which Luckman later said had worked like magic.[357]

On Monday, September 29, after more than four hundred advertising agency employees brainstormed solutions throughout the weekend, each team submitted its ideas, offering some one hundred different ad campaigns. The assemblage of advertisers converged on the Carlton Hotel, just two blocks from the White House. Luckman's secretary remarked that there were so many ideas snapping at you, "It was like being knee-deep in alligators. You never knew when one might reach out and bite you."[358] Luckman convened his hastily appointed committee the following day. Having polled 4,000 Americans, they found that most people, when told of Europe's dire situation, were willing to do what was needed. The team decided that the most effective campaign would be one of self-sacrifice. The slogan they selected was simple: "Save Wheat, Save Meat, Save the Peace."

A good slogan needs a symbol, and the winning entry drafted the bald eagle into service. Instead of facing an olive branch, this time the eagle was clutching a basket of food. Thousands of posters, placards, stickers, and billboards were immediately ordered. Billboards that normally required three weeks to produce were ready in three days. The Committee distributed these materials across the country, to schools, churches, public places, and shops – anywhere that would get the nation's attention.[359]

Posters and slogans would only be effective if they were connected to concrete plans. The Committee put forward a stringent four-point program. Americans would be asked to eat one less slice of bread per day, to eat no meat on Tuesdays, to eat no poultry or eggs on Thursdays, and (especially relevant to restaurants) to not offer bread and butter unless requested.

At 10 am on October 1, 1947, in the east wing of the White House, Truman spoke to the Committee, telling them in part: "You are here because millions of people in many countries are hungry and look to the United States for help. You are here because the United States, in addition to being a granary of bread, is even more a granary of hope."[360]

The President grasped that simply urging individuals to eat fewer slices of bread would never be enough. Truman had grown up in the farmland of Missouri. He knew exactly how grain is produced and how it is consumed. The key was to feed less grain to livestock and to cut down on waste. Some ten percent of all the food we buy, Truman said, is wasted. If Americans can reduce that level of loss, it would go a long way toward feeding hungry families abroad. The Committee could help Americans determine how to waste less, but everything depended on speed.[361]

Secretary of State George Marshall added his voice to the President's, urging swift action on the part of the public. The problem, he told the Committee, had reached the point where "only the immediate and concerted action of our people as a whole" can avoid disaster: "Every American, I am sure, will gladly share his bounty with the hungry men, women and children of Europe."[362] Marshall's faith in the country's goodness sprang from the sacrifices he had witnessed Americans make throughout the war. Luckman's task was to transform Marshall's faith into concrete actions. And the President was about to introduce the Boy Wonder to the nation.

Truman turned to a new medium to communicate the crisis. Television was just beginning to enter American homes, and though radio was still dominant, TV looked to have tremendous potential. In the first-ever televised address from the White House, simultaneously carried on all four radio networks, Truman outlined the emergency and the plan. He chose to make this address on a Sunday night, October 5, when most Americans would be at home and potentially in a charitable frame of mind, many having attended church that morning.

Truman's expression was somber, befitting the gravity of the situation. Standing at a lectern, the President outlined the suffering of average Europeans. Speaking frankly to the country, he explained that the nations of western Europe will not make it through the coming winter unless America steps in: "I know every American feels in his heart that we must help to prevent starvation and distress among our fellow men in other countries."[363] The crisis, he said, presented an opportunity for Americans to help. Truman led by example. He declared that the White House would comply with the Citizens Food Committee's four-point plan, as would all government restaurants and cafeterias across the country. He announced that he had ordered the Army, Navy, and Air Force to comply as well. But the effort could only succeed if every sector of society joined in – farmers, industry, and individual Americans: "From now on, we shall be testing at every meal the degree to which each of us is willing to exercise self-control for the good of all." The President was attempting to trigger the public's charity and compassion. Hungry people abroad are looking to us for help, he told the nation: "We must not fail them."[364]

With the President having launched the program, it was time for Luckman to assume the day-to-day operations. Things did not start smoothly. Luckman had assembled a top-notch team of prominent businessmen and civic leaders to aid in the food relief campaign. In their first meeting, each member demonstrated their remarkable ego. They talked at length, appearing more concerned about how the

Committee would affect their image rather than how they would be saving lives. The meeting adjourned with nothing resolved. Luckman then held his first press conference and discovered that Washington is not, in fact, a friendly town. He had kept the press waiting, and he was unprepared for the barrage of questions hurled at him. He had failed to gain his own Committee's approval for his initial plans, and he lacked specifics on how those plans would be implemented. It was a complete disaster. As Luckman put it, "I got murdered." The next day, the *Washington Post* reported: "Mr. Luckman, acknowledged to be a great salesman, found himself standing before the press with nothing to sell. He took a beating, but it must be said in fairness that he took it like a man."[365]

Luckman was not a politician. He had no familiarity with the brutality of the political arena. But he did possess an essential ingredient for success in any new endeavor: he was a quick learner. At his next press conference the following day, Luckman took command. Yesterday I listened to you, he told the press corps. Today you will listen to me. And then he laid out detailed explanations of how the grain-saving program would function. The newspapers delighted in his performance. Luckman was redeemed – for the moment.

Initially, Americans rallied behind the food drive. Citizen groups and organizations pledged their support of the President's plan. In southern California, women's groups declared that it was housewives who had done much of the conservation during the war, and they would be the ones to lead the way again.[366] In Boston, four out of five housewives reported not having served meat on the first Tuesday of the campaign, and across Boston sales of fish rose substantially.[367] The campaign got a boost when the military joined in. Commanding officers urged all soldiers, sailors, and airmen to obey the Meatless Tuesdays initiative. It warned that eating in restaurants that flouted the effort not only violated the spirit of the campaign but set a bad example to others.[368]

Most Americans were responding, but time remained the greatest enemy. More stringent measures were needed. Although a Gallup poll revealed that an extraordinary ninety-three percent of Americans knew about the food crisis and sixty percent claimed that they adhered to the voluntary food-saving measures, Truman and the Food Committee understood that the greatest savings would come from grain producers in the Midwest and the South, not from grain consumers. That fact was driven home when Agriculture Secretary Clinton Anderson committed his own press conference gaffe, thoughtlessly referring to the average citizen's actions as mere "symbols of sacrifice."[369] Truman and Luckman then had to double down on the program, insisting that every American was needed; every effort, no matter how small, helped save lives. But the truth was inescapable. The campaign absolutely required industry's support. And that was where Luckman came in again.

Luckman had to concentrate his persuasive powers on businesses and initially this too went smoothly. The nation's bakers showed that they would do their part. They agreed to stop producing baked goods that lacked sustained demand. They cut out three-layer cakes and pies with two crusts. They studied ways to produce smaller loaves of bread. But the largest savings came by ending the selling of baked products on consignment, a practice that allowed distributors to return those products that went unsold. The net effect of these new practices was to make nine million bushels of grain available for shipment overseas. One hundred million bushels were needed. Nine million was a start, but they had to find much more.

Restaurants made a major contribution to the effort by enforcing meatless Tuesdays and eggless Thursdays, and by reducing the number of items on their menus. Flour mills, syrup, corn starch, and breakfast cereal manufacturers took steps to cut fifteen to thirty million bushels.[370] Sector by sector, with Luckman's leadership, Truman's support, and sustained ad campaigns, the goal of one hundred million bushels was starting to seem possible. Americans were showing their true goodness, sacrificing for others in a time of need. But as always, another side of America wrestled with that charitable urge, and soon the backlash began.

The first grumblings of discontent came, not surprisingly, from steak houses. To serve no meat on Tuesdays effectively meant the loss of an entire day of income every week, while still having to pay rent and wages.[371] Next, 250 prisoners at a federal penitentiary launched a hunger strike in protest over meatless and eggless days, unhappy with their already unsatisfying meals.[372] But the first truly major opposition came from the country's poultry producers. Fearing a substantial loss of revenue, they strongly opposed Poultryless Thursdays, and the industry intended to fight it. To draw attention to the problem and simultaneously embarrass the President, they sent crates of live chickens to the White House, hoping that the cacophony of squawks would undermine the President's public relations campaign. The media instantly dubbed them "Harry's Hens," and "Luckman's Leghorns."[373] The battle for public sentiment was on.

In truth, the rushed, almost frenzied nature of Luckman's plans led inescapably to some ill-conceived ideas. The Committee was quickly forced to drop Poultryless Thursdays, and the press piled on about bureaucratic folly. From the Committee's perspective, it was attempting to save lives in a madcap race against time, while industry leaders and newsmen were sabotaging their efforts to win public support. In the end, Eggless Thursdays remained, and a new plan was hatched. After some fruitless negotiations between the two sides, the poultry industry representatives offered a grim but practical alternative. The largest consumers of grain were chicks, not people. Many of those birds would never be eaten, but feeding them required the use of vast amounts of grain. The solution was clear, though unpleasant. The chicks would have to be killed. With no better option at hand, the nation's poultry producers engaged in an act of mass extermination. Some 136 million baby chicks were culled, but this freed up thirty million bushels of grain. By reducing the turkey population, along with other measures, the poultry industry provided a total of fifty-six million bushels, more than half of the one hundred million bushel goal.[374] The Committee had nearly done it. With just one more measure, they would hit their target. But this last push seemed a step too far.

Distilleries consume vast quantities of grain to make alcohol. If they could be induced to shut down their operations altogether, if only for a limited time, it would easily make as much as twenty million bushels of grain available for Europe. But shutting them down meant that American workers would be laid off during the holidays for at least as long as the closures remained in effect. The union of distillery workers was outraged, claiming that the shutdown would cost 10,000 to 12,000 jobs.[375] Though the estimates were highly exaggerated, the workers' concerns were real. It was fine to help feeding the starving masses in Europe, but shouldn't the President be putting America first? This was certainly how it seemed to the union members whose lives were about to be disrupted. And it was not just union workers whom Luckman was infuriating. Business owners were growing increasingly irate.

Despite the constant battles, Luckman had good cause for optimism. His program, though controversial, was succeeding. The four-point plan had brought at least a significant part of the country into the effort. The poultry producers, restaurant associations, and other key sectors had, after savvy appeals to their patriotism and principles, contributed much of the needed grain. Luckman had also overseen a breathtakingly popular food drive in which a "Friendship Train" raced across the country, picking up donations in cities large and small. To unite the nation around the cause, film producer Harry Warner (of Warner Brothers Studios) took care to show Black Americans and Native Americans, not just white citizens, participating. The train netted twenty-two million bushels of grain and assorted nonperishable foods, while simultaneously raising the public's commitment to fighting hunger abroad. The Friendship Train ended in New York City, where Luckman jubilantly attended the ostentatious celebrations. He cheered the send-off as the collected grain and other foods were transferred to ships that set sail for Europe. On his return to Washington, he was feeling hopeful, though spent. The Committee was now so close to reaching the goal that initially seemed elusive. He had worked relentlessly to meet the one hundred million bushel target, and he needed rest. He arrived at his DC office to find a furious Lewis Rosenstiel waiting in the reception room.

Rosenstiel owned Schenley Industries, the largest liquor manufacturer in the country, and he feared that an industry-wide closure would curtail revenue. A domineering, driven, and wealthy man known for cut-throat business maneuvers, Rosenstiel was rumored to have ties to both FBI Director J. Edgar Hoover and organized crime.[376] Rosenstiel was used to getting his way. And at this moment, he was livid about the shutdown. Shouting invectives at the young sales executive, Rosenstiel threatened to ruin Luckman. He yelled that he would get Luckman's plans canceled and see Luckman fired by both the head of Unilever and the President. Luckman had had enough. Had he not been so exhausted, he might have thought better of what he next said: "Mr. Rosenstiel, I've been working night and day for months and I'm very tired. If you can get both Truman and my chairman to fire me, I will be grateful."[377]

Rosenstiel trembled with fury. Such effrontery, and from a man not yet forty, would not be tolerated. Shaking his finger at Luckman, Rosenstiel shouted, "Okay, kid, you'll be hearing from the president of the United States in five minutes," and stormed out.[378]

He was right. Truman swiftly summoned Luckman to his office. Rosenstiel was a major donor to the Truman campaign, and Luckman's insolence might have just cost the President a fortune. The coming presidential election was sure to be tough on Truman. His popularity had sagged, and his most likely opponent, New York governor Thomas Dewey, had organization, momentum, and money to spare. The President could scarcely afford to be losing wealthy backers. Knowing he had gone too far, Luckman resigned himself to his punishment.

"Do you know I'm supposed to fire you?" Truman asked. Luckman said that he understood and asked only how soon it would need to happen. But things were not as Luckman had assumed. Truman then revealed, "I let him go on for three minutes and then told the son-of-a-bitch to get the hell out of my office." Truman added that he told Rosenstiel he would be sending back his $100,000 campaign contribution.[379] Truman had promised Luckman when he took the job that he would have the President's complete support, and the President had just proved he was a man of his word.

That did not settle the matter, of course, because Luckman still had to persuade the nation's distillers to voluntarily close their doors for sixty days, and not one of them planned to agree. With the industry chiefs seated around a table, Luckman made his case. He explained again the desperate straits of Europe's women and children. He played on the industrialists' compassion, their kindness, their humanity, but the owners seemed unmoved. Luckman had sold soap to consumers. He had been dubbed the boy wonder of sales. But this pitch required more than mere salesmanship. It called for politics, and politics meant power. He could see that the discussions were going poorly. The group's resistance was strong. Soon he would have to call for a vote. And then, unexpectedly, Luckman was passed a note. It came from one of the industrialists in the room, the influential Armand Hammer. The note read: "Everyone in this room knows you have the complete backing of Harry Truman. Make them vote by name."[380]

Hammer was a man who understood power. None of the men in the room genuinely supported the shutdown, but not one would relish making an enemy of the President. They all knew that Truman had expended time, resources, and political capital to support the food relief effort. Blocking it as a group was one thing; being exposed as individual obstructionists was far more unpleasant. They could not count on every man in the room voting against it. And if some voted in favor, the ones who voted against would be vilified. Beyond earning the President's ire, they would be publicly exposed as shirking their duty when so many average Americans were doing their part. It could be a public relations disaster, for themselves and their businesses. Hammer had just handed Luckman a lifeline, and Luckman had the sense to grab it. When the roll call vote was taken, the tally was fourteen to seven. Luckman had won.

On October 25, production of alcohol in America slowed to a trickle.[381] It did not resume until December 24, giving the industry a welcome Christmas gift. The grain savings exceeded even the best estimates, yielding some twenty-two million bushels, pushing the final campaign's total over the one hundred million bushel goal. In the end, nearly 1,000 distillery workers lost their jobs as a result. The government agreed to find employment for these workers, but many had their lives upended by the stoppage. America was waging war on hunger, and in the cold calculus of this campaign, it was a simple choice between the loss of work or the loss of life. And though they were not American lives being saved, they were human nonetheless.

Fire

Luckman's "Friendship Train" had steamed across the country, brilliantly drawing attention to Europe's plight while rallying Americans behind a common cause. It was one of the few, perhaps the only, aspects of Luckman's schemes that did not face domestic opposition. Unfortunately, the simple act of American giving did have opponents abroad. The train's first shipments of food left New York harbor on December 8 and arrived in Le Havre, France, ten days later. Even the communist members of the National Assembly, who had been steadily objecting to American aid, publicly acknowledged their appreciation for this gift from the American people. France's Minister of Public Health declared that the gift had forged a chain of solidarity between the French and American people.

Then the dock workers started to unload the cargo. Some 144 cases of fruit juice were the first to appear on shore. Six young French women dressed in provincial costumes posed for pictures alongside the stevedores. One of the young women decided to climb a ladder to pose beside a sign on the ship reading, "Gift of Food from the United States." As she did, an American crewmember, not wanting to miss the chance, put his arm around the woman and offered her a kiss on the cheek as photographers snapped the shot. The crowd of dock workers and onlookers let up a cheer.[382] The scene bore a faint resemblance to the

Figure 16.1 American girls joining the nationwide campaign to donate food to starving Europeans. Scene captured in Harry Warner Studios "Friendship Train" documentary, 1947. Universal-International.

Figure 16.2 The crowd celebrating the arrival of the trucks carrying the food packages from the Friendship Train to the city hall in Paris, France, in December 1947. Photo by Keystone-France/Gamma-Rapho/Getty Images.

famous photograph of a French woman kissing an American GI upon the liberation of Paris.

The Friendship Train food aid was intended first for orphans and the elderly. Once those needs were met, the remainder would be distributed to the rest of the population. The entire complex operation, from Hollywood to Le Havre, had unfolded without a single hitch. Soon the bountiful American gifts could be distributed to hungry French families, as long as nothing went wrong overnight.

In the early morning hours before dawn on January 30, two explosions rocked the Paris warehouse containing Friendship Train supplies. More than 400 firefighters rushed to the scene. They struggled to salvage anything, battling the fire over the course of five hours, but it was too late. Only smoking walls, scorched metal, and rubble remained. The fire swept over 46,000 square meters causing heat so intense that homes in the vicinity had to be evacuated.[383] The flames consumed the entire stock of 2,500 tons of the train's donations. The warehouse also contained the donations of eight other American aid agencies. By the time the fires were extinguished, some 30,000 tons of food, clothing, and medicine had been lost. The head of the American aid agency in Paris announced that his organization was "completely wiped out." Total damages reached an estimated $4.5 million, the rough equivalent of $55 million today.[384] The fire bore the hallmarks of communist saboteurs.

Most likely acting on the orders of Moscow, communists across western Europe were opposing food aid from America, claiming that this represented a capitalist plot. Communist parties in France and Italy tried to block Marshall Plan aid. In southern Italy, when Friendship Train supplies arrived in Messina, hundreds of hungry Italians swarmed around the train to press handwritten notes into the hands of those on board. On these scraps of paper, they had written their home addresses. That morning, Messina's communists had spread handbills telling Italians that Americans had destroyed their homes through bombing, and now you deserve food aid. This led local residents to believe that the food would be distributed to them directly. Naturally, the food was earmarked for those most in need: at orphanages, homes for wounded veterans, and residents of other institutions. The hungry mobs who surrounded the Friendship Train had to be turned away empty-handed.[385]

The communists simply failed to understand how they were sabotaging themselves. By obstructing food aid to starving masses, they were casting themselves in the role of oppressor while allowing the Americans to present themselves as saviors. Throughout that winter, American shipments continued to reach average Europeans. In Vienna, people cheered as a Friendship Train rolled in carrying 1,100 tons of food and clothing. It had come from the northwestern states of Washington, Oregon, Idaho, Montana, and Alaska. The Austrian chancellor, Leopold Figl, gratefully received the donations. An American representative of charitable agencies in Austria even got a special cheer when she translated her own remarks into German.[386] At the port in Bremen, Germany, 2,000 tons of wheat arrived from American church groups, and many more ships followed. That food was distributed throughout Germany, Austria, Hungary, and Czechoslovakia.[387] The steady, reliable stream of food, medicine, and clothing to desperate peoples made a powerful impression on Europeans while the communists' actions were having the opposite effect.

No one realized what all this meant when the Friendship Train and Food Committee first began their work. Truman naturally hoped to stunt the appeal of communism on the continent, but something else was happening in the process. The racing of food to Europe, the selfless acts of giving by average Americans, the overcoming of communist sabotage, and the steady, reliable stream of American aid, all created the perfect playbook for another, even more dramatic rescue operation. The Friendship Train was, in a sense, a trial run. In the next showdown, supplies could no longer go by ship or rail. This time they would have to go by air.

17 RESURRECT

1948 was an election year, and almost no one thought Harry Truman had a chance, except, of course, for Harry Truman. Despite the advantages of being the incumbent, Truman's odds had to seem long. The Republicans, blocked from control of the White House since 1932, were desperate for a win. Thomas Dewey had lost in 1944, running against a popular, incumbent, wartime president. This time, Dewey knew, would be different. Truman had none of Roosevelt's charm, none of his oratory, and none of his elite breeding. The specter of the Depression had receded, and Truman's unpopularity was growing. In 1944, Dewey had managed to garner nearly forty-six percent of the popular vote, more than any previous Roosevelt rival. In 1948, running against Truman, Dewey was so confident of victory that he indulged in a rather leisurely campaign. And why shouldn't he? Every pollster throughout the year predicted his easy win. And those polls sent many Democrats into panic mode.

Within the Democratic Party establishment, prominent figures concluded that a Truman nomination would sink the Party's chances in November. They searched in desperation for anyone who could rescue them from their current leader. Eleanor Roosevelt, who still had little faith in her husband's successor, joined a growing campaign to draft General Eisenhower as the Democratic nominee. Although their effort failed, Truman faced far more serious opposition from another corner within his own party.

A segment of southern Democrats, outraged by Truman's advancement of Black American civil rights, broke away from the

Party to form the Dixiecrats. Led by South Carolina governor Strom Thurmond, the Dixiecrats resented Truman's passage of anti-lynching laws and his abolition of state poll taxes, which had been effectively used to prevent southern Black citizens from voting. The South had been a reliable Democratic stronghold for decades, and the Dixiecrats' defection threatened to bleed support away from the President.

But Truman faced still another threat to his election from the creation of an additional splinter group, the Progressive Party. Convinced that Truman's tough stand on communism was fueling the Cold War, former vice president Henry Wallace declared his candidacy for president. As Wallace saw it, not only the future of world peace, but also the soul of America rested on his shoulders. He would launch not a presidential campaign, but a crusade. He would be the true champion of the common man, the voice of oppressed minorities, and the only leader willing to uplift the downtrodden. He righteously proclaimed that all people, regardless of race, gender, social or national origin, were entitled to equal treatment and a dignified existence. And because he was right on the issues, he could not imagine how he could lose.

Wallace never forgot how he had been robbed of the vice presidency in 1944, when Party bosses, acting on FDR's wishes, maneuvered Truman onto the ticket. Wallace had been far more popular; most Americans knew almost nothing about Harry Truman, including Roosevelt. But Wallace's softness on communism made him a liability, and his notions of racial equality did not endear him to southern Party leaders. Now, in 1948, Wallace was striking back.

Henry Wallace was a man who stood so firmly on principle that he seldom moved forward. Compromise did not come easily to him. Socializing felt like a chore. He rarely mingled with the Washington crowd of policy wonks and gossipy socialites, once remarking that he preferred to deal with issues rather than people.[388] The sharp-tongued Alice Roosevelt, the daughter of Teddy Roosevelt, referred to him as "Farmer Wallace."[389] It was true that Henry hailed from the soil, having been raised on the farmland of Iowa. Wallace's father had served as President Warren Harding's agriculture secretary in the early 1920s. When FDR appointed Henry to fill that same post in the Roosevelt administration, Wallace proved to be a highly active secretary, doing more during eight years in that role on behalf of American farmers than any of his predecessors, including his father.[390] FDR shrewdly chose him as his running mate in 1940 to shore up support from the Party's progressive wing, but the vice presidency did not suit either his skills or his temperament. Overseeing Senate debates bored him. Sometimes he napped in his Senate seat. At other times he simply turned his duties over to the long-serving Senate majority leader Alben Barkley.[391] After deceptively dumping Wallace from the ticket in 1944 (never telling him directly of his intentions), FDR tried to mollify him by offering him his pick of Cabinet posts. Wallace chose commerce secretary. It was a peculiar choice – a position of far less importance and prestige than some others he could have selected, especially for someone who harbored grander aims.

Truman was not oblivious to the pain that his nomination as vice president in 1944 had caused. Though it had not been his idea or his intention, the Party bosses had cheated Wallace of the nomination, and by extension, of the presidency. Soon after that tumultuous convention, Truman visited Wallace in hope of smoothing things over. On the morning of August 3, Truman told Wallace that he had never spent such an unhappy week in his life as he had during the convention: "You know, this whole matter is not one of my choosing. I went to Chicago to get out of being Vice President, not to become Vice President."[392] Truman was keen to assure Wallace that he had not in any way maneuvered to bring about his own nomination, and he hoped that this situation would not damage their friendship. Wallace told him that he would do whatever he could to help the Party win the general election. But Truman sought more. He admitted that he was not a deep thinker like Wallace, and he asked for Wallace's help on policy during the campaign. Wallace was noncommittal.[393] It was an ominous augur of the tensions to come.

Once Truman acceded to the presidency, he retained Wallace as commerce secretary, but it quickly became evident to Wallace that his counsel was not sought. The two men were far apart in their visions of America's role in the world, and the breach in their relationship would inevitably come, sooner or later. It came sooner than either expected.

On September 10, Henry Wallace came to see Truman to show him the text of a speech he was planning to deliver in two days. Truman asked Wallace to summarize it. Truman did not notice anything amiss, but to be certain, he passed his copy to Clark Clifford, his chief counsel. Clifford did not react quickly enough. Neither did the President's press secretary, Charlie Ross. The debacle that followed was largely Truman's fault, but his aides also failed to protect him.

Wallace sent the media copies of his speech prior to delivering it. The reporters immediately noticed what Truman's aides had not. Wallace's ideas about relations with the Soviets were at odds with the President's positions. Truman was staking out a hard line; Wallace spoke of conciliation. At a press conference with Truman just hours before Wallace was to begin his speech, a reporter jokingly referred to Wallace as the secretary of state, and then quickly corrected himself to say commerce. The reporters chortled. They asked Truman if the Wallace speech reflected the policies of his administration. Not having read it carefully enough, Truman affirmed that it did. This gave Wallace ammunition. He could later claim that he had showed his speech before- hand to Truman, which he had, and that the President had approved it, which he did.

Word spread within the administration that Wallace was loose. Beyond the White House, the State and Navy Departments, the two major shapers of American foreign policy (along with the War Department), became alarmed. John Sullivan, the undersecretary of the Navy, marched over to meet with the man serving as acting secretary of state while Jimmy Byrnes was in Paris. Will Clayton understood immediately the damage that Wallace could cause. Both men agreed that Wallace had to be stopped. The United States could not afford to be sending mixed signals to Moscow. Stalin would exploit any sign of internal division with the government. Clayton rang Press Secretary Ross to demand that Wallace be prevented from giving that speech. Ross, not fully comprehending the problem, said it was too late to intervene. Wallace was soon to begin. At that point, John Sullivan grabbed the phone out of Clayton's hand and told Ross that if Wallace were not stopped, then the President would be forced to break publicly with either Wallace or Byrnes. There could be only one secretary of state.[394]

It was too late. The crowd at Madison Square Garden was eager to hear what the former vice president had to say. Despite his demotion to commerce secretary, Henry Wallace remained the nation's leading liberal. In New York City he had a devoted following. Ostensibly Wallace had come to speak in support of Herbert Lehman's bid for the US Senate. In reality, he was there to take the first step in creating a progressive party.

It was a powerful address, one of Wallace's most moving articu- lations of his deepest values. And in that speech, he revealed all that was best in him: a virtuous man convinced of the rightness of his cause for racial justice. He also exposed his gravest errors of judgment: the belief that Stalin and the communists should be left to dominate Eastern Europe as their rightful sphere. While it was true that the United States had little power to prevent the Sovietization of Eastern Europe, Wallace committed what many Americans viewed as an unpardonable sin by publicly suggesting a moral equivalence between the two sides. He entitled his address, "The Way to Peace."

Wallace began by pointing to the recent mass lynching of Black Americans in Georgia, calling it the kind of prejudice that makes war inevitable. Hatred, he declared, breeds only more hatred. He then linked America's racism at home with its policies for peace abroad:

> The doctrine of racial superiority produces a desire to get even on the part of its victims. If we are to work for peace in the rest of the world, we here in the United States must eliminate racism from our unions, our business organizations, our educational institutions, and our employment practices. Merit alone must be the measure of men.[395]

Wallace then laid out his ideas for constructing a lasting peace. They were notions at stark variance to those of the President. He proclaimed that a get-tough policy with Russia would fail: "The tougher we get, the tougher the Russians will get."[396] And then he made the remarks that would cost him his job. He asserted that America should not seek to check the influence of communism within areas already under Soviet control: "Russians have no business interfering in our sphere and we have no business interfering in theirs."[397] He tried to clarify that he did, in fact, see that Russian actions were oppressive, but the effect was muddled:

> On our part, we should recognize that we have no more business in the political affairs of Eastern Europe than Russia has in the political affairs of Latin America, Western Europe, and the United States . . . . We might not like what they do in Eastern Europe. It offends many of us, their suppression of civil liberties. But like it or not they will try to socialize their sphere as we try to democratize ours. We do the same in Germany and Japan.[398]

It sounded very much like the Commerce Secretary was mapping out a foreign policy position different from the one currently espoused by the President and the Secretary of State, and that could not be tolerated.

But that was not all. Wallace also insisted that the hard peace plan for Germany had to be maintained in order to mollify the Russians. Russia, he declared, must be assured that German industry could never again be able to manufacture the weapons of war. With these words Wallace planted himself unmistakably within the camp of those still demanding a punishing peace for Germany. Barely a week earlier James Byrnes had delivered his "Speech of Hope" remarks in Stuttgart, declaring that America's harsh policy toward Germany needed to change. Wallace was endorsing the Morgenthau Plan at exactly the moment when Truman's top advisors were attempting to rethink it.

Truman knew he had blundered by not having read Wallace's speech himself. He compounded the error by telling reporters that he stood behind the speech. It was a disaster of his own making. It gave the impression of an administration in disarray scarcely two months before the midterm elections. His approval rating plummeted from a once high-water mark of eighty-seven percent upon taking office to a measly thirty-two percent. Byrnes communicated from Paris and threatened to resign over the speech, as it undermined the policies he and Truman had been steadily advancing. After an angry encounter in the White House in which Wallace essentially refused to refrain from giving foreign policy speeches, Truman fumed. He had had enough. Wallace would have to go.

Sometimes Truman's temper overwhelmed him. That night he wrote an angry, ill-considered letter to Wallace and dispatched it without permitting any advisors to read it first. Immediately he regretted it. He realized that Wallace could easily publish the letter, which would be highly embarrassing. The next morning, Truman asked his chief counsel, Clark Clifford, to ask Wallace to return the letter. Wallace had read it, but in gentlemanly fashion, he resealed the envelope and sent it back as asked. According to Clifford, Truman destroyed the only copy. Wallace submitted his resignation with an arrogant note of his own, and the bad blood between them only worsened.

As electioneering intensified throughout the year, each of Truman's opponents became more wedded to their missions. Dewey believed that he would rescue the Republicans from their post-Hoover fall from power. Thurmond hoped to save southern white citizens from integration. Wallace was convinced he could combat racial hatred and ensure world peace. Each man saw himself as the savior of his people. And in the midst of this fractious campaign, Truman had to face a foreign crisis on which another world war might hinge.

Tensions with the Soviets had been mounting ever since the end of the war. One after another Eastern European nations fell under Moscow's control, typically by brutal means. Czechoslovakia was one of the few remaining semi-independent states until early in 1948, when the Soviets strengthened their hold. One night in March, Foreign Minister Jan Masaryk's body landed on the pavement, ostensibly tossed from his bedroom window. Investigations revealed a ransacked apartment, smashed belongings, and plaster beneath the victim's fingernails – a sinister clue that the Foreign Minister had desperately clung to the window sill.[399]

By early 1948, disagreements over the occupation of Berlin were heating up. The council of foreign ministers could not agree on administrative issues. Meetings in Berlin broke up in acrimony as the Soviet military representatives refused to compromise. Outside the angry meeting rooms, Americans were being kidnapped daily off the streets, driven to the Soviet sector, beaten, probed for information, and released to tell their tales. Anti-communist activists, or even those found reading anti-communist materials, were subject to this treatment. Moscow was closing its grip on the city. The United States had fewer than 9,000 troops in West Berlin. The Soviets surrounded them with 1.5 million.[400] If the Soviets chose to attack, Americans and their allies would be annihilated.

Fearing a sudden lurch toward war, and seeing herself as a champion of peace, Eleanor Roosevelt pleaded with Secretary of State George Marshall to sit down with the Russians to negotiate before it was too late. Of course, sitting down with the Russians was exactly what American representatives had been doing since the war's end, only to find that Moscow intended on control by force. But Mrs. Roosevelt wanted something more than just talk. She wanted to ensure that Germany would not be rebuilt in a manner threatening to Russia.

"I am sure that we have not been blameless and probably the Russians think we have done some things against them," she told Marshall. "I am sure they believe we are trying to build up Germany again into an industrial state. I sometimes wonder if behind our backs, that isn't one of the things that our big business people would like to see happen in spite of two World Wars started by Germany."[401] The former first lady had not altered her view in the years since Morgenthau had persuaded her that Germany had to be kept down. But there was little that either she or Marshall could do.

Eleanor Roosevelt never ceased espousing noble values. Unfortunately, she also never stopped to question some of the basic assumptions that drove her actions. This led her to misperceive the present danger. Deeply committed to the cause of peace, she assumed that accommodation with the Russians was necessary in order to avoid another war. It was an understandable assumption. The thought of another major conflict so soon after the horrors of the most recent one had to seem unbearable. And in truth, the Russians had suffered terribly during the last war. Even the die-hard capitalist Will Clayton found that many of Stalin's demands at Potsdam were reasonable and fair.[402] But soon after that conference, Stalin's actions across Eastern Europe and now in Berlin had grown increasingly authoritarian and cruel.

The former first lady also clung to two beliefs, both rooted in the virtuous ideal of preserving peace. She still saw German people as a threat, convinced that their culture of militarism could not change. But the Allied occupiers were actively reshaping German society, transforming education, promoting a free press, and supporting democratic leaders such as the aged anti-Nazi Konrad Adenauer, who would soon become the first chancellor of a West German republic. Mrs. Roosevelt also remained wedded to the idea (encouraged by her friend Henry Morgenthau) that the weapons of war are what produce war. But by insisting that German heavy industry be forbidden to rebuild, she was discouraging the economic recovery that would foster prosperity and stability. She wanted America to embody the principles of peace, but she failed to probe deeply into the causes of war.

Eminence Grise

Philadelphia is always hot in summer, but the summer of 1948 felt especially breathless for the 17,000 Republicans who packed into a frenetic auditorium in June. They had come to watch history in action. They had convened to nominate Thomas Dewey, a man they felt certain would win. After sixteen long years out of power, they were finally on the brink of recapturing the White House. They could not simply taste victory, they could see, smell, and touch it. But amidst the frenzied atmosphere of balloons and party favors, strategy and intrigue, hopes and expectations, they witnessed a stunning event, made even more shocking by its simple authenticity. Amidst this five-day extravaganza, the final speaker of the day approached the podium. As their hero made his way down the center aisle through the convention hall, something unexpected occurred. The crowd combusted in emotion. Their applause exploded into an outburst of appreciation. Soon the entire audience rose to its feet, stomped, and cheered. They whistled, they shouted, they screamed. Then the orchestra began to play "Glory, Glory, Hallelujah." The eruption of support could not be contained. Each of the forty-eight state delegations raised its standards high. Delegates began marching up and down the aisles as the band played on. But the man they were cheering was not Dewey. None of this had been rehearsed or planned. It was a purely spontaneous show of unbridled enthusiasm for the man they deemed a great American. Herbert Hoover had come home.

Speaker of the House Joseph Martin tried fruitlessly to gavel the crowd into order. They ignored him. Instead, they drowned him out with chants of, "Hoo-ver! Hoo-ver!" Then the orchestra took up the theme of Hoover's home state, "California, Here I Come," and the conventioneers sang along with abandon. The delegates kept on marching, cheering, and singing. As Martin helplessly tried to bring decorum to the crowd. More than ten minutes, then fifteen passed, before the tumult of affection for the old man settled down.[403] He had traveled the world to help bring food to the desperate. He had crisscrossed the country to ask Americans to give food to the hungry. He had returned to Germany to survey the terrible state of privation and furnish a plan for forgiveness. And now, he had come back to America to address his party.

And then came the next surprise. Hoover spoke to them not as Republicans. Naturally, he hoped for and expected the Party to win, but his speech rose above the political convention to a higher plane. He told the assembled partisans that something much grander was at stake than this one election. He was speaking of American values.

Fear, he told his listeners, has spread. Hope has dwindled, because liberty has been lost in countries around the world. The oppressors have revived government by hatred, torture, and exile. The men in the Kremlin threaten our civilization with aggression, while they steadily undermine it from within. Only as long as the United States is free and strong will liberty survive.

Hoover pointed to the strain on America's economy brought about by its relief efforts. Combined with the need to rearm, these two costs were like stilts. If we go any higher on them, "we'll break a leg getting down." Returning to his old metaphor of the Four Horsemen, he declared that two more have been added: high taxes and inflation. With full compassion for our friends abroad, they must understand that we can only provide the bare essentials. Hoover, who had done so much to create relief for Europe and Asia, now announced that America had its limits. We are straining our economy to the utmost, he insisted, and Stalin is hoping for our economic collapse.

And then, Hoover turned to Germany. He explained that Europe had to be reconstructed as a whole, and that meant rebuilding Germany. Though he did not mention the Morgenthau Plan by name or its embodiment in JCS 1067, he made clear that ongoing retribution toward the Germans would only impoverish all of Europe and America: "We need neither forget nor condone Nazi guilt, but a free world must not poison its concepts of life by accepting malice and hatred as a guide. Otherwise, not only will our efforts fail, but the American taxpayer will be bled white supporting an idle and despairing German people." The crowd offered only tepid applause. Hoover only riled up the crowd again when he turned his invective against domestic opponents, exactly what he said he would not do.

Our problem is not with the obnoxious communists in our midst, he asserted. Instead, it is with the fuzzy-headed liberals who think they can have liberalism without liberty. These people have allowed the creeping tentacles of totalitarianism to reach into our labor unions, our universities, our intelligentsia, and our government. It was a backhanded swipe at the Truman administration. He continued that line of attack with searing metaphors. These liberals, he opined, should note that in each of the European states that have fallen to the communists, "It has been the totalitarian liberals who provided the ladders upon which the communist pirates have boarded the ship of state." The old man, thinner and silver-haired, could still conjure up some cutting barbs, sharpened during years of practice from afar. He was clearly relishing the moment. Given his age, he assumed it would be his last convention, and he was determined to make this moment one to remember.

As he whipped up the crowd and pushed on to the conclusion, he invoked the classic American narrative – the story of America's goodness, which he entirely believed. America, he proclaimed, had earned the right to moral leadership in the world. We alone have taken no people's land. We have oppressed no race of man. We have faced all the world in friendship and compassion, in a genuine love of our fellow man. We have hated war and we have loved peace. What other nation has such a record? We have aided our enemies, and even the children of those who would do us harm. As he spoke those words, perhaps he thought back to his former partner, A. Stanley Rowe, who had years ago ruined their company through reckless speculation and whose children Hoover had helped support while their father was in prison. Whatever Hoover believed, he conveniently elided over America's brutal war in the Philippines, its denial of equality and independence to Filipinos, its acquisition of Mexican lands, Hawaii, Puerto Rico, Guam, and a host of island nations. He made no mention of America's oppression of Black Americans, nor its recent internment of Japanese Americans. And of course, he said nothing of the bomb. No, none of that would have fitted with the narrative he wished to tell, the narrative his audience wanted to believe. It was, however, an accurate articulation of the country he wanted America to be.

Building to a crescendo of patriotic piety, Hoover told his listeners that they were engaged in something far more crucial than selecting a nominee or adopting a platform. Their sacred task, he explained, was to rekindle a burning belief in American civilization: "You are here to feed the reviving fires of spiritual fervor which once made the word American a stirring description of a man who lived and died for human liberty." If you only parrot platitudes or pander to sectional and special interests, then you will have wasted your time and done nothing of historic significance. But if you recognize that "we are in a critical battle to safeguard our nation and civilization," then "you will be guided in every step to restore the foundations of faith, of morals, and of right thinking." As Hoover saw it, in the battle against Godless communism hung the survival of Christian civilization and the hope of human freedom. With stakes that high, his audience could only hope that he would declare their triumph certain. He did not. Instead, he ended with an exultation to "make yourselves worthy of victory."[404] And with those words, he was done.

To many of the delegates in that convention hall, Hoover's final words probably sounded like a call to readiness for their victory in November, but that was not what he meant. His entire address focused on the much larger campaign against communism. Hoover was calling Americans, not just Republicans, to gird themselves for battle against tyranny. Christian civilization, as he saw it, was in danger. Liberty was being extinguished, as he observed firsthand on his postwar tours of Eastern Europe. The true victory he hoped for was the one that would vanquish communism from the earth. He expected that struggle to extend far beyond November, whichever party won.

Two days later, the battle for freedom took a frightening turn.

18 UPLIFT

Intent on driving the Americans out of West Berlin, on June 24, 1948, just two days after Hoover's call for freedom, Soviet forces began severing transit lines into the western sectors, denying average citizens of food, coal, and medicines. West Berliners were now entirely at the mercy of the Soviets. Unless they succumbed to Soviet rule, they would not last. The city's inhabitants were barely surviving as it was. Hunger had damaged the health of nearly seventy percent of residents. Malnutrition was the third leading cause of death. Tuberculosis rates had doubled between 1947 and 1948. Jaundice had risen ninefold.[405] While some Americans still viewed Germans as the enemy, American occupiers could not be unmoved by the condition of civilians, especially the children, who suffered the most. The average child between age ten and fifteen was becoming permanently stunted from malnutrition.

Some of Truman's advisors urged withdrawal. They saw the situation through a military lens. America was severely outnumbered. Roughly half a million Soviet forces surrounded 160,000 American and 120,000 British troops.[406] If the Soviets chose, they could annihilate America's forces in West Berlin with relative ease. The western sectors, after all, were a democratic island floating in a Soviet sea, entirely surrounded by Soviet-controlled eastern Germany. The West was highly vulnerable, and the military sensibly argued that it would be better to withdraw to defensible ground. On June 28, Secretary of Defense James Forrestal, Undersecretary of State Robert Lovett, and Army Secretary Kenneth Royall convened in the President's office to discuss plans for evacuating the city. They all knew it was the unfortunate though reasonable course.

But Harry Truman was not reasonable. He viewed the crisis through a moral lens. The Russians had agreed to share Berlin, and now they were reneging on their word. That was wrong, and he refused to accept it. More than this, of course, Truman also saw the value of standing up to aggression, largely because of the lessons he drew from Munich. Toughness with an enemy was necessary in order to prevent greater conflict in the future. That was Truman's world view, and while it may have led to needless suffering in Hiroshima and Nagasaki, this time it served him well, though a good deal of luck and the American can-do spirit played their part.

Churchill was of the same mind, having drawn the same lessons from dealing with Hitler. While the French prime minister Robert Schuman urged conciliation, Churchill told cheering crowds that aggression must always be opposed.[407] Munich, he said, was the proof of this truism. It was one of Hitler's many tragic legacies that statesmen ever since have likened compromise to appeasement, and too many have believed that a military response is the only thing that aggressors understand. On this occasion, Truman proved them wrong. He stood up to aggression without firing a shot.

The first thirty-two planes landed in West Berlin's Tempelhof airport on June 26. They brought coal, medicines, milk, and one of the most vital foodstuffs of all, flour. Bread would help keep people alive and slake the gnawing hunger pangs, if enough could be delivered. It couldn't. The early days of the airlift barely fed a fraction of the population. West Berlin contained more than two million people. The Allies would have to increase efficiency while praying that the Soviets did not shoot them down. As days passed into weeks and then months, the Allies learned how to master the logistical challenges of an exceedingly complex operation. At its peak, the West had achieved what had previously seemed implausible, if not impossible. They were landing planes around the clock. They were sustaining an immense population entirely by air.

On July 21, Truman's advisors again met in the Oval Office, this time to persuade the President to transfer control of atomic weapons from a civilian agency to the military. Some of them believed strongly that the Berlin blockade would lead to war with the Soviets. In that event, the military would need control over nuclear arms. Truman disagreed. The previous week he had told Defense Secretary Forrestal that he intended to maintain full control over the bomb's use and would not have "some dashing lieutenant colonel decide when would be the proper time to drop one."[408] Forrestal might not have realized the full meaning behind Truman's words. The decision that both atomic bombs would be dropped as soon as they were ready, without a period of review after the first one, was determined by the military. Truman had not had a chance to think through the military's control over that aspect of the decision, though he could have called a halt after Hiroshima.[409]

Facing his military and civilian advisors, Truman sounded pensive, perhaps remorseful: "I don't think we ought to use this thing unless we absolutely have to. It is a terrible thing to order the use of something that … " and then he stopped in mid-speech, looked down at his desk and looked up at the group again, "that is so terribly destructive, destructive beyond anything we have ever had." He told them that the atomic bomb was not a military weapon: "It is used to wipe out women and children and unarmed people, and not for military uses. So we have got to treat this differently from rifles and cannon."[410] After some further discussion, Truman added: "This is no time to be juggling an atom bomb around."

Did Truman regret his decision to drop the atomic bombs on Japanese civilians after all? Truman had always maintained that he never lost a moment's sleep over the decision, but was that simply the face he showed to the world. When confronted with a second conflict in which the use of nuclear weapons was a possibility, did he hesitate because of what he had learned about the effects on the people of Hiroshima and Nagasaki? We will never know for certain.[411] We can only wonder and suspect. But we do know that throughout the blockade, at this first truly hot moment of the Cold War, Truman focused not on dropping bombs, but supplying bread. Some of the same planes and pilots who had devastated Berlin just three years before were now delivering food, supplies, and a lifeline to the German people. America was flexing its humanitarian muscle, and the entire world was watching.

The optics of the airlift could not have been more advantageous to the West. By cutting off the necessities of daily life to an entire population, the Soviets had cast themselves in the unmistakable role of oppressor. Foolishly, Stalin had made it easy for the Americans to assume the role of savior, as their planes descended from the heavens to deliver the Germans from Soviet-induced hunger. Truman's staff knew that the American people overwhelmingly supported his position. Press and radio commentary showed a willingness to negotiate, but only if a settlement did not violate the country's principles and national interests.[412] A British newsreel helped foster public support for the allied effort, portraying the airlift in heroic terms. In the face of "red obstruction," it explained, the Anglo-American airlift brought massive amounts of coal to keep West Berliners warm throughout the winter. "Endless cars of vitally needed coal are stalled by the Russian blockade of Berlin," the narrator intoned, "but that is only part of the story, as the red noose is drawn closer about the western sector of the capital."[413]

Figure 18.1 An allied Dakota plane brings aid to starving Berliners, 1948. Photo by Popperfoto via Getty Images/Getty Images.

In contrast to the red obstruction, the film showed scenes of the "candy bombers," pilots who tossed tiny parcels of chocolates and sweets to excited children down below. The joy of one young boy was unmistakable, as he ripped open the package and immediately crammed the confection in his mouth. The propaganda value was incalculable. The idea of dropping candy to children had not originated in the White House or the Pentagon. It was not concocted by a CIA public affairs officer. Instead, it emerged from a simple act of human kindness when Colonel Gail Halvorsen, an American pilot, encountered a group of German children behind a fence at Tempelhof airport. They had come to watch the planes arriving daily. There were almost thirty of them, all in old clothes, most without shoes. Halvorsen did not speak German, but some of the children could communicate in broken English. After chatting for a bit, Halvorsen realized he was late. He waved goodbye, and as he walked away, he put his hands in his pockets and noticed two sticks of chewing gum. He stopped. He knew what he should do, but part of him hesitated. He realized that these kids had grown up knowing only war. They had no access to candy. But they were Germans. Maybe they had been in the Hitler Youth. He struggled with the conflicting sentiments at war inside his heart. He thought of walking away, but in a moment of pure human compassion, he tore the two sticks in half and handed the pieces to four of the kids. Their eyes widened in amazement. The children's reaction was electric. Halvorsen tried to communicate with hand gestures that he would drop more candy to them on his next flight tomorrow. In order that they would know which plane was his, he stretched out his arms in imitation of a plane and wiggled his wings. Somehow they got the message, for the next day they were there, eyes gazing expectantly upward. And Halverson delivered. The phenomenon of the candy bomber was born. Soon the drops became a daily routine, as other pilots joined in the act.[414] As news spread across America of the pilots' good deeds, donations poured in. By Christmas time, vast crates of sweets were arriving in West Berlin, a gift from Americans to German children. By the operation's end, the crews had dropped an estimated twenty-three tons of candy over West Berlin.[415] America had won the war with the atomic bomb, and it was winning the peace with the candy bomb.

Upset

As badly as the Republicans craved the presidency, Harry Truman was equally determined to retain it. The campaign entered its final months, and Truman showed that he was willing to play dirty. Though he had seized the moral high ground over Berlin, he descended to old-fashioned mudslinging back home. He unleashed a relentless, at times rabid assault on both Dewey and the Republican-controlled "do nothing" Congress.

Because the polls continued to show Dewey with a comfortable lead, Truman's attacks became more virulent. His chief counsel, Clark Clifford, had helped design the campaign strategy, part of which included tying Dewey to the Congress, which had been unable to pass any major legislation. Dewey's advisors repeatedly instructed their candidate never to take the bait, to remain above the fray, acting presidential. As Truman went low, Dewey stayed aloof, not only from the attacks, but also from voters. He seldom engaged in the kind of handshaking, back-slapping activities at which Truman excelled. Henry Wallace spoke about a century of the common man, but Truman actually was the common man. As his whistle-stop train tour across America rolled on, his crowds began to grow.

Truman had nothing to lose. The predictions of his defeat were so total that not one pundit or pollster suggested otherwise. But the experts were speaking to each other, not to the average voter. At times Truman savaged the Republicans as being next to Nazis. At other times he labeled them the true communists. He threw any mud he could grab hold of, no matter how noxious or absurd. And all the while Dewey never hit back. Having seen what FDR did in his four election victories, Truman sometimes fell back on his predecessor's old playbook. In North Carolina he conjured up the specter of Hoover carts. He had to ask the crowd if they remembered what Hoover carts were. They were the automobiles that had broken down or run out of gas, and their owners could not afford to keep them running. Instead, they tied a mule to the front of the car and let the animal drag it along: "First you had the Hoovercrats, and then you had the Hoover carts. One always follows the other."[416] The worst of the Depression lasted for several years, and it left its scars on millions who lost their jobs, their savings, and in some cases, their loved ones.

Truman had to hope that he could still pin the Depression on the Republicans, despite that it was under his administration that inflation had risen, housing shortages became acute, and beef prices soared beyond reach. In the midterm elections of 1946, Republicans ran on the brilliantly terse slogan, "Had enough?" It worked. Republicans won fifty-four seats in the House of Representatives and eleven seats in the Senate, recapturing control of both houses. In 1948, inflation was still high, beef was still costly, and corn prices had plummeted, making midwestern farmers feel the pinch. Truman should have been vulnerable, but he artfully managed to blame all these ills on Congress for its inaction, and as a midwestern farmer himself, his words carried weight. Dewey did little to respond.

In the campaign's final month, Hoover foresaw what other Republicans could not – that Dewey's distant demeanor was turning off voters. He sensed that this would be the nominee's undoing.[417] Around this same time, Eleanor Roosevelt at last gave Truman her full endorsement, or as full as she could muster in light of the low regard in which she still held him. Her letter of unqualified support sounded more like a plea for Democrats to take back Congress, but Truman needed any endorsement he could salvage.[418] With her permission, he had her letter published in the press.

Almost nothing about the 1948 election occurred as predicted. At the start of the year it seemed certain that Henry Wallace's third-party campaign would split the Democratic vote and hand the election to Dewey. In fact, Wallace turned out to have helped Truman. By drawing all of the communists and communist sympathizers to the Progressive Party, Wallace inadvertently gave Truman cover. Republicans could no longer plausibly maintain that Truman was too far Left. It also enabled Truman to attack communism, denounce its supporters within the United States, and frame himself as an anti-communist, pro-working-man liberal. The effect was measurable. In the end, Wallace drew less than 2.5 percent of the popular vote. He was completely and unequivocally defeated. So, too, were his plans for full racial and gender equality, at least for the time being.

Parade

While the American presidential election reached its climax, the planes to Berlin kept landing. After Truman cheekily raised the newspaper above his head with the headline "Dewey Beats Truman," the flights continued. As the brutal winter of 1948 crept into 1949, still they flew. First they landed every five minutes, then every three, until finally they were landing every ninety seconds.[419] The ramshackle operation initially thrown together back in June had been transformed into a logistics masterpiece. The pilots brought more than just coal, medicines, milk, and flour. They brought hope to a desperate city. West Berliners felt comforted by the constant din of airplane traffic overhead. When, at times, the skies were silent, mainly due to fog, they felt a deep unease. Was it over? Had the Soviets found a way to intervene? Had the Americans given up at last? Would they starve to death, or would they live under Soviet control? And then the reassuring cacophony resumed, and West Berliners exhaled again. All the while, America was transforming itself in the minds of average Germans. Its image was shifting from conqueror to savior, from enemy to friend.

The shift could be seen in the pages of the popular weekly magazine *Der Spiegel*. Initially, the magazine's reporting on the crisis was purely factual and largely neutral in tone. But as the reporters came to see the actions of individual Americans, their stories became far more personal. They began to wonder who these people really were who were risking their lives and struggling under stressful, dangerous conditions to deliver food to their recent enemies. The profiles began with General Clay.

Just before the airlift began, *Der Spiegel* detailed the origins of some of the food aid coming to Berlin. The article opened with a lament, or possibly a complaint, that both Soviet and Western sectors of the city were entirely dependent on outside support. The children of the Soviet sector, the article proclaimed, thought as little about the origin of their food deliveries as did the children in the Western sector being fed by Hoover.[420] But by the close of July, while the airlift had been underway for a month, the magazine noted the peculiar behavior of General Clay. Each morning between 7 and 8 am, the General drove from his home to his office, taking down the addresses of occupying families (American and British), who had their lights on. In order to save electricity and maximize the benefits of the coal that the airlift was delivering, all West Berlin residents were required to have their lights turned off once the sun had risen. Those members of the occupying force who violated this rule would be punished, exactly like any other resident. There would be no special treatment for the occupiers, and Clay was a stern enforcer.[421]

Clay's rules applied just as equally to his own family, even his wife. Marjorie had moved homes with Lucius on twelve occasions prior to Clay's assignment to Berlin. Marjorie had not joined him there. When Clay's son Frank, who was serving in the Army and stationed in Berlin, married an American woman in Berlin, the rules stated that no one could enter the city for personal reasons. Every bit of space on the airplanes had to be devoted to supplies and crew or those on official business. Marjorie was not granted special permission to attend her son's wedding. The rules were applied equally to all. Impressed by this remarkable show of fairness from the commander of US forces in Germany, *Der Spiegel* declared, "Heute gehört auch Mrs. Clay zu Berlin" ("Today Mrs. Clay also belongs to Berlin"). It was a sentiment similar to the one in the French newspaper *Le Monde*'s declaration after the attacks of September 11, 2001, that "We are all Americans." Clay was forging a bond of solidarity with the German people, and the effects were palpable.

Over the course of the airlift, German reporting became increasingly personal. There were stories about Clay's chauffeur and even Clay's dog. Anecdotes about average American soldiers peppered the pages of the magazine, as German readers became more curious about those particular men. One airman, Marvin Eve, had been waiting for a set of false teeth, but he was ordered into action in the airlift before it arrived. Eve spent the next four weeks flying over Germany with no teeth at all.[422] Similar profiles of average American soldiers humanized the airlift for average Germans. The Americans were coming to be seen not as a group, but as individuals: to be thought of not as a foreign race, but as ordinary people. And as the Americans became more humanized in German eyes, the Russians grew less so.

The Soviets had tried everything short of war. They tried to seduce West Berliners with promises of fresh vegetables and meats. All that the West Berliners would need to do is exchange their ration cards for the Soviet ID cards of East Berlin. Though the cold and hunger sapped their strength, their spirit of resistance only thrived. Less than one percent of the city's inhabitants made the switch.[423] Then the Soviets turned to intimidation, ratcheting up threats, forcibly seizing municipal buildings, and imprisoning West Berlin officials. But the free people of Berlin would not yield, and the airlift carried on, month after month, as the world looked on in amazement.

The airlift was shaping perceptions of Americans and Russians not just among the German people. Those in other countries were taking note as well. Newspapers around the globe carried stories of the tense events of a city under siege. In August 1948, *The Scotsman* reported on the brutal Soviet arrest of a West Berlin police chief and five other policemen from within the American sector. The next night Soviet forces again crossed into the western sector to make more arrests. The Americans protested, but there was little they could do.[424] The Soviets were so oblivious or indifferent to the optics of their behavior that it almost seemed as if they wanted to undermine their own attractiveness as an alternative to the Western way of life. That same month, the *Times of India* reported on the crash of an American airplane as it tried to deliver supplies. The crew of two were both killed. The photos showed people looking on in horror at the broken rubble of a burned aircraft. It was the third crash since the airlift began.[425] The world was witnessing Americans sacrificing themselves to keep Germans alive. The role of savior was not metaphorical; it was evident in the smoking ruins of Skymaster planes.

On April 17, the Hong Kong-based *South China Morning Post* reported that the Anglo-American airlift had surpassed all previous records for the amount of goods delivered in a single twenty-four-hour period by flying an incredible 12,834 tons of food and coal into the city. Every pilot, every crewman, every participant was focused so intensively on the goal that they could think of nothing else. At one point on that momentous day, Lt. General William Tunner, commander of the airlift, asked a harried pilot for a ride back to West Germany, but Tunner's jacket was covering his insignia and rank. In his frenzied state, the pilot did not even recognize the commander. "You'll have to shake your tail and get aboard," he shouted at the General. "We are in a hurry." Tunner simply grinned and climbed in. He knew his men were making history. As the paper declared, this was a clear display to Russia that the Allies could supply West Berlin with all of its needs by air.[426]

At last, by the spring of 1949, after nearly a year of steady, reliable relief, the Soviets backed down. On May 12, they announced that normal transit into West Berlin could resume. It was a humiliating defeat for Stalin, and an extraordinary success for humanity.

That month, when it was clear that the airlift had succeeded, Lucius Clay came home. He never did see combat in WWII. His lifelong dream of heroically fighting in a war was never realized. At least, that was how he felt throughout the war, as his requests for transfer to the European theater were denied. And then, against his expectations, General Clay became a pivotal figure in a new kind of war, a cold one. Seen purely in numbers, the victory was stunning. In fifteen months the United States, with the aid of British, French, Canadian, Australian, New Zealand, and South African air forces, delivered 2,334,374 tons of supplies, a figure even greater than what Berlin had been receiving by road and rail before the blockade had begun.[427] America had led an international coalition that mastered a logistical conundrum, sustained that coalition's determination for more than a year, and managed to avoid another war. But the airlift represented much more than just an engineering or diplomatic feat. It symbolized America's commitment to its allies, its refusal to abandon free peoples to communist repression, and its humane values. Clay embodied all those noble traits, and the German people came to recognize it. Americans were just as eager to demonstrate their support.

On May 20, Clay rode up Broadway in New York toward City Hall as 250,000 people cheered and waved. Ticker tape poured down in streams upon the General in a show of enthusiasm not seen since Eisenhower's own triumphal parade. It was an outpouring larger and distinctly different from the fanfare that welcomed the Friendship Train more than a year before. Tenants along the route hung American flags from their windows as others leaned from balconies to watch the scene below. Police erected barricades to keep the densely packed crowd from mobbing the General's motorcade. At a luncheon in Clay's honor at the Waldorf Hotel, the indefatigable Herbert Hoover appeared again. He praised Clay as more than just a great soldier, but as a great statesman as well. Clay could not let the moment pass without sharing the praise for this victory. We would not have won, he told the audience, if Hoover had not enabled food to reach the Allied occupation zones. The General bore straight to the bottom line in summing up their success: "You cannot stop communism with starvation."

Clay was right. America could not win the Cold War with bombs alone. It would need to win by its attractive, soft power, through the magnetic pull of its principles. The Soviets had demonstrated in Berlin and across Eastern Europe that they engaged in brutal, inhumane behavior in order to seize and hold power. The United States had to show itself as a clear alternative. During WWII, America had strayed from its proclaimed principles of fair play by exacting revenge against the innocent. That deviation continued with its German occupation policy. Hoover, Truman, Clayton, and many others needed to undo that policy and bring America's actions back in line with its stated values. With the airlift, they succeeded beyond measure, but there was still much more to do. Something still had to be done about Japan.

19 ATONE

Reverend John MacLean told his congregation that he had a foolish suggestion, though in truth he knew there was nothing foolish about it. It was not the first time he had felt the Lord moving him to change his life. The first time came when God told him to give up his profession as a lawyer and become a Presbyterian minister. On a second occasion God led him to accept the leadership of the Ginter Park Church in Richmond, Virginia, despite not believing himself qualified. He trusted in the Lord's wisdom, and tried to lead as he thought God would want. On this third occasion, the Lord was directing him on a very different kind of mission – one that seemed likely to earn him the enmity of most Americans.

When the United States dropped the atomic bombs on Japan, MacLean did not rejoice at the mass slaughter. Instead, he accepted the notion that the bombs brought an end to the war, but he felt that America had a duty to help rebuild. On January 6, 1946, MacLean announced to his church that God wanted him to raise money among American Christians for the restoration of Hiroshima and Nagasaki. He chose not to declare the atomic bombings as right or wrong; he simply tiptoed to the edge of calling it immoral. He did not go as far as to claim that the United States needed to apologize for the nuclear attacks. He merely pointed out that "a Christian nation had not only killed many thousands of helpless civilians, but destroyed the homes of countless others, leaving them shocked, wounded, terrified and deprived of a means of livelihood. Many of these, especially the women and children, were as innocent of starting the war as are the citizens of Ginter Park."[428]

MacLean understood that anti-Japanese feelings still permeated the United States. It had been scarcely more than four months since Japan's surrender. But the Reverend reasoned that Christ had taught his disciples to love and forgive their enemies. If America's Christians would extend a hand in rebuilding what their country had destroyed, it would be a potent example of Christian principles to the rest of the world. Such an act might inhibit future wars and simultaneously give a boost to foreign missions. Once seized by the idea, MacLean knew he had no choice but to pursue it wherever it might take him. He actually thought it would be thrilling if his southern Presbyterian Church would "step out of its traditional conservatism" and take the lead in an effort that "might influence the whole world to be more Christian."[429]

To the Reverend's surprise, his "foolish suggestion" quickly gathered steam. Newspapers across America picked up the story of the minister who wanted to make up for what his country had done. The radical idea soon came before a national body. The Federal Council of Churches debated MacLean's suggestion, and that is where the idea came to rest. The Council agreed with the kind sentiment behind his plan. The act of Christian charity was noble, but the rebuilding of Hiroshima and Nagasaki had too many implications. We don't know exactly how or why MacLean's idea became transformed, but at a meeting of the Council in Columbus, Ohio, the national organization significantly altered MacLean's original idea.[430] The spirit of his intention should be channeled, they decided, into the building of a Christian university in Japan. It would be international in nature, employing faculty and drawing students from around the world, and grounded in Christian notions of peace and harmony. Classes would be taught in English, and a new generation of Japanese men and women would be educated in Western traditions of critical thinking.

The idea for an International Christian University (ICU) gained a powerful boost when Reverend Ralph Diffendorfer joined the cause. With his round glasses, wavy hair, and gentle gaze, the Reverend exuded a kindly disposition. An expert on missionary education, Diffendorfer quickly gravitated to the idea of a Christian university in Japan. He devoted himself to the project and became its most persuasive proponent. Diffendorfer recognized that if the campaign were to succeed, it would need a prominent person attached to it, and he could not be that person. They needed a man already known to many Americans. It had to be someone respected for his judgment. He had to be someone who could speak knowledgeably about Japan. And of course, he had to be a good Christian. There was only one plausible candidate. Former ambassador Joseph Grew simply had to be convinced to join the mission.

On November 9, 1949, Diffendorfer traveled to see Grew at his summer home on the north shore of Massachusetts. Grew's wife was not happy about it. She felt he was overcommitted already and hated to see him take on any additional obligations, especially an intensely time-consuming one. "Don't be your usual spineless self," she told him. During the meeting, Grew could clearly see what Diffendorfer was driving at. The Minister was laying out the case for Grew to head the new foundation. In effect, he wanted Grew to be responsible for overseeing the entire fundraising campaign. Partway through their meeting, Grew invited his wife to join them, knowing she would help shield him so that he could politely decline. But Diffendorfer turned out to be so persuasive, so convinced of the university's crucial importance to the future of world peace, and so ardent a proponent of Christian kindness, that when after a two-hour presentation Diffendorfer asked the ambassador point blank if he would head the campaign, Mrs. Grew said, "Joe, you can't possibly refuse. Get out of some other things. This is much more important than anything else you are doing."[431]

Diffendorfer's approach came at the right time. Since his speaking tour in 1943, when he advocated allowing Japan to retain their emperor, Grew had been labeled an appeaser.[432] The truth, of course, was that Grew had been highly vocal in his condemnation of Japanese militarists. The only thing "soft" about his position was his call to rebuild Japan as a democracy, rather than demanding the country's subjugation. Just as most sensible experts in government had argued that a rebuilt, democratic Germany would drive economic recovery in Europe, Grew recognized that a revitalized, democratic Japan would become a valuable trading and security partner of the United States. A strong Japan would also be a powerful check on the spread of communism in Asia. It was precisely Grew's fervent anti-communist attitudes that shaped his policy prescriptions. But the public and the media could not understand this. The press disparaged him, and calls mounted for him to be replaced. Sensing the shifting currents, the day after Japan's surrender Grew tendered his resignation. After forty-one years of government service, he was ready for a new beginning.

By any measure, Grew had excelled in his long career. He had served his country's diplomatic corps notably, attained exceptional knowledge of Japan, gained national prominence after his return from Tokyo, and rose to be acting secretary of state at the most pivotal moment in US–Japan relations. And in all those decades, he dealt skillfully with the prejudice of others toward his disability.

Joseph Grew was deaf. He had lost much of his hearing in both ears from an attack of scarlet fever he contracted as a small boy. If others enunciated clearly and face to face, he could make out their words, but he could not follow conversations, speeches, or quiet sounds.[433] He learned to work around it, accessing information in other ways. His natural talents and social status undeniably afforded him opportunities that other deaf people might never have enjoyed. Despite the advantages of class, he could not entirely escape the prejudice and pain that so often dogs the disabled. After graduating from Harvard, Grew was offered an exciting opportunity to be the private secretary to America's consul general in Korea, but when the Consul General learned of Grew's deafness, he swiftly rescinded the offer. Grew was so devastated that he contemplated suicide.[434] But soon other offers materialized once employers were convinced that Grew could handle the work. A clerkship in Cairo launched his long years of service abroad, bookended by a decade in Tokyo. Now, at age sixty-nine, he felt ready to give back to Japan, and the idea of creating a Christian university struck him as wholly appropriate.

But while Grew was open to Diffendorfer's offer, he had one vital caveat. No communists must be employed on the faculty. The university had to be a place of free and open discussion. Communists, as Grew saw it, would prevent the honest exploration of truth. Ideologues had to be screened out during the hiring process. In a follow-up letter, Diffendorfer expressed his strong agreement with Grew's opinion that communism and Christianity are completely opposed to each other. He acknowledged that academic freedom was essential, but he counseled that the word "screening" had rather negative connotations and suggested that a more neutral-sounding "advisory committee" could handle the vetting of faculty members. The Berlin blockade had just ended, the Cold War was heating up, and its tensions stretched into nearly every official activity.

As Grew threw himself into the task of raising funds for ICU, he began recruiting supporters and speaking to civic groups. In May 1950, he addressed the General Assembly of the Presbyterian Church in America, telling his listeners that Japan's youth were at a crossroads. Three paths lay open to them. They could fall back into the feudalism and militarism of the past. They could embrace communism, and follow it to the certain destination of mental and moral enslavement. Or they could follow the road toward democracy "built on high Christian principles and a high moral code." This new university could lead them there, if they could raise the necessary funds.[435]

Bringing Grew on board the ICU Foundation had been a true coup. The Ambassador possessed the perfect mix of gravitas and expertise necessary to garner public support. But Diffendorfer was not done. He always aimed high. He had yet another prominent person in mind for his mission. He knew it would be an even greater coup if he could enlist the support of America's most famous and respected woman.

Mrs. Roosevelt was not interested. The former first lady responded in the most noncommittal manner possible: "Dear Mr. Diffendorfer, I have your letter and the information you sent and I found it very interesting. With all good wishes, I am very sincerely yours."[436] It was a kindly worded, perfectly polite brush-off. But Eleanor Roosevelt had no idea of the force that was Ralph Diffendorfer. Three years later, shortly after the ICU welcomed its initial class of students, Mrs. Roosevelt found herself addressing the ICU faculty and students and marveling at what the university was building.

Once Grew was fully established in his position, he began recruiting other leading Americans to support the effort. It was essential to gain the endorsement of the supreme allied commander of the Pacific and de facto ruler of Japan, General Douglas MacArthur. MacArthur was happy to grant it, and he accepted the position as honorary Chair. Grew also recruited the five-star Fleet Admiral William Halsey to head the fundraising for the southeastern United States. But Grew needed still another ally in the daunting mission to raise ten million dollars to help launch the university. He needed someone with extensive ties to the business community who was also a well-known public figure. Fortunately, such a person was near at hand: his close friend and next-door neighbor, Will Clayton.

When Will Clayton spoke, people listened. His career had been remarkable for its diversity. He had managed to achieve extraordinary influence in both international business and international affairs. He had served as one of eight men on the Interim Committee, which recommended use of the atomic bombs. And now, in 1950, he found himself speaking to businessmen and community members about the need for a Christian university in Japan, a campaign that began as an act of atonement for the nuclear attacks.

On April 25, 1950, Clayton laid out the dangers in the current world situation for a group in Houston, his home town. We are in a global war of paganism against Christianity, he told them. America is the unquestioned leader of the Christian world, and must win this war because the Soviets want to destroy religion. Stalin is far shrewder than Hitler ever was, and he is guided by "oriental cunning."[437] At the moment, the Soviets are winning. They control an area five times as large and five times as populous as the United States. If they gain control of Germany and Japan, America will have lost. And then Clayton made the argument that his friend Grew had been making since his return from house arrest in Tokyo in 1942. The Japanese population cannot survive without free trade to support itself. This time, however, the argument had a new twist. During the war, the purpose of rebuilding Japan and reintegrating it with world markets was to keep the Japanese from the starvation that would follow if it were deindustrialized and cut off from foreign trade. Now, with the start of the Cold War, the reason for rebuilding and reintegrating Japan was framed as essential to prevent its fall to communism.

Like Hoover, Truman, and many of the leading American statesmen at the time, Clayton saw the blocking of communism as a humanitarian act. As Clayton framed it to his audience, the communists sought to set up the state as master, and the people as slaves. They want to destroy religion, the home, and human dignity. Japan must be made into a bulwark against godless communism, and the ICU was a major step toward that defense. The Supreme Commander of Japan fully agreed.

General Douglas MacArthur believed it his mission to reform Japanese society. That meant extirpating the roots of militarism while training the younger generations in democracy and Christian virtues. MacArthur had requested a study of Japan's educational system. The twenty-seven American educators who traveled to Japan to investigate found that teaching had been heavily controlled by the former authoritarian regime. Teachers had been told not simply what to teach, but how to teach it. There was no freedom of thought or free expression. The new

ICU would change that. MacArthur quickly signed on as its nominal head within Japan. It would not require church attendance nor seek to convert its students. Freedom of religion would be respected. The university's aim would be to create humanitarian leaders, grounded in Christian principles of peace and kindness, and dedicated to maintaining democracy once the occupation ends.[438]

MacArthur saw Christianity as the necessary ingredient to fill Japan's spiritual void. In order to undo the country's militaristic mindset, he invited missionaries to preach the Gospel. By 1950, more than 2,000 Christian soldiers, armed with Bibles and eager to spread the good news, marched into Japan. But MacArthur, like many of his peers, hoped that Christianity would also help to block the influence of communism. A Christian university would serve as one important brick in the spiritual defenses he aimed to construct.[439] As the Supreme Commander told the *Nippon Times* in grandiose terms at the close of 1946:

> Due to a vacuum which events have left in the spiritual phase of Japanese life, there now exists an opportunity without counterpart since the birth of Christ for the spread of Christianity among the peoples of the Far East. ... If this opportunity is fully availed of by the leaders of our Christian faith, a revolution of spirit may be expected to ensue which will more favorably alter the course of civilization than has any economic or political revolution accomplished in the history of the world.[440]

Every new university must first acquire land, and ICU's founders settled on the ideal location. On the outskirts of Tokyo stretched several hundred wooded acres, part of which had been central to Japan's war effort. The most appropriate site for this university, they realized, would be the former home of the Nakajima Aircraft Research Facility. It was here that Japanese engineers created fighter planes to wage their wars of expansion. The Japan ICU Foundation had made a boldly symbolic choice. ICU would transform what had once been a foundry of war into a crucible of peace.[441]

Rebuilding

While Clayton, Grew, and Christian missionaries were raising funds and crafting plans for a Christian university in Japan, and while

Hoover was attempting to rescue Europeans and Asians from starvation, Henry Morgenthau began humanitarian work of his own. The plight of Europe's remaining Jews was dire, and the former Treasury chief sought to raise money for their relief. Morgenthau said that "sacrificial contributions" from Americans were the only source of aid available to Europe's desperate Jews, as UNRRA had no responsibility for them.[44] At the start of 1947, he was named general chairman of United Jewish Appeal, and launched one of the largest fundraising campaigns in American history to that date. The goal was vast, but the needs were valid. He aimed to amass $170 million. Between 1947 and 1950, he raised nearly half a billion dollars – a testament not simply to his stature and abilities, but more to the goodness and charity of the American people.[443] Upon accepting the chairmanship, he declared: "I regard it as the moral obligation of every American man, woman and child to save from despair and destruction the pitiful remnant of Jews who remain alive in Europe."[444] The following year, he set off for the newly created state of Israel to survey how United Jewish Appeal's funds were being used to help settle Jews in the Holy Land.[445]

Morgenthau enlisted help from anyone who would assist. At one fundraiser in 1946, Albert Einstein joined in the campaign. The former Treasury secretary also obtained priceless support from an old friend. Eleanor Roosevelt appeared alongside him, urging average Americans to give whatever they could to aid Europe's Jews. In February 1947, she told a women's rally at the Waldorf Astoria that more must be done. America had not yet filled its immigration quota, and Europe's Jews needed a home. Later that day, both she and Morgenthau spoke at a luncheon to launch the United Jewish Appeal's Women's Division for New York. Morgenthau explained that one and a half million Jews were in desperate need, and we could not rely on UNRRA to care for them. He told his audience that it was entirely up to them to help those Jews survive.[446]

Eleanor Roosevelt's actions in the immediate years after the war remained largely focused on fostering the United Nations. She helped to draft the Universal Declaration of Human Rights and encouraged all countries to sign on. She continued her newspaper column, "My Day," through which she supported greater racial and gender equality. She also used her influence to press for social change through backdoor channels to those in power. In June 1945, scarcely two months after her husband's death, she was already at work analyzing the Democrats' political prospects in the upcoming midterm elections of 1946. She wrote to Robert Hannegan, Democratic National Committee chair, with her thoughts on election strategy. Her most vital message: you need to attract women voters. The Truman Cabinet has no women in it, she noted with regret, and she insisted that this omission be corrected. Women did not necessarily need to be in the Cabinet, she wrote, but they needed to be in positions of influence over policy, "not just for a brief time, but permanently." And then she spelled it out for him: "I know many men are made a little uncomfortable by having women in these positions, but I think the time has come to face the fact that you have to win as many women's votes as you do men's votes." Mrs. Roosevelt also encouraged Hannegan to appoint Black Americans to positions of power. She told the Party boss that these measures were not simply for the good of the Party, but the progress of the country as well.[447]

Because the former first lady believed so passionately in internationalism and peace, she promoted her views wherever she went. She traveled so widely that people started calling her, "The First Lady of the World." Publicly, her humanitarian instincts were never in doubt, but privately she held certain views that were sometimes seen as less than charitable. This was most true regarding her views of the atomic bomb.

Eleanor Roosevelt knew about the bomb's existence as early as 1943, when a scientist from the Manhattan Project revealed it to her and pleaded with her to have Franklin speed its development.[448] She never opposed its use on Hiroshima. In 1953, she traveled to Japan and was forced to confront the legacy of President Truman's decision. After speaking to the Tokyo Woman's Christian University, she was brought into a large room where some 300 men and women came to hear her thoughts. The former first lady was served green tea, dried seaweed, and pointed questions. They asked why the United States had used the atom bombs and how she felt about it. This was only the beginning of her attempts to defend the nuclear attacks.

The next morning she visited the newly opened ICU. Because the campus lies far from Tokyo's center, she passed through miles of streets flanked by small shops, many flimsily rebuilt after the war. Seeing the conditions for the first time, it occurred to her just how much destruction was caused during the war. She admired the industry of the Japanese in cleaning and rebuilding a shattered land.[449]

At ICU, she found a campus still in its infancy and gestating with potential. She noted that with the encouragement of Joseph Grew,

American Christians had been sending not only funds, but also tools and even cattle to graze its 365 acres. Those herds were used to produce milk for dairy products – a means of giving the university a degree of self-sufficiency. She praised the university's impressive president, Hachiro Yuasa. And she called the 150 members of its first freshman class, "among the most intelligent and alert group of students that I had met anywhere."[450] In a session with the new class of ICU students, she encouraged them to work toward international peace: "Never close your mind to the possibility of good in any people. Accept the reality of the world situation and always endeavor for greater understanding and greater ability to love our neighbors."[451]

On June 17, Mrs. Roosevelt traveled to Hiroshima, where she visited the Atomic Bomb Casualty Commission, an American research group that studied the effects of the nuclear attacks on bomb survivors. Many people had been injured by the fires that the bomb had caused. After her official meetings, some girls were waiting to see her. The girls explained that they did not blame her for the atomic bomb; they only wanted to impress on her the need to ensure that these weapons were never used again on human beings, given their effects. Although she did not say so directly, the girls may have been among those whose faces were permanently disfigured by the attack. This must have been a powerful encounter because Mrs. Roosevelt called it a "tragic moment." It led her to urge Americans to do more to help. Though she maintained that they were not America's direct responsibility, "as a gesture of goodwill for the victims of this last war, such help would be invaluable."[452]

The president of Hiroshima University, Tatsuo Morito, found Mrs. Roosevelt to be steadfast in her defense of the bomb's use, but sensitive to its impact. Roosevelt told a friend that she was actually "walking on eggshells" the entire time in Hiroshima. Reflecting on her overall experience in Hiroshima, she remarked privately in a letter to a friend that she had not wept, as some had reported. She called the Japanese newspapers unreliable, with a tendency to invent material: "I know we were justified in dropping the bomb, but you can't help feeling sorry when you see suffering."[453]

In her newspaper column, she reflected further, lamenting the terrible suffering of civilians. But instead of disavowing the decision to use the bomb or even regretting its use, she seemed to draw a moral equivalence between Hiroshima and Pearl Harbor. She remembered how she and Franklin first heard about the bombing of Pearl Harbor, out of which, she wrote, came Hiroshima. Though not directly stating it, she seemed to be telling her readers that the Japanese government's attack on armed forces at Pearl Harbor had made the atomic attacks on Japanese civilians necessary. Civilians did not only suffer in Japan, she observed. They suffered all around the world during the war. The only thing to do, she concluded, is to try to eliminate the causes of war, educate the people, use the United Nations to assist, and ask God to grant men greater wisdom in the future.[454]

The young people of Hiroshima held a different view. Students of that city wrote to Mrs. Roosevelt at the time of her visit to express their thoughts on the atomic bomb, which they called "the most cruel bombing that the world has ever seen." The students spoke of the peace movement in Japan, and their hope that Americans would learn the truth of the bomb's effects. They were collecting photographs of the city burning. They wrote of the children and elderly, the noncombatants, who died from this attack. And they wanted people to know about the young women whose faces were scarred for life. At the close of their letter, the students asked how a humane nation like America could have used such a weapon. Their English was imperfect, but their message was clear:

> If US government had known the miserable result of the A-bomb that were dropped in two cities of Japan and if US government had had a small amount of humanism, the A-bomb would have never been dropped on the heads of the man Because the spirit of the public international laws never permits to use the A-bomb. Do you think it is a crime to kill people without any strategic necessity? We want to know who is responsible for the crime of A-bombing.[455]

Open Doors

Ralph Diffendorfer did not live to see the opening of the ICU he had done so much to create. He died in 1951, one year before the official dedication ceremony. But Reverend MacLean did arrive in Tokyo for that occasion, held on April 29, 1952, one day after the end of the American occupation.

The tiny band of American Christians who devoted themselves to creating the ICU had come a long way from Reverend MacLean's foolish suggestion. They had started with a vision, a hope that an international university, guided by Christian ethics, could help train new generations of Japanese young people in humanitarian ideals. They aimed to break the spell of militarism that had for so long seized a substantial segment of the Japanese population.

In the inaugural newsletter outlining their initial steps on August 16, 1948, the editors selected a quote to inspire them. Since they chose only one quote to place at the close of their first issue, we can assume it was chosen with care. They did not cite the supreme commander, de facto ruler of Japan, General MacArthur. They did not quote the president, Harry Truman, nor even his far more quotable predecessor, FDR. Instead, they selected only six words from a man best known to many for his failures, but beloved by others for his goodness:

"Make yourself worthy of the victory."[456] (– Herbert Hoover)

20 AFTERLIFE

Herbert Hoover wanted America to change. He wanted the nation to embody kindness, charity, and the humane treatment of others, whether friend or foe. Victory had come at a steep cost, not only in lives and treasure, but also in spirit. He saw that the wartime acts of vengeance had damaged the country's moral character. He hoped that through humanitarian relief in the immediate postwar years, America could regain the moral high ground it had lost. What did it mean to make yourself worthy? To Hoover, it meant caring for the most vulnerable, whoever they might be. It meant ensuring the basic human dignity of all people. And it implied the willingness to change oneself, to become a better person, collectively becoming a better nation.

Not everyone was able to meet the challenge, including Hoover himself. He struggled to overcome his own ideological convictions, even as evidence of their limitations mounted. He vehemently opposed American entry into WWII.[457] Had he been president instead of FDR, Hitler and the Nazis might have succeeded, and the world would be a very different place today. His intense aversion to excessive government spending led him to oppose the Marshall Plan, which many historians and scholars now consider among the most successful American government programs of the twentieth century.[458] On two of the most pivotal issues of his time, Hoover simply got it wrong. But a person's life must be judged on the whole of their actions. Hoover's empathy and moral courage also drove him to leave an exceedingly positive mark on history, one that has been largely overlooked.

Hoover's food mission and Clayton's tour of postwar Europe helped prepare America for a massive reverse course. Their efforts combined to help undo the Morgenthau-inspired occupation plan. Clayton had been chair of the committee that oversaw the creation of that punitive peace. His change of heart sprang not simply from concern for the cost to the American taxpayer. He had empathy for the people whose suffering he witnessed. Both he and Hoover grasped that America's occupation policy was partly to blame for that suffering, and it had to stop. Both men also hoped to block the spread of communism, not solely to open markets to American goods, but also to save Europeans and Asians from the brutal, violent dictatorships that Moscow was erecting within its spheres. The Soviets repeatedly revealed their cruelty through the murders of political opponents, most of which went unseen by the world outside the Iron Curtain. But in 1948, when Czech foreign minister Jan Masaryk was thrown from his bedroom window to his death, the world could have little doubt as to the nature of Soviet rule. The Soviet attempt to strangle West Berlin by blockade only cemented this perception. As Hoover, Clayton, and many other American leaders saw it, to be anti-communist at that time was itself a humanitarian act.

These were the early days of the postwar world, when American power was unmatched, and its purported goodness was vigorously espoused. It was before the CIA fomented coups around the globe, overthrew democratically elected leaders, and experimented with psychedelics on unwitting subjects, all in the name of combatting communism. It was before the "red-baiting," black listing, and witch hunting of Senator Joe McCarthy.[459] It was before the overthrow of Left-leaning regimes, the propping up of repressive Right-wing tyrants, and the bombing of poor peoples in distant lands. It was before Operation Condor. It was before Vietnam. In those early postwar years, America tried to seize the moral high ground. It had worked hard to resurrect its image in the eyes of the world, to be not the nation known for internment, starvation, and nuclear attacks on innocent civilians, but the country that rescued strangers from starvation, funded economic recovery abroad, and sent candy to the children of their former foes. These were the actions that American leaders ardently hoped to highlight. They yearned to face the world and proclaim, "*This* is who we are."

Herbert Hoover never shook off the stain of the Great Depression, but his heroic actions during the international food crisis after WWII had a profound impact on both the alleviation of mass suffering and the securing of global stability. Accounting for his famine relief activities during and after both world wars, Hoover is estimated to have saved approximately one hundred million lives.[460] After WWI he was known as the Great Humanitarian. If the estimates of his lifetime work are even remotely accurate, he deserves to be remembered not simply as the "Great Humanitarian," but as one of the greatest humanitarians of all time.

Hoover witnessed a tumultuous century, and he played a significant part in creating America's soft power. His attention to the needs of children, whatever their race, nationality, or background, and his devotion to relieving the suffering of civilians, even former enemies, made America seem especially humane in the eyes of the world.

Hoover's own longevity astonished Americans, and probably even himself. He advised Republican leaders into the 1950s and 1960s. He spoke at every Republican national convention until declining health made attendance impossible. Despite all of the extraordinary good that Hoover accomplished in his lifetime, most Americans still blamed him for the Depression. When asked late in life how he dealt with his many critics throughout the years, he answered wryly, "I outlived the bastards." He died in 1964 at age ninety.

The other men and women who led America to its superpower status each continued along circuitous life courses, often changing and growing in their treatment of others. Henry Stimson, who had been at the center of all three wartime vengeful acts, died in 1950 at age eighty-two. Despite his best efforts to inject Christian principles of kindness and forgiveness into America's treatment of enemies, with respect to the three wartime vengeful acts, his efforts must be viewed as a failure. He ceded influence over Japanese-American internment to his deputy, John McCloy, who pushed hard for forced relocation. He never stood up to General DeWitt or Colonel Bendetsen, allowing them to override his better judgment that America "cannot discriminate among our citizens on the ground of racial origin." Of all of Roosevelt's Cabinet officers, Stimson was in the strongest position to block the internment. Had he shown backbone in February 1942, the entire miserable affair might have been prevented.

Germany represented another failure. Stimson tried repeatedly to combat Morgenthau's plans to cripple the German economy, and for the most part, Morgenthau got the better of him. The relentless

Treasury Secretary was simply more skillful at playing the Washington policy game. His personal relationship to FDR naturally afforded him even greater influence. Morgenthau knew how to badger, wear down, and eventually persuade others to his side. Stimson took a more high-minded approach, believing that reasoned arguments presented cogently would suffice. They didn't.

But over time, Stimson learned from his rival. Tired of losing, and fearing for the fate not only of average, innocent Germans, but also for the future of world peace, Stimson began adopting Morgenthau-style tactics. He engaged Felix Frankfurter in a behind-the-scenes campaign to undercut Morgenthau's ideas. He worked to turn Roosevelt's successor against the Quebec agreement. He privately urged his top generals to subvert, if not directly flout, their orders and disregard the harshest aspects of American occupation policy. In short, Stimson realized that his gentleman's etiquette no longer triumphed in such a combative arena. Too many lives hinged on the outcome of policy clashes. For the sake of the innocent, the civilians, and the children, he simply had to win. If the other side consistently played dirty, then he would have to fight in the mud. And if that meant engaging in at least a degree of manipulation and subterfuge, the ends would justify the means.

Stimson tried to maneuver Truman into accepting conditional surrender terms for Japan, abandoning the demand for unconditional surrender. He failed to overcome the President's objections. While Stimson did succeed in saving the city of Kyoto from atomic destruction, he ignored Ralph Bard's plea for a demonstration of the bomb that would not cause civilian casualties. If McCloy's postwar claims are correct, and there is every reason to believe them, Stimson agonized over the use of the bomb on innocent civilians. And though the use of atomic bombs, one or more, might have been necessary, we can never know whether an offer of conditional surrender or a demonstration might have obviated that need.

In fairness, throughout the war years, Stimson was weakened by illness, exhaustion, insomnia, and age. He was seventy-seven years old in 1945, far beyond the retirement norm. He was overseeing an army of eleven million men, conducting the largest war effort in human history. Tortured by piercing migraines, he sometimes functioned on will alone. If his rivals, generals, presidents, and underlings occasionally outflanked him, he still managed to fight back and sometimes win.

278/ This Is Not Who We Are

Stimson's singular success on German occupation policy came with his resurrection of Herbert Hoover back into the policy process. By convincing Truman to make use of Hoover's unique expertise in famine relief, Stimson played a pivotal role in the rescue of millions of Asians and Europeans from starvation. His maneuvering should be remembered as a noble act.

As for Henry Morgenthau, he never again achieved the stature and influence he once wielded while managing the nation's Treasury, but he did not retreat into obscurity. Instead, he took on a new mission outside of government service, raising money for Europe's surviving Jews. While he had served in government, Morgenthau seldom drew attention to his religion. His work on the Rescue Board had been conducted in secret. But now, with Hitler defeated, and with Holocaust survivors seeking exodus from Europe, Morgenthau felt impelled to embrace his Jewish identity. Though he never experienced any qualms about the harsh punishment of all Germans – regardless of whether they supported or opposed the Third Reich – he did feel a moral obligation to save the remaining European Jews from statelessness and starvation. To this day, he is remembered in Israel as a humanitarian hero of the Jewish people.[461] In America, his impressive achievements to help win WWII have largely been forgotten.

Eleanor Roosevelt remained the nation's most outspoken advocate for human rights, joining her friend Henry Morgenthau in the campaign to aid Europe's surviving Jews,[462] though her actions during the war were more complex. She had opposed her husband's directive on Japanese-American internment, but was caught in the seemingly impossible position of having to support it. If she had spoken out against internment, it is unlikely that she would have managed to stop it. In the process, she would have probably greatly lessened her influence on other issues. But of course this is always the argument for remaining silent. There is the possibility, remote though it may be, that her vocal opposition might have shifted public attitudes against the use of concentration camps. Naturally, we can never know what effect her personal intervention would have had. We can only acknowledge that her failure to speak out against internment did nothing to help, and her public support of evacuation on national radio lent a veneer of acceptability to a gross injustice. To her great credit, she visited some of the camps and pressed for the release of several thousand young inmates so that they could attend college. Although she could not slow the momentum toward internment, she did try hard to lessen its severity.

Mrs. Roosevelt consistently supported Morgenthau's plan for Germany. Even after the war she continued to warn against the revitalizing of German industry for the same reasons that Morgenthau had repeatedly articulated. Both of them feared that inherent militarism would eventually lead the German people to harness their country's industrial might for another war. She held the German people as a whole responsible for both world wars, maintaining that the wars sprang from the German character.

The former first lady had supported the dropping of the atomic bombs, because, like most Americans of her day, she was convinced that it was necessary. More than a decade after the war's end, she devoted one of her daily columns to the subject. She pointed to a recent article in a Catholic newspaper, circulated by the Quakers, which asserted that America must confess its guilt for Hiroshima and Nagasaki. Mrs. Roosevelt sternly refuted that assertion. She reminded her readers of the situation at the time, parroting the arguments that Stimson had laid out in his 1947 *Harper's* piece. The Japanese had to be convinced that they would be destroyed if they failed to surrender. Two bombs in quick succession were needed to convince them. The choice was between an invasion or the bombs. An invasion would have cost more than a million American lives. The bombs saved more lives than they cost. She proclaimed that we should have grief and pity for the innocent who suffered: "But if you had to make this decision, I do not think any decision could have been made other than the one that was made."[463]

That was what she told her readers in 1956, but a few years later she revealed something different. Initially she had thought that the second bomb had been unnecessary. In a letter to ex-president Truman in 1959, she reaffirmed her belief that Truman had had no other option than to use the atomic bomb. She confessed that she had harbored qualms about his decision to drop the second, but after visiting Nagasaki and speaking with a former prisoner of war, she had changed her mind. That man convinced her that the Japanese people would not surrender without another demonstration of American power.[464] Her writings reveal that the woman widely respected as "The First Lady of the World" had never truly grappled with the alternatives: offering the Japanese the chance to retain the Emperor (conditional surrender), or a demonstration of the bomb on an uninhabited island. In fact, Eleanor

Roosevelt's insistence on unconditional surrender might very well have influenced Truman's thinking, causing him to reject the proposals of nearly all of his military and civilian advisors to allow the Emperor to remain. For years after the war, Roosevelt did urge against the further development of nuclear weapons. She devoted much of the rest of her life to being a champion of the United Nations and a spokesperson for universal human rights.

Will Clayton underwent something of a transformation. He had initially opposed the Morgenthau Plan, but then came around to accepting some of it in principle. He chaired the intergovernmental committee, which forged the still punishing compromise that set US policy toward Germany for the first two years of occupation. But after the war, Clayton's survey of conditions in Europe led him to press for a complete course reversal toward Germany. For all his work on America's economic and foreign policy, he rightly deserves to be known as the brains behind the Marshall Plan.

Clayton's attitude toward the Japanese mirrored his behavior to Germany. Though he served on the eight-member Interim Committee, he said little to indicate support for a demonstration of the bomb before its use on civilians. After the war, however, despite his many other responsibilities, he assumed a leading role in fundraising for the creation of the ICU. To Clayton and the many others who fostered the university's establishment, ICU represented a bulwark against communism, a means of combatting Japanese militarism, and a way of injecting Christian principles into a Japanese society. But above all, his support for ICU enabled him to believe he was acting on his own Christian values of mercy and forgiveness.

The ICU welcomed its first class of students on April 29, 1953. It has continued educating students ever since. The campus still sits on the site of the former Nakajima Aircraft manufacturer, but after the war, that company transitioned to making automobiles. Today it sells cars under the brand name Subaru.

On April 29, 1961, the university invited a special guest to address the faculty and students. James Conant had become president of Harvard at age thirty-nine. An exceptional chemist, he had worked on the development of poison gases for the American military during WWI. After WWII, he served as America's first ambassador to West Germany. In his later years, he began to reflect and write on methods of education. His talk at ICU, delivered in the slow, deliberate manner of a man who had seen much, perhaps too much, in his eventful life, called for egalitarianism. He wished that class differences would not hinder young people from attaining a university education: "For surely in this strange, deeply divided world, the heavily industrialized nations need the most brilliant students."[465] It was a call for democratic education, equal opportunity, and fairness. No mention was made by Conant or his hosts of his leading role in the development and advocacy of the atomic bombs.

Following his complete trouncing in the election of 1948, Henry Wallace largely withdrew from public life. Once the leading voice of American progressives, the former vice president receded into history, mostly forgotten by textbooks and unknown to most Americans today. Had he obtained the vice presidential re-nomination in 1944, he would have succeeded Franklin Roosevelt as president and moved America much sooner toward racial and gender equality, universal healthcare, and other progressive causes. America might look very different today, if the Democratic Party bosses had not engineered a Truman nomination. But Wallace's position toward Soviet-style communism might also have led America down a path of cooperation with Stalin's brutal regime.

In 1952, Wallace publicly reflected on his poor judgment. In an article for *This Week* magazine, "Where I Was Wrong," he wrote that before 1949, he had believed that Russia genuinely wanted peace. Soviet actions in Czechoslovakia began forcing him to revise his assumptions. He had thought that the communists had the support of the people. He did not speak out when the communists forcibly took power in Czechoslovakia, throwing the foreign minister, Jan Masaryk, from a window to his death. He now saw his failure to denounce the coup as his greatest error. He admitted that he "failed utterly to take into account the ruthless nature of Russian-trained Communists whose sole objective was to make Czechoslovakia completely subservient to Moscow." And then, toward the close of his piece, Wallace at last acknowledged the true nature of Soviet rule: "More and more I am convinced that Russian Communism in its total disregard of truth, in its fanaticism, its intolerance and its resolute denial of God and religion is something utterly evil."

In a forward-looking passage, Wallace predicted that the future lay with China. At the moment, they were fighting in Korea with the backing of Moscow. One day, he mused, the Chinese will turn on the

Russians. Wallace hoped that the United States would someday convince the Chinese that through greatly increased production and trade, it could raise its living standards. The time for this was not yet ripe, but he insisted it would come.[466]

Earl Warren, who had risen to prominence as California's attorney general by championing the forced relocation of Japanese Americans, steadily gained national recognition through his political activities. From the governorship of his home state, Warren was Thomas Dewey's first choice as a running mate in 1944. But Warren was too savvy to challenge FDR at the height of the war, and he prudently demurred. Four years later, however, when Truman's popularity had sunk so low that a Republican victory appeared preordained, Warren accepted Dewey's offer of the vice presidential spot. Both men would be stunned by Truman's remarkable triumph. When Truman was succeeded by Eisenhower, the new president made Warren chief justice of the Supreme Court, and for nearly two decades Warren pushed through a surprising number of progressive decisions. The most famous of these was *Brown v. Board of Education of Topeka*, the decision that made segregated schools illegal. Thus, the man who had once vociferously attacked Japanese Americans as disloyal and worthy of internment in 1954 not only ruled in favor of a landmark civil rights case, but also worked behind the scenes to ensure that his Court's decision was unanimous. Years after his ugly efforts to stoke racial fears by demanding the internment of his fellow citizens, Warren reflected on his actions with regret:

> It was wrong to react so impulsively, without positive evidence of disloyalty, even though we felt we had a good motive in the security of our state. It demonstrates the cruelty of war when fear, get-tough military psychology, propaganda, and racial antagonism combine with one's responsibility for public security to produce such acts.[467]

Among the nine justices who ruled to desegregate America's schools was Felix Frankfurter. Frankfurter, who had opposed the Morgenthau Plan but supported the internment of Japanese Americans in *Korematsu v. United States*, found himself supporting desegregation. The Justice had come a long way in a short time on both civil liberties and civil rights. Nonetheless, he continued to advocate for judicial restraint, convinced that the Court should not limit the powers of the Executive or Congress.

Milton Eisenhower, who had briefly overseen the entire relocation and felt sickened by the task, left government service completely in
1943, putting the War Relocation Authority behind him. He followed in
his brother's footsteps, not as president of the nation, but as a university
president. He served as head of Kansas State, Pennsylvania State, and
finally Johns Hopkins. He could never undo what had happened to
Japanese Americans on his watch, but in 1953, he made a curious
suggestion. He proposed a new Friendship Train, this one for
Koreans. It would not only gather grain, but also clothes and toys. Its
long-term mission would be "to bring the American and Korean people
closer together and act as a catalytic agent for wider Asian-American
understanding."[468]

Dillon Myer, Eisenhower's successor as head of the War
Relocation Authority, presided over the internment until the camps
were eventually closed. In 1962, twenty years after FDR's executive
order that had set the internment process in motion, Myer was invited
to speak to the Japanese American Citizens League (JACL). Just as he
had done throughout the war, he attacked racism and racists, holding
up the camps as a model of humane treatment. He praised Japanese
Americans for their obedience, cleanliness, and orderly conduct during
the long years of internment: "My hat is off to all of you who so
unobtrusively carried on in spite of all of the discrimination, race-
baiting and name calling." And then, in a stunning show of the mixed
messaging that had characterized his entire anguished tenure as head of
the WRA, he described how some internees had allegedly enjoyed camp
life. He told of women who had been spared the hard work of household
chores for the first time in their lives, able at last to "indulge" in "leisure-
time activities." Some of the men, he explained, had enjoyed their time
in the camps so much that they had to be persuaded to leave them when
the war ended.

Reflecting on some of the internment's tensest moments, including the riots, Myer admitted that the pressures of wartime and need to
act quickly led to mistakes. And then he lauded the American people for
their postwar efforts to remedy the injustices done to the Japanese-
American community. "The good people in our democracy sometimes
move more slowly than the people of ill will," he told his audience, "but
when they become convinced that the bill of rights and all of our
guidelines for democratic action have been set aside, they do move to
rectify the situation and they keep at it until the job is done."[469]

He was right. The American system did enable a degree of restitution, but it would take another twenty years before a full accounting could begin. In one final awkward irony, Myer concluded his remarks to the JACL by naming the individuals who deserved the greatest appreciation for their efforts during the internment. Some of them were truly deserving of praise, such as Clarence Pickett and the Quakers, but among his select list of friends of Japanese Americans was John McCloy, the man largely responsible for both establishing internment and suppressing evidence to ensure that the Supreme Court would not overturn it.

As for General John DeWitt, a key figure in the internment drama, his career proceeded smoothly. After overseeing the evacuation and relocation of Japanese Americans, he led the Army and Navy Staff College (predecessor to the Naval War College) in Washington, and retired from the military not long after the war. In 1954, a special act of Congress elevated DeWitt to a full general, a rare honor given for his services to the nation. Colonel Karl Bendetsen, a principal instigator of internment, remained unrepentant to the end. In 1982, a reporter from the *Washington Post* conducted a lengthy private interview with Bendetsen, which he recorded. Though slow in speech, the Colonel seemed mentally agile, able to perform remarkable contortions of the truth. The internees, he insisted, were never held against their will. They were free to leave the camps whenever they wished. The barbed wire was not meant to keep people in, it was intended to keep cattle out, lest the animals disturb the camp. He never asked to be tasked with the thankless assignment of devising the evacuation and internment policies, and he did not enjoy one minute of it, he maintained. Forty years later, he was still declaring his actions both necessary and humane.[470]

Fred Korematsu, the shy young man who had defied the internment order to remain with the woman he loved, lived for forty years with the stigma of having been convicted of a crime. Because of his criminal record, he had difficulty finding work after his release from detention. Lacking a college degree, he took manual labor where he could find it. He married a white woman, but as a mixed race couple, they found it hard to find people who would rent to them. Only a Jewish landlord agreed to rent them an apartment. He never spoke about his case with his children, who only learned about it in school. He remained throughout his life a soft-spoken, modest man, who never stopped believing that it was pure racism that had led to the gross mistreatment of Japanese Americans.

And then, one day in 1981, Korematsu received a call from a law professor in New England. Peter Irons said that he had been researching the now forty-year-old case and unearthed some previously unseen materials. They showed that the case against Korematsu had been rigged. Evidence had been suppressed. The intelligence reports to FDR concluding that the Japanese and Japanese Americans living on the west coast posed no security threat had intentionally not been submitted to the Court. And there was more. Some reports had been altered to draw the opposite conclusion to their author's intent. With this discovery, Irons explained, Korematsu's case could be reopened and his conviction overturned. More than this, the wrong done to thousands of Japanese Americans could at last be righted.

What followed was a complicated series of legal gambits designed to bring the case back before the Supreme Court. Once Korematsu's legal team announced the case at a heavily covered press conference, a new battle was on. Korematsu's lawyers were claiming that the government had been engaged in the suppression of evidence and a cover-up. These were not inconsequential oversights but serious crimes. The government tried its best to minimize the negative publicity. Its legal representatives offered to pardon Korematsu, but he would not accept. A pardon would be an admission of guilt, and Korematsu knew that his only crime was in being Japanese American.

As his case wove its way through the court system, Korematsu also faced pushback from one of America's most respected and influential establishment insiders. In 1980, Congress established a commission to investigate the internment issue. The aim was to discover whether the surviving internees deserved compensation for a denial of their civil liberties. Throughout the second half of 1981, a nine-member commission held hearings across the country, taking testimony from roughly 750 Japanese Americans. On August 5, George Takei (the actor who played Sulu in *Star Trek*) gave his testimony. He was impressed by the scene of so many elderly citizens, who had been silent for so long, finally being heard. Though many were stooped and frail, they delivered their accounts of suffering and privation in the hope that justice would at last arrive. But then Takei saw another group of citizens approach the bank of microphones. These were white Americans who told how they had lost loved ones at Pearl Harbor and in the brutal war with Japan. Takei boiled in anger. He felt incensed that after so many decades, those people still did not understand that Japanese Americans were Americans and not responsible for the actions of Japan's military regime.[471] One month later, the man who had done more than any other to produce the internment took the witness stand.

On November 3, 1981, the Commission called to the Senate hearing room the eighty-six-year-old former assistant secretary of war. It seemed as though an entire era had passed since his days working for Henry Stimson. After the war McCloy returned to private legal practice, and in 1947, he became president of the World Bank. In 1950, President Truman appointed him as the first civilian governor-general of occupied West Germany. McCloy had opposed Morgenthau's harsh peace plan, and then found himself in charge of transitioning West Germany to a self-governing democracy. Among his most controversial actions involved the early release of imprisoned war criminals. Eleanor Roosevelt, still clinging to her critical views of the German people, wrote to McCloy asking, "Why are we freeing so many Nazis?"[472] McCloy was unmoved. He did not alter his decision, a decision which made him popular among some within Germany, but which raised questions over whether he had gone too easy on war criminals. By granting clemency, he released from prison many who had been found guilty at Nuremberg, including concentration camp guards and industrialists who had requested Jewish slave labor at their facilities. Decades later, McCloy had to answer for an even more controversial decision.

For four hours the former lawyer responded to questions, which at moments must have felt like both an interrogation and a trial. For a man who had long been shown deference throughout his lengthy career, this experience had to be a shock. The Senate room was filled with Japanese Americans, the survivors and children of survivors of internment. As McCloy insisted that the relocation had been necessary and prudent, his comments repeatedly met with hisses of disgust from the crowd. McCloy said that he had visited the camps and found that the residents were not distressed. This was not the experience of most survivors, as evidenced by their extensive testimonies.

When Judge William Marutani, the only Japanese-American member of the Commission, questioned the elder statesman, both men became highly agitated. Maybe it was because of the intense discomfort of the situation, or maybe it was just the result of an exhausting emotional exchange. But finally, after forty years, McCloy said it. The relocation was implemented, he blurted, as retribution for Pearl Harbor.

And there it was. Marutani stopped the proceedings and asked the stenographer to read back McCloy's statement. McCloy asked to retract the word "retribution," but it was too late. Neither his comment, nor the internment, could be undone.[473]

At least, that was how historian Peter Irons presented it, but the transcript of his testimony is more muddled. What McCloy actually said has to be viewed in the context of Judge Marutani's examination of him. The Judge asked McCloy to acknowledge the distress that the internment caused to Japanese Americans. McCloy tried to say that all Americans shared in suffering. "I don't think the Japanese were unduly subjected to distress during the war." McCloy insisted that the impact of the surprise attack led them to take the measures they did, and it was not possible to distribute evenly all of the distress. He argued that we cannot now, forty years after that attack, try to readdress what happened. It was within this context that McCloy uttered his chilling remark.

MCCLOY: I didn't say we all shared equally, no. I said it is impossible to make equal distribution. You can't do it. I say that I don't think the Japanese population was unduly subjected, considering all the exigencies to which, to amount that they did share in the way of retribution for the attack that was made on Pearl Harbor.[474]

Was McCloy actually saying that Japanese Americans were being punished as retribution for the Empire of Japan's attack on Pearl Harbor? Judge Marutani certainly thought so, but McCloy's words are so unclear that it is difficult to know for certain. Only one thing was clear. The experience of being hounded by a judge and hissed at by an angry crowd was deeply distressing for McCloy.

McCloy was not finished. He felt deeply disrespected by the frequent interruptions of his testimony. He told Senator Charles Grassley that he considered the experience "a horrendous affront" to the American tradition of fair and objective hearings. Grassley invited McCloy to testify again when Grassley's Judiciary Committee would be conducting further hearings on the question of compensation, and

McCloy readily agreed. Before that rematch occurred, McCloy published an op-ed in the *New York Times* denouncing the investigation. He had a strong motivation to do so. McCloy had pushed harder than anyone else in President Roosevelt's inner circle for the forced relocation of Japanese Americans. It was he, after all, who had manipulated and suppressed evidence to ensure the Supreme Court's decision in his favor. Whether he secretly influenced, pressured, or merely persuaded his close friend Justice Frankfurter to support the War Department's side (or to lobby for McCloy's position among the other justices) may never be known. In 1983, McCloy was in the final years of his long and distinguished life. The reopening of the Korematsu case presented him with an opportunity to admit his wrongdoing, acknowledge the enormous harm it caused to more than a hundred thousand innocent people, and apologize. He could have done what Earl Warren did by publicly repudiating his own actions in support of internment. Instead, he chose a different path.

In his op-ed, McCloy argued that blame for the internment rested squarely with the wartime government of Japan. Its "sneak attack set in train the dislocation, death and misery of millions, including the privations suffered by the innocent ethnic Japanese on the West Coast." McCloy fell back on a tired and faltering defense: we feared the threat of sabotage, it was impossible to separate the loyal from the saboteurs, and the Supreme Court upheld the decision on grounds of military necessity. But as we now know, military and FBI intelligence concluded that there was no necessity of relocation. The few potentially dangerous individuals were under surveillance, and the overwhelming majority of Japanese Americans posed no threat at all. McCloy suppressed those reports from reaching the Supreme Court's justices. This was a serious crime, and McCloy made no mention of it. Instead, he ended his piece with a pitiful lamentation over how the times have changed: "What have we come to when Americans are asked to shoulder the blame, to finance and conduct inquiries into their 'guilt' and pay for the consequences of an indisputable act of aggression by Japan?"[475]

Given his lifetime of public service at the highest levels, McCloy had certainly earned the chance to be heard. On June 21, 1984, at age eighty-nine, McCloy entered the hearing room to testify before the House panel on compensation. This time he would be treated with extreme deference. He had every opportunity to voice his position for the record, and he showed not a scintilla of regret.

Calling it a "grotesque charge" that President Roosevelt and others had acted with racist intent, McCloy full-throatedly objected to the claim. There was not a drop of racial prejudice in Roosevelt or Stimson. The internment decision was entirely about security. McCloy became emotional as he defended the administration's actions. He deployed every argument he could muster. Our military leaders acted in the country's best interest. It is a disgrace to impugn their motives. No one on the Relocation Commission served at the time. They cannot know what we knew. The lobbyists are out to get money from the government. The Canadians had interned their Japanese as well, but no one ever mentions this. We believed that Japan had a network of saboteurs along the west coast. There was no way to distinguish the loyal from the disloyal. All those people in the camps who refused to swear their allegiance proved their disloyalty. We were acting to defend the nation.

The entire scene appeared shockingly anachronistic. The past was colliding with the present, and the two simply could not see eye to eye. McCloy repeatedly insisted that the men who led the country during the war were the finest statesmen. Some Congressmen tried to explain that no one denied their stature. All respected and admired them. But even the finest statesmen sometimes make mistakes. McCloy could brook no criticism. And then, as if to underscore the distance that America had traveled since McCloy's time, Congressman Barney Frank took his turn to question the elder statesman.

Barney Frank knew something about prejudice. At the time of this hearing, he had not yet come out, though three years later in 1987 he would become the first openly gay Congressman in American history. In his treatment of McCloy, Frank afforded the elder statesman the respect he deserved for the service he had given to his country. But the gap between the two men's perspectives was unbridgeable, not simply because of the generations between them, but also because of their divergent life experiences. In what would quickly be evident as a fruitless exercise, the Congressman tried in vain to make McCloy see that the rounding up of all Japanese Americans was both unnecessary and prejudicial, though he tactfully avoided using the word racist.

CONGRESSMAN FRANK: The indication that there might have been some small percentage in a given population of people prepared to be disloyal, for that to then be the basis for rounding everybody up solely on their common racial ancestry, that is the concept that many of us find to be very frightening. We do feel it would not have been applied to a similar geographic group or some other group.

MCCLOY: Well, I think you would be surprised to find what groups we did apply it to. At the time of World War II we applied it to some of the Germans that were down in South America. They were brought up here to – what was it, Crystal City – interned in Crystal City and Ellis Island –

FRANK: Were these American citizens?

MCCLOY: No; they were Germans. They were Germans, but –

FRANK: But we're talking about Americans, Mr. McCloy.

It was as though McCloy could not recognize that Japanese Americans were in fact Americans. Frank tried at length to explain.

FRANK: But I think the point we want to get across is not that we think Franklin Roosevelt, or Judge Patterson, or others were racially prejudiced in a personal way. On the other hand, I think many of us feel the decision to take that action, based solely on a racial criterion for the people involved, was, in fact, objectively a kind of prejudicial action, and that while we understand the fear – and I'm not saying that these were bad or vicious people; they are people I greatly admire – I think one of the lessons we should learn is that in times of war, and because there are racial feelings in all of us, we have to guard against even the best people taking actions that don't conform to our democratic traditions.

Taking everyone in a particular racial category, without evidence, and subjecting them to some form of dislocation, assuming them to be guilty and putting on them the burden of then proving their innocence, is the thing that bothers us. We are saying we really don't want that to happen again.

McCloy was ready for Frank's remarks and responded with what must have struck him as a perfectly compelling analogy. He suggested that if Cuba were to attack the United States in Florida, it would be reasonable to move the Hispanics out of that area. Probably taken aback by McCloy's suggestion, Frank responded with a articulation of his opposing point of view. First, he said that our national security need not come at the expense of our people's civil liberties. And then he elaborated:

FRANK: I want to say that we will protect our installations with as much police power as it takes, that we will fortify the installations if necessary, we will give very severe security checks to anyone who works there, and we will act on evidence that any individuals are likely to commit sabotage. But no, we will not round up all of the Cubans or all of the Salvadorans and relocate them. That, we think in hindsight, was not a good idea, not necessary, and in fact contributes to people thinking of other American citizens in racial categories, which is something we want to get away from.

McCloy again insisted that his colleagues did not act out of racism. Congressman Frank tried one last time to explain why an apology was warranted.

FRANK: My last statement, Mr. McCloy, I will not impute to them racial prejudice. But I think it can be very good in a democratic system to say yes, we apologize, that we think, in all good faith, that an error was made. I think that is a reasonable statement.

John McCloy arguably did more to shape American superpower than any other unelected official in the twentieth century. His

Figure 20.1 President Reagan and John McCloy talk during a Rose Garden ceremony on April 2, 1985, honoring McCloy, a longtime US diplomatic troubleshooter, who was celebrating his 90th birthday. McCloy said to Reagan, "Compared to me, you're a spring chicken." Reagan replied, "You've made my day." Photo by Bettmann/Getty Images.

efforts to end the war with Japan without dropping the atomic bombs on civilians, though unsuccessful, stand out as noble. His attempts to ameliorate the effects of the Morgenthau Plan undoubtedly saved innocent German lives. As the high commissioner for Germany after the war, he helped to transition West Germany from occupation to independence and cemented positive relations with the United States. His role as one of Washington's "wise men" of foreign policy placed him at the fulcrum of pivotal moments in American history. As such, he was one of those whom every American president from Roosevelt to Reagan called upon for advice. John F. Kennedy enlisted McCloy to help negotiate with the Soviets a peaceful settlement of the Cuban Missile Crisis. When Lyndon Johnson turned to him during the Vietnam War, McCloy advocated escalation in 1965, as did nearly all of his peers. In the 1980s, McCloy had the opportunity to publicly admit his willful withholding of evidence from the Supreme Court in the Hirabayashi and Korematsu cases. It was a chance to set the record straight, but he could not do it. He still saw his actions as necessary for safeguarding the nation, despite overwhelming information to the contrary. The passage of decades only hardened his view. He had the chance in his final years to act with

Figure 20.2 US President Bill Clinton stands with Fred Korematsu awarding him the Presidential Medal of Freedom, the nation's highest civilian honor. Photo by Paul J. Richards/AFP/Getty Images.

honor, but he simply lacked the ability to recognize his actions as wrong. McCloy died in 1989, just months before the start of the Soviet Union's collapse. He missed the moment when America emerged as the world's sole superpower, the situation he had been striving to create throughout his long and remarkable life.

Fred Korematsu's case ultimately ended in his complete exoneration and the government's admission of guilt. The case also prompted the government to make restitution to those who had been forcibly interned. The Civil Liberties Act of 1988 provided $25,000 to each surviving victim. At the signing ceremony, President Ronald Reagan told the onlookers that they were gathered "to right a grave wrong." He declared that the internment had been based solely on race: "No payment can make up for those lost years. So what is most important in this bill has less to do with property than with honor. For here we admit a wrong. Here we reaffirm our commitment as a nation to equal justice under the law."[476]

Toward the end of his life, Fred Korematsu became something of a folk hero to those interested in civil liberties and social justice. Though in fragile health, he continued to speak with students and civic groups around the country in the 1980s and 1990s. Shortly before his death, Korematsu received a surprising honor. In 1993, President Bill Clinton invited him to the White House. Korematsu's once thick, dark hair was now thinned and white, but he still retained the habit of clasping his hands behind his back and leaning in to listen. And this was a moment worth listening to. The man who in his youth had been imprisoned for his defiance of a presidential order now found himself receiving the Presidential Medal of Freedom.

One other person deserves mention in the long story of America's struggle between vengeance and virtue. In the summer of 2019, Americans learned that conditions for children at the southern border had not improved since the Trump administration's separation policy had been exposed the year before. In fact, the situation had worsened. Along the Texas border in the sweltering summer heat, thousands of migrants still languished in holding centers, including hundreds of children. The stench of sweat, filth, and human excrement suffused the squalid cells. In quarters so tightly packed that the occupants could not sit down, some children stood atop toilets where the air was slightly less fetid.

Outraged by these appalling conditions, attorneys brought suit against the United States government for violating the law that minors must be kept in safe and sanitary conditions. The Trump administration's Justice Department lawyer disagreed. Sarah Fabian argued that the government was not in fact required to abide by the Flores Settlement, the precedent that dated back to 1997, when the courts established the safe and sanitary rules. Unfortunately for Fabian and the Justice Department, the three judges on the Ninth Circuit Court of Appeals rejected Fabian's arguments, none more ardently than the Court's most senior judge, and with good reason.

The Court's most senior judge was A. Wallace Tashima. As a young man, Tashima had enlisted in the United States Marine Corps.

Following his military service, he pursued an education, graduating from UCLA and then from Harvard Law School. In 2019, at age eighty-five, Judge Tashima found himself adjudicating a case distressingly familiar to him. During the oral arguments, he challenged Ms. Fabian:

JUDGE TASHIMA:	It's within everybody's common understanding that if you don't have a toothbrush, if you don't have soap, if you don't have a blanket, that's not "safe and sanitary." Wouldn't everybody agree to that? Do you agree with that?
FABIAN:	Well, I think it's – I think those are – there's fair reason to find that those things may be part of "safe and sanitary."
JUDGE TASHIMA BORE DOWN:	Not may be . . . . Why do you say "may be"? You mean there's circumstances when a person doesn't need to have a toothbrush, toothpaste and soap for days?

It was a bad day to be arguing for internment. The Trump administration lawyers had landed in the wrong court, with the wrong judge, on the wrong side of decency. America's cruelty in WWII was colliding with its present-day abuses, and on this day at least, humanity prevailed. That was because Judge A. Wallace Tashima was also known as Atsushi Tashima – the little boy mentioned at the start of Chapter 3. He was just eight years old in 1942, when he was among the thousands of children forcibly relocated to an internment camp. Now, in the latter years of his long career, Atsushi Tashima found himself confronting another case of cruelty toward innocent children. This time, however, he possessed at least some power to make things right.

America had decisively defeated tyranny in WWII, but more than seventy years later it was still struggling to make itself worthy of the victory.

ACKNOWLEDGMENTS

My first debt is to my editor at Cambridge University Press, Cecelia Cancellaro, whose belief in this project has been steadfast. I am equally indebted to numerous archivists, including those at the Presidential Libraries of Franklin D. Roosevelt, Harry S. Truman, and Herbert Hoover. Randy Sowell of the Truman Library consistently strove to help me find the records that would answer arcane questions. Tom McAnear of the National Archives and Records Administration went out of his way to dig up records from the short-lived Office of Facts and Figures, and Timothy Duskin at the Naval History and Heritage Command patiently answered my questions regarding the Ralph A. Bard papers. Margaret Dakin of Amherst College's Archives and Special Collections kindly assisted me with access to the papers of John McCloy. A fellowship from the Japan ICU Foundation enabled me to spend time in Tokyo at the university's archives. The ICU Library staff were exceedingly diligent in their efforts to provide me with materials and assistance in my searches relating to the university's early years. I was truly impressed when they located an aged audio cassette recording of a speech at ICU by the former Harvard President James Conant, and then managed to track down a cassette player on which to hear it.

I am especially grateful to the staff of the Hoover Institution on War, Revolution, and Peace. Sarah Patton and the Hoover staff provided documents, photographs, and audio recordings in digital formats, while making other records accessible to me, including the substantial food mission diaries of Ambassador Hugh Gibson. The Hoover Institution provided generous support during the final phase of this project, for which I am truly thankful. The librarians at the Dudley Knox Library of the Naval Postgraduate School and the University of California at Berkeley were always helpful and professional. Greta Marlatt of Knox Library helped me in my hunt for surveys of American attitudes and rare footage of the aftermath of the atomic bombings. It is clear why she was named Federal Librarian of the Year. Jennifer Dorner of Berkeley's Doe Library frequently assisted me in locating materials, taking extra time to offer tips on using the library's search tools.

While researching and writing this book, I have been fortunate to have worked with numerous outstanding assistants, primary among them being Jason Altwies. For several years, Jason has been a steady, reliable fixer of more problems than I wish to recall. His tenacity and devotion to professionalism have left me endlessly impressed. Many others have helped facilitate my research, including Carina Hinton, Cynthia Huang, Aaditee Kudrimoti, Alec Medein, Teja Pattabhiraman, Riley Seow, Femke van der Drift, and Michelle Yoshimoto. I profited from the able assistance of Akshara Cholla. She deserves considerable thanks for her dedication to my many projects over the course of several years, all the while studying to enter medical school. Her care and patience will make her a wonderful physician. In the final stage before submitting the manuscript, I had the good fortune to work with Alessandra Maranca, who went far beyond my expectations to help me tie up loose ends.

My colleagues and the staff at the Naval Postgraduate School facilitated my research in various ways, which helped to make the completion of this work possible. Jeroen deWulf and Gia White of UC Berkeley's Institute of European Studies have been consistently in my corner, and my talks at the Institute helped to make this a stronger book. As with many previous projects, John Connelly of Berkeley's history department provided invaluable advice and ideas. Peter Zinoman, also of Berkeley's history department, encouraged me in this project from its outset.

The remarkably talented Adam Hochschild provided extremely useful guidance and support based on his long experience writing for audiences beyond academia. He scrupulously read the entire manuscript, offering trenchant tips to vivify the scenes and humanize the characters. I am indebted to Fredrik Logevall, who not only read parts of the manuscript but also encouraged me as I brought the book to publication. Dayna Barnes read many early chapters and generously offered me her expertise and insights into the Roosevelt administration's postwar planning. Greg Robinson graciously and tirelessly talked me through many of the thorny issues surrounding the Japanese-American internment. I always marveled not merely at his knowledge but also at his ceaseless passion for the topic. Jonathan van Harmelen shared with me documents he had gathered during his graduate research into the internment and alerted me to other records that proved of great value. Michael Kort sent me important information on casualty estimates for the planned invasion of Japan. George Nash, the leading expert on Herbert Hoover, provided his thoughts and pointed me toward useful sources of Hoover's views. Several anonymous reviewers contributed suggestions that substantially improved the text.

I have been blessed with many good friends who took the time to read and comment on parts of the manuscript. Amrit Dhir, Leslie Chang, and Scott Saul each gave valuable feedback. Elliot Neaman read several chapters in progress and offered excellent suggestions for improvement. As with so many of my previous books, Kristin Rebien did more than just lend her expertise. She also found numerous ways to enhance the language, which has always amazed me, since English is not her native tongue. I still don't know how she does it. Elizabeth Miles used her exacting eye to help me avoid numerous errors. To all of these people I am immensely grateful.

NOTES

Prologue: The Friendship Train

1. "Television: TV's Job on Friendship Train at Hollywood Is the Tops," *The Billboard*, November 15, 1947.
2. Film footage of these desperate scenes of hunger can be viewed in the documentary, "We Fed Our Enemies." Hoover Institution Archives. 62008_f_0012444_r-2.
3. John Ward, "America's Friendship Train," *The Palestine Post*, November 28, 1947.
4. "Film Stars Send the Friendship Train Eastward," *New York Herald Tribune*, November 8, 1947.
5. "Load Is Tripled as Friendship Train Rolls East," *New York Herald Tribune*, November 10, 1947.
6. Ibid.
7. Dorothea Kahn, "People's Gifts Swell Relief Train," *Christian Science Monitor*, November 13, 1947.
8. Ibid.
9. "Friendship Train Arrives Here Sunday," *Cleveland Call and Post*, November 15, 1947.
10. To view the fourteen-minute documentary that Harry Warner produced about the Friendship Train, see www.youtube.com/watch?v=BfxWYNf97Hg.
11. Kahn, "People's Gifts Swell Relief Train."
12. "Kansas Gifts Top Peak in Relief Train," *Christian Science Monitor*, November 26, 1947.
13. "Friendship Train Now 184 Cars," *Los Angeles Times*, November 17, 1947.
14. Charles Grutzner, "City Hails Friendship Train," *New York Times*, November 19, 1947.
15. Ibid.
16. "First Shipment of Friendship Train Food Off," *New York Herald Tribune*, December 8, 1947.
17. *Final Report*, US Citizens Food Committee, January 15, 1948. www.google.com/books/edition/Final_Report/Upw8AAAAMAAJ?hl=en&gbpv=0.
18. "Thanks Given for Packages from CARE: Letters Acknowledging Receipt Overseas Are Received," *The Hartford Courant*, May 20, 1948.

Introduction: From Vengeance to Virtue

19. "He Saw the Panic: The Afghan Men Who Fell from the US Jet," *The Guardian*, September 16, 2021. https://apple.news/Avd9N2zA-TOemuWXbK6j1Kg. For more on Zaki Anwar, see Laila Rasekh, "The Falling Man of Kabul," *Foreign Policy*, August 28, 2021.

20. See 2021 Kabul Airport Attack, Wikipedia. https://en.wikipedia.org/wiki/2021_Kabul_airport_attack.

21. Not all Americans objected. A sizeable minority, twenty-seven percent, supported it. Dylan Matthews, "Polls: Trump's Family Separation Policy Is Very Unpopular – Except among Republicans," June 18, 2018. www.vox.com/policy-and-politics/2018/6/18/17475740/family-separation-poll-polling-border-trump-children-immigrant-families-parents. In one poll, ninety-one percent of Democrats opposed the policy, but fifty-five percent of Republicans supported it.

22. Soviet wartime losses remain uncertain. Some twenty million deaths was the official figure during the Soviet era, including roughly 8.7 million military deaths. Both estimates have been disputed. For a summary, see "World War II, Casualties of the Soviet Union." https://en.wikipedia.org/wiki/World_War_II_casualties_of_the_Soviet_Union.

23. In a recent study, John E. Schmitz argues that while racism was prevalent, the internment of Japanese Americans was not primarily based on race because German Americans and Italian Americans were also interned. While I cannot agree with his conclusion, his study is worth considering as it spotlights the national security concerns of policy makers as well as the experience of many Americans of German and Italian descent. See John E. Schmitz, *Enemies Among Us: The Relocation, Internment, and Repatriation of German, Italian, and Japanese Americans During the Second World War* (Lincoln: University of Nebraska Press, 2021).

24. Adam Taylor, "In Japan and America, More and More People Think Hiroshima Bombing Was Wrong," *Washington Post*, May 10, 2016. It is entirely conceivable that if more Americans learned the true effects of the bombs on civilians and were taught that alternatives to its use existed, the percentage supporting this decision would fall even lower.

25. It was not until the presidential campaign of 1928 that Hoover's supporters assigned him the "Great Humanitarian" label.

26. The list of US government actions that fostered suffering in this period is undeniably long. It fire bombed Japanese cities, burning thousands of men, women, and children to death. It devastated German towns, most infamously Hamburg and Dresden, again inflicting mass suffering on civilians. During and after the war, it backed European colonial regimes, which in turn savagely repressed resistance movements. It supported the openly racist regime in South Africa. These are but a few of the foreign policies that the US government pursued, which belied its avowed support for democracy and freedom. Its domestic policies, from segregation to other legal forms of discrimination, also fostered suffering, particularly for minorities. But its system did allow for the gradual, much too gradual, advancement of equality and individual rights.

27. John W. Dower, *War Without Mercy: Race and Power in the Pacific War* (New York: Random House, 1986).

28. Stephen Wertheim, *Tomorrow the World: The Birth of US Global Supremacy* (Cambridge, MA: Harvard University Press, 2020).

1 Concentrate

29. *Detroit Free Press*, December 7, 1941. www.newspapers.com/newspage/98269070/. See also United States Congress, House Committee on Un-American Activities, *Report on the American Slav Congress and Associated Organizations, June 26, 1949* (Washington, DC: US Government Printing Office, 1950), p. 13.
30. Address of Attorney General Francis Biddle to the American Slav Conference of Michigan, December 7, 1941. www.justice.gov/ag/speeches-0.
31. For a gripping and insightful study of violence committed against immigrants and others during World War I, see Adam Hochschild, *American Midnight: Democracy's Forgotten Crisis, 1917–1921* (New York: Mariner Books/HarperCollins, 2022).
32. The literature on the Japanese and Japanese-American evacuation, relocation, and internment is vast, but in my view the best work on the subject has been done by Greg Robinson. See, for example, *By Order of the President: FDR and the Internment of Japanese Americans* (Cambridge, MA: Harvard University Press, 2001), especially ch. 3.
33. Greg Robinson, *A Tragedy of Democracy: Japanese Confinement in North America* (New York: Columbia University Press, 2009), p. 116.
34. Peter Irons, *Justice at War: The Story of the Japanese American Internment Cases* (New York: Oxford University Press, 1983), p. 20.
35. Robinson, *By Order of the President*, p. 3.
36. Ibid., p. 85.
37. "Pacific Coast Attitudes Toward the Japanese Problem," RG 208 NC-148 3-D Alphabetical Subject Files, 1939–1942. Box 7, located at: 350/71/12/6. File: "Polling Division, rpt, 2/28/1942," National Archives and Records Administration, Washington, DC.
38. Biddle referred to this survey in his postwar autobiography, but he gave the date as March 9, 1942. He almost certainly meant the one conducted from February 7–13. Francis Biddle, *In Brief Authority* (Garden City: Doubleday, 1962), p. 224.
39. In June 1942, the Office of Facts and Figures was renamed the Office of War Information, devoting itself to psychological influence campaigns at home and abroad.
40. I have drawn here on the intriguing argument developed by Marc Trachtenberg in *The Craft of International History* (Princeton: Princeton University Press, 2006), ch. 4.
41. For a recent study of Hitler's decision to declare war on America, see Klaus H. Schmider, *Hitler's Fatal Miscalculation: Why Germany Declared War on the United States* (Cambridge: Cambridge University Press, 2021).
42. Robinson, *By Order of the President*, p. 122.
43. Diary of Henry L. Stimson, February 3, 1942 (hereafter Stimson Diary). Yale University Library holds the original Stimson diary and related papers, and microfiche versions of the diary are available to scholars through other university libraries.
44. Stimson Diary, February 10, 1942.
45. Robert Dallek, *Franklin D. Roosevelt: A Political Life* (New York: Penguin, 2018), p. 6.
46. Stimson Diary, December 7, 1941.

2 Sabotage

47. Kai Bird, *The Chairman: John J. McCloy & the Making of the American Establishment* (New York: Simon & Schuster, 1992), p. 121.

48. Stimson Diary, December 7, 1941.
49. The Belgian Army in 1914 consisted of approximately 120,000 regular soldiers and some 65,000 reservists. https://en.wikipedia.org/wiki/Belgian_Army_order_of_battle_(1914). The American Army, in contrast, comprised roughly 98,000 troops. An additional 27,000 troops formed the National Guard. https://spartacus-educational.com/USAarmy.htm.
50. For a detailed description of the attack and the story behind it, see Chad Millman, *The Detonators: The Secret Plot to Destroy America and an Epic Hunt for Justice* (New York: Little, Brown and Company, 2006).
51. For more on von Papen and the Night of the Long Knives, see Zachary Shore, *What Hitler Knew: The Battle for Information in Nazi Foreign Policy* (New York: Oxford University Press, 2003), particularly ch. 2, "The Longest Knife."
52. Robinson, *A Tragedy of Democracy*, p. 85.
53. Ibid., pp. 50–51.
54. Pan-American Coffee Bureau Series-Program #16. January 11, 1942. Franklin D. Roosevelt Presidential Library.
55. Doris Kearns Goodwin, *No Ordinary Time, Franklin and Eleanor Roosevelt: The Home Front in World War II* (New York: Simon & Schuster, 1994), p. 296.
56. Pan-American Coffee Bureau Series–Program #21. February 15, 1942. Franklin D. Roosevelt Presidential Library.
57. The audio recording of her address, while scratchy, distinctly reveals that she placed emphasis on the word "all."
58. Greg Robinson offers thoughtful reflections on Eleanor Roosevelt's awkward position with respect to internment. See Greg Robinson, *The Great Unknown: Japanese American Sketches* (Boulder: University Press of Colorado, 2016).
59. Goodwin, *No Ordinary Time*, p. 326.
60. "Japanese-American Relocation Reviewed, Volume II: The Internment," Online Archive of California. https://oac.cdlib.org/view?docId=ft1290031s&doc.view=frames&chunk.id=doe8284&toc.id=doe8284&brand=oac.
61. For more on Galen Fisher, the Protestant missionary who played a leading role in the Fair Play Committee, see David A. Hollinger, *Protestants Abroad: How Missionaries Tried to Change the World but Changed America* (Princeton: Princeton University Press, 2017).
62. John McCloy Diary, December 1, 1941 (hereafter McCloy Diary).
63. Hadley Cantril, *Public Opinion, 1935–1946* (Princeton: Princeton University Press, 1951), p. 380.
64. Some of the scholarship citing the ninety-three percent and fifty-nine percent support for internment include the following: Nicholas Taylor, "The American Public's Reaction to the Japanese American Internment," *West Virginia University Historical Review*, Vol. 1, No. 1 (2020), Article 8; Donna K. Nagata, *Legacy of Injustice: Exploring the Cross-Generational Impact of the Japanese American Internment* (Berlin: Springer Science & Business Media, 2013); Adam J. Berinsky, *In Time of War: Understanding American Public Opinion from World War II to Iraq* (Chicago: University of Chicago Press, 2009), pp. 127–152; Gary Y. Okihiro and Julie Sly, "The Press, Japanese Americans, and the Concentration Camps," *Phylon*, Vol. 44, No. 1 (1983), pp. 66–83. The survey was also cited in the government's official 1983 report on the internment. See Commission on Wartime Relocation and Internment of Civilians, *Personal Justice Denied: Report of the Commission on Wartime Relocation and Internment of Civilians* (Seattle: University of Washington Press, 1997), p. 112. The survey is also cited on the website of the US Holocaust Museum. https://encyclopedia.ushmm.org/content/en/article/japanese-american-relocation.

65. Office of Facts and Figures, "Pacific Coast Attitudes Toward the Japanese Problem." February 28, 1942. RG 208 NC-148 3-D. Alphabetical Subject Files, 1939–1942. Box 7, located at: 350/71/12/6. NARA, Washington, DC.

66. Office of Facts and Figures, Bureau of Intelligence, Division of Intensive Surveys. "Exploratory Study of West Coast Reactions to Japanese (Preliminary Results). For administrative use only. Confidential." February 4, 1942. For the survey that found support of internment at only 10.5 percent, see Office of Facts and Figures, Bureau of Intelligence, Division of Intensive Surveys, "West Coast Reaction to the Japanese Situation." NARA, Washington, DC, 1942.

67. My thanks to Greg Robinson for relating this fact to me by email on October 27, 2021, and for his permission to cite his email in this context.

3 Coordinate

68. Sakura Kato, "Judge A. Wallace Tashima: A Judge Who Looks Like Us," Discover Nikkei: Japanese Migrants and Their Descendants, August 6, 2014. www.disco vernikkei.org/en/journal/2014/8/6/judge-tashima/.

69. The stories of Donald Nakahata and Mary Tsukamoto are drawn from the testimony given by hundreds of Japanese Americans from 1981 to 1983, as part of the congressionally mandated investigations into the wartime relocation program. A sampling of this testimony can be found in John Tateishi, *And Justice for All: An Oral History of the Japanese American Detention Camps* (Seattle: University of Washington Press, 1999).

70. David Michaelis, *Eleanor* (New York: Simon & Schuster, 2020), p. 448. From Biddle, *In Brief Authority*, p. 219.

71. Robinson, *By Order of the President*, p. 138. Robinson maintains that Morgenthau held an ideological objection to the seizure of Japanese-owned property.

72. John Morton Blum, *From the Morgenthau Diaries: Years of War, 1941–1945* (Boston: Houghton Mifflin Co, 1967), p. 2.

73. Ibid., p. 4.

74. Robinson, *By Order of the President*, p. 144.

75. Blanche W. Cook, *Eleanor Roosevelt*. Volume 3: *The War Years and After, 1939–1962* (New York: Barnes & Noble, 2016), p. 421. Other estimates are lower, $67 to $116 million in 1945 dollars, more than half a billion dollars in 2019.

76. Robinson, *By Order of the President*, p. 131.

77. Eleanor Roosevelt, "My Day, March 21, 1942," *The Eleanor Roosevelt Papers Digital Edition* (2017). www2.gwu.edu/~erpapers/myday/displaydoc.cfm?_y=1942&_f=md056139.

78. Brief Historical Report of the Pacific Coast Committee on American Principles and Fair Play. October 1 1941–December 15 1945. https://oac.cdlib.org/ark:/13030/k6fr0325/?brand=oac4.

79. Ibid.

80. Cook, *Eleanor Roosevelt*, p. 418.

81. McCloy Diary, April 6, 1942.

82. *Japanese Relocation*, film produced by Office of War Information, Bureau of Motion Pictures. www.youtube.com/watch?v=Gric3lTanQU.

83. Address by Dillon S. Myer, director of the War Relocation Authority, over the National Broadcasting Company network at 10:45 pm, EWT, Thursday, July 15, 1943. Truman Library, in the collection The War Relocation Authority & the Incarceration of Japanese-Americans During World War II. www.trumanlibrary.gov/library/research-files/speech-dillon-s-myer-over-national-broadcasting-company-network-july-15-1943.

84. "Obligations of Our Heritage," a talk by Dillon S. Myer, director of the War Relocation Authority, given before the Rotary Club of Lawrence, Kansas, and broadcast over Station WIEN, Lawrence, Kansas, Monday, October 18, 1943. Truman Library, Folder, The War Relocation Authority & the Incarceration of Japanese-Americans During World War II. www.trumanlibrary.gov/library/research-files/speech-obligations-our-heritage-dillon-s-myer-rotary-club-lawrence-kansas.

85. Records of the War Relocation Authority, National Archives and Records Administration, Washington, DC. https://aad.archives.gov/aad/record-detail.jsp?dt=3099&mtch=1&cat=WR26&tf=F&q=raymond+muramoto&bc=,sl,sd&rpp=10&pg=1&rid=52845. My thanks to Prof. Greg Robinson for sharing this record with me.

86. Robinson, *A Tragedy of Democracy*, pp. 154–166. I have drawn on chapter 4.

87. Allan W. Austin, *Quaker Brotherhood: Interracial Activism and the American Friends Service Committee, 1917–1950* (Urbana: University of Illinois Press, 2012), p. 127.

88. Robinson, *A Tragedy of Democracy*, p. 181.

89. Ibid., pp. 181–182.

90. Austin, *Quaker Brotherhood*, p. 129.

91. Herbert Hoover to Stanley Washburn, July 1, 1943. Post-Presidential Individual File (PPI), Hoover's personal papers, Herbert Hoover Presidential Library, West Branch, Iowa.

92. I have not dealt here with the Japanese American Citizens League, largely because it chose to cooperate with the government on internment, and I wanted to focus on those Japanese Americans who resisted. However, the JACL must have struggled with its decision, just as the Fair Play Committee did, along with many others. Neither course, cooperation or resistance, was without risk.

93. For more on Fred Korematsu's background, see Lorraine K. Bannai, *Enduring Conviction: Fred Korematsu and His Quest for Justice* (Seattle: University of Washington Press, 2015).

94. Ibid., p. 42.

95. Mrs. Franklin D. Roosevelt, "The Democratic Effort," Common Ground, Spring 1942, pp. 9–10. The drafts of this article can be found in Box 1412 of the Eleanor Roosevelt Papers, Franklin D. Roosevelt Archives.

96. Joseph C. Grew, *Ten Years in Japan* (New York: Simon & Schuster, 1944), pp. 565–571.

97. An Intelligence Officer, "The Japanese in America: The Problem and the Solution," *Harper's*, October 1, 1942.

98. Drew Pearson, "The Washington Merry-Go-Round," *Washington Post*, February 7, 1943.

99. George H. Gallup, *The Gallup Poll: Public Opinion 1935–1971, Vol. I* (New York: Random House, 1972), p. 361.

100. For an interesting study of other individuals and groups opposing anti-Japanese sentiments, see Robert Shaffer, "Cracks in the Consensus: Defending the Rights of Japanese Americans during World War II," *Radical History Review*, Vol. 72, No. 3 (1998), pp. 84–120.

4 Cover-Up

101. Irons, *Justice at War*, see ch. 11, particularly pp. 283–287.

102. Ibid., p. 202.

103. Ibid., pp. 207–211.

104. James F. Simon, *The Antagonists: Hugo Black, Felix Frankfurter and Civil Liberties in Modern America* (New York: Simon & Schuster, 1989), p. 55.

105. Ibid., p. 113.

106. Dewitt allegedly made this remark at a news conference on April 16, 1943. Although it was uttered long after the evacuation order of February 1942, it reflected the sentiment of those who had initially called for the mass removal. John DeWitt, Densho Encyclopedia. https://encyclopedia.densho.org/John_DeWitt/.

107. Kai Bird supports this observation in Bird, *The Chairman*, p. 167.

5 Disintegrate

108. Dean Acheson, *Present at the Creation: My Years in the State Department* (New York: W. W. Norton, 1969), p. 740. Other colleagues used the nickname as well. See Peter Moreira, *The Jew Who Defeated Hitler: Henry Morgenthau Jr., FDR, and How We Won the War* (New York: Penguin, 2014), p. 18.

109. Acheson, *Present at the Creation*, p. 22.

110. Henry Morgenthau Jr., *Germany Is Our Problem: A Plan for Germany* (New York: Harper & Brothers, 1945), p. 6.

111. Ibid., p. 32.

112. Jeffrey Herf, *The Jewish Enemy: Nazi Propaganda During World War II and the Holocaust* (Cambridge, MA: Harvard University Press, 2006), p. 97. Litvinov's birth name was Meir Henoch Mojszewicz Wallach-Finkelstein. www.britannica.com/biography/Maksim-Litvinov.

113. Ben Shephard, *The Long Road Home: The Aftermath of the Second World War* (New York: Penguin, 2012), p. 69.

114. Joseph Grew, Address at the Annual Banquet celebrating the 90th anniversary of the Illinois Education Association, Chicago, at 8:00 pm, December 29, 1943. www.ndl.go.jp/constitution/e/shiryo/01/003/003tx.html.

115. *Our Enemy – The Japanese*, film produced by the Office of War Information and the United States Navy, 1943. www.youtube.com/watch?v=3bmS4FWpGXM.

116. Blum, *Morgenthau Diaries*, p. 342.

117. Michael Beschloss, *The Conquerors: Roosevelt, Truman and the Destruction of Hitler's Germany, 1941–1945* (New York: Simon & Schuster, 2002), p. 72.

118. Ibid., p. 100.

119. Blum, *Morgenthau Diaries*, p. 360.

120. Henry L. Stimson and McGeorge Bundy, *On Active Service in Peace and War* (New York: Harper Collins, 1948), p. 569.

121. Ibid., p. 570.

122. Ibid., p. 570.

6 Collude

123. Just two weeks after the Octagon meetings, Fala would rise to national prominence when FDR's Republican opponents concocted a story that the President had left his dog behind on the Aleutian Islands and ordered her to be brought home at a cost of millions to the American taxpayer. Taking the advice of Orson Welles, Roosevelt turned the accusations into a joke at the Republicans' expense, declaring that while he and his family did not object to the Republicans' attacks, Fala did. His audiences laughed along with him, bolstering his substantial popularity nationwide.

124. Interview with Andrew Meier regarding his forthcoming book, *The House of Morgenthau*. Meier has spent the past ten years researching the Morgenthau family and is convinced that Churchill, Roosevelt, Eisenhower, and others publicly disavowed the vengeful Morgenthau Plan yet privately endorsed its treatment of Germany. Interview on November 5, 2018. Michael Beschloss maintains in *The Conquerors* that Churchill's initial objections faded as he quickly came to see the benefits of the plan to Britain.

125. The final two sentences of Morgenthau's memorandum on Quebec read: "This programme for eliminating the war-making industries in the Ruhr and in the Saar is looking forward to converting Germany into a country primarily agricultural and pastoral in its character. The Prime Minister and the President were in agreement upon this programme." Box 126, "Morgenthau, Henry Jr., and Morgenthau Plan," Hoover Library.

126. Michael Beschloss makes this argument with respect to Roosevelt. See *The Conquerors*, p. 131.

127. "Samson in the Temple," *Washington Post*, September 26, 1944.

128. James Kanegis, "Letter to the Editor: Morgenthau Plan," *Washington Post*, October 3, 1944.

129. William A. Coates, "Morgenthau Plan," *Washington Post*, September 29, 1944.

130. J. L. Hudson, "Letter to the Editor: Morgenthau Plan," *Washington Post*, October 4, 1944.

131. Beschloss, *The Conquerors*, p. 160.

132. Goodwin, *No Ordinary Time*, p. 544.

133. Stimson Diary, September 16–17, 1944.

134. Box 126, "Morgenthau, Henry Jr., and Morgenthau Plan," Hoover Library.

135. Stimson and Bundy, *On Active Service*, p. 581.

136. Letter from Secretary of War Stimson to the President, September 5, 1944. https://teachingamericanhistory.org/document/documents-regarding-the/.

137. Eleanor Roosevelt, "A Challenge to American Sportsmanship," *Colliers*, Vol. 112 (October 1, 1943).

138. Bird, *The Chairman*, p. 169.

139. Ibid., p.120.

140. McCloy Diary, December 1, 1941. The diaries of John J. McCloy are now available for download through Amherst College.

141. Ibid., December 7, 1941.

142. Ibid.

143. Ibid.

144. *Korematsu v. United States*, 323 US 214, December 18, 1944.

145. Simon, *The Antagonists*, p. 46.

146. Roger K. Newman, *Hugo Black: A Biography* (New York: Pantheon, 1994), p. 280.

147. "The Power of Fiery Dissents – Korematsu v. US," United States Courts. www.uscourts.gov/educational-resources/educational-activities/power-fiery-dissents-koremastu-v-us.

148. Richard Drinnon, *Keeper of Concentration Camps: Dillon S. Myer and American Racism* (Berkeley: University of California Press, 1987).

149. Dillon S. Myer, "Racism and Reason," An address to be delivered by Dillon S. Myer, Director of the War Relocation Authority at an interfaith meeting sponsored by the Pacific Coast Committee on American Principles and Fair Play, at Los Angeles, California, on October 2, 1944. Truman Library Collection, The War Relocation Authority & the Incarceration of Japanese-Americans During World

War II. www.trumanlibrary.gov/library/research-files/speech-racism-and-reason-dillon-s-myer-interfaith-meeting-sponsored-pacific.

7 Deny

150. For more details surrounding this episode, see Robert Ferrell, *Choosing Truman: The Democratic Convention of 1944* (Columbia: University of Missouri Press, 1994), pp. 11–14.
151. David Pietrusza, *1948: Harry Truman's Improbable Victory and the Year That Transformed America's Role in the World* (New York: Sterling, 2011), p. 43.
152. Ibid., p. 43.
153. "Favors Resettling Japanese Locally; Bricker Tells Californians It Is a Matter for Towns, with the Disloyal Deported," *New York Times*, April 18, 1944.
154. Rebecca Erbelding, *Rescue Board: The Untold Story of America's Efforts to Save the Jews of Europe* (New York: Doubleday, 2018), p. 206.
155. Pietrusza, *1948*, p. 47.
156. Stimson and Bundy, *On Active Service*, p. 569.
157. Erbelding, *Rescue Board*, p. 57.
158. Stimson Diary, February 1, 1944.
159. Bird, *The Chairman*, p. 231.
160. Blum, *Morgenthau Diaries*, p. 407.
161. Ibid., pp. 408–412.
162. Ibid., p. 414.
163. Moreira, *The Jew Who Defeated Hitler*, p. 274.
164. Beschloss, *The Conquerors*, p. 88.
165. Ibid., p. 137.
166. Max Freedman, ed., *Roosevelt and Frankfurter: Their Correspondence of 1928–1945* (New York: Little Brown, 1967). Frankfurter to FDR, June 4, 1940, pp. 524–525.
167. Stimson Diary, December 1, 1941.
168. Ibid., December 8, 1941.
169. Ibid., January 1, 1942.
170. Beschloss, *The Conquerors*, p. 113.
171. Harlan B. Phillips, ed., *Felix Frankfurter Reminisces* (New York: Reynal & Co., 1960), pp. 146–147.
172. Blum, *Morgenthau Diaries*, pp. 418–419.
173. Harry S. Truman, *Memoirs of Harry S. Truman*. Volume I: *Year of Decisions* (New York: Oxford University Press, 1955), p. 17. See also Albert Baime, *The Accidental President: Harry S. Truman and the Four Months That Changed the World* (Boston: Houghton Mifflin Harcourt, 2017), p. 50. As Baime and others have described the scene, Mrs. Roosevelt calmly placed an arm around Truman's shoulder and told him, "Harry, the President is dead." Truman was shocked. He knew that Roosevelt was ill, but he thought that the president was recovering at Warm Springs. It took him a moment to find his voice. "Is there anything I can do for you?" he asked her, fighting off tears. Eleanor responded simply: "Is there anything we can do for you, for you are the one in trouble now."
174. Steve Neal, *Eleanor and Harry: The Correspondence of Eleanor Roosevelt and Harry S. Truman* (New York: Scribner, 2002), p. 22.
175. Memorandum of the Secretary of State to President Truman, *Foreign Relations of the United States, Diplomatic Papers, 1945, Volume II*, April 16, 1945.

176. Telegram, The British Prime Minister Churchill to President Truman, *FRUS, Diplomatic Papers, 1945, European Advisory Commission, Germany, Austria, Volume III*, April 18, 1945.
177. John Dietrich, *The Morgenthau Plan: Soviet Influence on American Postwar Policy* (New York: Algora, 2002), p. 86.
178. Truman, *Memoirs*, Volume I, pp. 47–49.

8 Maneuver

179. For a thorough biography, see Herbert P. Bix, *Hirohito and the Making of Modern Japan* (New York: Harper Perennial, 2001).
180. Premier Kuniaki Koiso's New Year's Address, Foreign Broadcast Intelligence Service, Federal Communications Commission. www.ibiblio.org/pha/policy/1945/450101a.html.
181. Ibid.
182. Bird, *The Chairman*, p. 233.
183. Truman, *Memoirs*, Volume I, p. 27.
184. For a thoughtful study of the unconditional surrender policy, see Marc Gallicchio, *Unconditional: The Japanese Surrender in World War II* (New York: Oxford University Press, 2020).
185. Waldo Heinrichs Jr., *American Ambassador: Joseph C. Grew and the Development of the United States Diplomatic Tradition* (Boston: Little, Brown, 1966), p. 4.
186. Ibid., pp. 4–8.
187. Ibid., pp. 374–375. Heinrichs does not believe that Grew sought conditional surrender in order to avoid use of the atomic bomb. See fn. 48, p. 438, but he did conclude that Grew thought that not using the bomb would be preferable.
188. Stimson Diary, see May 1–4, May 11–13, May 16, May 18, and May 29, 1945.
189. Timothy Walch and Dwight M. Miller, *Herbert Hoover and Harry S. Truman: A Documentary History* (Worland: High Plains, 1992), p. 35.
190. Kenneth Whyte, *Hoover: An Extraordinary Life in Extraordinary Times* (New York: Knopf, 2017), p. 579.
191. Stimson Diary, May 13, 1945.
192. Michael Kort, *Columbia Guide*, "Hoover Memorandum to Truman," May 29 or 30, 1945 (undated), Document A-19/B, p. 271.
193. Joseph C. Grew, "Memorandum for the President," Analysis of Memorandum Presented by Mr. Hoover," June 13, 1945. https://nsarchive2.gwu.edu/nukevault/ebb525-The-Atomic-Bomb-and-the-End-of-World-War-II/documents/023.pdf.
194. For more on John Rabe, the Nazi Party member in China who tried to protect civilians against the Japanese Army's savagery, see John Rabe, *The Good Man of Nanking: The Diaries of John Rabe* (New York: Vintage, 2000). For a popular account of this episode, see Iris Chang, *The Rape of Nanking: The Forgotten Holocaust of World War II* (New York: Penguin, 1997).
195. For some interesting reflections on the morality of aerial bombing in World War II, see Charles S. Maier, "Targeting the City: Debates and Silences about the Aerial Bombing of World War II," *The International Review of the Red Cross*, Vol. 87, No. 859 (September 2005). www.icrc.org/en/doc/assets/files/other/irrc_859_maier.pdf.
196. Notes of the Interim Committee Meetings, June 18, 1945. https://history.state.gov/historicaldocuments/frus1945Berlinv01/d598.

197. McCloy's anecdote can be found, for example, in Baime, *Accidental President*, p. 350; Tsuyoshi Hasegawa, *Racing the Enemy: Stalin, Truman, and the Surrender of Japan* (Cambridge, MA: Harvard University Press, 2005), p. 103; Bird, *The Chairman*, p. 246. See also Peter Wyden, *Day One: Before Hiroshima and After* (New York: Simon & Schuster, 1984), p. 171, and also William G. Hyland, "John J. McCloy: 1895–1989," *Foreign Affairs* (Spring 1989). The original source appears to be an interview McCloy gave in 1964–1965, which was published in Fred Freed and Len Giovannitti, *The Decision to Drop the Bomb* (New York: Coward-McCann Inc., 1965), p. 136.

198. Regarding Truman's recommendation that the proposal be discussed with James Byrnes, Tsuyoshi Hasegawa argues that this was Truman's way of killing proposals he disagreed with: feigning to agree and then suggesting that those proposals be discussed with others whom he knew would block them. In this case, Hasegawa argues that Truman knew that Byrnes would oppose conditional surrender. I am not convinced that Truman had fully determined his view on conditional surrender at this stage. See Hasegawa, *Racing the Enemy*, p. 105.

199. Dayna Barnes, *Architects of Occupation: American Experts and the Planning for Postwar Japan* (Ithaca: Cornell University Press, 2017), p. 173. I am grateful to Dayna Barnes for sharing her archival notes and extensive expertise with me.

200. Stimson Diary, May 16, 1945.

9 Regret

201. Albert Einstein to Franklin Roosevelt, August 2, 1939. www.atomicarchive.com/Docs/Begin/Einstein.shtml.

202. Martin J. Sherwin, *A World Destroyed: Hiroshima and Its Legacies* (Stanford: Stanford University Press, 2003), p. 27.

203. "The Franck Report," Memorandum to the Secretary of War, June 12, 1945. https://fas.org/sgp/eprint/franck.html.

204. Gar Alperovitz, *Decision to Use the Atomic Bomb* (New York: Vintage Books, 1996), p. 226.

205. See Harry S. Truman Presidential Library for a calendar of appointments. www.trumanlibrary.gov/calendar. The calendar reveals five meetings between the President and Bard in the spring of 1945, but not after July 13, and none that were one-on-one.

206. Michael Kort, *The Columbia Guide to Hiroshima and the Bomb* (New York: Columbia University Press, 2007), p. 165.

207. Naval History and Heritage Command Archives, Ralph A. Bard Papers, "Letters Relating to Resignation," Box AR/204.

208. For more on the Lippmann–Frankfurter friendship, see Brad Snyder, *House of Truth: A Washington Political Salon and the Foundations of American Liberalism* (New York: Oxford University Press, 2017).

209. See Richard B. Frank, *Downfall: The End of the Imperial Japanese Empire* (New York: Random House, 1999).

210. Tsuyoshi Hasegawa maintains that it was Russia's declaration of war on Japan, more than the nuclear strikes, that proved decisive in convincing the three-member "war faction" within Japan's Cabinet to surrender. See Hasegawa, *Racing the Enemy*.

211. Barnes, *Architects of Occupation*, pp. 35–36.

212. Stimson Diary, July 3, 1945.

213. Grant Madsen, *Sovereign Soldiers: How the US Military Transformed the Global Economy After World War II* (Philadelphia: University of Pennsylvania Press, 2018), pp. 86–87.
214. Ibid., p. 87.
215. See Robert Jay Lifton and Greg Mitchell, *Hiroshima in America: A Half Century of Denial* (New York: Avon Books, 1996), p. 4. For the version just one week prior to Truman's announcement, see draft statement on the dropping of the bomb, July 30, 1945. Truman Papers, President's Secretary's File. Atomic Bomb-Hiroshima. www.trumanlibrary.gov/library/research-files/draft-statement-dropping-bomb.

10 Fallout

216. Wanting to document and preserve the horror of these attacks in order that the world would know the truth of what had happened, Japanese film crews criss-crossed Hiroshima and Nagasaki, taking footage of what they saw. When the American occupation authorities discovered this, they confiscated the film and locked it away. Flouting orders, one member of the film crew saved a copy of the film and hid it in an attic, where it remained undiscovered for decades. The full length of that film is said to be housed in the National Archives in Washington, DC, but sixteen minutes of it can be viewed on YouTube. "Hiroshima, Nagasaki: Original Footage," www.youtube.com/watch?v=ZPCJvLhDEAg. The Soviets also took footage of the devastation and presented this rare record to Japan's Prime Minister Shinzo Abe in 2016. www.dailymail.co.uk/news/article-3725520/Nuclear-disaster-seen-Russians-Rare-footage-filmed-Soviet-researchers-shows-utter-devasta tion-Hiroshima-Nagasaki-shortly-atomic-bombs-flattened-cities-1945.html. See also Greg Mitchell, "Hiroshima Film Cover-up Exposed," *Asia-Pacific Journal*, Vol. 3, No. 8 (August 3, 2005). https://apjjf.org/-Greg-Mitchell/1554/article.html. The US Air Force also produced a film, drawing on original footage of the aftermath. "The Effects of the Atomic Bomb on Hiroshima and Nagasaki," www.youtube.com/watch?v=QUvM2uQR1cA&feature=emb_logo.
217. Michihiko Hachiya, *Hiroshima Diary: The Journal of a Japanese Physician, August 6–September 30, 1945* (Chapel Hill: University of North Carolina Press, 1955), p. 15.
218. Harry S. Truman to Richard Russell, August 9, 1945. Truman Papers, Official File, 197: Japan. https://catalog.archives.gov/id/40020053.
219. Truman may have had conflicted feelings about the bomb, despite his consistent public statements that he never doubted the decision. Vice President Wallace recorded in his diary on August 10 that Truman wanted a halt to any future uses of the atomic bomb without his express approval. According to Wallace, Truman said that "the thought of wiping out another 100,000 people was too horrible. He didn't like the idea of killing, as he said, 'all those kids.'" John Morton Blum, ed., *The Price of Vision: The Diary of Henry A. Wallace, 1942–1946* (Boston: Houghton Mifflin, 1973), p. 474.
220. Gallup, *Gallup Poll*, pp. 521–522.
221. Ibid., p. 477.
222. Ibid., p. 522.
223. Robinson, *A Tragedy of Democracy*, pp. 257–258.
224. Neal, *Eleanor and Harry*, p. 50.
225. For a thorough account of articles and reports on the bombs' effects prior to Hersey's piece, see Lifton and Mitchell, *Hiroshima in America*.

226. John Hersey, "Hiroshima," *New Yorker*, August 23, 1946. www.newyorker.com/magazine/1946/08/31/hiroshima.

227. Michael J. Yavenditti, "John Hersey and the American Conscience: The Reception of 'Hiroshima,'" *Pacific Historical Review*, Vol. 43, No. 1 (February 1974), pp. 24–49.

228. Ibid.

229. Sean L. Malloy, "A Very Pleasant Way to Die," *Diplomatic History*, Vol. 36, No. 3 (June 2012), pp. 515–545. https://academic.oup.com/dh/article-abstract/36/3/515/363398?redirectedFrom=fulltext.

230. Ibid.

231. "Memorandum from Dr. Compton to Truman with Related Correspondence," October 4, 1945. Truman Papers 1-A-21. Japanese Post-War Economic Considerations," 21 July 1943, in *The Occupation of Japan: US Planning Documents, 1942–1945* (Bethesda: Congressional Information Service, and Tokyo: Maruzen Publishing, 1987), microfiche.

232. Karl Compton, "If the Atomic Bomb Had Not Been Used Was Japan Already Beaten before the August 1945 Bombings?" *The Atlantic*, December 1946. www.theatlantic.com/magazine/archive/1946/12/if-the-atomic-bomb-had-not-been-used/376238/.

233. Robert Lifton described in detail how Conant essentially re-wrote Stimson's first draft of the article. See Lifton and Mitchell, *Hiroshima in America*, pp. 100–101. The authors also revealed Stimson's qualms about the article itself.

234. Joseph Grew was not happy with Stimson's *Harper's* piece and wrote to the aging war secretary to tell him so. Grew resented being overlooked in the article, since he had played a major role in trying to persuade Truman to let Japan retain the Emperor. With trenchant words he noted: "the almost unique position you enjoy before the American people gives any statement of yours a conclusive character and crystallizes history." Heinrichs, *American Ambassador*, p. 379.

11 Reckoning

235. The question of casualty figures is covered in many scholarly works, but two particularly useful studies are by D. M. Giangreco, "Casualty Projections for the US Invasions of Japan, 1945–1946: Planning and Policy Implications," *Journal of Military History* (July 1997), and "'A Score of Bloody Okinawas and Iwo Jimas': President Truman and the Casualty Estimates for the Invasion of Japan," *Pacific Historical Review*, Vol. 72, No. 1 (2003), pp. 93–132. As with many of the subjects covered in this book, the literature on the atomic bomb is substantial. Readers seeking other intriguing studies might consult the following works: J. Samuel Walker, *Prompt and Utter Destruction: Truman and the Use of Atomic Bombs Against Japan* (Chapel Hill: University of North Carolina Press, 1997); Barton Bernstein has written extensively on these issues, see, for example, "Understanding the Atomic Bomb: Little-Known Near Disasters and Modern Memory," *Diplomatic History*, Vol. 19, No. 2 (Spring 1995), pp. 227–273; Campbell Craig and Sergey Radchenko, *The Atomic Bomb and the Origins of the Cold War* (New Haven: Yale University Press, 2008); Wilson D. Miscamble, *The Most Controversial Decision: Truman, the Atomic Bombs, and the Defeat of Japan* (New York: Cambridge University Press, 2011); Richard Rhodes, *The Making of the Atomic Bomb* (New York: Simon & Schuster, 1986); for a provocative interpretation, see Alperovitz, *The Decision to Use the Atomic Bomb*.

236. Stimson, "Decision to Use the Bomb," *Harper's*, February 1947. http://afe.easia
    .columbia.edu/ps/japan/stimson_harpers.pdf.
237. Truman, *Memoirs*, Volume I, p. 445. Truman claimed that military experts esti-
    mated that the invasion would cost at least half a million American casualties. In
    Lifton and Mitchell, *Hiroshima in America*, p. 179, the authors showed that
    Truman's estimates of lives saved varied widely over time. During his presidency,
    he used figures of 200,000 and 250,000 lives. (For an example of the quarter
    million figure, see Truman's news conference on August 14, 1947.) Later, the
    first draft of his memoir used 500,000. At other times, he raised the estimate to
    one million.
238. Giangreco, "A Score of Bloody Okinawas," p. 106.
239. Stimson Diary, May 13, 1945.
240. Whyte, *Hoover*, p. 579.
241. Stimson Diary, May 16, 1945.
242. D. M. Giangreco, "A Score of Bloody Okinawas and Iwo Jimas," in Robert J.
    Maddox, ed., *Hiroshima in History: The Myths of Revisionism* (Columbia:
    University of Missouri Press, 2007), pp. 76–155, at p. 96. See also Kort,
    Columbia Guide, p. 159.
243. Groves's account of this episode stressed the amicable relations between the two of
    them. Groves related that he continued to press for Kyoto as a target, even having
    Stimson's aide, George Harrison, cable the War Secretary at Potsdam to reconsider.
    Stimson then spoke with Truman about it and convinced him to keep Kyoto off the
    target list. Groves let the matter drop after that. His postwar memoir insisted that
    Stimson never tried to silence him, which is no doubt true. But other accounts
    suggest some tension. See Leslie Groves, *Now It Can Be Told: The Story of the
    Manhattan Project* (New York: Harper, 1962), ch. 19.
244. Rhodes, *The Making of the Atomic*, p. 640.
245. *Foreign Relations of the United States: Diplomatic Papers, The Conference of
    Berlin (The Potsdam Conference), 1945*, Volume II. Editor: Richardson Dougall.
    The Secretary of War (Stimson) to the Acting Chairman of the Interim Committee
    (Harrison) from Folder "Use of atomic weapons in the war against Japan"
    (Documents 1307, 1308). July 21, 1945.
246. Hebert Feis, *Japan Subdued: The Atomic Bomb and the End of the War in the
    Pacific* (Princeton: Princeton University Press, 1961), pp. 73–74.
247. Stimson had specifically called in General Arnold, head of the Army's Air Corps
    (the United States did not have an independent Air Force until 1947) to instruct him
    to ensure precision bombing. Stimson was concerned about the civilian casualties
    caused by indiscriminate fire bombings. Arnold explained that it was nearly impos-
    sible to conduct precision bombing, as Japanese industries were scattered among
    civilian homes. Several days later Stimson told Truman that he (Stimson) was
    attempting to hold the Air Corps to precision bombing for two reasons. The first
    was purely humanitarian: "I did not want to have the United States get the reputa-
    tion of outdoing Hitler in atrocities; and second, I was a little fearful that before we
    could get ready the Air Force might have Japan so thoroughly bombed out that the
    new weapon would not have a fair background to show its strength." See Stimson
    Diary, June 1 and 6, 1945. These two contradictory reasons encapsulate Stimson's
    conflicted feelings about the enemy.
248. After the war, the Strategic Bombing Survey, a report issued by a group of non-
    military experts authorized by Stimson to assess the effectiveness of bombing
    campaigns in both the European and the Pacific theaters, concluded that
    Japanese leaders would have surrendered by the end of 1945, and possibly by

November 1, 1945, even without the use of atomic bombs, or the Russian declaration of war, or an Allied invasion. These findings were later found to be highly suspect. See Strategic Bombing Survey summary: https://en.wikipedia.org/wiki/United_States_Strategic_Bombing_Survey#On_German_production.

249. Baime, *Accidental President*, p. 250.
250. First Message of President Truman to the Congress, April 16, 1945. www.ibiblio.org/pha/policy/1945/450416a.html.
251. Truman, *Memoirs*, Volume I, p. 80.
252. Harry S. Truman, Farewell Address, January 15, 1953. https://millercenter.org/the-presidency/presidential-speeches/january-15-1953-farewell-address.
253. Harry S. Truman, *Memoirs of Harry S. Truman*. Volume II: *Year of Trial and Hope* (New York: Doubleday, 1956), p. 8.
254. Bird, *The Chairman*, p. 263.
255. Whyte, *Hoover*, p. 580.

12 Rescue

256. Norman Lewis, *Naples '44: A World War II Diary of Occupied Italy* (New York: Carroll & Graf, 2005), p. 39.
257. Ibid., p. 131.
258. Ibid., p. 169.
259. "Is UNRRA Doing Its Job?" Transcript of NBC Radio Broadcast, October 21, 1945. Hoover Institution Archives, William L. Clayton Papers, Box 2, Folder 20. https://archive.org/stream/departmentofstatx1345unit/departmentofstatx1345unit_djvu.txt.
260. Ellen Clayton Garwood, *Will Clayton: A Short Biography* (Austin: University of Texas Press, 1958), p. 29.
261. Kathleen McLoughlin, "Allies Asked to Pool Food to Avert Crisis in Germany," *New York Times*, March 1, 1946.
262. Walch and Miller, *Hoover and Truman*, p. 67.
263. Edward T. Folliard, "Newsmen Find Hoover Fit, Vigorous," *Washington Post*, March 2, 1946.
264. Felix Belair Jr., "New 'Famine' Board Asks US to Cut Wheat by 25%; Conferring on the Problem of Feeding Overseas Needy," *New York Times*, March 2, 1946. www.nytimes.com/1946/03/02/archives/new-famine-board-asks-us-cut-wheat-use-by-25-conferring-on-the.html.
265. Walch and Miller, *Hoover and Truman*, p. 71.
266. Ibid.
267. "Hoover Bids US Save 500 Million in Famine Nations; Radio Appeal Calls Upon Every Family to Take 'Invisible Guest' to Its Table He Flies to Paris Today May Visit India, but Russia Is Off Itinerary as Result of Offer to France," *New York Times*, March 17, 1946. www.nytimes.com/1946/03/17/archives/hoover-bids-us-save-500000000-in-famine-nations-radio-appeal-calls.html.
268. Walch and Miller, *Hoover and Truman*, p. 72.
269. Glen Jeansonne and David Luhrssen, *Herbert Hoover: A Life* (New York: New American Library, 2016), p. 339.
270. For an account of this episode, see Herbert Hoover, *Freedom Betrayed: Herbert Hoover's Secret History of the Second World War and Its Aftermath*, ed. George Nash (Stanford: Hoover Institution Press, 2011), p. 36.
271. Whyte, *Hoover*, p. 579.

272. Years later, Hoover would thank Truman for enlisting him back into public service and correcting some of the "disgraceful" actions that had gone before. See Whyte, *Hoover*, p. 599.

13 Sacrifice

273. FDR was the first American president to fly while in office, and Harry Truman continued to use the Sacred Cow during his presidency. Truman signed the National Security Act of 1947, which created the Air Force, while on board the Sacred Cow. The term "Air Force One" was not created until the presidency of Dwight Eisenhower.
274. Lee Nash, *Understanding Herbert Hoover: Ten Perspectives* (Stanford: Hoover Institution Press, 1987), p. 91.
275. George H. Nash, *The Crusade Years, 1933–1955: Herbert Hoover's Lost Memoir of the New Deal Era and Its Aftermath* (Stanford: Hoover Institution Press, 2013), p. 31.
276. Andrew Preston, *Sword of the Spirit, Shield of Faith: Religion in America in War and Diplomacy* (New York: Alfred A. Knopf, 2012), p. 293.
277. Saul Friedlander, *The Years of Extermination: Nazi Germany and the Jews, 1939–1945* (New York: HarperCollins, 2007), p. 304.
278. Nash, *Understanding Herbert Hoover*, p. 95.
279. Hugh Gibson, *The Food Mission Diaries of Hugh Gibson* (hereafter Gibson Diary), March 20, 1946. https://digitalcollections.hoover.org/images/Collections/56000/gibson_diary_1946_vol_1.pdf.
280. Ibid., March 29, 1946.
281. Ibid., March 30, 1946.
282. Hoover, *Freedom Betrayed*, p. 1278.
283. Gibson Diary, April 12, 1946.
284. Felix Belair Jr., "Four Calls to Country," *New York Times*, April 19, 1946.
285. "Truman Joins Hoover in Plea for More Food," *Washington Post*, April 20, 1947.
286. For more on the development of Truman's speaking style, see Clark Clifford, *Counsel to the President: A Memoir* (New York: Random House, 1991), p. 74.
287. Walch and Miller, *Hoover and Truman*, pp. 74–75.
288. Morgenthau, *Germany Is Our Problem*, p. 16.
289. Ibid., p. 96.
290. Ibid., p. 68.
291. It is certainly true that although many Germans opposed the Nazis, many others did, in fact, support the regime. Still others came to support their government as the war dragged on. For a study of German attitudes, see Nicholas Stargardt, *The German War* (New York: Basic Books, 2015). For a provocative argument that many Germans supported Hitler because of the financial gains they received from looted Jewish property and funds, see Götz Aly, *Hitler's Beneficiaries: Plunder, Racial War, and the Nazi Welfare State* (New York: Metropolitan Books, 2007).
292. James Bacque, *Crimes and Mercies: The Fate of German Civilians Under Allied Occupation: 1944–1950*, (Vancouver: Talonbooks, 2007), p. 111. James Bacque claims that in the same month, November 1945, Eisenhower's deputy, General Lucius Clay, prevented Red Cross food aid from entering the American occupation zone, allegedly saying, "Let the Germans suffer." The quote derives from a source that Bacque himself was unable to verify. Bacque's allegation seems unlikely. If Clay did harbor the strong anti-German sentiments prevalent at the war's end, he quickly changed his attitude, as evidenced by his journey to Brussels on April 6,

1946, to meet with Herbert Hoover to discuss remedies for the starvation of average Germans. Many of Bacque's allegations in this vein have been discredited. See S. P. MacKenzie, "Essay and Reflection: On the 'Other Losses' Debate," *The International History Review*, Vol. 14. No. 4 (November 1992), pp. 717–731. www.jstor.org/stable/40107116.

293. United States Government, *Pocket Guide to Germany*, 1944. https://archive.org/details/pocketguidetogeroounit/mode/2up. Andrei Cherny, in his excellent popular history of the Berlin airlift, depicts the *Pocket Guide* as a harsh document, reflecting the victors' intention to punish the German people. While it does contain language stating that justice should be strict and fraternization with Germans should be limited, I read the document as a reflection of American intentions to be both fair to average Germans and supportive of Germany's revival. See Andrei Cherny, *The Candy Bombers: The Untold Story of the Berlin Airlift and America's Finest Hour* (New York: G. P. Putnam's Sons, 2008), pp. 84–85.

294. Walch and Miller, *Hoover and Truman*, Byrnes to Truman, March 12, 1946, p. 69.

295. Walch and Miller, *Hoover and Truman*, pp. 80–81.

296. Ibid., p. 84.

297. Herbert Hoover, Radio Address, May 17, 1946. The audio of his speech can be heard on YouTube: www.youtube.com/watch?v=1BPPzILlXbk. https://hoover.archives.gov/sites/default/files/research/ebooks/b3v5_full.pdf.

298. Herbert Hoover, *Memoirs: Years of Adventure, 1874–1920* (New York: MacMillan, 1951), pp. 347–348.

299. Gretta Palmer, "Can America Be Prosperous in a Sea of Human Misery?" *Ladies Home Journal*, May 1946.

300. Eleanor Roosevelt, "My Day," June 3, 1946. www2.gwu.edu/~erpapers/myday/displaydoc.cfm?_y=1946&_f=md000355.

301. Walch and Miller, *Hoover and Truman*, p. 90.

302. Dietrich, *Morgenthau Plan*, p. 106.

303. American soldiers did engage in violence against civilian populations. For one account focused on France, see Mary Louise Roberts, *What Soldiers Do: Sex and the American G.I. in World War II France* (Chicago: University of Chicago Press, 2013).

304. JCS 1067. Directive to Commander-in-Chief of United States Forces of Occupation Regarding the Military Government of Germany. October 17, 1945. https://en.wikisource.org/wiki/JCS_1067.

305. Jean Edward Smith and Lucius D. Clay, *An American Life* (New York: H. Holt, 1990), p. 6.

306. Oral History Interview with Lucius Clay, July 16, 1974. Harry S. Truman Library. www.trumanlibrary.org/oralhist/clayl.htm.

307. Ibid.

308. James F. Byrnes, "Stuttgart Speech, September 6, 1946," *Documents on Germany under Occupation, 1945–1954* (London and New York: Oxford University Press, 1955), pp. 52–60.

309. Ibid.

310. Roosevelt, "My Day," October 13, 1945. www2.gwu.edu/~erpapers/myday/displaydoc.cfm?_y=1945&_f=md000155.

311. Walch and Miller, *Hoover and Truman*, p. 94.

14 Reform

312. Wolfgang Borchert, "Das Brot," *Das Karussell*, 1947. http://users.skynet.be/lit/borchert.htm.

313. After the war, the US Strategic Bombing Survey found that the bombing of German industrial targets was of mixed effectiveness in ending the war. Germany's economic recovery is partly attributed to the lack of total destruction by the Allies. However, food production remained a severe problem for several years following the end of hostilities. Some scholars have criticized the survey's findings. See Strategic Bombing Summary: https://en.wikipedia.org/wiki/United_States_Strategic_Bombing_Survey#On_German_production. One window into the debate over the Allied bombing campaign's failure to destroy the German economy can be found at: www.stern.de/politik/geschichte/bombenkrieg-barbarisch–aber-sinnvoll-3346830.html.

314. Tony Judt, *Postwar: A History of Europe Since 1945* (New York: Penguin Press, 2005), p. 21.

315. Eleanor Roosevelt, *My Day: The Best of Eleanor Roosevelt's Acclaimed Newspaper Columns, 1936–1962* (New York: Da Capo Press, 2001), p. 125.

316. Gibson Diary, February 10, 1947.

317. Jeansonne and Luhrssen, *Herbert Hoover: A Life*, p. 17.

318. Whyte, *Hoover*, p. 96.

319. Anne Applebaum, *Iron Curtain: The Crushing of Eastern Europe, 1944–1956* (New York: Doubleday, 2012), p. 145.

320. Ibid., p. 355.

321. Gibson Diary, February 8, 1947.

322. Ibid., February 11, 1947.

323. John Connelly, *From Peoples Into Nations: A History of Eastern Europe* (Princeton: Princeton University Press, 2020). In Connelly's magisterial account, the author describes the appeal of communism to many East Europeans. Americans have often failed to grasp the powerful appeal of political movements that promise equal access to land. This lack of understanding would be repeated in Vietnam and Afghanistan. See Jeffrey Race, *War Comes to Long An: Revolutionary Conflict in a Vietnamese Province* (Berkeley: University of California Press, 1972), and Carter Malkasian, *War Comes to Garmser: Thirty Years of Conflict on the Afghan Frontier* (New York: Oxford University Press, 2013).

324. Herbert Hoover, *Addresses Upon the American Road, 1945–1948* (New York: D. Van Nostrand, 1949), p. 285.

325. Hoover, *Freedom Betrayed*, p. 1264.

326. Ibid., p. 285.

327. Ibid., p. 103.

328. Fred Smith, "The Rise and Fall of the Morgenthau Plan," *United Nations World*, March 1947. Box/Folder 126: 7 Morgenthau, Henry, Jr., and Morgenthau Plan, 1944–1948, Hoover Library. The same article asserted that the idea for the Morgenthau Plan received its strongest spark from General Eisenhower, who insisted on a tough treatment of the German people, not just the Nazi leadership. Viewing all Germans as guilty, he allegedly said that he wanted to "see things made good and hard for them for a while." The author of this article may have been the same Fred Smith who served on Morgenthau's staff at Treasury, in which case his presentation of Eisenhower's views toward Germany might be suspect. Michaela Hoenicke Moore makes a compelling argument that during the war there was no clear consensus on how to view the Nazi threat. She points to the many efforts to distinguish between average Germans and Nazi leaders. However, Moore makes a peculiar argument that Morgenthau was not bent on revenge against Germans, suggesting instead that his plan was motivated by the spirit of New Deal reforms. This argument seems untenable in light of the extensive efforts Morgenthau exerted

to block any attempts to soften his plan, his travel to London to lobby General Eisenhower to reduce the number of calories that Germans would receive under occupation, his constant pressure on President Roosevelt to hold fast to a hard line against those who spoke of a soft peace, and his sustained bureaucratic maneuverings to ensure that the harshest interpretations of his plan were implemented, even going as far as transferring his close supporter, Col. Bernstein, onto General Clay's staff after the war. See Michaela Hoenicke Moore, *Know Your Enemy: The American Debate on Nazism, 1933–1945* (New York: Cambridge University Press, 2010).

329. The preceding quotes are drawn from Herbert Hoover, "Report No. 3."
330. "Voters Favor Hoover Report on More German Food Relief by George Gallup Director, American Institute of Public Opinion," *Washington Post*, March 22, 1947.
331. Ibid., p. 112.
332. Ibid., pp. 113–114.

15 Revive

333. William L. Clayton. Memorandum by the Under Secretary of State for Economic Affairs. Foreign Relations of the United States, May 27, 1947. The British Commonwealth; Europe, Volume III. https://history.state.gov/historicaldocuments/frus1947v03/d136.
334. Garwood, *Will Clayton*, p. 54.
335. Ibid., p. 60.
336. Ibid., p. 61.
337. Ibid., p. 63.
338. Ibid., p. 60.
339. Ibid., p. 145.
340. Ibid., p. 91.
341. "Cotton & King," *Time* magazine, August 17, 1936.
342. Gregory A. Fossedal, *Our Finest Hour: Will Clayton, The Marshall Plan, and the Triumph of Democracy* (Stanford: Hoover Institution Press, 1993), p. 63.
343. Garwood, *Will Clayton*, p. 110.
344. Ibid., p. 19.
345. Ibid., p. 116.
346. Ibid., p. 117.
347. For a detailed account of Russian rapes, see Norman Naimark, *The Russians in Germany: A History of the Soviet Zone of Occupation, 1945–1949* (Cambridge, MA: Belknap Press of Harvard University Press, 1995).
348. Donovan Memorandum for the President, September 5, 1945, in "Office of Strategic Services – Donovan – Chronological File – September 1945," Box 10, Truman Papers, Rose A. Conway Files, Harry S. Truman Library, Independence, MO.
349. Hoover, *Addresses*, pp. 121–122.
350. Ibid.
351. For a thorough elaboration of the original study, see Paul C. Light, *Government's Greatest Achievements: From Civil Rights to Homeland Security* (Washington, DC: Brookings Institution Press, 2002).
352. "The Immediate Need for Emergency Aid to Europe," September 29, 1947. Truman Library, President's Secretary's Files, Folder: "The Immediate Need for Emergency Aid to Europe" Collection: Truman and the Marshall Plan. www.trumanlibrary.gov/library/research-files/immediate-need-emergency-aid-europe?documentid=NA&page number=2.

16 Hunger

353. "Knee-Deep in Alligators," *Time* magazine, October 13, 1947.
354. Ibid.
355. The Andrews Sisters performed a version of Berlin's song here: www.youtube.com/watch?v=A66oPN2rkPw.
356. The song can be heard at: www.youtube.com/watch?v=oLW1uDEezpU.
357. Charles Luckman, *Twice in a Lifetime: From Soap to Skyscrapers* (New York: W. W. Norton, 1988), p. 208.
358. "The Administration: Knee-Deep in Alligators," *Time*, Monday, October 13, 1947. http://content.time.com/time/subscriber/article/0,33009,933706–2,00.html.
359. For a thorough account of the Committee's activities, see "Final Report," US Citizens Food Committee.
360. Harry S. Truman, "Remarks to Members of the Citizens Food Committee," October 1, 1947. www.presidency.ucsb.edu/documents/remarks-members-the-citizens-food-committee.
361. Ibid.
362. Ibid.
363. Harry S. Truman, Address to the Nation on Food Emergency. Truman Library. www.trumanlibrary.gov/library/public-papers/202/radio-and-television-address-concluding-program-citizens-food-committee. Video: www.youtube.com/watch?v=qPj3NRyrxj4&list=PLpz8_szloU8L2X5xwQXT3onEXiWcSHA1W&index=2.
364. Ibid.
365. Luckman, *Twice in a Lifetime*, p. 210.
366. "Cooperation Pledged on Meatless Tuesday," *Los Angeles Times*, October 7, 1947.
367. "First 'Meatless Tuesday' Termed Successful Here," *Boston Globe*, October 8, 1947.
368. "Meatless Tuesdays and Armed Forces," *Baltimore Sun*, November 22, 1947.
369. "The Administration: The Chicken & The Egg," *Time* magazine, October 20, 1947.
370. The preceding information is drawn from *Final Report*, Citizens Food Committee.
371. "First Meatless Tuesday Diets Observed Here," *Chicago Daily Tribune*, October 8, 1947.
372. "250 Convicts Go on Hunger Strike," *Baltimore Sun*, December 9, 1947.
373. "Poultryless Thursdays Cancelled," *Los Angeles Times*, November 7, 1947.
374. Details of the mass chick culling can be found in "Final Report," US Citizens Food Committee.
375. "Distilleries Close for Sixty Days, Backing Truman on Wheat Saving," *New York Times*, October 26, 1947.
376. Lewis Rosenstiel, Wikipedia entry: https://horatioalger.org/members/member-detail/charles-luckman/.
377. Luckman, *Twice in a Lifetime*, pp. 212–213. In his autobiography, Luckman incorrectly referred to Rosenstiel as Sidney, misremembering Rosenstiel's actual first name, which was Lewis.
378. Ibid., p. 213.
379. Ibid.
380. Ibid.
381. There were four exceptions made to the shutdown. Two distilleries in California, one in Michigan, and one in Pennsylvania, all of them small-scale producers, were permitted to remain in operation. See *Final Report*, Citizens Food Committee.

382. Volney D. Hurd, "Grateful French Hail Arrival of Food Ship," *Christian Science Monitor*, December 18, 1947.
383. "US Gift Parcels Lost in Fire: Arson Suspected," *The Guardian*, January 31, 1948.
384. David Perlman, "30,000 Tons of U.S. Relief Burns in Paris," *New York Herald Tribune*, January 31, 1948.
385. Joseph G. Harrison, "Humble Gratitude Greets Relief Train in South Italy," *Christian Science Monitor*, January 27, 1948.
386. "Vienna Cheers US Gifts," *New York Times*, March 24, 1948.
387. "Loads 'Friendship' Grain," *New York Times*, March 2, 1948.

17 Resurrect

388. Ferrell, *Choosing Truman*, p. 15.
389. Henry Agard Wallace, *The Price of Vision: The Diaries of Henry A. Wallace, 1942–1946* (Boston: Houghton Mifflin, 1973), p. 10.
390. Ibid., p. 15.
391. Ibid., p. 23.
392. Ibid., August 3, 1944, p. 373.
393. Ibid.
394. Clifford, *Counsel to the President*, p. 118.
395. Wallace, *Price of Vision*, p. 662.
396. Ibid., p. 664.
397. Ibid., p. 665.
398. Ibid.
399. Cherny, *Candy Bombers*, p. 202.
400. Berlin Blockade. Wikipedia: https://en.wikipedia.org/wiki/Berlin_Blockade.
401. Eleanor Roosevelt to George Marshall, March 13, 1948. https://erpapers.colum bian.gwu.edu/eleanor-roosevelt-george-marshall-march-13-1948.
402. Fossedal, *Our Finest Hour*, p. 175.
403. Willard Edwards, "Delegates Cheer Hoover and Speaker," *Chicago Daily Tribune*, June 23, 1948. See also "Republicans Pay Honor to Herbert Hoover: Hoover Given Mighty Ovation," *Los Angeles Times*, June 22, 1948.
404. For the text of Hoover's speech, I have drawn on the original audio recording. Herbert Hoover, "This Crisis in American Life," June 22, 1948. Discs 19–22: Address Before the Republican National Convention NBC, Philadelphia. Reference number: 62008_a_0002925. Hoover Institution Archives, Stanford, California.

18 Uplift

405. Cherny, *Candy Bombers*, p. 227.
406. Norman N. Naimark, *Stalin and the Fate of Europe: The Postwar Struggle for Sovereignty* (Cambridge, MA: Harvard University Press, 2019), p. 223.
407. Cherny, *Candy Bombers*, pp. 256–257.
408. James Forrestal, *The Forrestal Diaries*, ed. Walter Millis (New York: Viking Press, 1951), p. 430.
409. Lifton and Mitchell, *Hiroshima in America*, p. 161.
410. David E. Lilienthal, *The Atomic Energy Years, 1945–1950, Vol. II* (New York: Harper and Row, 1964), p. 391. I am grateful to Andrei Cherny for helping me to trace the source for this episode.

411. See Lifton and Mitchell, *Hiroshima in America*. These two authors explored this question in their penetrating book, but they could not reach a definitive conclusion. Only Harry Truman knew the answer, and he never shared it directly with anyone, as far as we currently know. He did, however, express publicly his humane desire not to use the atomic bomb because it would harm the innocent. At a news conference in 1950, responding to a question about the bomb's possible use in the Korean conflict, Truman said: "I don't want to see it used. It is a terrible weapon, and it should not be used on innocent men, women, and children who have nothing whatever to do with this military aggression." Truman News Conference, November 30, 1950.
412. "Report on US Public Opinion on the Berlin Situation," July 29, 1948, President's Secretary's Files, Berlin Airlift Collection, Truman Library. www.trumanlibrary.gov/library/research-files/report-us-public-opinion-berlin-situation?documentid=NA&pagenumber=2.
413. British Movietone News 1949. www.youtube.com/watch?v=_nHdB1vJNsg.
414. I have drawn heavily on an exquisitely told account of the airlift and of Gail Halvorsen's role in it. See Cherny, *Candy Bombers*, pp. 299–300.
415. The estimate of twenty-three tons of candy comes from Gail Halvorsen. Wikipedia: https://en.wikipedia.org/wiki/Gail_Halvorsen#Operation_"Little_Vittles".
416. Pietrusza, *1948*, p. 345.
417. Ibid., p. 369.
418. Eleanor Roosevelt to Harry S. Truman, October 4, 1948. https://erpapers.columbian.gwu.edu/eleanor-roosevelt-harry-s-truman-october-4-1948.
419. Cherny, *Candy Bombers*, pp. 347 and 464.
420. "Viel Bauchweh," *Der Spiegel*, June 19, 1948.
421. "In Berlin Ergraut," *Der Spiegel*, July 31, 1948.
422. *Der Spiegel*, May 19, 1949.
423. Cherny, *Candy Bombers*, p. 345.
424. "Russians Violate Berlin Boundaries. Arrest Six Policemen in US Sector," *The Scotsman*, August 21, 1948.
425. "Air Crash in Berlin," *Times of India*, August 3, 1948.
426. "Berlin Airlift: Anglo-US Planes Set New Record, Blockade Fails," *South China Morning Post* (from Reuters), April 17, 1949.
427. Berlin Blockade. Wikipedia: https://en.wikipedia.org/wiki/Berlin_Blockade.

19 Atone

428. Reverend John A. MacLean, "Suggestion – As Foolish as the Teachings of Jesus of Nazareth," January 6, 1946. Ginter Park Presbyterian Church, Richmond, Virginia.
429. Ibid.
430. "Preacher's 'Brainstorm,'" *Richmond Times Dispatch*, November 27, 1949.
431. Address of Joseph C. Grew before the 162nd General Assembly of the Presbyterian Church in the United States of America, Cincinnati, Ohio, May 23, 1950.
432. Hasegawa, *Racing the Enemy*, p. 22.
433. Heinrichs, *American Ambassador*, p. 10.
434. Ibid.
435. Address by Joseph C. Grew to the General Assembly of the Presbyterian Church of the United States of America, Cincinnati, Ohio, May 23, 1950.
436. Diffendorfer to Eleanor Roosevelt, March 1, 1950, and Roosevelt to Diffendorfer, March 30, 1950.
437. Address of William L. Clayton, Japan International Christian University, Houston, Texas, April 25, 1950. Hoover Institution Archives, Box 20, Folder 36.

438. Ibid.
439. For more on this topic, see Ray A. Moore, *Soldier of God: MacArthur's Attempt to Christianize Japan* (Honolulu: University of Hawaii Press, 2011).
440. M. William Steele, "The Cold War and the Founding of ICU," *Asian Cultural Studies*, Special Issue, No.21 (March 2016). https://subsite.icu.ac.jp/iacs/en/call-forpapers/no21-/No21.html.
441. For an interesting popular account of American efforts to devise an effective bombing campaign during World War II, including its failed attempts to destroy the Nakajima aircraft manufacturing facility, see Malcolm Gladwell, *The Bomber Mafia: A Dream, a Temptation, and the Longest Night of the Second World War* (New York: Little, Brown and Company, 2021).
442. "Little Aid to Jews by UNRRA Reported," *New York Times*, May 15, 1946.
443. See Jewish Virtual Library entry on Henry Morgenthau Jr. www.jewishvirtuallibrary.org/henry-morgenthau-jr.
444. "Morgenthau Gets Jewish Aid Post," *New York Times*, January 3, 1947.
445. "Morgenthau to Israel," *New York Times*, October 3, 1948.
446. "Mrs. F.D. Roosevelt Aids Jewish Drive," *New York Times*, February 20, 1947.
447. Eleanor Roosevelt to Robert Hannegan, June 3, 1945. https://erpapers.columbian.gwu.edu/eleanor-roosevelt-robert-hannegan-june-3-1945.
448. Goodwin, *No Ordinary Time*, p. 621.
449. Roosevelt, "My Day," June 1, 1953. www2.gwu.edu/~erpapers/myday/displaydoc.cfm?_y=1953&_f=md002551.
450. Roosevelt, "My Day," September 8, 1953. www2.gwu.edu/~erpapers/myday/displaydoc.cfm?_y=1953&_f=md002641.
451. Eleanor Roosevelt, Speech at the International Christian University, Tokyo, Japan, May 27, 1953. Japan ICU Foundation (JICUF). www.jicuf.org/eleanor-roosevelt-speech-at-icu/.
452. Roosevelt, "My Day," June 17, 1953. www2.gwu.edu/~erpapers/myday/displaydoc.cfm?_y=1953&_f=md002565.
453. Joseph Lash, *Eleanor: The Years Alone* (New York: Norton, 1972), p. 224.
454. Roosevelt, "My Day," June 16, 1953. www2.gwu.edu/~erpapers/myday/displaydoc.cfm?_y=1953&_f=md002564.
455. "A Message to Mrs. Roosevelt from Hiroshima Students Association of the United Nations," 1953. Eleanor Roosevelt Papers Project, George Washington University. https://erpapers.columbian.gwu.edu/message-mrs-roosevelt-hiroshima-students-association-united-nations.
456. Newsletter of the Japan International Christian University Foundation, August 16, 1948. ICU archives. The exact quote of Hoover was, "Make yourselves worthy of victory."

20 Afterlife

457. Hoover did not consider himself an isolationist, but rather a noninterventionist. He did not perceive a direct threat to the United States from Nazi Germany. For a more detailed account of his views on the subject, see Hoover, *Freedom Betrayed*, Editor's Introduction.
458. Light, *Government's Greatest Achievements*.
459. America's experience with harsh anti-communist measures can be graphically seen three decades earlier during World War I with the infamous Palmer raids, but the 1950s and beyond witnessed a renewed and expanded anti-communist frenzy.
460. Whyte, *Hoover*, p. 2.

461. One cooperative farming community in Israel even named itself Tal Shahar, Hebrew for "morning dew," the meaning of Morgenthau in German. "Henry Morgenthau Jr.: Americans and the Holocaust." https://exhibitions.ushmm.org/americans-and-the-holocaust/personal-story/henry-morgenthau-jr.

462. "Mrs. F.D. Roosevelt Aids Jewish Drive," *New York Times*, February 20, 1947.

463. Roosevelt, "My Day," May 31, 1956. www2.gwu.edu/~erpapers/myday/display doc.cfm?_y=1956&_f=md003498.

464. Neal, *Eleanor and Harry*, p. 262.

465. James B. Conant, Address at the International Christian University, April 29, 1961. Audio recording, ICU Archives.

466. Henry A. Wallace, "Where I Was Wrong," *This Week* magazine, September 7, 1952. https://delong.typepad.com/sdj/2013/02/henry-a-wallace-1952-on-the-ruth less-nature-of-communism-cold-war-era-god-that-failed-weblogging.html.

467. Bannai, *Enduring Conviction*, p. 136.

468. "Milton Eisenhower Urges a Korea Friendship Train," *New York Herald Tribune*, June 18, 1953.

469. Speech of Dillon S. Myer, July 27, 1962. Truman Library. Folder: "Speech of Dillon S. Myer, to be delivered July 27, 1962, Pioneer Banquet, 17th Biennial National Convention, Japanese American Citizens League, Seattle, Washington", from the Collection "The War Relocation Authority & the Incarceration of Japanese-Americans During World War II". www.trumanlibrary.gov/library/research-files/speech-dillon-s-myer-be-delivered-july-27–1962-pioneer-banquet-17th-biennial.

470. "Interview with Karl Bendetsen about the Japanese American Internment Camps, December 6, 1982," Karl Bendetsen Papers, Hoover ID 75100_a_0010376, Hoover Institution Archives.

471. George Takei, *To the Stars: The Autobiography of George Takei, Star Trek's Mr. Sulu* (New York: Pocket Books, 1994), p. 348.

472. Bird, *The Chairman*, p. 365.

473. Irons, *Justice at War*, p. 353.

474. Testimony of John J. McCloy, November 3, 1981. CWRC, RG 220. National Archives and Records Administration, Washington, DC.

475. John J. McCloy, "Repay US Japanese?" *New York Times*, April 10, 1983.

476. Bannai, *Enduring Conviction*, p. 195.

SELECT BIBLIOGRAPHY

Below is a selection of primary and secondary sources used in developing this book. Because the literature on WWII and the Cold War is enormous, I have chosen to restrict the bibliography to those works I found especially valuable for understanding the specific questions I sought to answer. The following list is by no means comprehensive, but those seeking to delve deeper into the topics I covered in this book might find some of these sources to be useful entry points. Additional references and details may be found in the notes.

Archives

Bancroft Library, University of California at Berkeley. (Of particular value are the Japanese Evacuation and Resettlement Survey.)
FDR Presidential Library & Museum Archives
Harry S. Truman Presidential Library & Museum
Herbert Hoover Presidential Library & Museum
Hoover Institution Library & Archives
International Christian University Archives
National Archives and Records Administration
Naval History and Heritage Command Archives

Unpublished Diaries

Gibson, Hugh. *The Food Mission Diaries of Hugh Gibson*. Stanford: Hoover Institution Library Archives.

McCloy, John J. *Papers*. Amherst College Archives and Special Collections.
Stimson, Henry L. *Diary of Henry L. Stimson*. New Haven: Yale University
   Library.

Newspapers and Journals

Asia-Pacific Journal
Baltimore Sun
Billboard
Boston Globe
Chicago Daily Tribune
Christian Science Monitor
Cleveland Call and Post
Common Ground
Der Spiegel
Detroit Free Press
Guardian
Harper's
Hartford Courant
Japan Times
Ladies Home Journal
Los Angeles Times
New York Herald Tribune
New York Times
New Yorker
Palestine Post
Richmond Times Dispatch
Scotsman
South China Morning Post
Time
Times of India
Vox
Washington Post
Week

Published Primary Sources

Acheson, Dean. *Present at the Creation: My Years in the State Department*.
   New York: W. W. Norton, 1969.

Biddle, Francis. *In Brief Authority*. Garden City: Doubleday, 1962.

Blum, John. M. *From the Morgenthau Diaries: Years of War, 1941–1945*. Boston: Houghton Mifflin, 1967.

Clifford, Clark M. *Counsel to the President: A Memoir*. New York: Random House, 1991.

Commission on Wartime Relocation and Internment of Civilians. *Personal Justice Denied: Report of the Commission on Wartime Relocation and Internment of Civilians*. Seattle: University of Washington Press, 1997.

Final Report, US Citizens Food Committee, January 15, 1948.

Foreign Relations of the United States

Forrestal, James and Mills, Walter. *The Forrestal Diaries*. New York: Viking Press, 1951.

Freedman, Max. *Roosevelt and Frankfurter: Their Correspondence of 1928–1945*. New York: Little Brown, 1967.

Gallup, George H. *The Gallup Poll: Public Opinion 1935–1971, Vol. I*. New York: Random House, 1972.

Grew, Joseph C. *Ten Years in Japan*. New York: Simon & Schuster, 1944.

Groves, Leslie R. *Now It Can Be Told: The Story of the Manhattan Project*. New York: Harper, 1962.

Hachiya, Michihiko. *Hiroshima Diary: The Journal of a Japanese Physician, August 6–September 30, 1945*. Chapel Hill: University of North Carolina Press, 1955.

Hoover, Hebert. *Addresses Upon the American Road, 1945–1948*. New York: D. Van Nostrand, 1949.

Freedom Betrayed: Herbert Hoover's Secret History of the Second World War and Its Aftermath, ed. George Nash. Stanford: Hoover Institution Press, 2011.

Kort, Michael. *The Columbia Guide to Hiroshima and the Bomb*. New York: Columbia University Press, 2007.

Lewis, Norman. *Naples '44: A World War II Diary of Occupied Italy*. New York: Carroll & Graf, 2005.

Lilienthal, David E. *The Atomic Energy Years, 1945–1950, Vol. II*. New York: Harper and Row, 1964.

Luckman, Charles. *Twice in a Lifetime: From Soap to Skyscrapers*. New York: W. W. Norton, 1988.

Morgenthau, Henry Jr. *Germany Is Our Problem: A Plan for Germany*. New York: Harper & Brothers, 1945.

Neal, S. *Eleanor and Harry: The Correspondence of Eleanor Roosevelt and Harry S. Truman*. New York: Scribner, 2002.

Roosevelt, Eleanor. *My Day: The Best of Eleanor Roosevelt's Acclaimed Newspaper Columns, 1936–1962.* New York: Da Capo Press, 2001.

Stimson, Henry and Bundy, McGeorge. *On Active Service in Peace and War.* New York: Harper Collins, 1948.

Tateishi, John. *And Justice for All: An Oral History of the Japanese American Detention Camps.* Seattle: University of Washington Press, 1999.

Truman, Harry S. *Memoirs of Harry S. Truman.* Volume I: *Year of Decisions.* New York: Doubleday, 1955.

Memoirs of Harry S. Truman. Volume II: *Year of Trial and Hope.* New York: Doubleday, 1956.

Von Oppen, Beate R. and Bullock, Alan. *Documents on Germany under Occupation, 1945–1954,* New York: Oxford University Press, 1955.

Walch, Timothy and Dwight M. Miller. *Herbert Hoover and Harry S. Truman.* Worland: High Plains, 1992.

Wallace, Henry A. *The Price of Vision: The Diaries of Henry A. Wallace, 1942–1946.* Boston: Houghton Mifflin, 1973.

Secondary Sources

Alperovitz, Gar. *Decision to Use the Atomic Bomb.* New York: Vintage Books, 1996.

Applebaum, Anne. *Iron Curtain: The Crushing of Eastern Europe.* New York: Anchor Books, 2013.

Austin, Allan W. *Quaker Brotherhood: Interracial Activism and the American Friends Service Committee, 1917–1950.* Urbana: University of Illinois Press, 2012.

Bacque, James. *Crimes and Mercies: The Fate of German Civilians Under Allied Occupation: 1944–1950.* Vancouver: Talonbooks, 2007.

Baime, Albert J. *The Accidental President: Harry S. Truman and the Four Months That Changed the World.* Boston: Houghton Mifflin Harcourt, 2017.

Bannai, Lorraine. *Enduring Conviction: Fred Korematsu and His Quest for Justice.* Seattle: University of Washington Press, 2015.

Barnes, Dayna. *Architects of Occupation: American Experts and the Planning for Postwar Japan.* Ithaca: Cornell University Press, 2017.

Beschloss, Walter M. *The Conquerors: Roosevelt, Truman and the Destruction of Hitler's Germany, 1941–1945.* New York: Simon & Schuster, 2012.

Bird, Kai. *The Chairman: John J. McCloy & the Making of the American Establishment.* New York: Simon & Schuster, 1992.

Bix, Herbert P. *Hirohito and the Making of Modern Japan.* New York: Harper Perennial, 2016.

Borchert, Wolfgang. *Das Brot.* Berlin: Das Karussell, 1947.

Cherny, Andrei. *The Candy Bombers: The Untold Story of the Berlin Airlift and America's Finest Hour*. New York: G. P. Putnam's Sons, 2008.

Connelly, John. *From Peoples Into Nations: A History of Eastern Europe*. Princeton: Princeton University Press, 2020.

Cook, Blanche. W. *Eleanor Roosevelt*. Volume 3: *The War Years and After, 1939–1962*. New York: Barnes & Noble, 2016.

Dallek, Robert. *Franklin D. Roosevelt: A Political Life*. New York: Penguin Random House, 2018.

Devine, Thomas W. *Henry Wallace's 1948 Presidential Campaign and the Future of Postwar Liberalism*. Chapel Hill: University of North Carolina Press, 2013.

Dietrich, John. *The Morgenthau Plan: Soviet Influence on American Postwar Policy*. New York: Algora, 2002.

Dower, John W. *War Without Mercy: Race and Power in the Pacific War*. New York: Random House, 1986.

Drinnon, Richard. *Keeper of Concentration Camps: Dillon S. Myer and American Racism*. Berkeley: University of California Press, 1987.

Erbelding, Rebecca. *Rescue Board: The Untold Story of America's Efforts to Save the Jews of Europe*. New York: Doubleday, 2018.

Farrell, Robert. *Choosing Truman: The Democratic Convention of 1944*. Columbia: University of Missouri Press, 2013.

Feis, Herbert. *Japan Subdued: The Atomic Bomb and the End of the War in the Pacific*. Princeton: Princeton University Press, 1961.

Fossedal, Gregory A. *Our Finest Hour: Will Clayton, the Marshall Plan, and the Triumph of Democracy*. Stanford: Hoover Institution Press, 1993.

Frank, Richard B. *Downfall: The End of the Imperial Japanese Empire*. New York: Random House, 1999.

Gaddis, John Lewis. *George F. Kennan: An American Life*. New York: Penguin Press, 2011.

Gallicchio, Marc. *Unconditional: The Japanese Surrender in World War II*. Oxford: Oxford University Press, 2020.

Garwood, Ellen C. *Will Clayton: A Short Biography*. Austin: University of Texas Press, 1958.

Gladwell, Malcolm. *The Bomber Mafia: A Dream, a Temptation, and the Longest Night of the Second World War*. New York: Little, Brown and Company, 2021.

Goodwin, Doris K. *No Ordinary Time, Franklin and Eleanor Roosevelt: The Home Front in World War II*. New York: Simon & Schuster, 1994.

Hasegawa, Tsuyoshi. *Racing the Enemy: Stalin, Truman, and the Surrender of Japan*. Cambridge, MA: Harvard University Press, 2005.

Heinrichs, Waldo H. *American Ambassador: Joseph C. Grew and the Development of the United States Diplomatic Tradition*. Boston: Little, Brown, 1966.

Hitchcock, William I. *The Bitter Road to Freedom: A New History of the Liberation of Europe*. New York: Free Press, 2008.

Hochschild, Adam. *American Midnight: Democracy's Forgotten Crisis, 1917–1921*. Boston: Harper Collins, 2022.

Hollinger, David A. *Protestants Abroad: How Missionaries Tried to Change the World but Changed America*. Princeton: Princeton University Press, 2017.

Irons, Peter. *Justice at War: The Story of the Japanese American Internment Cases*. New York: Oxford University Press, 1983.

Jeansonne, Glen and Luhrssen, David. *Herbert Hoover: A Life*. New York: New American Library, 2016.

Judt, Tony. *Postwar: A History of Europe Since 1945*. New York: Penguin Press, 2005.

Karabell, Zachary. *The Last Campaign: How Harry Truman Won the 1948 Election*. New York: Knopf Random House, 2000.

Lash, Joseph P. *Eleanor and Franklin: The Story of Their Relationship Based on Eleanor Roosevelt's Private Papers*. New York: Smithmark, 1995.

Lash, Joseph P. and Roosevelt, Eleanor. *Love, Eleanor*. Garden City: Doubleday, 1982.

Lifton, Robert J. and Mitchell, Greg. *Hiroshima in America: A Half Century of Denial*. New York: Avon Books, 1996.

Light, Paul C. *Government's Greatest Achievements: From Civil Rights to Homeland Security*. Washington, DC: Brookings Institution Press, 2002.

Madsen, Grant. *Sovereign Soldiers: How the US Military Transformed the Global Economy After World War II*. Philadelphia: University of Pennsylvania Press, 2018.

Malloy, Sean L. *Atomic Tragedy: Henry L. Stimson and the Decision to Use the Bomb Against Japan*. Ithaca: Cornell University Press, 2008.

McCullough, David. *Truman*. New York: Simon & Schuster, 1993.

Millman, Chad. *The Detonators: The Secret Plot to Destroy America and an Epic Hunt for Justice*. New York: Little, Brown and Company, 2006.

Miscamble, Wilson D. *The Most Controversial Decision: Truman, the Atomic Bombs, and the Defeat of Japan*. New York: Cambridge University Press, 2011.

Moore, Michaela H. *Know Your Enemy: The American Debate on Nazism, 1933–1945*. New York: Cambridge University Press, 2010.

Moore, Ray A. *Soldier of God: MacArthur's Attempt to Christianize Japan*. Honolulu: University of Hawaii Press, 2011.

Moreira, Peter. *The Jew Who Defeated Hitler: Henry Morgenthau Jr., FDR, and How We Won the War*. New York: Penguin, 2014.

Morris, Sylvia Jukes. *Price of Fame: The Honorable Clare Boothe Luce*. New York: Random House, 2014.

Naimark, Norman M. *Russians in Germany: A History of the Soviet Zone of Occupation, 1945–1949*. Cambridge, MA: Belknap Press of Harvard University Press, 1995.

Stalin and the Fate of Europe: The Postwar Struggle for Sovereignty. Cambridge, MA: Harvard University Press, 2019.

Nash, Lee. *Understanding Herbert Hoover: Ten Perspectives*. Stanford: Hoover Institution Press, 1987.

Newman, Roger K. *Hugo Black: A Biography*. New York: Pantheon, 1994.

Osada, Arata. *Children of the A-Bomb*. San Francisco: Verdun Press, 2015.

Philips, Harlan B. *Felix Frankfurter Reminisces*. New York: Reynal & Company, 1960.

Pietrusza, David. *1948: Harry Truman's Improbable Victory and the Year That Transformed America's Role in the World*. New York: Union Square Press, 2011.

Preston, Andrew. *Sword of the Spirit, Shield of Faith: Religion in America in War and Diplomacy*. New York: Alfred A. Knopf, 2012.

Rhodes, Richard. *The Making of the Atomic Bomb*. New York: Simon & Schuster, 2012.

Robinson, Greg. *A Tragedy of Democracy: Japanese Confinement in North America*. New York: Columbia University Press, 2009.

By Order of the President: FDR and the Internment of Japanese Americans. Cambridge, MA: Harvard University Press, 2001.

Schmitz, David F. *Henry L. Stimson: The First Wise Man*. Wilmington: SR Books, 2001.

Schmitz, John E. *Enemies Among Us: The Relocation, Internment, and Repatriation of German, Italian, and Japanese Americans During the Second World War*. Lincoln: University of Nebraska Press, 2021.

Shephard, Ben. *The Long Road Home: The Aftermath of the Second World War*. New York: Anchor Books, 2012.

Sherwin, Martin J., *A World Destroyed: Hiroshima and Its Legacies*. Stanford: Stanford University Press, 2003.

Shore, Zachary. *What Hitler Knew: The Battle for Information in Nazi Foreign Policy*. New York: Oxford University Press, 2003.

Simon, James F. *The Antagonists: Hugo Black, Felix Frankfurter and Civil Liberties in Modern America*. New York: Simon & Schuster, 1990.

Smith, Jean E. and Clay, Lucius D. *An American Life*. New York: H. Holt, 1990.

Snyder, Brad. *House of Truth: A Washington Political Salon and the Foundations of American Liberalism*. New York: Oxford University Press, 2017.

Stargardt, Nicholas. *The German War, a Nation Under Arms, 1939–1945: Citizens and Soldiers*. New York: Basic Books, 2015.

Steil, Benn. *The Marshall Plan: Dawn of the Cold War*. New York: Simon & Schuster, 2018.

Takei, George. *To the Stars: The Autobiography of George Takei, Star Trek's Mr. Sulu*. New York: Pocket Books, 1994.

Trachtenberg, Mark. *The Craft of International History*. Princeton: Princeton University Press, 2006.

Utley, Freda. *The High Cost of Vengeance*. Dublin, Ireland: Omnia Veritas, 2016.

Walker, J. Samuel. *Prompt and Utter Destruction: Truman and the Use of Atomic Bombs Against Japan*. Chapel Hill: University of North Carolina Press, 1997.

Wertheim, Stephen. *Tomorrow, the World: The Birth of US Global Supremacy*. Cambridge, MA: Belknap Press of Harvard University Press, 2020.

Whyte, Kenneth. *Hoover: An Extraordinary Life in Extraordinary Times*. New York: Knopf, 2017.

INDEX

Entries in **bold** font refer to the major topics of the book
Page number in *italics* refer to content in figures